Er

MW01241615

Publishing

Watch for More Titles
from Carl von Isenburg

and *Empower Publishing*

Elephants Have Right of Way

By

Carl von Isenburg

Empower Publishing
Winston-Salem

Empower

Publishing

Empower Publishing
PO Box 26701
Winston-Salem, NC 27114

First Empower Publishing Books edition published December, 2022
Empower Publishing, Feather Pen, and all production design are trademarks.

For information regarding bulk purchases of this book, digital purchase and special discounts, please contact the publisher at publish.empower.now@gmail.com

Cover design by Pan Morelli

Manufactured in the United States of America
ISBN 978-1-63066-522-7

DEDICATION

Mum, you were the personification of Patience. Fortunately so, for if you hadn't been, you might have had to be an ax murderer.

Valerie, Stephanie, Charles and Megan, you might wonder how or why I had the good luck to live through the hum-drum set of accidents and incidents - the mishaps and the haps, perhaps, that I've described. I can only think that they were all necessary to bring me to America and to you. I often wonder how I deserved that good luck. I hope I have let you all know just how lucky I believe myself to be.

I am grateful to my very good friend Jim McCracken for providing the impetus to move a stack of paper in a three-ring binder into this present form.

Thank you all for your love.

—Carl von Isenburg

TABLE OF CONTENTS

ILLUSTRATIONS

Map of the Region.

1

Carl von Isenburg

The Ruwenzori Mountains and Evirons of Kagando.

2

William Davidson ("Paga") in his late 80s

Mum & Dad in their 50th anniversary portrait.

Granny "Sims" and Jock (The only surviving photo).

The Farmall Tractor

Recent satellite photo of Rongai farm, the left to right cultivate stripe across the center, showing the contour lines we laid out in the 1950s still being followed. Our house was roughly at the lower end of the light coloured field; 3° 5' 16" S, 37° 3' 43" E.

Recent satellite photo of where Kagando Plantation would be, if it hadn't reverted. The white line is approximately along the Lamia River, the Congo/Uganda border and boundary of Kagando; 0° 36' 47" N, 29° 57' 13" E

In Nairobi, all cleaned up for the interview with The Nation.
Rear: John, Pauline. Front: Richard, Carl, Bill.

Also after we left Congo, but more like how we would have
appeared at Kagando. L-R: Richard, Pauline, Mum, Dad, Bill,
John.

PREFACE

One day, when my father was a few days shy of his eighty-fifth birthday and I was in my fifties, I finally did something that he had wanted me to do since I was old enough to talk: I spoke to him in his own language. At the time neither of us dwelt very long on the immensity of the moment. Since then I have had time to reflect on it, though more in terms of its poignancy than of its immensity. He has not.

Dad's earliest efforts to teach me his language were at the dinner table. I would counter those efforts, he often liked to remind me, by a look that said: "You can't fool me!" and the lecture: "Forkses is forkses, forkses is not *Gabels*! *Ngombes*[1] is *ngombes*, *ngombes* is not horses!" He was quite aware of the selective application of this logic, because we all readily switched back and forth between Swahili and English. *Ngombe* is Swahili for cow, and it was our word for cow, even when we were speaking English among ourselves. But then, logic has little to do with things like this. All the same, some of Dad's language seeds must have taken root, for I can remember, at later dinner tables, some occasional efforts as deep as: "Please cut me a slice of bread", and some daring, bedtime piecings together of words from those same lessons, shouted just not loudly enough to carry across the house to the living room, or maybe just gigglingly enough to be ignored: "Daddy, *du bist ein Esel!* You are a donkey!" In this context, I discount all of those episodes, for they were self-conscious and not really attempts to communicate.

Apart from the few lapses at dinner and bedtime, I had always resisted speaking German. I spent some time growing up in my Scottish Granny Sims' house, so I had a well-

---

[1] The 'ng' is pronounced like the 'ng' in singer: NGO-mbays. This is a complicated one, because ngoma, a drum, is pronounced as in finger. Don't worry about this one, it's not very serious. Do see the Notes on Swahili Pronounciation for some more punctuation rules, some of them are serious.

7

developed case of English speakers' dread of sounding silly. Of course, I had heard German spoken nearly all of my young life, either in Dad's efforts to teach it, or in overhearing his conversations with his German friends. I'm not sure that familiarity made the language any more appealing to me. After all, what is a young man supposed to think of a language in which his father introduces his oldest boy as *"...mein ältester Bub ..."*, with the last word pronounced uncomfortably like 'poop'? Even, for that matter, if it was pronounced 'boob'?

Dad suffered several other linguistic indignities at the hands and tongues of his loved ones. When he was introduced to Sims for the first time, she listened to his wonderful collection of aristocratic German names and titles that had been passed on to him by long generations of ancestors, of which, and of whom, he was very proud. She pronounced those names too awkward. Henceforth, she said, he would be called "James". As usual, she was right. He was.

None of us could see why Dad should speak to us in German, after all, he could speak English. And we knew we really didn't have to speak German with Dad. The whole family, including Mum, had a foolproof way of avoiding it. When he spoke to us in German it was not always consciously, it was just that that was the language in which he happened to be thinking. He was usually so wrapped up in what he was saying that if someone introduced a different language into the conversation, any language with which he was even slightly familiar, he would continue, quite happily, even if sometimes quite erratically, in the new one.

On That Day, though, when Dad spoke German, the trick of speaking in English didn't work for me. I had called to find out how he was, after I got a letter from Mum in which she told me that he was back from a short stay in the hospital. He'd been in the hospital before and survived it, so I hadn't thought this was any more serious. One of those previous times, when he was already in his eighties and in the intensive care unit for treatment for a mild heart attack, the nurses had begged Mum to take him home. They thought it was a bad example for a patient in that place to be pestering them for a telephone, particularly a telephone to be used for business. I imagine his booming bass voice calling them, following them down the corridors the way it used to follow his children around the coffee plantation. The voice would be organizing them to provide various secretarial functions so that its owner could continue to conduct his own, personal campaign to keep Africa and, thereby, the rest of the world free from Communism.

That Day, I had telephoned my parents in Germany, but, apparently, I had dialed the wrong number. I had expected to be greeted by that same loud, vocal surprise and pleasure that always met my calls. The cheerful greeting would be followed by descriptions of the latest plans for speaking tours, by questions about which American Senator would be the most receptive to or most worthy to approach with its owner's latest cause, by plans for another fact-finding trip to South Africa and by a discussion of plans to visit the States to see American grandchildren. Instead, I was greeted by a voice that seemed to belong to a confused, frail, little, old, German lady whom I must have wakened from her late afternoon nap. So I apologized and I ended the call.

I sometimes still make the mistake of dialing my aunts' number instead of my parents', particularly if I dial from memory, so I checked the number and dialed again. The same small voice answered and I soon became even more confused than its owner appeared to be. I asked for my father, by name, trying German.

The owner told me, softly but proudly, in German, that *she* went by that name. My German is poor, but not so poor that I could make a mistake like that, so I asked, again, in English. I got the same answer, in German.

I tried: "Aunt Maggie?"

"Nein! Hier Ernst!" The weak voice was beginning to show signs of impatience with this dense caller, even though we had exchanged fewer than ten words each.

I was certain that this time I had dialed the right number, and just as certain that we were not going to progress very far in either German or English, so I asked for Mum, by name. In a few seconds, I was speaking with her.

From Mum I learned that it was indeed Dad who had answered the phone. *This* nurse knew, from a lifetime of experience, which battles can be won and which battles are simply not worth fighting, and she had let Dad have his telephone at his bedside. Which phone he was, of course, insisting on answering, even if he had to waken from a medicated sleep to do so.

A few minutes later I was trying to talk to him again. Since he was not taking the English bait, I was struggling, a little sheepishly, in my best but inadequate German. He didn't know me, but was nonetheless very pleased that I had called to wish him well. Did I know he was "...a bit out of sorts? ... just back from the hospital ... some friends have been in to see [him]... very nice ... very kind of them ...So nice of [me] to call ..."

I did call again and spoke to him a few times, over the next few days. Those times, he was awake when I called and he was much more himself. He recognized my voice the moment I said "Hello, Dad!", and speaking to him in English worked. He told me that he had set up meetings with his associates, so that his work could be passed on to them while he rested a little. We talked about how I would visit him, right after Christmas, when transatlantic seats would be more readily available and other plans not so hectic. We talked about how, perhaps, he could bring Mum to the States, when he was better.

I recognized this man who always had plans, always had a project or a campaign to right some wrong, who always looked to the future. But I did not recognize his voice. His voice which used to find me a mile away had become a strained whisper. It sounded, in fact, like the voice of a frail little old lady. It was hard, talking with that voice.

But, back to the conversation on That Day. If his English was out of order, so was my German. I wanted to ask him a bit more about how he felt and if he was in pain. I came up with: *"Was ist los?"* That is a very colloquial "What's up?" What was up, he told this unrecognized but slightly familiar caller, was that there were these things wrong with his liver, his pancreas and some other organs.

He had not used the word, but "these things" were cancers, and they killed him, not a week later.

Dad could ride a donkey through a herd of elephants and walk home through a pride of lions. He had once, reputedly, shot a lion dead, in mid leap, as it attacked him[2]. Dad survived

---

[2]We grew up with the lion skin rug in the living room. It certainly looked shot and dead, though not any longer in mid leap. Dad never told us the story, perhaps we told ourselves, but we believed it and frequently re-enacted it for ourselves.

the unavoidable natural forces of destruction in tropical diseases, plagues, droughts and floods. He survived the probably just as inevitable, and to him, just as natural ones that lie in saying the wrong things to or about Hitler, getting entangled in any way with British colonial politics, eating the wrong mushrooms and drinking his own pineapple wine. He was a survivors' survivor.

I regret, though I do not blame myself, that I did not grasp that he was not going to survive 'these things' and that to see him alive once more I would have to go sooner than our holiday plans and airline bookings seemed willing to allow. I didn't grasp it even though he used the words 'if I'm still here' while we discussed the plans. He had often sounded melodramatic, and for twenty years he had talked about making sure that Ona (his nickname for Mum) would be taken care of after he was 'gone'. I regret, also, that my last conversations with him were so strained, and that I was unable fully to appreciate how bad it was for him. But I'm positively embarrassed to remember my weak, trite performance in his cherished German: *"Was ist los?"* indeed, to a dying man!

Isn't it odd how the natural laws that govern airline seat availability and just general plan-making work so that one can't find a seat sooner than six weeks to go see a loved one alive, but one can somehow get one to go to a funeral only days later? Perhaps it is the same laws that saw to it that Dad's funeral was the first time in twenty-seven years that Mum had her five children under the same roof at the same time!

Perhaps not unnaturally, for a year after Dad's death I reminisced even more than I usually do, much of it out loud. My children suggested, perhaps in self-defense, that I write some of that stuff down, just as I have asked Mum to write some of her stuff down and wish that I had known to ask her mother and father and others to do so with their stuff. Whenever anyone suggested to Mum that she write down some of her experiences, she said that she would not - could not - do it until most of the people in the stories were dead. That time is probably already here, and she can't put us off anymore. Somehow I have expected Mum to be ready to start though I know I am not, even as I start writing.

But then I think of Dad's approach to things. I can count seven or eight times that he had to start again, after he had been financially ruined by, among other things, political upheaval, change of climate and misplaced trust. One of these times he started again, literally, from ashes. He explained his Phoenix-like new starts by saying that you can't beat a man who doesn't know when he's beaten. That may be true, but I would add that it was more that he just had a compulsion to act. When he could not act, he planned what he would do as soon as he could act, but planning was usually a poor second best to acting, and usually happened only during long hours of driving or other periods of forced inactivity.

The period that the following reminiscences are concerned with covers one new start which began in 1958, Dad's fifty second year and my nineteenth, though, in order to put it in perspective I have had to go back a bit. I think it helps to know what the devil we were doing in Africa, anyway. When my children ask me to explain something, they usually preface the question with: 'In five words or less, what ... ?' This time, they didn't. Nevertheless, thankfully I found it possible to start the story just this side of the Flood.

For this new beginning, Dad moved us, lock, stock and barrel, to a new country, which had a new language, where we were to create a coffee plantation out of a parcel of virgin land located about 300 miles by road from the nearest real town. He knew it would be five years before the first crop and that there was the equivalent of only $10,000 in the bank.

He was not exactly courting success or 'good luck'. Although by this time he had already had more than his share of bad luck, I never heard him call himself anything but a lucky man. After all, he had been able to maintain his principles and was still alive, he had good health and he had a family which he loved and of which he was proud. That is an enviable list of blessings.

Despite being a very principled man and a great talker, he didn't spend much time during my youth lecturing me about his guiding principles, so he taught me very few lessons, in words, about life. I think there are three or four one-sentence lectures that fall into that category, and he admitted that they were borrowed. The ways he did teach me were, first, by expecting, really presuming, success in impossible or improbable tasks and, second, through example, and these approaches were worth volumes. I recall being put on the milk lorry that we had flagged down somewhere along the road, to go the forty miles in to town to run an errand or get a part, and to find my way back the same day or, failing that, the next. It doesn't sound like a lot to expect, but I was twelve. Was it expecting a lot of a twenty year old girl and her eighteen and seventeen year old brothers to leave them alone for six weeks somewhere at the end of a jungle track, a thousand miles away from home, with not much more than a few instructions, to start a coffee plantation? It may happen every day, in some places. We weren't even surprised when he did it to us.

Dad did not believe that life just happened to him. He believed that he had to take control. He never, ever, was without a project that required his total attention. He never, ever, got involved in anything without it just about consuming him. Of course, if it consumed him, it should be consuming everyone else, concurrently and equally. People who have lived with him will tell you that he never got involved in anything without driving everyone else to distraction. It is appropriate that one of his few one sentence lessons to me applies to this facet of his personality: 'You must always take people for what they are and not for what you would like them to be.' One had to take Dad the way he was, for there was no force on earth that could change him.

This is not a story about Dad, but since he was the central figure in our lives and in almost all of the experiences we had when we were growing up in Africa, it is full of him, just as our lives were. More than a year after I had left Africa for the first time, and was at university, I was asked by a fellow student who was conducting a study for his thesis, to describe myself in several different ways. I was to list the most important one first, least important last. My first description was: "I am my father's son." I don't know exactly what I meant, or what this says about him, or about me, or about our relationship. It would still be somewhere on my list if I were to redo it now.

Nor is this a story about me, even if the first person singular is overused in it, a fact for which I apologize; I am lazy, and it is just easier to report my own memories and impressions rather than those of others. And it is not a novel, requiring a plot and a neat conclusion.

It is a collection of memories of an era that was short and is over. We happened to have been led by Dad to start a coffee plantation in the Belgian Congo. We were there in the last two years before the colony gained its independence and for six months after that. We did not do anything earth-shaking, but few people lived the same experiences and none will live them again. Not exactly the same, even though the headlines in the world's newspapers suggest that things are not much more settled in the Kivu Province of Zaïre[3], over three decades later.

I have reported some conversations as well as I can remember them, not claiming that any are verbatim, acknowledging that several of them are reconstructions and that some are totally invented to make a point in a more interesting way or for a change of pace. However, the conversations in the latter category *could* have taken place. Also, at the risk of it becoming intrusive, I intentionally use the old names of the countries and other words as we would have used them in that period; they were part of that time and part of the experience.

I have looked on the writing about those experiences and that time as one way of celebrating Dad's life, of not letting go of him, yet. And I have hoped that, perhaps, by the time it is done, during my ninetieth or hundredth attempt to learn German, I will be brave enough to attempt some better conversational gambits in that language. The only way that will have happened is that I will have reminded myself of and will have followed his example in his approach to language. You must never be intimidated by the rules of grammar. If you wait until you are perfect in a foreign language before daring to speak in it, you will never say a word, and you will never have communicated.

Come to think of it, his approach to life was somewhat similar. If you don't act because plans or opportunities are not perfect, you will never do anything. He didn't ever guarantee that this approach would bring success, but neither did he ever contemplate failure.

If I wait until I am ready to write, it will never happen. Maybe if I do get started and write some of that stuff, however imperfectly, Mum will do some, and we will start to be able to share a family's rather unusual experiences and remarkable history with Mum and Dad's daughters-in-law and

---

[3] Now, in 1997, again named 'The Republic of The Congo'.

grandchildren. We used to have opportunities to hear stories about earlier days from our parents and grandparents, that modern lifestyles and the intrusion of television have made rare. This is an important justification for attempting to write this. It is my excuse.

Maybe, if we get the hang of this, one day we will be able to do justice to Dad's own story. It is a good one.

The history of the European in the Congo is mostly bad. Fortunately, for the Congolese, the worst of it was short. The worst of the worst ended in the first decade of the twentieth century, fifty years before we went there. Peter Forbath has written an excellent, honest book about the exploration of the river Congo and the exploitation of the country and its people, and his Epilogue would serve well as a backdrop for my story. If you are at all interested in understanding more, I strongly recommend that you read the book.

The history of Zaïre since the European left is not much happier. That history is still being lived and made. Thirty-seven years haven't changed much of anything.

—CvI, Winston-Salem September, 1997

P.S.
Dad:
Iko shauri moja, Mzee Mbogo, there's just one thing, Elder Buffalo. I like to think that had I seen you after Christmas, as I had hoped, I would have said something that I don't think I ever did actually say to you. It's not that we didn't know how to talk, we talked plenty - at least some of us did. Maybe we didn't think we needed to say some things, because we each knew what we would have said. Maybe that was just a rationalization for not saying them; sentimentality and all that soppy stuff didn't fit comfortably on any of us. Be that as it may, I never doubted your pride in and love for me and for all of your family. I hope you never doubted my pride in and love for you. While I think this story says it, it is an oblique way of saying it and it might well be masked in the fun I can't seem to resist poking at you. So I'll say it, not in German, yet, it won't ring true and I can't allow another linguistic whimper:

"Dad, thank you for the sometimes maddening, usually frustrating, always hectic, but nonetheless great experience of

15

being your son! I love you, just the way you were!"

—CvI, Winston-Salem September, 1997

Now, sixty years after the events that ended our time in the Congo, I look back at what I wrote nearly thirty years ago. A few things come to mind.

First, the region has not yet seen peace, not even for a short time.

Second, I was reminded of Dad's comments to the effect that the so-called democracies have had seven centuries to work on it, and haven't yet got democracy right, so we shouldn't be surprised if the Congolese didn't get it in a period of a few months. Now I live in the country supposed to have the only democracy continuous for over 200 years. The fantastic claims of the Congolese political candidates in 1960 seem pale in comparison to some of the claims bandied about by elected politicians and talk show hosts today. We came close to losing it in January this year. I wonder if we can last a couple more decades longer, let alone centuries.

—CvI, Durham, NC
May, 2021

PART ONE

KAGANDO
AT NGANDO'S PLACE

CHAPTER ONE

The day on which Dad finally came back with Mum, her father and a menagerie of animals, we found that a family of buffalo had visited the new camp we had just built. They had come the night before as though to give it a final inspection and had left calling cards in the living room. The presence of the piles of droppings could have been taken as a bad omen, but didn't have to be. In some tribal customs, any part of a person's body, or anything to do with the body, is good material for casting spells. It is a gesture of trust and friendship, even a form of blessing, to spit on a person you wish to honor, for in fact you put your very life in his hands by doing so. In this light, it is much more meaningful to spit on someone in greeting than to offer the right hand. The latter really only means "Look!, I'm not holding any arms in my right hand." So, if a little gob of spit is a blessing, what generous wishes of good fortune were there in the huge piles of gesture that the buffalo delegation left us?

It had taken a year for the family to prepare for and to make the seven hundred mile move from Tanganyika[4] to this raw, thousand-acre chunk of The Belgian Congo that we were to try to coax into becoming a coffee plantation. It had taken nearly two weeks for Pauline, Bill and me (aged 20, 17 and 18, respectively) to unload the parts of a tractor, several ploughs and other equipment from our lorry and its trailer, for Dad to hire about two hundred Watalinga[5] and Wanandi tribesmen,

---

[4]Now Tanzania.
[5]In Swahili, a *Mtalinga* is a member of the *Watalinga* or *Talinga* tribe, which speaks *kitalinga*. If you're a purist, their home is probably *utalingani*, however, purity was not an issue here. In this area, as in many others, 'b' is substituted freely for 'w', and they refer to themselves as the

and then to walk us around and over the land, dispensing instructions as he went. It had taken Dad less than ten minutes to pack to leave to fetch Mum and Paga.

It took less than three minutes after he shouted a departing promise to be back in about three weeks, for Dad's VW pickup, our link with the world, to be gone from our sight.

It took only moments after that for the three of us to feel terribly lonely.

We shouldn't have felt lonely. There were three of us, and we were surrounded by two hundred people. The two hundred people were very friendly, if their broad smiles and grins were any indication, and they spoke a language in which we should be able to make ourselves understood. If we didn't know where to get food, there were plenty of people who did (even though it would not be from a grocery, the nearest one being in Beni, 60 miles away). If we were unfamiliar with the area, there were plenty of people who knew it well. If we needed protection, there were plenty of people to provide it. We'd have to be pessimists to worry! I mean, what harm could possibly come to us, and what could we possibly be nervous about?

We must have been three pessimists, though not one of us would have admitted any worries to anyone else, yet. But, in our frame of mind, the surrounding felt rather claustrophobic. Weren't some of those teeth we saw behind the smiles filed to sharp points? Hadn't the hero of one of the stories in [our uncle] Jock's old boys' magazines known that this was a sure sign of cannibalism? How clear could we make ourselves in *Kinguana,* really only a distant cousin of Swahili? We understood that *machetes* were necessary tools, but weren't there rather more than necessary bows and arrows and sticks in the crowd? If we were going to need protection, from whom were we to be protected?

How long were the three weeks going to be?

Believe us, you can feel extremely lonely, even in a crowd.

Hey! It was all in our minds! To take our minds off our lapse,

---

Batalinga. The Belgians used the 'w', not that they were purists, nor that they knew enough to be right, they just did it, the way they just did lots of other things. I'm doing it because it comes more naturally to me. If I slip and use a 'b', and you catch me, don't worry about a new tribe moving in, and don't ask for a prize.

18

we compared notes about the instructions and the parts of The [verbal - *very* verbal] Grand Plan that Dad had left us with. Among the myriad details, four things stood out very clearly.

"First, we have to start putting the men to work clearing the *matete*[6], and don't forget Dad's Mulching System," said Pauline.

Dad believed in mulch so fervently that he committed fifty percent of the land to its production. We were to follow a pattern that cleared and left alone alternating, parallel strips. Thirty meters would be room for ten rows of coffee trees and thirty meters of *matete* would produce mulch. No mulch would have to be carried farther than fifteen meters. This was the backbone of the Mulching System. It followed that the first strip would be fifteen metres of *matete*. It followed, further, that you could drive or walk right past much of our work of the next two years and not see it. The Mulching System was not for providing a view of our coffee trees, it was to give us Superior Grades of Coffee. We had heard about the Superior Coffee every time Dad had thought of telling us about it, which had been every time he had thought about it, which had been often.

"I've got to finish putting the tractor together and take the trailer into de Jaeger's *coup de bois*," said Bill. This was a certain area in the jungle where our neighbor had a timber concession from the government. "We have to get poles for the camp and check on the stuff at the mission."

We were to cut what we would need, haul it out of the forest and up on to the hill and build a temporary, thatched-hut camp. The camp would serve the family until we could make bricks and build a real house. In consideration of the extreme heat and humidity, Dad had told us to "...build it on top of that two-hundred-foot-high hill, over there, overlooking the plain. And design it to Catch Every Breath of Moving Air!"

The stuff at the mission was almost all of the first load of our personal possessions, that we had left in the shelter of a de-consecrated church at the Catholic mission, ten kilometres away, close to the *coup de bois*. With not a single structure existing on our land, this ex-church was the only shelter

---

[6]ma-TAY-tay. *Matete* is also known as elephant grass. It is so named because an elephant - actually, several herds of elephants - could and often did hide in it.

available, within one hundred kilometers, to unload the lorry into. Its major problems were that it was not close to our *gîte*[7], and it had no doors or windows. It had no walls either, so I suppose doors and windows didn't matter much. But, it would be easy to check on it every time we went for a load of poles. And then, for ten minutes, or however long we cared to stay there on our way to haul poles, the stuff would be perfectly safe. For the rest of the time, it would be open hunting season on it. To add slightly to its security and to compensate for the fact that Père Jean had removed his Catholic *dawa,* or spell, we had left a couple of young fellows in charge of the church and its contents. One was named Pascali, who was going to be our house servant and cook, when we got a house and a kitchen, and the other was Sengerengabo[8], a laborer. Since they were Warundi, not Watalinga, we thought that they would be able to avoid having to be nice to their brothers and sisters by letting them help themselves to our things. Their brothers and sisters were three or four hundred kilometres away, and we assumed that it would take them more than three weeks to find new brothers and sisters in this new place. Still, it behooved us to look in on them, once in a while, lest they forget our interest in the stuff.

Third, we were to stay in the new *gîte,* which had been erected, hastily, by Basikania, chief of the local branch of the Nandi tribe. This *gîte* was constructed like a native hut. It had a beaten earth floor, mud walls, a single entrance, no windows and a thatched roof. It was a two mile walk from our future home. It was one hundred yards from the real *gîte,* the one we had planned to use, but that the two young Flemish *colons* (colonials), who had taken the neighboring properties and had made their move into the area quicker than we did, were occupying while they built their respective houses.

"Fourth, and not least," Pauline reminded us, "he said we must be Polite, But Distant with our two neighbors. I don't think he really expects that I might get romantically involved with one of those Belges in three weeks. Do you?" We thought

---

[7]A *gîte* is literally a resting place. The word is used in the colonies for a structure used by visiting officials. Sometimes it is a government owned structure, with kitchen and bath. Not always.
[8]Pronounce the 'g' this time, 'ng' as in finger: seng-gereng-GAH-bo.

not. Rather, we believed it to be a reaction to the fact that for all of the thirty years that he had lived in British East Africa, he had never been treated as an aristocrat. One, he was a German, a rotten Hun. Two, he had the effrontery to marry one of their own, a beautiful Scottish girl. While he did make some very close friends across all nationalities and races, many British colonials never really forgave him for either of those two crimes. Three, the British have their own brand of aristocracy and, to them, since they have forgotten that their current crop and several before it were borrowed heavily from the Continent, they look on everyone else's brand, particularly if it's from the Continent, as being merely a pale imitation of their own. In East Africa, when people addressed him as "Prince", it was almost condescending; they were being good sports and playing along with his little pretense. Now, in The Belgian Congo, even the authorities spoke to him respectfully. His mother was a Princess, and a Belgian national, after all, and they were representatives of King Baudouin. She was not a Princess *of* Belgium, she was a Princess *and* Belgian. Dad understood such things, we didn't. Anyway, he felt at home and comfortable with this fresh treatment. With respect to our neighbors, he merely wanted us to maintain the appropriate dignity and decorum befitting our recently dusted off status.

In retrospect, we actually addressed all of the things that he had listed, with varying degrees of success, albeit in a different order, in the **six** weeks that it took Dad to return.

Of high priority, on the personal shelter and survival front, was setting up our *gîte* to fit our needs. Comfort was not the question; basic needs were. We worked on that in the evenings, after putting in long hours in the *matete,* in close to 100-degree heat, and walking two miles back to our hut. We would head back, soaked in sweat, hot and thirsty. As we came up the hill and within shouting distance, one of us would call out: "Nivari, *lete maji!* Bring water!" and our self-appointed interim cook would come out to greet us with large pans of cool water. We would quaff gallons, before thinking of doing anything else.

Our arrival in the little village of Njadot[9] must have been the

---

[9]njah-DOUGH. The spelling is courtesy of the French language. If you want to know how good it can get, compare 'Houphouét Bouagny' and 'Ufwe Bwanyi'. Or 'Ouagadougou' and 'Wagadugu'

event of the decade for the villagers, for we were constantly being watched by hundreds of pairs of eyes. For the first week, we would have to push our way through the crowd to get in through our front entrance - there was no door, as such. Most of the time, we got just a blank stare so it was hard to tell if we caused the watchers pleasure or pain. Every now and then, though, something we did would cause some pointing, some comments in *Kinandi* or *Kitalinga* and some merriment. We never knew what, or we might have repeated it for them, from time to time. Bill and I were lucky that, even in front of that audience, we could shed our shirts to cool off. Pauline felt that it was far too public for her to be able to do so. Considering the dress of some of the onlookers themselves, I'm sure that had she been brave enough to join us the audience would not have blinked.

When the sun goes down at the Equator, it gets dark very quickly. All that we had for lighting was a couple of well used *fanusis*, hurricane lamps, so once we had drunk our water and taken our bows in front of the audience, we had little time to sit around before trying to make the hut habitable. There were no windows. There were two divisions, hardly rooms, in the hut. One was slightly less public than the other, so Pauline got it as her bedroom. The other space became the boys' bedroom and the living room. You can't really clean an earth floor, so we were saved some of the effort that would have been spent in cleaning it. That was the good news. Storing food, clothing and other personal items on a dirt floor, with no furniture, does present some difficulties. That was the bad news. We just had to use our ingenuity. We found places to hang things.

There was no electricity and no telephone. There was no running water, so it follows, there was no indoor plumbing, no showers, no baths, no toilets. There was a poorly screened pit latrine behind the hut. Given the always-present gawkers, it was not easy to be discreet about some very private activities.

Each evening, as soon as it began to get dark, we followed a ritual. We took soap, towels and clean clothes and walked down the track to the ford at the river. We went upstream and Bill and I stopped at the first slight bend so that the *matete* on the bank hid us from view, Pauline went on past the second bend, and we bathed. We bathed fast. It is not that we were shy, or afraid of the wild animals for we had not yet come across them.

22

As we rushed through our first of many such baths, Bill said, through chattering teeth: "It's n-nice to be able to c-cool off, but I didn't ask for it to be *that* c-cold!"

I said: "The river source is high up in the mountain, which is high enough to have snow and ice on it several times a year, even though it is right on the equator. At least, they say it has, under all that cloud."

My school companions, even as far back as Arusha School, had been so impressed by my knowledge about all manner of diverse subjects, that they had nicknamed me "Professor". Bill was much less impressed. He offered his own theory that had something to do with artesian wells fed from glaciers in Antarctica. With my puffery properly deflated, we went back up the hill, already sweating from the heat.

Food was an interesting problem. The nearest supermarket may have been in another continent. The nearest grocer was in Beni, our Provincial capital. To get to Beni, we would have to go one hundred kilometers, or sixty miles, over an unpaved road. The choice between doing it in miles or in kilometers and the state of the road were all academic. We had no car and the tractor was not suitable for this kind of trip. Were we not being Polite But Distant with our neighbors, we might have arranged to go with one of them, but we were, so we didn't. There was nothing for it but to live off the land. This is where Nivari came in. Although he was a Mtalinga, from down in the forest, and we were in the mountain dwelling Nandi's village, he knew his way around enough to be able to look for food. Soon the word got out, and the crowd that gathered at our door every evening would hold a few people with an egg or two, a few handfuls of locally grown rice tied in a scrap of cloth, or perhaps a chicken or a bunch of bananas to sell.

"What! You don't want to buy my eggs?!"

It was a combination of question and exclamation. These folks didn't have degrees in marketing, but we understood. We would pay the going rate, usually a *rumée* (a quarter of a franc, or half a penny) per egg, about a penny or two for a kilo of rice, a few cents for a bunch of bananas.

Bananas are easy to store, you hang the bunch from something. We found a rafter near the door to be most suitable. It was near the light from the doorway and we could see it and avoid bumping into it. We also could not forget we had it. Rice presented a different challenge. The seller would want to take the cloth or bowl back with her. Containers were a precious commodity in most of rural Africa; bottles and tins would be used over and over. The only container we could come up with for the rice was my spare pajama pants. With a knot in the end of each of the legs, they were transformed into a neat double sack. When we sat the pajamas astride a rafter, the rice was kept nicely off the floor.

Without refrigeration, the only way to keep a chicken until we needed it was to keep it alive. We just had to be careful that Pauline didn't give it a name!

Before Dad left, our landlord, Chief Basikania had been to visit us, to see how well we were getting settled in to his *gîte*. He was accompanied by his son and two men. One man he introduced as Augustin, whom he was offering to us for the position of *ndombe* or combination of headman and clerk, since he could read and write in Swahili, French and Kinandi, and, presumably, could be counted on to report back to Basikania anything that he thought his chief should know. His name was pronounced Augustin, Agostino, Agosta and Costa, in the same conversation. The other man was pulling a small black pig along on a rope tied to one of its forelimbs. This pig was Basikania's welcome gift to us. We were probably supposed to slaughter it, immediately, cook it and invite Basikania to sit down and eat it with us, but we didn't. At least we should have offered him beer, and, perhaps even his entourage, including the man who had led the pig, who had probably been its owner until it was raised to the status of Welcome Gift for the *Wazungu*, the Europeans. We didn't. We did not even have beer, which was unusual for *Wazungu* in the Congo. So we all sat around for a few hours, which felt like weeks, sipping tea, while Dad described to a bewildered Chief and entourage, a) his pedigree, part of which had to do with his mother being a Princess, whatever that was, and at the same time something called a Beaufort-Spontin and, yet again at the same time, a Belgian, (the latter was particularly puzzling, for why would he want to claim connection to the Belgians? It probably was not true, anyway, or was a misinterpretation, since there was no beer here. Beer and Belgians are usually found together!), b) the Mulching System

24

and c) how appropriate it would be for us to have about two more acres of land, on top of that hill, over there, so that we could be among the hill people (after all, we had just left the tallest mountain in Africa, yes, even taller than the Ruwenzoris) and, incidentally, so that we could build our house to Catch Every Breath of Moving Air. Basikania apparently was flattered that this person, who, among the *Wazungu* was almost as important as was Basikania among the Wanandi, appeared to want to be in the hills with his superior people, rather than in the low land of the Watalinga. It was agreed that we could build on the hill. We would settle the details later.

Basikania's son, Paul, pronounced Apollo (to show they could be consistent, the locals nearly always addressed Pauline as Appolina). He was a young teen-ager, who went to school across the river, in Uganda, then under British rule. His father was very proud of his ability to speak English.

Just about exactly every fifteen minutes, no matter who was speaking, or what was being said, Apollo demonstrated this prowess by asking out loud: "WHATee time eeZEET?"

We later asked each other if it was an amazing coincidence, or what? His appearance and that of his god-ish namesake, at least our conception of what his namesake's appearance should be, bore a striking lack of similarity!

But this is about food and the pig! During the tea-sipping and the talk of ancestors and hill sites, Pauline announced to Bill and me: "The pig's name is Dagobert!"

We knew what that meant. Dagobert might become the centerpiece of our growing menagerie of chickens, roosters and goats that was our larder-on-the-hoof, but he was never to become the centerpiece of a roast pork feast, for somewhere, it is written: 'Thou shalt not eat an animal which has acquired a name.' I suppose it suited Bill and me. Although we would be talked into hunting, neither of us had the stomach to kill our dinner in hand to hand combat. Even if it is done by proxy, there is something different between telling Nivari to cook *a* chicken and telling him to dispatch *this particular,* named animal.

Within a week or two of Dad's departure, we had settled into our hut and into a routine. Evenings, just before our walk down to the river for our baths, we would sit in the pool of light near the doorway and wind down, largely succeeding in

25

ignoring the diminishing crowd of Wanandi in front of the hut and trying vainly to ignore the increasing clouds of mosquitoes around our legs.

On one such evening, Bill and I were shirtless, as usual. I had one pair of pajama bottoms on over my khaki shorts and tucked into my laced up army surplus jungle boots, in a vain effort to protect my ankles from the marauding mosquitoes. The other pair of pajama bottoms, full of rice, was sitting astride the low rafter near to and visible from the doorway. The bananas were hanging beside the rice, at eye level. Dagobert was snorting around the door, looking for whatever it is pigs look for. Some of the chickens were scratching around, doing chicken things and making chicken noises. Pauline was doing something with the body of one chicken that, earlier in the afternoon, Nivari had permanently discouraged from scratching by separating it from its head. She had the non-head and featherless part in a pot, on the kerosene cooker. The cooker was also in the light near the door, on the floor.

Pauline muttered out loud: "Where is Apollo when you need him? Four times 'whatee time eezeet' would make an hour. That should be just about enough time to soften up this old bird!"

I was fishing out a cupful of rice through the fly of my pajama pants, the ones I was not wearing, which in the dim light, looked like part of a body hanging in the rafters.

There was a polite cough outside. We looked up to see M. Paepe, one of the neighbors from the comfortable *gîte*. He apologized, most politely, in French, for disturbing us, and went on to ask if we could lend him something.

We looked at each other. I had had quite few years of classroom French, but my ear was not yet tuned in to the dynamics of the spoken language. "He wants to borrow a sailor," I translated.

He looked surprised and said: "Non! A 'amma! For to 'amma *clous*."

When we 'ad cleared up the differences in spelling, pronunciation and utility between French sailors and French 'ammers for 'ammering nails, 'e went on with a few pleasantries. He was obviously rather taken by the whole scene. He was finding it very difficult to keep a straight face.

I felt that I might improve the situation by offering an

explanation for my unusual outfit. *"C'est contre les moustiques, vous comprenez!"*

But he did not seem to find it any easier to accept this explanation of my semi-nudity than to keep his composure. He left after a few more minutes of polite, not very distant, but strained conversation.

Pauline continued to do some more things to the chicken. She had been given a wild pepper plant, pulled out by the roots. It had on it a hundred tiny red chili peppers, each no longer than half an inch. The donor, one of the workers, had suggested that the peppers did wonders for flavor if they were thrown in the pot with a chicken. Looking at the scrawniness of the chicken, we all thought that anything that would help turn that bird into a meal would be doing a notable wonder. We were all partial to hot chicken curries and so Pauline had decided to make us a treat, that night, in place of whatever Nivari would have boiled for us. Curry powder being unavailable, the chilies would turn this into a sort of hot chicken stew, the next best thing to hot chicken curry.

While she did the things necessary to complete turning the chicken and some of the pajama-rice into dinner, we congratulated ourselves for being so diligent in doing Dad's bidding by being Polite But Distant with poor M. Paepe. And we laughed until it hurt.

"I wonder if he understands that these mosquitoes really do like my ankles better than my arms or my back!"

"Don't worry! What does it matter if he doesn't! He's going to be polite but distant from us, after this!"

"A sailor! He doesn't look the type to need a sailor!"

"D'you see his expression? Why d'you never have a camera when you need one!"

We were still laughing about the spectacle we must have presented when we hunkered down around the packing box that was our table, to eat hot chicken stew.

One mouthful later, the tears of laughter turned into tears of another kind! The chicken was so hot that we couldn't keep it in our mouths.

Pauline told us, her eyes streaming: "He said put a few *pilipilis* in with the chicken, maybe six. I thought that we'd need more than a few, they're so small, and we're used to Mum's hot curries!"

27

Bill asked: "How many is 'more'?"

"Oh! I think I started with about twenty. I may have added more, later."

I don't know when we stopped laughing, that evening. We fell asleep with our mouths seared and sides still aching.

As far as work was concerned, there seemed to be no end to the things to be attended to. Each of them was the most urgent. The smart thing would have been to split up the duties, but it was still our first few days at this level of responsibility, so we still were leaning a bit on each other and did many thing for the first time together. One advantage was that, this way, many of our early experiences were shared.

The first thing we did was to start to lay out the pattern of 30 meter clearings, known as *kipaniyés*[10] so we could put the laborer's to work. This was a chore at which we would spend many an afternoon and evening, over the next two years, so that the men would be able to go to work as soon as they appeared each morning. It soon was to become one of those things that are not so hard to do but are dreaded because of their inevitability.

Second was to set a team of men to cut a road through the *matete,* towards the famous hill. We laid out our path to be wide enough for one vehicle to pass at a time and to head straight towards the hill. The land on the plain was relatively flat and the going was smooth for the first half mile. We went off to check on something else. When we came back, we noticed that the path made several rather jagged turns that seemed unnecessary, before stopping at a small spring that was more like a swamp, right at the foot of the hill. The swamp drained out into the flat land through a narrow neck only ten feet wide. It seemed that any access to the top of the hill had to go across this neck of the swamp, or all the way around it. We got across, retrieved one or two boots from the mud, and put the men to work to continue the path, slanting up the side of the hill.

At this point, Joseph (pronounced josEPH), a short man

---

[10]key-pah-nee-YAYs. I have no idea if this is a kinguana word, or where else it might come from, or how it is spelt, for that matter. The 'ki' part might be a diminutive, or it might not. The closest I can come to the word it in the French dictionary is 'panneau', panel. Its better than 'panier', basket, don't you think?

with filed teeth and a very official looking cap, volunteered: "I am not a laborer, I have been a *capita*, or headman, in the *Departement de Travaux Publiques*. I know the work of roads, and will cut the road up the hill." Several voices supported his claim, so we thought we could leave him to do that.

So we did, but not before saying: "You must make it easy for the *camion* (the lorry), and the *tracteur* to climb this steep hill, even with a big load."

Indignantly, pulling himself up to his full five feet, two inches of height, he said: "*Bwana!* Have I not done this for many years, since even before you were in your mother's belly? Did I not become M. Unpronounceable's right hand? Did he not say to the whole *Departement*, on *siku ya posho,* the day for giving out rations: 'Joseph, your skill in finding the easy way is exceeded only by that of *tembo,* the elephant.' And you know that the elephant always looks for the easy way up a hill! Bwana, the entire road from Beni to here followed the tracks made by *tembo*. Do *I* know how to do it?....Why..."

If he had just said: "Trust me! I know what I am doing," in precisely those words, we would have been suitably warned not to. He didn't, and we weren't, so we did. So we left the continuation up the hill to Joseph and the bridging of the water to later, and took some time to check on some of the other pressing things.

We walked back down the path together. On the way, we stopped to check out those curves in the new road.

Bill said: "It looks like the road was coming along too fast, couldn't stop and pranged into the hill."

Indeed, this end of the road looked crumpled. As we walked through the curves, which were really too tight for the lorry, we peered into the *matete* to see what was going on. We noticed that there were many paths through the thick grass, some covered in buffalo footprints. At each of the road's abrupt changes in direction, there was a hole in the ground, mostly hidden by the *matete*. The holes were typically six feet long, two feet wide at the top and about six feet deep. You'd get a nasty shock if you fell into one, particularly if you were an elephant! When we asked him, later, Augustin explained that the shape and size were just right to get an elephant immobilized long enough to kill it with spears. Sometimes, there would be wooden stakes in the bottom, which would

29

help. The stakes, he explained, did not last long in the holes, being attractive to swarms of wood-hungry termites. The elephants, we imagined, did not last very long in there either, being attractive to swarms of meat-hungry Watalinga.

A few days later, Bill had already done one trip to fetch poles from the *coup de bois*. He wondered if the rest of us wouldn't like to come along, so we would know the way, too. Also, it was a bit of a trick to get the tall, gangling Farmall M tractor and the big trailer into the forest, along a track that had not been cleared for months. Any suggestions on how to make it easier would be welcome. We thought it a good idea, and promised to go along, the next day.

I was, of course, quite willing to show my younger brother how easy it really was. I took the driver's seat as we started into the narrow green-black tunnel going into the forest, leading at right angles from the edge of the road.

"I'll go ahead and show you where the turns are," offered Bill.

The workers all jumped down and headed onto the track, ahead of the tractor, laughing, leaving only Pauline, who stood on the drawbar behind me and held on to the seat.

"And I'll show you how to make the turns!" said I.

"Happy lot, Bill has on this job!" Pauline and I agreed, as I let out the clutch and the tractor lurched down the track.

Because of my high seat, my head was in the overhanging branches and the track was almost invisible to me. Even so, I was able to get the cumbersome tractor around most of the bends without any problem. How difficult could this have been for Bill? As the trailer followed on its tighter radius, its tall sides scraped along most of the trees. Its uprights, one after the other, caught onto and shook each tree thoroughly, almost as though they were designed to do so. The shaking caused a fine shower of particles to rain down on us from the trees. Bill turned around and looked at us, with exaggerated nonchalance, just as Pauline and I yelled, together:

"HEY! I'm on fire!" "What IS that?"

We had ants all over us. Biting, stinging fire-ants. Down our shirt necks, in our hair, in our shoes. We had ants in our literal pants. The road back was awash with disturbed fire-ants. The road ahead wasn't blocked, so we left the tractor and ran. But running away from them didn't help. Even if we could

30

convince ourselves that we didn't want the poles, we had to get the tractor out. And there was no question, we had to get the poles. And then, when we had the poles, we had to get back out, along the same track, with the now loaded trailer even less maneuverable than before.

When we got out, finally, and had shaken, dusted and beaten the ants off our bodies, and had given the ants that had fallen on the tractor and the trailer and its load time to disperse, we decided to stop in to check on Pascali, Sengerengabo and the stuff at the Mission.

When we were approaching the Mission, we saw Pascali walking awkwardly along the edge of the road. We soon saw why he was unsteady. He had had a little too much *pombe*, native millet beer, and he was wearing some shoes that were too narrow for his wide feet. Getting closer, we recognized the shoes as Dad's. This made me very angry, first, that he had abandoned his post, second that he was drinking when he was supposed to have been on duty and third, that he was using and abusing our property which he was charged with protecting. After checking that Sengerengabo was at his post, I ordered Pascali to get on the trailer and come with us. As we drove along, I thought about what we were going to do about him.

Pascali had been Dad's house servant and cook in Urundi where he had been doing a stint of contract labor recruiting the previous year. He had asked to come along on the next trip to Tanganyika, to see the world. Dad had agreed, but since Pascali was taking up a paying seat, the agreement was that he would work for his keep and fare, but not get wages. Pascali had bid his young family farewell and had left for what should have been two to three weeks. On this trip, however, the sale of our farm and other things to do with our move had come to a head and the next recruiting trip to Urundi was canceled so that we could prepare for our move to the Belgian Congo. Pascal had decided to stay on with us, waiting for our move, which would bring him closer to Urundi. The two-week trip had lasted seven or eight months and it was not over for him, yet, and his wife probably had no idea that he was even alive.

He was a cheerful, likable person. It was hard to get angry with him, but this sort of dereliction of duty couldn't be tolerated, particularly by someone so newly come to such a position of authority. I worked on my indignation for the two hours that it took to drive to the building site, unload the trailer and walk home to the *gîte*.

It must have helped that the ants had already been under my skin that afternoon, because I found myself quite able to perform. He was given a real treatment. I warmed up by telling him how disappointed I was in him. I walked back and forth in the small space near the door. Distracted by my concentration, I bumped my head on the ever-present bunch of just ripe bananas and put my hand up to steady it. I became more caught up in my eloquent expressions of disappointment, disillusion-ment, surprise, sorrow, anger, indignation - by now, righteous indignation - and all those things that I rightfully should have felt, in the circumstances. I paced back and forth, lecturing as I went. At first, Pascali did seem impressed, though not very contrite. Soon he seemed much more amused than impressed.

Perhaps it was the *pombe*. It makes some people dead drunk, some mad drunk and some people happy drunk.

"Perhaps it was the bananas," said Pauline, pointing to the bunch, or to where the bunch had been. There was only the stem left. A couple of dozen bananas had disappeared in the course of Pascali's disciplining. These were small, dessert bananas, a third of the size of the variety imported to Europe and North America; delicious, sweet and tender when ripe. "You ate one every other time you walked past the bunch!"

One has to find ways to show who is in control and to make an impression on an unreceptive audience on matters concerning morals, duty, betrayal of trust and such!

To Pascali, what he had done was not wrong. He had not stolen the shoes, for they were still there. He probably could have guessed that Dad would not have been pleased to see him using them, but not that I would get so worked up about it. Anyway, to make a point and to help him remember it, we made him walk back to the Mission. Six miles seemed to us, in our wisdom, to be a good sentence. We kept the shoes. Had we been wiser, we would have made much more of a lasting impression if we had waited until his hangover had set in and then made him wear the ill-fitting shoes to walk the six miles! But then, Amnesty International frowns on torture, doesn't it?

The Camp to Catch Every Breath of Moving Air was laid out and built just below the summit of our hill. We wanted to save the very top of the hill for the permanent house. We learned from Augustin, the geographer, that the hill was known as "Kagando." Long ago, a chief named Ngando had had his compound there. *Kwa* Ngando[11], meaning Ngando's place, had devolved to Kagando.

Ngando had good taste. To the northeast, straight up the Western Rift Valley, we could see more than fifty miles, to Lake Albert. This is one of many lakes that are part of the Nile's system. It is fed by the Semliki, which we had to cross to get to our new home and which was itself fed by the Lamia river. The latter was the boundary between the Belgian Congo and Uganda and was also the eastern boundary of our property. Lake Albert is also fed by the Victoria Nile, which, on our move, we crossed at Jinja, where it leaves Lake Victoria. All in all, we felt connected to that patch of shimmering light near the horizon.

Still to the northeast, but below the view line to the lake, was a small, densely populated part of the Kingdom of Toro, in Uganda. It was referred to by our local folk as *ngambo*[12], sort of: "yonder" or "over there." There we could see hundreds of plots of dense green banana trees and the smoke of hundreds of cooking fires.

To the west, we saw the western wall of the Western Rift Valley, rising over the valley of the Semliki River. This was only the first forty miles of the Ituri Forest, a jungle that didn't stop before it reached the Atlantic Ocean, perhaps a thousand miles away. The Parc National Albert was a large part of this view. (Albert got around, one might think, but one might be wrong. The Park was named after Roi Albert, King of the Belgians and the son or grandson of infamous Roi Leopold II. The lake was named for Queen Victoria's Consort, before the other Albert succeeded to the Belgian throne).

To the southwest, we could look along the Ruwenzori Mountains' foothills. There was a mile-wide break between the Ituri forest and the forest of the mountain. I have no idea if this was a result of the human habitation or if it was natural. What was certain is that the two forests were very different and

---

[11] This 'ng' as in 'finger'.
[12] Back, again, to 'ng' as in 'singer'. Ngambo has a definite sence of being across or over some barrier.

plants at higher altitudes in the Ruwenzoris are unique. In this direction lay the village of Kiesegeta. Bill and I had our eyes on the area as a possible location for the second and third plantations, on which we might get started once we got this first one going.

In all of those directions, the hill stood about two hundred feet above the surrounding plain. The plain then fell away towards the Semliki in the west and to Lac Albert in the northeast. From east all the way round to southwest, the ground fell away slightly before joining the mass of the Ruwenzoris, which filled this view. The Ruwenzoris are just north of the equator; on the map, they seem to be supported on it, like a tight rope walker. The peaks are almost always covered in cloud and mist. They are so shy they would put Greta Garbo to shame. We were not to get our first glimpse of them until several months had passed. When they did show themselves, it was a beautiful sight. We were so close to the foothills that we were looking through them, up the valleys, towards the peaks. This foreshortening disguised the distance. The green foreground contrasted dramatically with the colours of the diorama view that it framed; the distant vegetation appeared dark, a deep blue, which faded where the vegetation itself faded, to a gray-blue. The dainty little peaks, several of them, distributed in three or more clusters, glittered like jewels in the sunlight. The peaks are about the same height as Mt. Kenya, which also hugs the Equator and also boasts year-round snow and ice on its peaks.

The view, as I have described, was spectacular, but an equally fine thing about the location was the natural air conditioning that was the result of being up out of the still air on the plain. Also, it seemed that mosquitoes did not like to fly up to that height. Dad had an unerring eye for this kind of detail. He had decided that this was where the house would be built, even though the hill was outside of the boundaries of our concession. Along with his unerring eye, he had developed an unfailing faith in his ability to cause things to be changed, even through the colonial bureaucracy. We had no title to the top of the hill, but neither did any other white man or white men's government. We had Basikania's promise. For Dad that was enough. He knew that the matter would be settled. We built it where he pointed.

The design of the camp was simple. It had one main hut for

cooking, eating, sitting and relaxing in front of the view. There were three smaller huts, one for Mum and Dad, one for Paga and one that was divided, one end for Pauline, the only girl, the other for her four brothers; Bill, whom you've met, already, John (then 15) and Richard (12), who were away at school when this adventure began, and myself. There was an irregular plaza between the huts. Twenty yards down the hill was a pit latrine. It was not camouflaged under a convenient tree, the way King's Club, the outhouse at Rongai was, but it would do. Baths were to be taken in an old galvanized tub in Pauline's room, in water that would be carried in kerosene cans on Pascali's head and heated over a fire between three stones, still in the cans but no longer on Pascali's head. There was no point in spending any of our precious resources on anything very elaborate or permanent, since we planned to start to build the new brick house almost immediately after the first revenues came in from our soon to be planted crops.

The huts were built from poles and a cord made from the peel of certain rushes from M. de Jaeger's *coup de bois,* and from *matete* stalks and thatch from grass from our own land. The floors were of beaten earth. There were about three full-height doors and a couple of "Dutch" doors between us, which had made the first trip from Tanganyika. The main hut got no doors. The boys' hut got the lower half of a Dutch door.

The common hut was on the point of a secondary summit, about fifteen feet lower than the true summit, the others snuggled a little back into the crease between the two. The living room had a verandah from which most of the view could be seen The hut was light and airy, with the minimum of structure visible. We did not want anything to obstruct the view. And, above all, we wanted to catch Every Breath of Moving Air.

It was a beautiful and peaceful spot.

We looked forward to witnessing Mum, Paga, John and Richard's first sight of this wonder, and Dad's first sight of our execution of his broadly described vision of what was to be our home.

We and a buffalo family looked forward.

CHAPTER TWO

The Watalinga area was like those "lost valleys" of fiction. It had only one practical way in, and its sole link to civilization was through one remote and obscure colonial administrative post on the edge of a jungle.

This post, perhaps from some beneficent oversight or benevolent exaggeration, was named Beni. Beni itself boasted only three ways in, or, cynics and visitors (and I know some who were both) might have observed, only three ways out. One unpaved road ran in a north-south direction right through the middle of town, and another came in from the Uganda border to the east to meet it at the only intersection, just on the northern edge of town. I vaguely remember another road which came in from, or went out towards the west. I don't remember where it entered or left Beni. Nor do I know what was at the other end of it. Something, I suppose.

Standing boldly at Beni's intersection, Germain's Petrofina fuel pumps gave their silent, antiseptic, bright blue welcome, and offered relief to anxious, fuel-gauge-watching travelers coming into town from the north or the east. At the same time, the pumps gave notice to travelers leaving town in those directions, that if they did not avail themselves of the service, they would have to hope that they could reach the next pumps in Bunia, about 200 kilometres to the north, or in Katwe, well past the Uganda border, over 100 kilometres to the east.

At the same intersection, a little less boldly and much less easy to see behind a row of banana trees, decidedly less silent and even less antiseptic, stood a thatched hut which gave its own message to its own constituency of travelers. Before the hut held court a man who called himself *Papa ya Roma,* the Pope of Rome, and from it blared a wind-up gramophone, continuously repeating the latest John Bosco hit tune. Travelers who stopped here were attracted less by Papa than by what the sounds of John Bosco promised. If visitors were not looking for indulgences from the Pope when they arrived they would surely have earned the need for them by the time they left. The hut housed an African *hoteli,* or *kilabu* (as in hotel or club), which usually offered beer, food and "ancillary personal services" perhaps better not described here. Papa (no one knew his real name) was the village idiot, whose sole, self-imposed, I could say self-designed, occupation was to write down vehicle license numbers on scraps of paper, and to attempt to collect a "tax" for doing so. He collected frequently enough to need no other occupation, so what kind of a fool was he? Travelers who passed up the opportunity to stop at this *hoteli* would have to hope that they could last until they found a similar facility, which would not be for at most another kilometre or two, in any direction.[13]

In fiction, we would have gone in to this *hoteli* to find it run by a large, jovial but wise African madam with a heart of gold, or a petite, shopworn, fallen but wise French madame, say a night club singer, with a similar heart. Either of these ladies would drag a grizzled, drunk "white hunter" out of a back room to tell us of the dreadful dangers ahead, which telling would set the stage for a wild and woolly adventure and some hair raising, explosive climax. Alas, life never quite seems to live up to fiction. No European woman, fallen or not, and no European man, grizzled or ungrizzled, drunk or sober, would have gone into one of those places.[14] And in the end, although

---

[13]The network of these institutions would, a couple of decades later, be one of the principal vectors for the spread of AIDS. At the time we're talking about, AIDS wasn't yet recognized, if indeed it existed, so they had to be content with spreading traditional social diseases, hangovers, news, rumours and political awareness and with providing local colour to my story. The order of the list is random, as was the process.

[14]Perhaps the French or the Belgians would have. Certainly not anyone who was brought up among the British, anyway. The British managed to govern their empire whose natives outnumbered them, hundreds to one, partly by establishing and jealously guarding a very big social gap between the races, reminiscent of their class structure at home, while treating them at least a little like humans, if paternalistically, all the same. They called it something like 'keeping their respect', and it pretty well precluded fraternization. The Belgians' approach was not as genteel: they called the Africans *macaques,* to their faces. When you think about that, you wonder if the Belgian *colons* thought they needed a bigger gap than the Brits did, or if they recognized, as I'm sure the British did, that Belgians started at a lower point on the scale than that occupied by their

some hair got raised on the way, the climax to our story was much more like the fizzle of a wet firecracker. Ah, well!

The main, unnamed, unpaved and unique street was wide and had a row of six lamp posts down its centre. At night, these lights were powered by a diesel generator which could be heard crump-crumping, somewhere behind the buildings which stood one row deep along the street, and they would flicker, momentarily brighter with each crump. On most Fridays, during the day, when the lights were not otherwise preoccupied with keeping time with the struggling generator and could more easily dodge traffic, a big, red Berliet truck would come lumbering down the hill from Butembo in a cloud of dust, carrying some freight and the mail. The truck was the only scheduled transportation connection with the outside world. A few hours after it arrived, it would groan its way past Germain's pumps, and head northwards to Bunia, its own noise drowning out the siren call of the *hoteli*.

There was no telephone in Beni, but the *Administrateur* had a radio. His boss, at the District Office, a half day's drive away in Goma, would listen to his radio at noon on Fridays, in case during the week either of them had thought of anything interesting to say to the other.

That means that both things that happened in Beni happened on Friday. That demonstrates either a singular breakdown in planning, having everything happen at once, or else a stroke of genius, making it unnecessary for people to get all excited twice each week. Perhaps those two events weren't all that exciting to me, for despite the fact that neither of them happened at the intersection, it is a picture of that intersection that comes to mind when I think of Beni. Elephant grass on either side of the approaching road, some banana plants and a thatched roof to the left, behind the Pope, and the blue pumps straight ahead.

Apart from Germain's garage, the *hotelis* and the administration offices, Beni had a clinic manned by Congolese paramedics, a bank, a grocer, a second, competing garage, two European hotels (which attracted far fewer travelers than any of the *hotelis*) and a half dozen stores.

---

neighbours across the Channel and therefore had to push the natives even lower to maintain an appropriate gap.

One most immediately noticeable difference between Beni and East African towns of its size was that all the clerks were Africans rather than Goans. Another difference was that the stores were run by Greeks, not Indians, and they were built of cement blocks, rather than the corrugated, galvanized iron *mabati* that the Indian *duka wallahs* favoured.

The presence of a Pope notwithstanding, Beni was pretty far from what would pass as civilization. If it was the Watalinga's link to civilization, it was a tenuous one!

Then you must take into account that the Watalinga area was another hundred kilometres beyond Beni, down a jungle track. When we first went there, we had to wait on the muddy banks of the 100-metre-wide, slow, brown Semliki River, to be carried across on a raft made out of empty oil drums. At this point, the river was infested with, one got the impression it was defended by, in descending order of aggressiveness, mosquitoes, hippos and crocodiles.

As Mum and Sims would say, Watalinga "is at the Back of Beyond!"

To understand how a family of eight Europeans, none of them with the ready motivations or excuses of missionaries, came to look forward to moving there, it is necessary to go back a little in time. Then we'll go forwards again, to look at what made them so willing to leave.

William Davidson was born in 1877. Half a world away, Henry Morton Stanley was shooting rapids and unfriendly natives by turn, on his famous discovery trip down the Congo River. Stanley's trip was intended only to disprove Livingstone's theory that the Nile's source was Lake Tanganyika, but it also, inadvertently, opened up the heart of the continent to exploitation of its resources and its people.

While Leopold's minions and Tippoo Tibb's[15] successors were still demonstrating that they were more savage than any of the 'savages' of the Congo jungle, Bill Davidson was facing major decisions. He was, with many before and after him, part of what was the biggest single export commodity of his native

---

[15]An Arab slave trader who worked in Tanganyika. He accompanied Stanley only far enough to see that the Congo River was a highway into the interior from Tanganyika, abandoned him and returned to exploit his knowledge.

Scotland: a youth facing limited opportunity at home, obliged to go overseas to find it. Some of his friends and relatives went as far as Australia, New Zealand and Canada. Some went to Sea.

Bill chose Africa. He landed in Durban, on New Year's Day, 1901, in the month that he turned 23. After spending a few years working in a haberdashery in Durban, he went home and somehow inspired his half cousin, Agnes (Nan) McIntyre to join him. She did, they were married and moved to Pretoria, where Fiona (Mum) and her brother John (Jock) were born.

By 1923, Nan's health dictated a move to a high, dry climate. They heard of someone selling some land on the foothills of Mt. Kilimanjaro, in the new British "Mandated Territory" of Tanganyika. Without seeing it, they bought a parcel and headed off up the coast in a steamer. Mum was six and Jock was an infant. They had the assurance of the seller that, if they did not like the parcel they had bought, which he could not imagine, they could swap it for the very one that he had reserved for himself. Well, when they arrived, several weeks later, they didn't like their land. It had no water. It was not irrigable, anyway, being on the top of a hill, and it had poor soil. However, they did like the area and the alternative parcel looked fine. They were assertive enough to remind the seller of his promise to trade. Surprisingly, if reluctantly, he honoured it and they took possession of the better farm.

There is some irony here. They moved to Tanganyika for health reasons. Only a few decades earlier, David Livingstone, a fellow Scot, had his health destroyed, and eventually, his life taken by the diseases that were rampant there and against which the Europeans had little resistance. It says something about the advances of medicine in that short time, particularly the use of quinine against malaria, but it also says rather a lot about the bravery of the family.

The 750-acre farm they settled on touched the Kilimanjaro forest reserve on the east, was bounded by a small, part time river on the south, and had a few of its westernmost acres in the Sanya Plains, which are contiguous to Amboseli and Serengeti. Situated between two dormant volcanoes, it was in an area of spectacular views.

One of these volcanoes, Kilimanjaro, the highest mountain in Africa, had year-round snow on its tallest peak, Kibo. The other, Meru, significantly shorter, was of almost perfectly classical cone shape. One wall of Meru's crater, on the side facing the farm, was so low that, from the thirty mile distant but higher vantage point of the farm, one could see inside it for a surprise sight of a second cone within the first one. There were hills and mountains within the view, each with a wonderful Maasai name. We could see Longido, over fifty miles away, where, years later, when formal roads were cut through the plains, the road to Nairobi would cross the border between Tanganyika Territory and Kenya Colony. We faced Lolowai, much closer, a landmark on the way to Olmolog, if one needs a landmark with Kibo overwhelming every view. Sometimes, on rare days when the haze and the dust allowed it, one could even see Oldoinyo Lengai, an active volcano about a hundred miles away, in the Rift Valley. It was the home of the Maasai god, Lengai. One could certainly see its smoke and ash when it blew. More than anything, though, the area was notable for its wildlife. I can remember that, even twenty years later, there were a hundred or a thousand times more animals than people. In a half hour evening stroll, we would see dozens of ostrich, zebra and giraffe, and perhaps hundreds of either of the two most common species of antelope. Where there are so many grazing animals, there are jackals, hyenas, lions and leopards not far away. Elephants, too, would come down into the grassy plains, from time to time, when it was too wet in the forest. At some point or another, Fiona and Jock would have, as pets, one or more of many of these species, excluding, for perhaps obvious reasons which might include a poorly hidden lack of parental enthusiasm, elephants, giraffes and all carnivores.

The region was named Ngare Nairobi, Maasai for Cold River, after the largest river in the area. That river and all the others there were cold for they were fed by rains and melting ice from high up on Shira, the group of older, lower peaks that made up the western part of the Kilimanjaro massif.

Our river was named Ngare Rongai, or Little River, and the Davidsons named the farm Rongai. It was a fitting name, at 750 acres it was small for the area. The river was more like a large brook. It ran down onto the plains and disappeared. Its water was clear and sweet. The family drank water straight from the river, or from a furrow fed by it. Jock learned how to tickle trout in it.

The soil was red, mineral rich and exceedingly fertile. In that soil, with the strength of the sunlight being amplified by the 5,500 feet of altitude and the proximity to the Equator, it was guaranteed that you could grow anything. All it needed was water. The abundant rainfall and the river supplied it.

Fortunately, the coolness caused by the altitude made the area unattractive to mosquitoes. There was no malaria and anti-malarial medicine was not necessary. The small price we paid for this was that for a good part of the year we needed pullovers, particularly in the evenings. A fireplace was essential and was used often.

The Davidsons added on to a stone house that had been built by a German settler. Some of the materials had to come from Moshi, forty miles away. At the time, there were only two vehicles powered by internal combustion engines in the whole province, so the materials were carried out on the heads of porters.[16]

The porters and the farm labour came from 12 miles away, from Kibongoto, one of several population centres of the Chagga tribe. Ngare Nairobi had no native residents to be seen, other than the nomadic Maasai tribesmen who wandered past once in a while. There must have been a stable population, at one time. There were some round hillocks that looked suspiciously like burial mounds. Dr. Louis Leakey came by, once, and dug in one of them, revealing some human bones. He was going to come back, but never did. Olduvai Gorge, a little over a hundred miles away, was yielding signs of much earlier, pre-human life that kept him very busy.

---

[16]One of these porters, Tengia, become the cook and stayed with the family for many years. He would tell us how he had first acquired his bald patch on his head by carrying, on that same head, the roof that we were sitting under, all the way out from Moshi, each trip taking four days. Over forty years later, Dad was in the train station in Hanau, Germany, when he saw a young man, standing, waiting for a train. From his general appearance, he was obviously African and not one of the American GIs, and from his physiognomy, obviously a member of the Chagga tribe. Dad was never able to resist the slightest temptation to engage anyone in conversation, I mean anyone, so said to the stranger, in Swahili, "You are, without any doubt, a Mchagga!" The surprised young man pleaded guilty and, under cross examination, was found out to be Tengia's son, now a doctor, visiting Germany to take some courses.

The European population, however, were more and more to be seen[17]. Some of them had children. Nan was among the people who got together to organize a school. Fiona and Jock would walk to this school, about three miles in each direction, with only each other for company and for protection. The protection they needed was from the wild animals, which were to be seen every day, and from Ngolomiko and General Earbiter. The latter two, not so often seen, were characters from Maasai or Chagga mythology and from Jock's fertile mind, respectively. Ngolomiko got around, a bit, so he was quite likely to be away on an errand of mischief, however, General Earbiter really liked to hang around the ford at the Rongai river and you were lucky if you escaped him. Fiona and Jock had a tremendous run of luck; in the years that they walked that path, they never once encountered either of the two mischievous characters. Jock was good enough to warn us, though, so we, in turn, kept a look out for them and were able to avoid trouble.

One day, Bill Davidson went to meet them on the hill across the river. On his way, he spotted a *kongoni*, a tawny antelope, lying in the grass a few yards from the track. *Kongoni* spend most of their lives standing, even when they're asleep. He was curious and went closer to take a look. When he got closer there was no *kongoni*; he was face to face with a lion. He later explained his survival on a couple of things. First, he was too surprised to be frightened. Second, remembering something he'd read, somewhere, he stared at the lion, right in the eyes. It worked. The lion decided to get up and move away. He used that same look on us, later, to get his way. It often worked on us, too. Fiona and Jock continued to walk to and from school, along the same track. While some mothers admonished their children to avoid the puddles and to button up their coats, their mother would be warning Fiona and Jock to let sleeping *kongoni* lie, *kongoni* and anything that looks like *kongoni*.

---

[17]I asked one of my young playmates why Europeans were called *wazungu*. His explanation sounds good and may have some basis in truth. He said: "The old people used to say 'If you turn in this direction, you see them there. If you turn in that direction, you see them there. If you turn in any direction, you see them there! They are in every direction! They surround you!'" *Kuzungua* is the verb 'to turn', in Swahili.

There was little to amuse young people, so Fiona and Jock had to be resourceful. Trees took on characters and names. The two thorn trees that straddled the approach road, at the bottom of the hill, were named "The Portals" by their mother, but Fiona and Jock would fly in the one of them that they knew as "Aeroplane Tree". Jock invented a whole town full of people about whom he had a complete story. One of the characters was Granny Sims. Somehow, that name got transferred to his mother, perhaps when she became a granny. She innocently accepted it, probably grateful for small mercies. She might not have been quite so happy with the name of some of the other characters, say that of Obberibuck bin Strawberrybasket. But then, she was safe, because chances are he was a man. There was no written history of this community, so I've had to guess the spelling. In Swahili, 'bin', pronounced 'been', means 'son of' ('binti' means 'daughter of'). Of course, it might really have been 'Bean' or 'Been', which leaves the question open, again. Sims has a better sound to it, anyway.

You might guess that Jock was a collector or specialist in funny names. He might have enjoyed knowing that someone would coin the appropriately convoluted term "comiconomenclaturist[18]" for people like him. He was not the first, nor the last, but a card-carrying member of the club, nonetheless.

He also loved to play games with people's names and things to do with their names. In Swahili, *'bwana mkubwa'* means 'the big boss'. To Jock, that was 'banana cooper'. It was inevitable that some years later he would become friends with a man named Cooper, and that Cooper would never understand what connection he had with the yellow plantain whose name he had come to share. It was fortunate that Jock got that one out of his system by the time he married Diana Cooper, who was not related; father Cooper didn't share Jock's sense of humour.

Sims and Mum had a friend whose name we heard often, Kitty Parker. But think! *Paka* is 'cat', in Swahili. You see how it might work, don't you? Jock may not have had anything to do with her name, he may never have met her. But I wonder if

---

[18]Peter Bowler, *The Superior Person's Book of Words.* David R. Gordine, Boston, 1982

her name really was Kitty, or Parker. How could you trust a name like that, any more.

Once, when I was four or five years old, I was waiting for Dad with Sims on the verandah of the New Arusha Hotel, when a man came by and spoke to her. She introduced him as Mr. van Ennemis. I had never met him, but I immediately recognized his name from a recent discourse by Jock, who had been watching me dip my toast fingers into my soft-boiled egg, during which he had very earnestly told me that there was a man named Mr. Egginamess, and how he got that name. Of course, it had been shortened for convenience, through laziness or natural evolution, to van Ennemis.

I tugged at Sims' skirt: "Granny, is that the man who ...?"

"Shh!"

Why is it so difficult to attract grown-ups' attention when there are more than one of them present? "Granny, is that ... ?"

"SHHHH! Please run and see what the clock hands are pointing to now."

I ran into the dining room, looked at the clock on the wall and ran back. "The big hand is on the four and the little hand is on the six." Sims must have thought she had distracted me. "Granny, is *that* the man who *stirs* his *eggs* with his *fingers*?"

Van Ennemis probably didn't think anything of it, but Sims could have been more embarrassed only if Willem Malan had come along instead of van Ennemis. Jock had named his big fat gray cat "Well I'm Damned Malan" after him.

Here is some more evidence to be considered. Jock swore that his first son was going to be named Oliver. Oliver Ploom, that is. This was to be in honour of the lady who fed the students at the school their cooked lunches. One day, many years before our time, as she was coming out of the kitchen carrying the stewed fruit that was intended to be dessert (and doubtless also to maintain the young people's regularity, for if matrons don't think of these things, no one will), something jogged her arm, sending the bowl and its contents to the floor and leaving purple juice all down her front.

With a dismayed look she stepped back, and into history by gasping "Eee! I'm alloverploom!"

If being quoted by several people each year is what it takes to have a place in history, she was already assured hers. I think

45

it was she who was once seen putting back on the plate some food that had fallen on the floor, muttering the never to be forgotten words: "If they don't close their teeth too hard, they won't notice!"

Jock never had a son. I think I would have liked him, anyway, even if his father had gone through with his plan.

It is obvious from this that Jock was actually inventing funny names rather than collecting them. That makes his avocation more like paranomasia[19], word play of the punning kind, rather than true comico-nomenclature, but I'm not going to report him.

At some point, Fiona and Jock went off to boarding school in Kenya, ending up in the Limuru Girls' School and The Nairobi School, respectively. After finishing there, Fiona went on to teach at the Arusha School and Jock came back to help on the farm.

As a young man, coincidentally, 23 years old, Ernst Prinz von Isenburg completed his service as an officer cadet in the German Navy. He had served on a steel-hulled sailing ship which had taken him to the East Indies and to the East African Coast. On this tour, he had seen and been intrigued by coffee and cocoa plantations in Indonesia. On the return voyage, he had visited and been captivated by Bagamoyo, the old Arab enclave and dhow port on the Tanganyika mainland, across from Zanzibar. He had promised himself that he would revisit Bagamoyo, and, if he ever had a family, to take them there.

He came home to the family estates in Hessen, Germany with a lot of ideas and enthusiasm. He soon grew frustrated with the way his conservative family would not let him experiment with agriculture on some of the properties. Had his father not been so inconsiderate as to be the younger son, Ernst would have been the heir to massive estates. As it was, he was not in line to inherit much, nor, it appeared, to have his ideas listened to.

In 1929 he decided to go to Africa to make his fortune there, growing coffee. He remembered Bagamoyo and chose Tanganyika. The family, still not known for its ready acceptance of new ideas, wanted to be a little less uncertain that this was not a passing fancy but something he really

[19]Ibid.

46

wanted to do. He was to receive his share of a small inheritance to invest, but only after he had spent a year working gratis for a German coffee planter named Landgrebe, who was the friend of an uncle, and who had a plantation in Ngare Nairobi, in Tanganyika. During the probation period, though, occasional news reports would appear in Europe of trouble somewhere on the "Dark Continent." The "somewhere" may have been thousands of miles from where Ernst was, but each of the reports would further undermine the already weak confidence the family had in his silly idea. And, if it was not one thing, it would be another that would give them reason not to release the funds, despite Ernst's earnestness.

Soon, the Depression struck. Any effort to farm or plant was thwarted by the economy. It cost more to plant and harvest a crop than you could get for it on the market. Healthy young men sat around doing nothing because doing anything lost money. One day, someone said he had heard that there was gold in the hills behind Namanga, out beyond Longido, halfway to Nairobi. Ernst said that he had heard that gold could be divined the same way that water could, with a green twig. That was obviously a ridiculous idea and his friends set out to make sure that he should enjoy some of the ridicule himself. They took the few things he had in the way of gold - signet ring, watch, cuff-links, etc. - and challenged him to find them, out there in the field, where they had buried them. In half an hour he had uncovered them all. He had proved, to his own satisfaction, and perhaps to his own surprise, that he had the touch.

Never comfortable sitting and doing nothing for long, Ernst packed a tent, some supplies, tools and some African labourers into a lorry and set off to Namanga to look for gold.

There was no road, as such, to Nairobi or to Namanga. There was a tangle of several somewhat parallel, interconnected tracks leading in the same general direction, each born when something in an existing track went beyond being a mere obstacle and became an impassable barrier. You could go along a track that was quite passable the last time you used it, and find that a ford had got washed out, rain had turned the dust into axle-deep mud, a large tree had fallen, blocking the way, or that buffalo had turned the road into a wallow. You would then back up, or turn around, if you could, and try along another track. Perhaps you'd be lucky on that attempt, perhaps not. If you thought that you could improve your odds by following fresh wheel tracks, you were wrong. Fresh tracks indicated only that someone had tried to go through, not that he had succeeded. The fresh tracks could easily have been your own, that you made only hours ago. The 170-mile trip to Nairobi could take two days. It took longer if you got stuck or broke down.

Ernst parked his lorry on the edge of one of the tracks, where it crossed a likely looking river, and went up the dry riverbed with his divining rod. At a certain point, his rod told him to dig. He told his men to dig. They dug. They hit solid rock.

He had foreseen this, and had brought the right tools and some dynamite. To drill a hole for the dynamite, one man stood in the pit to hold a steel bar, and another stood on the surface to wield a sledgehammer. Late one day, when the pit had become quite deep, something went wrong and the sledgehammer hit the man in the pit right on the head, knocking him unconscious.

Ernst got very concerned. It was nearly night, the way to the lorry was unfamiliar, there were thorns, wild animals and snakes along it. The lorry was the best part of a day's march away and Nairobi another day's drive beyond that, if the engine started, and if everything else went well. The other men said not to worry, he wasn't dead, look, he was breathing, he'd be OK. Just give them an aspirin for him to take when he woke up. Ernst left him, conscious, but groggy, in the care of his colleagues, and worried all night.

He got up early in the morning, ready to strike camp, knowing that he'd have to start out for the lorry and Nairobi. But the invalid was up and, though he complained of a headache, he was ready to work. "Only, this time, bwana, *I* stand up here, with the hammer. *He* (pointing with his tongue) goes down there!"

They blasted through a few feet of rock and the hole filled with water. The water filled the hole faster than they could empty it. The rod kept on saying that this was the right place, but it couldn't tell him what to do about the water. Without a pump, they could dig no further. Without money to buy a pump, they gave up.

Ernst marked the place and went back and sat on the farm, and the conversation turned to other things.

For many years, he insisted that he knew that there was gold there, waiting to be dug up by someone with the right financing and equipment. At the end of his expedition, though, given the problems he had had, the risks they were taking and the depletion of their supplies, he had had enough. I think he lost his conviction that the rod knew the difference between gold and what, in most of Africa, is worth its weight in gold: water.

In Germany, Hitler came into power. The politics of the Nazis soon began to be reflected, in Kenya and Tanganyika, in the relationships between Germans and fellow Germans and between Germans and British. Ernst soon began to be criticized by his compatriots for not behaving the way they thought a son of the Fatherland should.

At some point, Ernst was invited by some distant relatives and their connections, to start a promising business in the importation of diesel trucks from Germany. The company was set up in Nairobi. Before he could do much, he was frustrated in this, as in everything, by the reluctance of his family to send out his money. In 1935 he went back to Germany to see if he could free some of his funds. He left the management of his affairs in the hands of a German man, going so far as to give him a power of attorney. He hardly knew the man, but he was strongly recommended by the leaders of the German community. Ernst, possibly naïvely thinking that he might deflect some of the criticism, accepted their recommendation.

In Germany for the first time since he left in 1929, he stopped at the home of relatives who, being childless, wanted to adopt him to keep their property in the family. There, he ran into some people stomping around in black boots and brown shirts and being rude to the lady of the house. He threw them out. Within twenty-four hours of arriving in Germany, he was a marked man. Later in the visit, when he did not like the way the ubiquitous brown shirted louts were behaving, he said so, loudly and publicly. He compounded his error by declining a pointed invitation to make amends by using his family's position to the advantage of the Nazi Party by leading the local Hitler Youth. Not only did he decline the invitation, he had the temerity to explain why, and to follow that with a lecture on

49

the evils of totalitarianism. At social gatherings he would be talking (do bears sleep in the woods?) and suddenly become aware that he was talking to himself; because everyone would slink away from him as soon as he got on to certain subjects. Ernst never tried to avoid those certain subjects.

As a result of his willingness to express his thoughts, and his unwillingness to behave in the way expected in the new Germany, he was given an opportunity to leave the country, under the cover of night. It happened, much the way it did for the von Trapps in the famous movie, the night before he was to have been picked up by the Gestapo or the SS. A family friend tipped him off and helped him over the Swiss border. Sometime later, for good measure, he was stripped of his German citizenship and of any property that he might have in Germany. Fortunately, the little he had was in France.

The childless relatives were forced to look for a less controversial relative to adopt.

After checking with the German anti-Hitler movement, who said that they could not use a volunteer with so high a profile, he made his way back to Tanganyika. Back in Tanganyika, Ernst found that the man he had left in charge had embezzled all of the cattle and many of the possessions left in his care. For some reason that history does not relate, it seems that he felt he had no recourse. I think the British authorities told him that it was a matter between Germans, don't bother them with it.

Ernst had managed to free up some of the inheritance from France and had put the money into the truck import business. Immediately after that, he found that the business could not be continued. Official Germany was simply galled by the fact that the two brothers that he had picked as partners, on the basis of their business acumen, were Jewish. It also was impossible for Germany to sanction trade with a man who was now a political embarrassment. The company died, which it would have done, anyway, at the outbreak of the war.

He found himself a target in other, more direct ways, of the resident Nazi faction. Tanganyika had been *Deutch Ost Afrika* and many *Deutcher* remained. Only a few of them were rabid Nazis, but only a few of the majority were strong enough to stand apart from them. Some of the bullies would ambush him when he was alone or accompanied by Fiona and Jock, the latter only in his early teens and therefore not much of a deterrent to them. There were several such attacks on his body and on his reputation. I believe that there was a price on his head. The presence of the British Administration of Tanganyika rather cramped the Nazis' style. They wanted him back in Germany, where they could deal with him in their own special way. The authorities appealed to Ernst's father to recall him to Germany. This prompted his mother to write a letter to Sims, which survives, pleading with her to do all she could do to convince him *not* to come back to Germany.

On several occasions, in several ways, Ernst could have bent a little to make life easier for himself. Had he worn a brown shirt and taught youths to bully little old ladies and Jews, or even just looked away when they did, there would have been nothing to impede his inheriting a fortune. A little flexibility would have made his life very different. He did not bend for lesser things, so it was not likely that he could have bent for things to which he was so fundamentally opposed.

When he first pronounced: "My children would rather have a poor father and a proud one than a father who cannot hold his head high!" he had no children to speak for, so he couldn't ask them, even if he'd thought of it. When he said it after he had children, he didn't think to ask them.

He did not have to.

Ernst had left Ladgrebe, by this time, and had gone to work with the Davidsons, on Rongai Farm. He was living in their first house, about a mile lower than the one they had modified and moved to. Evenings, he'd walk up to the other house to join the family for dinner. I believe it was when he started courting Fiona. One night, he was walking home when he felt a presence in the darkness. After a while, he made out the shape of a lion or lioness, walking parallel to his direction, a few yards off, in the bushes.

He stopped. His companion stopped.

He walked on. His companion walked on.

His companion was as interested in him as he was now interested in it. There was only one thing to do. He kept on walking, at a very steady pace, all the way home.

The next night, he was not about to miss his meal or his visit, nor to cut the latter short, so he found himself walking home, again in the dark, and again he enjoyed the same escort.

51

And the next night, it was the same. The fourth night, apparently the animal was bored and it stayed away. If walking with lions to see your sweetheart isn't a good test of love, there isn't one. I suspect it is also a test for other attributes, too. How about bullheadedness?

The economy was still in a shambles. Ernst's presence enabled Bill Davidson to move into Moshi, to get a paying job, leaving Sims and their children, when they were not away at school, on the farm.

Early in 1937, Ernst married Fiona, but not before his mother in law to be had picked a new name for him. His funny-sounding, unpronounceable names did not please her. He had seven names she could have chosen from, but she picked one of the few names which his parents had not thought to give him: James. He didn't mind, or never gave anyone reason to think he did. I think Fiona called him James to the day he died.

At that time, there were few young Europeans about. Another pairing that occurred was between two other members of the small group of friends: Margareta Malan married Jack Williamson. These two couples maintained their close friendship throughout all the changes in their lives and their children were to feel related to each other, almost like cousins. We Isenburgs were not to know our real cousins until we were grown.

The Depression was not yet over in East Africa. It still cost more to produce crops than one could sell them for. One did whatever one could to earn a living. Ernst had learned that there was a demand for labour in the coffee and sisal plantations around Kilimanjaro and knew that there was underemployment in the centre of the country. He put his new bride into his diesel lorry, Belinda, the only thing he had been able to salvage from the importing business, and they headed off, across country, literally, for there were still few roads, to spend their honeymoon recruiting labour. This trip yielded a great story about the lorry getting stuck on the rails, with a train coming along the track. In the absence of television and radio, the telling and retelling of such stories would serve for many years as evening and dinner table entertainment for their children.

Pauline was born at the end of 1937 and I followed at the end of 1939, just after the war broke out. Sometime after

Pauline's arrival and before mine, Dad's mother came out to visit. I have no recollection of ever hearing what she thought of the life her son found himself living. No other member of his immediate family ever made it out there.

Sometime around this time, in one of her first pronouncements, Pauline said "Paga" for Grandpa. Bill Davidson became Paga.

With the war, Dad was, technically, an enemy of the British administrators of Tanganyika Territory. He was put in a detention camp, along with all the other "Huns", including the local Nazi bullies, leaving Mum with her two children at Rongai, with Sims and Jock, who was then a teenager. When the complaints of the Nazis were not successful in keeping Dad's odious presence from sharing the same roof with them, they attempted to do him bodily harm. After all, he was a traitor to his German-ness, and so on.

He was a traitor, and he had exhibited bad taste by marrying an enemy. On top of that, the enemy clan had a perverted sense of humour. Jock would drive Mum to the camp to see Dad on Sundays. Dad's fellow campers would look up, in surprise, when a Scots accented voice shouted out: "Ribbentrop! Here! Goebbels! Here!" It would be Jock, calling the two dachshunds back "from their quick reading of the dog newspaper". The inmates' expressions would change from surprise to puzzlement and, finally, to a frown when they began to suspect that the choice of names just might not have been motivated by respect for Hitler's Generals. Maybe that suspicion earned Dad more bruises than his own earnest political stands.

Fortunately, the British Camp Commandant soon recognized the gravity of the situation. Dad was sent to manage a transportation unit for the government, in Tabora. This was a different form of detention. Sixty-odd years earlier, this was the most important inland town for the Arab slave traders and one of Dr. Livingstone's bases. Apparently it was still a major hub. Major is a relative term. It was, and still is, in the middle of a large, tsetse fly infested, arid region of Tanganyika. Later, he was sent to manage a coffee plantation near Oldiani[20], for a British family whose men were away in the war. The plantation

---

[20]Pronounced: 'ol-de-AH-nee'

was known by the grand name of Glenmalure Estates, and was in a place named Karatu. You might, possibly, find Oldiani on a large scale map. You won't find Karatu. Oldiani had two Indian *dukas*. Karatu had one, run by C. M. Patel.

Bill was born in Moshi, while Dad was away on one of these assignments, probably still Tabora.

The family went with Dad for part of the time in Tabora and all of the time in Karatu. Because of Dad's status we needed a permit to leave Karatu. The restriction was a bit academic, given that most of the time the only practical transportation we had was some donkeys and a horse. The administrative restriction and the lack of practical transportation were quite effective in minimizing our movements; we only ever got to the Ngorongoro Crater once, when Jock visited, despite it being virtually in our back yard. The local Administrative Officer, who was the source of the permits, has his name indelibly etched on our memories, since it was mentioned in just about every conversation among the Germans. It was one of few words that stood out and were heard through the stream of German. He was never "Mr. or Herr Austin", just "Austin". The tone that it was said in must have delivered a subliminal message. Many years later I would have to overcome a deep prejudice before I warmed up to the Austin vehicles we were to own. Another word we heard often was *"schweinerei."* It was used to describe many things done in the name of His Majesty, by the local administration and by the Custodian of Enemy Property, or CEP. The CEP was unlikely to make many friends, given the nature of its work, the administration of properties confiscated from citizens of Britain's enemies.

The Germans whom we came across in Oldiani were not locked up, because they were relatively harmless. At least, they couldn't have been rabid Nazis. Dad got on with most them fairly well and with some of them extremely well.

We came to know the von Kalckstein family. They were also sent to Oldiani, from Moshi, to keep them out of the way for the duration of the war. They could hardly have posed a threat. Hans Georg, the father, was a painter. Inge, the mother, had been a champion tennis player and was a skilled piano player. The whole family was very musical and artistic. The only slightly dangerous thing about any of them was Inge's temper.

54

At one point, Hans Georg was very depressed and Dad asked him to do him a great favour and paint him a picture of Kilimanjaro. He painted the most realistic depiction of that mountain that any of us has ever seen. Looking at it you can feel the heat on your skin and the dryness in your nostrils. You can feel the grass crackle under your feet and smell the dust. He did it entirely from memory, since it was a hundred and fifty miles away, and he did it with the added handicap that he was colour blind.

I believe that Dad was somehow instrumental in preventing a *schweinerei* that was to be perpetrated on the von Kalcksteins, by writing to Buckingham Palace. At the end of the war, they were to have been expropriated and deported, despite being as harmless and peaceful a family as you could meet. Fortunately, they were able to stay on. I don't know the story, but I wouldn't be at all surprised if Dad's letter to His Britannic Majesty did have something to do with the result.

The Kalckstein children were mostly a few years older than we were, but they were very open and accepting and forgave us our youth. They were our first friends. We thought they were All Right, the highest praise we knew how to give. We are still in touch, from time to time, with the surviving members of the family. Hans Georg died of complications from diabetes, all but three of the rest of them have died in vehicle accidents.

Dad was not immune, himself, from threats of, or at least fear of deportation from the British controlled country. Enough so that he bought a blue and yellow book with the title "Teach Yourself Portuguese." Dad would say that the Portuguese, through their diplomatic office, had extended an open invitation to His Serene Highness to go to settle in Angola or Mozambique with his Serene family, any time. It may have been that he asked them if it was possible to move there, and they said "Yes". Dad was not above such artistic license. We were into the first few chapters and asking "where is the pen of the gardener of my aunt?" or something equally useful, before it blew over. Imagine *that* future!

Another German family in the area was suffering the effects of the war. Voigt was a skilled cabinet maker. He had had no work for years and, like Hans Georg von Kalckstein, was suffering personally from the loss of his professional and artistic outlet. Dad used the same approach, giving him the means to cure himself. He commissioned him to make a desk and a cabinet to hold the old wind-up gramophone and the records, out of local *mvuli* wood. Voigt went to work with a vengeance and produced a handsome, serviceable desk and, for the records, a piece about four feet high, three feet deep and six feet long. It had about eighteen drawers. It was beautiful. It was big! We called it "The Monster".

Dad used to get around Glenmalure Estates on Mrs. Quellhorst's mare, Lady, or on his donkey, Peppy, mostly the latter. One day, he went up to the place the water furrow inlet took the water from the river, way up the hill, in the forest. This was something that had to be done, from time to time, just to check if the stinging nettles had to be cleared, or if any repairs were needed. On the way back Dad let Peppy find the way home while he let his mind work on some sort of project he was going to tackle. He became aware that Peppy was a little excited and looked up to see that they had ambled into the middle of a herd of elephants. He made a quick, three-way deal with the elephants and his mount. Elephants normally dictate the terms, but if you think fast, you can sometimes get your way. If he pretended not to notice them, they would pretend not to notice him, Peppy would pretend that he wasn't frightened and they would be allowed just to amble on through. Just as long as they didn't make any sudden moves or any noise, no one would have to do anything unpleasant and no one's dignity or pride would suffer.

By the end of the war, when we all could return to Rongai, there were five children. Pauline, Bill and I had been born in the European Hospital, in Moshi, but John and Richard were delivered at our temporary home, in Karatu, a hundred miles from a hospital. Doctor Stern[21], a German missionary, doctor and dentist delivered John and Richard. He had a pedal-operated dentist's drill that he used on me, once. He must not have needed the drill for the midwifery procedure, because he

[21]Thirty years later, Dad was telling his favourite chiropractor in Hanau about the only other person he had ever met whose skills as a diagnostician could come close to hers, one Doctor Stern. She harrumphed and said some good-naturedly disparaging remarks about him. It turned out that they had been engaged to be married, but that he had broken off the engagement to go be a missionary doctor in Africa.

walked over to our house rather than have Mum go to his makeshift facility in Oldiani. At that time Mum would have had to walk or ride Peppy. The only wheeled transportation available was the engine-less hulk of a lorry, to which Dad would hitch a span of oxen. It was not elegant, but it worked for short trips. Had she been able to wait a year or two longer, Mum could have been driven to Dr. Stern's in an ex-military 1939 model, 3 ton Chevrolet lorry, still painted olive drab, which Dad drove home one night, towards the end of the war. However, these things don't wait, particularly not for the participants' convenience, in fact, these things actually seem to be designed to make the participants wait, and it was probably better for everyone to have Dr. Stern walk to Mum than for her to be bounced to him in an ex-military lorry, or an ex-engined lorry, or even an ox-engined one.

While either John or Richard was coming, Pauline, Bill and I were sent off, taking turns on Kingo's shoulders and walking, to go the mile or two to spend some days with "Uncle and Auntie Limmer." The Limmers had no children, but they had a way with them, and plenty of patience. Much of our entertainment became self-entertainment after we discovered Uncle Limmer's trumpet and he made the mistake of showing us how to get sound out of it. We might have spent a few days, a few weeks or only a few hours there, but to us kids, it seemed forever. Imagine what it must have been like for the Limmers.

Somebody, somewhere, knew that there were several 'us kids' growing up in the difficult circumstances of the war. A large wooden box with a red cross on it came. It was full of bandages, dressings, M&B powder, aspirins and other things. All of them quite welcome, I'm sure, though we probably would have lived if they hadn't come. Perhaps from this treasure trove, perhaps from some other source, Mum used to give us a daily Kalzana tablet. She should have taken some of them herself, to replace the calcium that her five pregnancies were taking from her own teeth and bones, but she didn't. She told us that it was to strengthen our teeth and make us grow big. After the first reluctant time, there was no problem in getting us to line up for the tablets because we found that they were slightly sweet. One day I complained to Mum that Bill had gone around for a second one. I was indignant that he should have got away with it.

I was also worried. "Mum, do you think he'll turn into a jant?"

Mum didn't think so and said so in the most reassuring way she knew. I wasn't sure. I watched Bill. I think I was right to worry. He's by far the tallest of us all. By the time I had proof, it was too late to do anything about it, I'd finished most of my growing.

One day, I can remember it clearly, we were walking along one of the tracks around Karatu. We came across Mr. Gabler, one of the community of banished Germans. For the last several weeks, perhaps months, every time we had seen him he had said: "The war is over! No, really, this time, it's really over!"

This time he said it again, but added: "You see, I have the absolute, final proof! Look what I got in the shop!" He brandished an apple.

Apples didn't grow in most parts of Tanganyika, so I had never in my life seen one. They were a mystery to me, an exotic, foreign fruit. 'A' was for them, I knew, and in the colouring books that Dad's sisters sent us from time to time they were a red that gave me a headache. Now they became even more mysterious and intriguing, since I knew that they could signal things like when to stop wars.

The apple was right. Sometime after this incident, we moved back to Rongai. It must still have been a while, because Richard was born in Oldiani in early 1946. Maybe it wasn't a very powerful apple, it had had to come a long way.

Just before we moved to Rongai, we took a trip to Dar-es-Salaam. We went in the lorry, and essentially lived in it for a few days and nights. I don't know the ostensible reason for the trip, but I remember three or four things about it. We carried with us some *debes* of coriander oil extracted by a neighbour, which *debes* leaked. The close quarters made it impossible to avoid the aroma, and I developed a horror for the smell or flavour of coriander which lasted for decades. Another thing was that we went to Bagamoyo, where we stayed while Dad went back and forth to Dar, about twenty miles away. Bagamoyo, remember, the place Dad saw on his naval duty. We slept on the beach for a night or two, until someone invited us in to one of the old Arab houses. It had been owned by one of the famous Arabs, could it have been Tippoo Tibb? And, not surprisingly, I got a sunburn that gave me blisters as big as saucers.

At Rongai, we became a three-generation family again. We loved that experience; it is one that everyone should have the good fortune to share. And we loved getting to know the place that had all along been our home, even if we hadn't been allowed to live there.

We set about becoming acquainted with 'Aeroplane Tree' and other features that Mum and Jock had enjoyed. We got to know the season for the best wild *manka* berries and the best trees to climb. We discovered rocks that had big black crystals in them. We looked for potsherds and obsidian arrow heads. We found and collected magnetic black sand. We learned from Mum that one persistent and loud bird was threatening or boasting: "I'll eat your mealies! I'll eat your mealies!" We learned from Jock that it was really saying something else, something to do with a body function.

We ate guavas, persimmons, custard apples and mulberries, in their respective seasons, until we should have been sick. We agreed, with Mum, that we should know when we were getting old: it would be when we could no longer eat and enjoy green guavas. Waiting for fruit to ripen in the trees in Sims' five acre orchard and garden was not possible; first, there was the problem of patience, then there was the reality that the birds or the workers would get them if we left them one moment too long.

Mum showed us how to make boats out of the seed pods of the flame trees and how to make "pop guns" from the smaller branches of a giant tree in the garden. With these, we could shoot, with a very satisfying "POP!", harmless wads of paper torn, when he wasn't looking, from Dad's Farmer's Weekly, and chewed to the right consistency. We were told to shoot only targets. We followed the rule to the letter. Pauline was my target, I was Pauline's target. Bill was a smaller target and offered a greater challenge. John and Richard served as targets for the three of us. Then they got bigger and learned to shoot back.

Our African playmates, children of the servants and farm workers, showed us how to scratch a certain creeper to make it ooze a white latex which would curdle into rubber. If you were clever and very patient, you could make a hollow ball that

59

actually bounced. My solid balls bounced, but I never succeeded in making a hollow one bounce. Nor did I ever make a successful potato whistle out of clay. I did learn from the Chagga boys, who told me that was how the herdsmen communicated with their herds, how to whistle, at least to make whistling noises, twenty different ways, using my fingers or my cupped hands and my lips.

The same playmates showed us how to make 'soap box' cars out of sticks, whose wheels were slices cut from logs. The cars would look familiar to anyone who has seen 'The Flintstones' cartoons on TV. The only way we could coax these cars to roll down even a steep slope was to lubricate the axles, lavishly. The lubricant of choice was the only one that both worked and was available in quantity: fresh cow dung. Mud had the wrong consistency, was too sticky and dried too quickly. Just as the racers in our adventure books got covered in a film of oil, grease and road dirt, so did we end up wearing more than a trace of the materials to which we were exposed. When we came home from our car rallies, Mum would intercept us before we got too far into the house and suggest to us that we go down to play in the river. Normally, playing in the river was not strongly encouraged, because the water was ice cold. We could get a pass into the house only after a half hour of teeth chattering play in that water had frozen and shaken off some of the characteristic trademarks, colours and smells of our sport.

The same African playmates used to eat one big meal each day, usually when their fathers came home from their work on the farm. If we happened to be around, we might go with them to collect their daily *kibaba,* or ration of *posho,* about a pound of maize meal, and then we would watch them cook the *ugari,* a stiff porridge, in iron or aluminum pots balanced on three stones over an open fire. The mothers were probably at home in Kibongoto, looking after the smaller children, the homestead and the *shamba,* the field, so the sons who were our age cooked for their fathers. Africans share and we were, naturally, invited to eat. Everyone would sit on the ground, in a circle around the communal pot. Very politely, in your turn, you'd dig a chunk of the *ugari* out of the pot, mold it into a ball, make a dimple in it with your thumb, scoop a little bean or vegetable sauce into the dimple and pop the whole thing into your mouth. You'd wash it down with water from a shared enameled tin cup or empty tin salvaged from our kitchen. All this, you'd do with one hand, the right hand. The left hand was not supposed to come near the food; it was the hand people used for dirty jobs, like going to the toilet. Our hosts never apologized for the fare, or the lack of meat, nor did they contrast their offerings with whatever fancy food might be on the *mzungus'* table that night, though they would joke about the tenderness of our fingers with the steaming hot, sticky *ugari*. When we did sit down to our own meal, less than an hour later, with this lump of *ugari* sitting solidly in our stomachs, it was impossible to pretend to have an appetite. Mum must have wondered, sometimes, why she bothered to make soup, a main course and some kind of pudding for us.

We played a lot, but we worked, too, sometimes. The nature of the work at any time was governed by the seasons. There were the 'long rains', which lasted from about March to about June and the 'short rains', which came in November and December. Obviously, you wanted to plant before the long rains set in, and you had to plough before you could plant. Then, if there was a crop to be harvested, you needed to get it in before the next rains came and ruined it. If there was a crop, and you were having any difficulty in bringing it in, that would surely be the year that the short rains would not fail. We were still quite small when we started going into the fields at planting time. If the mechanical planter was not performing, either because it was broken or because the soil was too sticky for it after the first rain had fallen, all able-bodied men, women and children were called out and we planted non-mechanically. You don't need to be very big to plant. You carry a basket of pre-soaked maize seed and walk along a line. You make a hole with your heel, drop three grains into it and cover them with a sideways push of your foot. This work was usually done in cloudy, chilly weather.

Harvest time was usually nice weather, and though we didn't usually have as much to do, we would be involved in small ways, holding gunny sacks, *gunias*, to be filled, or sewing them up when they were full. We had a reaper-binder, which cut the ripe wheat and formed it into sheaves. It tied the sheaves with twine, finishing the knot with a delicate bow, and threw them out onto the field. The sheaves were then collected and brought to the thresher, in a yard close into the store house. At various times, this was done by ox wagon, by tractor and trailer and by lorry. One particular year, Dad and the headman, Melile[22], were discussing the problem of keeping the dust in the yard down, and the problem of sweeping up the spilled grains of wheat without having to winnow it again to get the dust out of it. Melile said he had a solution, leave it to him. Dad did. Melile used an old native method. He took dried cow dung, made a thin paste out of it and coated the whole yard. He was right. There was little dust, and we didn't have to winnow any *dust* out of the swept-up wheat.

Nearly all of our running around on the farm was done barefoot. Every couple of days, after our baths, there was a session with Mum, whose gentle touch with a sewing needle could coax a thorn out of a heel or a jigger out of a toe. Jiggers liked to burrow under the skin to lay their eggs. They particularly liked the creases behind and between toes and anywhere around or under toenails. As they went in, they started an awful itch, but that was nothing compared to the itch that developed as the eggs matured. Thankfully, that meant that there was no chance that that they would escape your notice long enough for the eggs to hatch. Getting the sac of eggs out whole was a delicate feat, requiring sharp eyes, a sharp needle and a steady hand on the part of the operator and absolute stillness and self-control on the part of the operatee. If the sac broke, it was a mess that could easily turn septic.

Mum was as competent at doing things as Dad was at planning them, and she was much quieter at it. When we needed a stick pulled out of a thigh, a dog's teeth extracted from an arm, or some other such ministration, we ran to Mum, not Dad. She often told us that she had usually gone to her Dad, not her Mum. She asked us if we wouldn't like to try it. We didn't seem to want to; we kept on bringing our little crises to Mum.

When Mum wasn't teaching us or ironing clothes with a charcoal-burning iron or sewing and mending with the hand-cranked sewing machine, she might have been found syringing an animal's wounds from an encounter with a leopard, pulling porcupine quills out of a dog's nose, patching workmen,

[22]Pronounced: 'may-lee-lay', it means 'eternity'.

workmen's families and her own children, or otherwise doing unimaginable things. The Wambulu and some of the other tribes had a fondness for sticks. They were ostensibly defensive weapons, but frequently became quite offensive. Mum patched the head of many men who got in an argument over the beer.

One night she had to bring Melile into the house and try to treat him for severe head wounds suffered at the hands of a drunk worker. She was home, alone, or with John and Richard, who would have been very young at the time. There was no vehicle and no phone. There was no ambulance to call, anyway. The nearest clinic was twelve miles away, in Kibongoto. Melile died on my bed before dawn. We knew about, and were sensitive to, but didn't follow the native custom of burning the house down following his death in it. We heard about and were quite sensitive to the bafflement of the natives over this much ballyhoo-ed British justice, when at the end of the ensuing trial the killer was let free and a prosecution witness was jailed for some unrelated thing.

Melile had been a headman for Dad, before the war. When Dad was put in the detention camp, Melile went off to serve his king by enlisting in the Kenya Police, the Kings African Rifles, known affectionately as the KAR, or both. One day, sometime after the war was over and we were back in Rongai, he appeared again, for all we knew having walked the 250 miles from his home in Kenya where he had been demobbed, to say: "I'm back!" Dad put him in charge of all the workers, planned the crops with him, planned the herd development and breeding program with him and trusted him totally. With Melile there, Dad at one point even felt able to make an extended trip to Germany. At about the time the Mau-Mau uprising broke out in Kenya, we were suffering a lot of visits from cattle rustlers. The rustlers were Maasai, who really were only claiming what was rightfully theirs; Lengai had given all the cattle in creation to the Maasai people, and it was their right, even their duty, to reclaim them. We and our puny efforts to thwart them were only small inconveniences thrown in the way of the fearless Maasai warriors in the pursuit of their holy grail. Our thorn bomas and watchdogs were no deterrent. Our watchmen were no deterrent. Our watchmen were either cousins of the marauders or conveniently on the other side of the boma when they came. So the Maasai came and went as they pleased. Melile suggested that the visits might be discouraged if it were known that he was armed. He also thought that it might deter the thieves who, without the divine right of the Maasai, were breaking into our stores and stealing tools and *posho,* the maizemeal that was rationed out daily. Dad put his shotgun in Melile's care without a moment's hesitation, even while Europeans in nearby Kenya were under siege. There were many Africans like Melile, who cast their lot with the *Wazungu*, probably not because they liked *Wazungu* in general, but because of a personal loyalty to the individual or family. Sometimes this commitment was made at great personal cost.

Melile died, probably first because he was utterly incorruptible and therefore a nuisance, and only second because he had been careless about how much beer he allowed himself to drink on his last weekend. But he should have known that you can't drop your guard when you are among people of a different tribe.

We used Mum's ironing time for some deep, philosophical discussions with her, since she was captive. She could have let one of the servants do the job, but she had some things that she preferred to iron herself, because the charcoal-heated iron was unforgiving. She might well have let the servants do it had we got much more creative in our discussions.

Pauline talked girl things, and we boys probably avoided those conversations. Bill talked about how he wanted to marry someone with gold toenails. I was sure that I'd marry someone who could *really* cook spaghetti. Mum pointed out that Bill might have to marry an Indian to achieve his goal, while I might find mine easier to fulfill, there were plenty of Italians around, close, as we were, to Somalia. Had Dad been part of the conversation, he would have pointed out that his/my/our great-great-grand-something is/was/were Italian, and we would have changed the subject.

Much later, after a visit with or by Paga, John commented to an ironing Mum: "You know, Paga is surprising!"

Mum agreed.

John went on: "You know, at his age, you'd expect him to be suffering from senile decay, wouldn't you?"

Mum probably nodded.

"But he isn't, at all, is he?"

Mum agreed. She also wondered where this had come from, John may have been seven, or younger, at the time.

One day, probably again later, Richard was looking very thoughtful as he hung around Mum, watching her work away with the iron. He wasn't very old then, either.

He said: "Mum, I want to ask you something about marrying and all that stuff."

Mum thought to herself: 'Oops! This doesn't sound like the same gold toenail and Mediterranean cuisine type of discussion!' and said: "What do you want to know?"

"Well, you see, I'm just thinking: say you don't *want* to get married ... "

"That's OK. Some people don't marry."

"Yes, but what can you do if you *say* you don't want to get married, but somebody just comes along and marries *you*?"

Jock was our hero. He was so *old*. He must have been sixteen or seventeen years older than Pauline. Yet he was not *so* old that he couldn't do wild and wonderful things. He once made a jeep out of the remnants of a car. Which car, or whose car, I do not know. Dad once made some rueful comments about how Jock learned all he knew about cars, and those comments might have given me a hint, had I been of the hint hearing persuasion at the time. Jock took everything off the frame, because jeeps do not have roofs and doors. For a seat he balanced a wooden box on the planks that were the only thing between the occupants and the road. The result had some of the attributes sought in a jeep, it certainly inflicted the expected brutal bodily punishment on its passengers, but there was a problem. Authentic jeeps have the controls on the left, not the right. Jock's solution was simple. He turned the front-end linkages upside down, or back to front, or both, to put the controls where he wanted them. In solving the one problem he created another. To turn the car to the left, he had to turn his steering to the right, and vice versa. This new problem bothered other people, but not Jock. He had no problem, whatsoever, enticing his non-driving niece and nephews to ride with him, and no luck, whatsoever, with the adults. We didn't understand why, and we didn't care.

The Davidsons had inherited a water wheel on Rongai. It powered a flour mill and some other minor machinery. Jock maintained it and it worked smoothly, but at some point, he

65

decided that it was inadequate or was in the wrong place. He decided to replace it with a single cylinder, stationary, internal combustion engine. No such engine was available, so he adapted a four-cylinder car engine, maybe while Dad wasn't looking. He didn't take all of it, anyway; he only cut off a slice, so to speak. He and his Chagga assistant and friend, Kiboko, spent days working away, pushing and pulling at hacksaw blades with their bare hands, to affect this metamorphosis, wishing volubly that they hadn't started. The exposed ends of the water jacket and oil galleries, they patched with cement. The contraption worked, though I don't know how well and for how long. I think more than one season of milling was done using it. The water wheel may have outlasted the engine, eventually, but it didn't outlast my admiration for Jock's ingenuity. Jock was a magician.

Jock had a motorcycle. I learned, from observation, roughly where the sun was in the sky when he would be likely to be coming home at the end of the day, and I would lie in wait for him at the Portals. If he saw me, he would stop, swoop me on to the tank in front of him, and I'd ride home the remaining quarter of a mile, beaming. I was shy and never had the courage to ask for a ride; he had to offer. Even as I lay in wait for him and planned how to make him find it difficult to miss me, I would be torn between my awe of him and my desire - my need - to get the ride. Need usually triumphed over awe. I used the same tactic to get rides with him on an old Fordson tractor.

He also had a .22 rifle. When I turned five he taught me how to fire it. We "aimed" at a rock at the bottom of the garden. Much to Mum's consternation, to say nothing of my own, something went wrong. The breech hadn't closed properly and I got a powder burn under one eye. I have fired thousands of rounds since then, and it has never happened again. Jock very quickly took care of my condition by finding the Very Big Chip that my shot had split from the rock. It was a miraculous bullet, because I don't think it could have come within five feet of the rock. It took him a lot longer, and much more talking, to take care of Mum's condition. She eventually got over it and I certainly gained a very healthy respect for guns.

Hero worship usually extracts a price, at some point. Jock's suggestions had a weight or an authority that he probably didn't even suspect they possessed. Some of it was the hero thing, some of it was that he had been places and done things that we couldn't imagine. I suppose that is part of being a hero. One evening, at supper, I declined Mum's kind offer of some spinach, even after she mimicked Paga's stock phrase "It's VERRy good FORR you!" because I didn't like the bitter and sour and green and wet and gloppy stuff. Declining such invitations usually was a waste of time; this time, it was also a mistake. Jock stopped feeding cherry tomatoes to the dik-dik (he liked the surprised expression it got every time it bit one, when the juices squirted out of the side of its mouth), and told us, again, about Popeye the Sailor Man. He had seen a Popeye cartoon at the flicks, and could relate the entire cartoon, word for crazy word. I wound up with all of the spinach on my plate. Everyone else seemed willing to make the sacrifice. Despite my most valiant effort, there much of it remained. Spinach didn't taste good in the little serving we usually got. Popeye and Jock notwithstanding, it didn't get better in as big a pile as sat there and stared malevolently back at me. I don't think I ate enough to get as strong as Popeye, even momentarily, or else I was not of a mind to notice if I did. Nor did I make particular note of any lesson in life. But I have noticed that it wasn't until I was married and there was someone else in my life whose suggestions carried quite as much authority as Jock's, that I could bring myself to try spinach again. Now I like it. I guess I have another, different kind of hero.

Some years later, other cartoons appeared at the flicks. Jock would come home on his visits and tell us, frame by frame, the adventures of Tom and Jerry. Fortunately, neither of them used - or abused - vile tasting, green substances, and we could just hang by Jock's eyelashes and enjoy the good, clean mayhem.

When Jock wasn't passing cherry tomatoes to the dik-dik, he might have been spooning out for it the sugar left in the bottom of his coffee cup. The expression that this treat brought on was of sublime transportation, rather than surprise.

Or, he might have been going through his routine, for the dozenth time, about the hunting scene depicted on a series of faded tapestries that must have come along with Dad from Europe.

"There's a magpie in that scene. It's just out of the picture. Bet you can't find it."

One of us would point to the knot in a tree: "Is this it?"

We'd no idea what a magpie should look like, but a knot? Jock would just shake his head.

Someone else would try a shadow under the bush: "Is *this* it?"

Or: "I know! It's just behind the tree!"

To all of these guesses, he had the same answer: "No. You're not listening. It's just out of the picture."

We'd just look harder. "This shape, here, *this* must be it!"

After a while, we got as far as to ask on which side it was just out of the picture.

If Dad was around, this conversation would be his cue to tell us about the "stonen men" who stood guard at one of the gates in Schloss Büdingen. He pointed to them in a water colour of that gate, painted by his mother, which hung in the dining room.

"Every night, when the two stonen men hear the clock strike midnight, they get up and change places."

"Did you see them do it? If I'm ever there, I'm going to stay up and watch!"

"I know! Someone comes out and moves them!"

"How can you tell that they've changed places? Are they different?"

You are free to imagine the rest of the conversation. You are also free to anticipate the way such naïvete was later to be welcomed in boarding school.

Once in a while, on a trip into Moshi we would spend the night in Paga's flat. That was almost as much fun as riding on one of Jocks contraptions. We loved Paga, and seeing him was a treat in itself, but there were so many things that were different, that the whole trip became an experience. First, you didn't have to bother with kerosene lamps, there was electricity. Then, there were those fans hanging from the high ceilings, that were so absolutely quiet but could deliver a wonderful cooling breeze. Moshi was at an elevation of two thousand feet, considerably lower than Rongai, which made the air there very different; it was sticky and hot in a way it never was at home. The word *moshi* means smoke, and we were told that the place got that name from the haze that was usually in the air.

Because there was malaria in Moshi we slept under

mosquito nets, which added to the strangeness and to our appreciation of the fans. Above the fans, on the ceiling, were a family of geckos which chased mosquitoes and moths. We'd watch them swallow insects. I mean it literally. They evolved on the ceilings of caves and flats in Moshi, out of the sunlight, so they had translucent, almost transparent skins, and we could see the dark patch go down their throats and join the line of dark patch meals that traced their innards. The electric light in Paga's cave wasn't strong enough to bother their pigmentless skins.

Then there was the water. When you got yourself a glassful of water from the tap (instead of from a ceramic filter, as we did at home), it turned milky white for a minute, then it would slowly become normal. The water was under pressure, so as soon as the pressure was released, air came out of solution in tiny bubbles.

And there were the unnatural noises. At home, we went to sleep with the sound of insects, frogs, monkeys, small, nocturnal, tree dwelling creatures called bush babies, hyenas and sometimes even of larger wild animals. In Moshi, instead, there were strange traffic noises. Paga's flat was close to the traffic roundabout in the centre of town, which some wag had nicknamed Piccadilly Circus. Much of the traffic going anywhere went through this circle, and it seemed like an endless stream; there could be ten or twenty vehicles in one evening. We could recognize the sounds of ex-military Ford lorries whose third gears whined characteristically, other Fords, with snub noses, dubbed Ford Canadas, whose gears were all noisy, the far fewer Chevys which sounded like ours and the UK-made Albion and Dennis lorries, with their low-pitched diesel engine rumble. Closer to home we could have guessed, from its sound, whose lorry was going by, and we'd usually be right. We had much less luck with the cars, their sounds were less distinctive. In town, though, there were just too many vehicles for us to know them all; we didn't even try to guess who was going by.

Before we got into bed to lie and listen to the strange sounds and to the absence of the familiar ones, we would have enjoyed a treat for supper. We would have had canned baked beans on toast, just like we knew cowboys had when they camped on the range. We knew because Jock told us, that's how. In the morning, we'd wake up to another treat for breakfast: eggs and bacon or sausages, with tomatoes and bread fried in the fat. We loved the Rongai breakfast staple of maize meal porridge, even though we had it every day, but this Moshi breakfast, *this* was living!

Sims had a garden. It was big. It covered about five acres. In it she had vegetables, fruit, flowers and a veritable arboretum It was where she spent much of her time. When she spent time in the garden, we did too, our "help" commensurate with our age.

If we helped too much, or did anything harmful, we'd be admonished or corrected quite quickly, though quite kindly. Perhaps the kindness obscured the message.

One day, Mum heard Pauline's two-year-old voice (it must have been before the banishment to Tabora) saying, oh so sweetly: "Don't step on Granny's peas! Don't step on Granny's peas! Don't step ... "

She looked over to see Pauline, very, very carefully stepping on each tender plantlet in a row of peas, saying, with each step: "Don't step ... "

Sims used to enjoy a late afternoon walk. She liked to do a loop of a bit less than a mile. We'd often all go along, Mum, children, dogs and other pets and all, making up a rather undisciplined parade, with some of us trailing along, getting farther behind as we looked at butterflies and dung beetles or collected bits of obsidian. On one such walk, I lagged a bit farther than usual, daydreaming or otherwise distracted. I was brought back to the present and propelled back into line quite suddenly and very unceremoniously. Ngenenia, a pet Thompson's gazelle, named after the Maasai who had given him to Sims, was lagging even farther behind than I was. He got the idea, perhaps instinctively, being the dominant buck there, that I shouldn't wander from the herd like that. He let me know it by butting me on my rump. He actually didn't butt me, he hit me with what would have been the point of one of his horns, if that horn hadn't been broken. Had it been whole, or had he used the other horn, he would have impaled me. (Would that have made him an Impaler, rather than a Tommie?). The incident was firmly imprinted on my memory, if my memory resides in my brain. I had trouble sitting for weeks, with a bruise the size of an egg right where, later, one of my boarding schoolteachers helpfully confided in me I'd find my brain, if I'd care to look.

Ngenenia had a pal named Ngoili. You got it, he was named after his donor, Ngoili. They both lived with us, in the house, with the dogs and cats, quite peaceably. The same dogs were happy to go hunting wild gazelles, antelopes, rodents and warthogs with the herdsmen. They saw no inconsistency in their behaviour towards these two animals. After all, they were family!

At one time we had eight cats and five dogs, all at the same time. We rarely closed a door or a window, so they came and went as they pleased, along with the dik-diks, the Tommies and whatever else was resident. One golden retriever/ridgeback mix had the colouring of a lion. His appearance earned him the proud name *Simba*. His behaviour earned him another name. In Sims' orchard, there were avocado trees that were sixty feet tall. The lowest branches were ten feet up. When the fruit ripened, it was out of reach. To harvest them, we had to rely on the heavy landings of the hornbill birds who came to eat, to shake the ripening fruit loose. Hornbills are as big as storks, but have shorter legs and necks and are clumsy. Their landings are controlled crashes. From the house, we would hear the swish-swish of the wings as they broke their speed to land, and we would start running as we heard the impact of the bird on the branch, even before we heard the crash of the fruit falling through the leaves and branches and the thump as it hit the ground. For Simba also was tuned in to those sounds. He loved avocados as much as we did and had the advantage of a more sensitive nose to lead him and twice as many legs to propel him to the treasure. Simba's advantages usually only helped him to find the first, and perhaps the second avocado. While he feasted, we would collect the rest. If there were only two avocados, guess who lost, but there were usually plenty. In season, we had dozens of them completing their ripening, ranged along the top of the dining room window's valances, the sideboard - anywhere out of dog-reach. We enjoyed them best with plenty of salt, pepper and vinegar, mashed and piled so high on a slice of bread that our noses got covered in green. We would look much like Simba did after he ate his treats, but we didn't have to be satisfied with not-quite-ripe fruit and no seasoning, so we had the last laugh.

71

Jock started calling Simba "Stinker", because he won so many of the races. Stinker by name, but not by nature. When Dad was away, he would automatically come to sleep on the floor, at the foot of Mum's bed. As soon as Dad was back, he would return just as automatically, to his spot on the living room floor by the front door.

Jessie was a bitch of about the same generation as Stinker. Her first litter consisted of a single, still-born pup. She kept trying and trying to lick it and nudge it awake or to life. It took us two days to get it away from her. On the day that we finally got rid of it, a herdsman came up to us with a baby dik-dik. He had killed its mother while he was out tending the cattle. This was not uncommon, for them to bring the foundlings to us, they knew that we were soft-hearted and would ransom the little creatures. Someone, I think Mum, had the idea of offering this one to Jessie. Jessie understood, immediately, that this was not a morsel intended as a snack. For months, our visitors were astonished to see a dog nursing a dik-dik. The other dogs never bothered it, just as they had never bothered Ngenenia and Ngoili.

One day, John woke up to find blood stains on the windowsill, right over the spot on his bed where Bobby, a dachshund, used to sleep, but no Bobby. Mlavi or Marisha, whoever was the houseboy at the time, followed the blood trail and found leopard footprints. For a while, we closed some windows.

Not long after, Mum woke up to find that the wall that held that same window had fallen. Though it fell outwards, it left a stone bigger than John's head in the spot where his head would have been, had he not crept into her bed during the night with a tummy ache or "bad dreams".

That gave Dad an excuse to rebuild virtually the whole house. He used the same materials as the original structure, river stones with mud mortar and lime and cement pointing for the walls, corrugated galvanized iron for the roof and cement for the floors. While the stone *fundis* were finishing the masonry, carpentry *fundis* worked on making doors and windows from local woods. We 'helped' and learned how to use hand tools.

A short while after the nice new *mvuli* front door was hung in its place, it was left open during a day of rain. It swelled so

72

much that we were rarely able to close it. That front door stayed wide open for years, despite Bobby's fate, despite the weather and, later, despite even the Mau-Mau troubles in Kenya.

With the rebuilding, the verandah became part of the living room. A family of swallows which came from Europe each year to build their nest there lost their favourite spot, and we lost the passion fruit vine that had been intertwined with the 'golden shower' trumpet vine that had graced the verandah. Granny and Mum saw silver linings where we didn't, they noted that Jock could no longer drive his car onto the verandah.

We boys moved to the far side of the house. It was nice, in ways, to have our own room, just for the four of us, on our own wing of the house, but when we got our bad dreams, there was an awfully wide expanse of dark house to get through to reach Mum. We still didn't get indoor plumbing, the toilet was still an outhouse, which Jock had dubbed[23] "King's Club". We learned to plan ahead before we turned in for the night, and, also, not to need to go very frequently. Under certain circumstances, we'd climb out of the window, do our communing with nature and climb back in.

In the rebuilding, Dad got a one hundred and twenty square metre living room, not quite as big as the great hall in Langenselbold, and a fireplace not quite big enough to sit in, as you could in the ones in the castles back home. But they were grand enough for him to consider them steps in the right direction.

Dad nearly didn't get to enjoy his new, grand living room. He woke up one morning, early in the rainy season, to find that the whole hillside below the cattle *boma*, usually tinged a little green from the manure washing down the slope, had turned quite white. Tens of thousands of mushrooms had sprouted overnight. Dad immediately sent us all out to gather them. All of them, we didn't do things in half-measures. We would feast on mushrooms and then dry what was left. One of Dad's favourite themes was self-sufficiency.

---

[23]This is a pun. People on the wrong side of the Atlantic, or on the wrong side of the Channel, might miss it. I'd hate to think it was wasted. The WC was often called the dub.

Something (could it possibly have been in one of the many helpings of mushrooms that he ate in those days?) was almost sufficient to do Dad's self in. He was so sick I truly wondered if he would survive. He lay in bed for a week, vomiting and otherwise manifesting how sick he was, with Mum and the rest of us running back and forth with the bed pan. We'd report to him, occasionally, how the drying was going. He probably didn't care, but we were trying to think of things that would let him know that there was a reason to go on living.

After the third or fourth day of spreading the soggy mushrooms out on the old coffee drying trays, an awful stench started to develop, and it had nothing to do with Dad's condition, not directly, though one might be forgiven for making the olfactorial connection. Drying meant sun-drying, since we had no other method available. The sun wasn't co-operating. It was on holiday for the duration of the rainy season, and wouldn't be back for several weeks. The air itself was cold and saturated, and couldn't do the job.

Eventually, we were forced to find a place to bury the rotten, slimy mass. When we reported the fact to Dad, he looked pained. It could have been because of the loss of such a treasure. Or it could have been another stomach cramp. It would have been impossible to tell.

While we're on the theme of self-sufficiency, we can think about why we are lucky we were born who we are.

One day we had just had some ham or *Wurst*, and were discussing smoking as a means of curing meat. That means, Dad was telling us about it. Before the discussion was over, we were digging a trench up the side of the slope in front of the kitchen and covering it with twigs, leaves and earth. At the low end, we dug a hole in which a fire would be set. At the upper end, about twenty feet away, we placed an empty *debe,* a paraffin can. The smoke from the fire, we were told, would know to go up the gently sloped, almost horizontal chimney formed by the trench, cool itself as it went, and arrive at the *debe* ready to cure the meat which would be waiting there for it. We nodded wisely and went off to play. We had witnessed several things like this, and they had all been forgotten before long.

Very shortly after this particular demonstration, we found ourselves in the middle of a flurry of unpleasant activity. A pig

74

had been slaughtered, and Dad was going to make full use of it and the model smoker. Some of the pig was cut into ham-like chunks, while other bits were being shoved through Mum's hand-cranked meat mincer which had a horizontal funnel-spout like thing, a sausage attachment, that could be mounted on it. Someone was dispatched to find the right amount of onions and things to mix into the *Wurst,* someone else to clean the gut which would become the sausage skin. Someone else was probably looking for some salt to rub into the hams.

When Pauline was offered the opportunity to get involved, perhaps to clean some gut, she demurred. Her demurral was fairly polite, I thought. Most of it was.

Dad didn't seem to think so. He was quite upset that she should decline this opportunity to complete her education: "Why, *every* Bavarian countess knows how to dress a boar!"

Pauline pointed out that she was *not* a Bavarian countess. Fortunately, in her opinion. She added something about the perversions that seemed to amuse some of the idle rich and made herself scarce.

The smoke was not Bavarian, either, and didn't know what was expected of it; it never made it all the way to the *debe.* The meat never made it all the way to being cured; it turned into roasts and things, instead. Or, maybe we were just lucky enough to have to go back to school before the exercise was over. I just can't remember eating any *Wurst* from it, or ham, or bacon. One would remember such an experience, I think.

Be thankful you aren't a Bavarian countess. Be ever thankful you aren't a pig!

Mum and Jock had started their education literally braving the wild animals to walk to school. That school did not survive. It evolved or was subsumed into the only European elementary school in the Province, The Arusha School, in Arusha, sixty miles away. Later, Mum taught there for a short time. We, the next generation started out with school coming to us. We sat at home and were taught by Mum and Sims, who also had been a schoolteacher. That is, we ran around the farm, barefoot, until we made the mistake of coming close enough to hear the bell ring. Then we would come in, reluctantly, and sit and be taught. Every month, a new set of correspondence lessons came in the mail. We were genuinely excited when we received each new package in a soon familiar

75

black cloth bag, wrapped in brown paper and tied with yards of string for the parcel post. We did the exercises and read the books, and, some weeks later, were genuinely glad to wrap each package up again, in its black bag and saved brown paper and string, and send it in to Paga in Moshi, to be mailed for grading. "The Correspondence School, Dar-es-Salaam", was an adequate address. After about 4 or 5 years of this, we would each go on to boarding school, inevitably but fittingly, the Arusha School.

After a short flurry of preparation, including the acquisition of tin trunks, which Paga had painted black and had ceremoniously decorated with our names in big, perfect white letters, Pauline and I were driven to Arusha in the lorry. In January, 1949, it was still in its military paint. Dad drove and Mum rode in the front. Pauline and I rode in the back, as usual, enjoying our last chance for a while to see if we could do the whole trip standing without touching the sides. When we tired of that, we climbed down onto the chassis through the hole that the tractor's front wheels had punched through the floor.

We didn't fully comprehend what was in store for us, so we might even have been naïve enough to sing. If we did sing, it was probably some snatches of the Mbulu traveling song we could parrot, without comprehending the meaning of the words. Fitting, in a way.

We might well also have sung a folk song that goes:
"Naomba ruksa, bwana, kwenda Kilindini.
Baba yangu mgonjwa sana, mimi vile vile!"
The tune is reminiscent of, but not identical to Yankee Doodle Dandy. It is in *kisettla*, the settler version of Swahili, in which grammar and spelling rules are largely ignored. It says, with its tongue in its cheek: "I beg permission, boss, to go to Kilindini. My father is very sick, and so am I!" It has several verses, one for each possible problem that could befall each member of the extended family, with no limit to the number of misfortunes that any one member could suffer. The last line of the last verse is: *"Baba yangu kufa jana,* (my father died yesterday), *mimi vile vile!"*

We might also have sung a folk song that Mum taught us, in English, which I remember imperfectly:
"As I went down to Derby, to ring the High Church Bell,

I met the biggest ram, sir, that ever was fed upon hay!
"Sing jorum, sing jorum, sing jorum dandalay,
It was the biggest ram, sir, that ever was fed upon hay!
"It had a great big hoof, sir, it was so large and round,
That when he put it down, sir, it covered an acre of ground!
"Sing jorum ..."

Then there were some more verses dealing with horns, and things, and one that Mum had started to teach us, when, demonstrating that she could tease every bit as well as Jock, she had a sudden failure in her memory. It was a mystery which intrigued us greatly. The only clue we had to go on was the end of the last line:

"..., they all washed away in the flood!"

We might also have sung one of Jock's songs, say, to the tune of 'My Bonnie ...'

"My breakfast lies under the ocean,
My dinner lies under the sea,
And if we continue this motion,
Oh, what will become of my tea?"

As Dad drove through the avenue of impressive eucalyptus trees, which impressed us mostly with how very, very small we were. We went from the sun into a deep shade, and our mood changed. It would stay changed for years. When we sang again, it was on the trip away from school, three times each year. Our songs would be things like 'Pack up your troubles in your old kit bag." I think we lost something.

Dad pulled up in front of the school. We climbed down and someone put our new trunks on the driveway. Mr. Morgan was the Assistant Headmaster. Mum knew Cuss Morgan from when she taught there, when the eucalyptus trees were less tall. He saw us arrive, shouted for "Sieghardt and Thor!" (I'm not joking!) to "...look after the new boy and get somebody to look after the new girl." Turning to Mum and Dad, he said: "It's better if you go. Now!" They went. We didn't go in for much of that sort of mushy stuff, so there were no hugs or kisses. It was a good thing. I would have been mortified had they done that to me in public. It seemed to us that three minutes had not passed from when we entered the gates until we were abandoned in the driveway of this frightening, strange place full of strange people. As far as we could remember, we had in our whole lives spoken to no more than half a dozen English

77

speaking people our own age (Pauline had just turned eleven, and I nine), if you don't count our own family and the von Kalcksteins. Those few people whom we had met had been inclined to be friendly. That left us totally unprepared for the viciousness and cruelty that other kids are capable of showing towards anyone who hasn't yet learned how to stand up to it. And, to cap it all, among all the other indignities, we were expected to wear shoes! All day! Every day! Before every meal, we were lined up for inspection: hair combed? faces washed? behind and inside ears clean? back of hands, fingernails, front of hands and knees clean? shoes freshly shined? -- Shoes? If, in the hurry to get into the line to subject myself to the indignity of the inspection before breakfast, I forgot to put on my new and uncomfortable shoes, I could expect the Matron to be quite insensitive and say all kinds of rude things, right in front of all the others. Life had definitely taken a sudden turn for the worse. Nothing to sing about here!

The first night, I was so utterly, miserably homesick that I ached, and I cried. I cried really hard, and I cried out loud, because I hadn't yet learned not to cry, even when I really had to. Worse, I hadn't learned that even when I absolutely had to cry, it was worth my life to let anyone know that I was doing so. My weakness did not go unnoticed; it led to my being given endless opportunities to entertain the troops, over the next three years. Over thirty years later, when he was about the age that I was that night, Valerie and I left our son, Charles, at a summer camp where he would be alone with strangers for the first time. At the last moment, when he saw the place and the other boys, he didn't want to be left. You just know that I would remember my own experience and relent, to save him from emotional scars that might turn him into a pathological killer. Sorry! Parenthood does not of itself impart wisdom or unlimited sensitivity. We left him there, literally pushing him out of the car as we drove off. I remember vividly the drive home and the long week that passed before we went back to pick him up, so whatever sensitivity I have must be of the 'too little, too late' variety. He isn't a pathological killer, yet, and even seems not to lack social skills. It is perhaps less thanks to fathers' sensitivity and more to youth's innate ability to overcome such sanity-threatening experiences that this race was not snuffed out a long time ago.

78

At Arusha, they used to give out stars to people who did well in class or in tests. This was done in assembly, in front of the whole school. One morning, during the first few weeks, the Headmaster called out a name three times, and nobody came up.

Then the boy next to me shoved me. "Hey! Eisenberg! That's you."

And so I started to get used to the further indignity of hearing my name mispronounced every time it was used.

About the time that Pauline and I went to Arusha School, Jock moved away, to earn a better living in Arusha. A year or so later, Granny Sims took a trip to Scotland. It was the first time she went "back home" since she left, about forty years earlier. We children were aware that she was going, in part, for medical reasons. When she came back, she had shrunk. In her shoes, she was barely five feet tall, so she started out short, but cancer made her just tiny. Each time we came home for holidays, we noticed dramatic changes in her. She lost so much weight that I would carry her on my own, from her room to the living room. She had no wheelchair, so I would pick up her wicker chair, with her sitting in it, and carry them both. I was ten.

A few weeks after going back to Arusha for a new term, Bill and I were called in to see the Headmaster. "Going to see Cuss Hamshere" was usually bad news. We wondered what we could be guilty of. Bill was two standards behind me, so I couldn't be seen with him much, so we couldn't be in trouble for the same thing. The Head's expression was serious, but did not fit with trouble for us, certainly not serious enough for a punishment, anyway. We were relieved, but still apprehensive. Then we were told that our grandmother had died, and we got a long - it seemed long - discourse on how she had been instrumental in creating Arusha School, and how everyone in the School community would share and feel the loss. We didn't hear any of it. We just wanted to get out and be alone. When we did get out, we were not very composed, as one might imagine, and we were not very alone. The school community didn't seem to be sharing our grief. We were teased immediately for our tears, ironically, first by a girl whose parents knew Granny well and was even one of the few children we had met, once, before coming to school. As the older brother, it should have been my instinct to help Bill through the next few hours. I have not been able to forget that my instinct, which I followed, was to go where even Bill couldn't see that I was crying and let him take care of his problem his own way. Boarding school does not do much to develop the human side of ten year olds.

A few years after that, Bill and I were again in school together, but now in Nairobi. Jock had taken an unplanned trip to the UK, also to seek treatment for cancer. After I had read a letter from Pauline, who, through with school, was home at the time, I walked into Bill's dormitory, more like a barracks, where he was lying on his bed for the regulated 'rest' in the afternoon.

I handed him the letter, said: "Jock died," and walked away, leaving him to handle his grief in front of twenty-six fellow resters.

If I had stayed, I might not have kept my composure, and that just would not have done; I was a prefect and this was the junior dorm of our house. Bill might not have managed any better, either, with me there. Under the circumstances I may have done him a favour by leaving immediately. Boarding school doesn't improve the chances for people to be human when they're sixteen-year-olds, either. Bill has never said that he resented either occasion. If he accepts that behaviour as normal, I have to conclude that he is as warped as I am.

After Arusha School, we all went on to secondary schools in Nairobi: Pauline to the brand new Kenya Girls' High School, affectionately known as the Heifer *Boma* (the Heifer Corral), Bill and I to Jock's old school, by then named The Prince of Wales School, known as Prince o', or the Cabbage Patch, and John and Richard to Saint Mary's School, "Saints" or the "Fairies" (the modern connotation of this word was not then in use). Fortunately, we boys all avoided being sent to the Duke of York School ("Duke o'", or the "Duck Pond").

I saw the papers that admitted me to Prince o'. I asked Mum what were those letters, MCA, before my name. I had a horrible feeling that I knew, but I could hope I was wrong. She told me they were just my initials, well, some of them. I nearly died. Maria Carl Alfonz. How long did I think I was going to survive in a boarding school with a name like that? Couldn't they at least have dropped the Maria?[24] Couldn't they have chosen some other names from the nine I'd been given?

Had we been crows, we would have been able to fly the 170 miles to Nairobi in a few hours. We weren't crows, nor were we able to find anyone interested in giving up two days at a time to drive us. We had to go by train. It was a trip of 300 miles that took 18 hours that felt like 18 days. On this unchaperoned trip, the favourite sport of the bigger boys was to grab someone younger and smaller and to hang him out of the window by his heels. Next favourite was to stand him, or another one like him, on the sink and induce him to sing by threatening his toes with one of the plentiful empty beer bottles. Particularly attractive as victims were *pongos*,[25] the newcomers from the UK. *Pongos* were easily recognized, their too-long shorts were a dead giveaway every time, that and their propensity to have been given money by their loving parents to order bed linen for the overnight ride - and then actually using it for that purpose. The East African born (they wouldn't have called themselves "native") boys toughed it out; whatever sleep they got was not with the aid of bed linen! There were only so many pongos, not nearly enough to go around, really, so all smaller boys were at risk. No boys, anywhere, ever wished or prayed more fervently that they would grow bigger, faster, than did the unfortunate twelve year olds who had heard these stories (perhaps even from their own Uncles Jock!) before they faced their first ride on that infamous train from Tanganyika to the schools in Nairobi. Any boy whose first name was Maria had a bunch more to hope for. Even so, history does not relate that anyone was ever seriously hurt, anywhere other than in his ego (or if he was a reluctant singer, in his toes). The Prince o' train

---

[24]Dad was away, in Germany, when I actually left to go to Nairobi. He had explained to us, earlier, how we came by the good fortune to be named that way, in honour of our Lord's mother, the patron saint of the family, just like all of the lineage, masculine, feminine or neuter, back through the generations. When I got copies of the names of that lineage, years later, I found that either he was wrong, or, if he ever believed that line himself, he had been tricked. I think the tradition went all the way back about three generations!
[25]Swahili for bush buck, a shy, almost effeminate, forest or thicket dwelling antelope.

even prided itself in having a worse reputation than those of the Duck Pond and the other schools. The behaviour of the group on my very first trip earned everyone on the train six weeks of "gating" or "grounding", including me, and I think I had hardly dared to peek out of my cabin.

I didn't mind the gating. I'd survived the trip. And no one seemed to care, yet, what that dreaded initial, 'M' stood for.

The gating calmed things down, for a while. Gating is serious stuff; there are no leave passes to see the flicks in town, to visit the Boma, or even to get a coveted space on the once-weekly shopping lorry into town to break the routine. Three or four years later, though, shortly after term started, two boys from the Tanganyika train went to see the matron at the sanitarium, to get relief from what seemed to be '*dhobi*[26] rash' which comes from wearing shorts incompletely rinsed after being washed in the locally made, caustic, blue, laundry soap. Matron examined the rashes. She called the school doctor. The school doctor called the Headmaster. The Headmaster called the boys in to his office. He then called their parents to invite them home, for good. It seems that they had looked for some other kind of entertainment, off the train, during the three-hour stopover in Voi.

We were invited, in small groups, to talks about things that didn't include the price of eggs and were sent off to be good boys and not let the school and Tanganyika down. Which we promised fervently to do and not to do and went on to draw the conclusion that the earlier ideas of entertainment were more acceptable, after all. They certainly had lesser repercussions.

Expulsion and gating were the most dreaded punishments. Caning was much more common, and there were others even more common. Caning was delivered (executed?) by school prefects, themselves students, for minor offenses, by the Housemaster for more serious offenses and by the Headmaster for the worst cases. I once get four strokes for whispering to someone else, a fellow Tanganyikan: "There goes the City of Nairobi," as the *chura* lorry whined its way past our common room while we were doing our homework assignments, "prep", it was called. I knew the silence rule. It's

---

[26]The Hindi word for laundry or launderer.

just that I thought it funny that the only place we frequently saw the name of our host city was on the side of the truck which came every other day to empty out the latrine buckets of Junior House. The "temporary" wooden barracks, left over from the war, had been our home only the year before. We now enjoyed flush toilets in Intermediate House and could feel quite superior. Superiority comes before a whack on the behind.

I also once got six strokes for sharing a few puffs of a cigarette with Westy, a chap I had befriended. I probably got the six strokes more for having befriended him than for having puffed on his cigarette. He was one of those kids who seemed to attract trouble, despite themselves. My Housemaster told me that I shouldn't spend any time with him, he was a bad influence, and so on. My Housemaster was probably right, but I hardly looked on Westy as a role model. I just didn't see why he should be denied friendship. Besides, his name was Charles and we shared our birthday. I was told, never by him, that he had been separated from his family during the war and had lived for a while as an urchin on the streets of London. That could be one explanation for some of his social problems. He once invited Bill and me to his parents' home twelve miles away, in Kiambu, a coffee growing district near Nairobi. He had spent most of the preceding holidays helping his father build a swimming pool and wanted to show it off to us. On a Sunday, duly armed with leave passes, we hitch-hiked to his home. There, in front of thirty of her guests and his own two guests, Westy's mother shouted at him that she didn't want him there, couldn't he see she had guests, she was having a pool party, what was wrong with him, get out, get lost, drop dead, etc., etc. I think we came closer to understanding what was the real cause of most of his social problems.

The cane was a very physical punishment, on a very immediate level. Then there was an insult that was added to the injury. Every now and then a van would drive up with the legend "H.M. Prisons" done in gold leaf on the side. The driver would step out with a dozen new rattan canes and deliver them to the Headmaster's office, for further distribution by him to the eight Housemasters. We were being corrected with the same instruments with which justice was meted out to common criminals, native criminals. And they didn't care if we knew it. I mean, if they were in the slightest way concerned

83

about our sensitivity, they could have sent them by Parcel Post, couldn't they, or delivered them in an unmarked car, or a plain brown wrapper, or something?

One defining experience of the early part of my time at Prince o' occurred in a Scout camp. It goes beyond telling about the school. It says things, not all of them flattering, about several institutions. It was in 1952, before the Mau Mau activities had developed to the point that the Governor declared the State of Emergency. We could still have camps. Boy Scouts from all the local schools were involved in this week-long affair at the Agricultural Show grounds. We pitched our tents in the surrounding forest and scouted. We had our area, the Asians had theirs and the Africans had theirs. Technically, we did things by troops, not by race, but since there was a troop for each European school, one for each Asian school, etc., what's the difference? We all did our scouting apart, until the last night, when we had a bonfire. We sat around the bonfire, separately, in our troops, and each troop was asked to do a little thing to entertain the rest. The Africans sang some songs, in a strong, four-part harmony totally natural to them, and did several clever skits. We watched them for fifteen or twenty minutes, patronizingly, amused by their accents when they sang in English. Then the Asian troop did an extremely inventive production that involved every one of their members. The group was, at different times, raw KAR (King's African Rifles) recruits, soldiers being sent off on campaign, the Kenya Bus Service bus that took them and various obstacles that it met on the way. The only props they used were a sheet, a couple of flashlights and a bicycle pump. All of this while they sang the marching song *"Funga Safari, Pack up and go,"* in Swahili and delivered a commentary in Swahili, Hindi and English. We watched them for twenty minutes, we wouldn't have admitted it, jealously. The non-European troops performed well, each in three languages. We wondered what our troop was going to do that could be cleverer. We, who were wondering, were the first-year members, the juniors, the "rabble". It was not our place to think or suggest. While the Asian troop was winding up, the seniors said something like: "You, you and you! Do something!" One of the yous was me! We did the entire planning of our own skit in as long as it took one *pongo* to remember a thing he had done as a Wolf Cub, half of his life ago. We didn't have time to rehearse and it wouldn't have helped. Our skit involved a wet washcloth and it went over like a wet fire cracker. Thankfully, it lasted only fifteen seconds, from the time we stood up to the time we sat down again and I could crawl away and hide.

As soon as the skit was done, but before the campfire was over, one of the scouts who had been you-ed with me was sent by one of the you-ers, Hodges, the head scout, a senior boy, not a master, to wash the cooking utensils at our camp. Richard Martin was a fellow rider of the Tanganyika train and a friend, so I joined him to help. I guess nobody noticed that two of us went. It took a fair amount of time and when we were finished, we decided to stay in the camp rather than find our way through the dark forest to the fire.

When everyone came back, only fifteen minutes later, Hodges called for Richard. Why hadn't he, Martin, come back to the fire? Had he, Hodges, said that he, Martin, could stay away? No? Then why had he, Martin, a rabble (the collective noun was used for a singular person in this important application), taken it on himself to disobey the head scout, and a school prefect, at that? Come and see him, Hodges, at his tent at half past seven.

At half past seven, I went with Richard to his, Hodges', tent. I waited outside, wondering if I should go in, too. I heard him, Hodges lecture Richard for a long time. He would turn and ask another older boy who was there with him, for confirmation and support, which he appeared to get.

Then he said: "On your Scout's honour, you are not to tell anyone about this! Bend over!" I no longer wondered if I had done the right thing in not going in with my friend.

He gave Richard six strokes with a switch that he had cut on his way back from the campfire. I was ten feet away in the dark and I heard the cane whistle through the air on each stroke. I heard it land and I heard Richard catch his breath each time. I think I felt each stroke, myself. My friend came out of the tent and we walked together, slowly, silently and, one of us, quite gingerly, to our own tent. I suggested, only half seriously, that we should tell the scoutmaster. Richard thought not and I didn't press the point.

A sadistic bully could get away with that kind of thing

because he had put his victim on his honour not to tell. And, should the victim have harboured, for just one moment, the thought of 'cliping' he would soon have brought himself to his senses and decided that he'd rather live more peacefully in the future, or just live, than seek justice.

That perverted behaviour, the perverted sense of what honour meant and the cowardice that I displayed, after all I had not been bound by that one-sided vow, were not isolated examples of boarding school life.

The experience in boarding schools should have made the British more sensitive to the plight of the African colonial subjects, shouldn't it? Actually, what it did was turn out generations of people who had been somewhat desensitized and could have no glimmer of understanding of that plight.

After saying all that, I must also say that I did make some very good friends at Prince o'. I got my second paying job from Gianfraco Benetti, one of those friends. If fate hadn't scattered us all in different directions, I don't doubt we'd still be good friends, some of us. I guess it was not all bad.

I also should say that some of the teachers were respected, liked, even admired by many of the students, even by me. Some, understandably, were not, not even by me. The teachers, too, were scattered by similar fates. One evening, not long ago, we were entertaining three couples at our home in Winston-Salem. One of the guests turned out to be the niece of Mr. Salmon, my geometry teacher in Form III A, over forty years ago. He was a respectee because he was a respecter. He'd walk in the door and drawl: "Sit daown and pipe daown!" but then he proceeded to treat us like humans. I remember the long argument we had about one particular problem, in which I refused to be wrong. He was gracious enough to allow me, eventually, to be right. He was also sensible and sensitive enough to help me to avoid making a habit of being right. He's now living in Canada, his excuse being he's Canadian. He must be in his eighties.

That must make "Flakey" Fletcher, the Headmaster, over a hundred and five, or so. We respected Flakey. Even while we asked each other if anyone had seen a little old man with no red hair, we respected him. In a way, he was the Prince o'. He knew all six hundred boys by name. I bet he'd remember Bill and me, immediately, if we were to meet him today. Even at one hundred and five. If I were to see him now, even at a hundred and five yards, I think I'd instinctively reach down to pull up my socks before his frown could hit me. I can't imagine that he isn't there, somewhere in retirement land, perhaps with even less red hair than he didn't have in the fifties, but walking just as tall and straight and purposefully through the Lake District or along the cliffs in Cornwall as he did through the school grounds. It was Flakey who noticed, one term, that Bill and I had come to school without the traditional fifty shillings (50/-) each for pocket money (which would be deposited with the Housemaster to be meted out over the next three months, all but 20/- which would have gone immediately into the School Fund), and had asked us about it. Dad was particularly low in cash at the beginning of that term and couldn't give us anything before he headed off on a long trip to investigate an alternative way to make a living. Flakey found a hundred shillings, "in a special fund", for us to put in for pocket money like everybody else. He did it quietly, so we could retain our dignity. Students' dignity is not commonly a concern in boarding schools. Bill says Flakey took it from his own pocket.

At the same time that Flakey was doing that for Bill and me, John and Richard must have been under similar circumstances at Saint's. Father Kelly was Saint's Bursar. He was also the lucky priest who used to come up to Prince o' on Monday afternoons, to teach the Catholics about our one and only true faith. We were, after all, suffering the deprivation of being "educated" at a government school in a Protestant country, and we could not just be ignored, lest our souls be lost.

During one class, he wanted to make the point about the infallibility of the Pope. One had to follow the teachings of the Church hierarchy, one couldn't make up rules for one's self. "Just because a man travels to the Belgian **Congo**, it doesn't mean that he can change the rules to suit him**self**! Just because he has visited the Congo doesn't mean he is any better than anybody **else** and can have things changed to suit **him**! … "

Bill and I looked at each other. We knew exactly what was on his little mind. We knew he knew we were related to this man who traveled to the Congo, and who from time to time didn't do exactly what people expected, even powerful people like Father Kelly, Bursar. We didn't give Father Kelly the pleasure of having to discipline us for walking out on his class. I just walked out on his institution. I think I have not been back in a Catholic church purely on my own initiative more than twice since then. He found a way to avoid losing my soul by the simple expedient of chasing me away. But I shouldn't give him all of the credit. He had had a lot of help from other Fathers Kelly along the way, but that is another story.

There was a short, stout, strutting man who taught algebra and called himself Colonel something, let's call him Forrest. He was smaller than his battle ax of a wife. His wife intimidated some basic French into us. There were others who said they had also been officers and didn't think they needed to go around calling themselves Major, or Captain. There were probably others who didn't think they needed to go around calling themselves Corporal, or Private, either. None of them were married to Mrs. Colonel Forrest, so they had different agenda. There was Mr. (Captain) Chadwick, who had been a tank commander in the desert of North Africa and had a long, thin nose. He taught Latin and history, and about once each term, instead of all those dates and reasons for the War of Jenkin's Ear, he'd talk about THE war. He had seen action and had seen his friends and colleagues incinerated in their tanks. He told us about his part in the Battle of El Alamein. Riveting! When he talked dates and reasons for the War of Jerkin's Ear, and whatever else there is to talk about in history, we used to count how many times he pulled his nose, how many times he walked up and down the platform, sat down, stood up, sat down, walked again, and how many times he tossed and caught his keys. He walked between five and ten miles a week just in the three periods he had our class, and he taught six classes. When he talked tanks, we didn't count.

There was Mr. (Colonel) McGregor. His right arm had been destroyed by a bullet through the shoulder. He taught physics left-handed, with the aid of a metre rule, which he brandished during the first class. "I brrreak a' least one perrr yearrr on the ferrrst perrrson to give me a rrreason! I do, too!"

Willie Mac never, ever, had a discipline problem in his class, even after he forgot where he had put down the metre rrrule. He didn't break a metre rule our year, and nobody else ever reported seeing him do it. Even if he did tell us a lie, he had a twinkle in his eye, taught well, and we liked him.

There was Mr. Heathcote, who also taught physics. His only discipline problem was his own son, who was in our class. Mr. Heathcote had worked on systems to make ships trick magnetic mines into not exploding under them, and on the early development of radar. He made an oscilloscope and a wire recorder, with his own two hands. He also used a couple of boxes, some wheels, wires, valves and other metal and glass parts. Both of these things worked. He also made a gizmo which looked like a music box. It was going to ring the school bell at preset times. I never saw or heard it work, but I'm told it did.

And there was M. Larthe de Langladure, who charmed some advanced French into us. Loved him. He had been in the underground, we believed. Not the *métro*, you understand, the *résistance*. Occasionally, we could get him to talk about something other than French, sometimes about where his activities had taken him, but never about the activities themselves. Did you know that in Czech the word for neck is krk? Explains why that's where we get cricks, doesn't it? M. Larthe said he had once weighed fifteen stone (210 pounds, but the man we knew was small and thin. He had only half of his innards, the rest lost to ulcers. The part he had left couldn't support a big body. The man we knew must also have lost most of his ties. The patterns of the one he had left are apt to reappear when I doodle, nearly forty years later.

One night, late in my first year at Prince o', we were all lying in bed, not quite asleep, listening illicitly on our crystal sets to Ray's a Laugh, The Goon Show, or a request programme, or whatever it was. The drone of a cluster of piston-engined military transport planes coming in low, drowned out the unamplified headphones. Minutes later, another formation followed. Then another, and another. We counted dozens of waves over several hours. We almost didn't mind missing our show, something exciting was happening. The next morning we were told that there was a state of emergency in the colony. The Mau Mau uprising had got out of hand, and several units of the British Army had been called in and had been flown in to Eastleigh, an RAF air base.

The Emergency started in 1952, my first year, and it ended

89

in 1959, over a year after I had left. During most of the time at Prince o', it was a fact of life, and it affected our life. Sandbags and barbed wire appeared around our dormitories. We were not to go "off concrete" after dark, unless there were five or more of us. Armed Kenya Police *askaris* patrolled all night long. Our popular driver, Harrison, was not there one new term. They had him in jail for being a Mau Mau general. Our head cook, too.

Our activities in the CCF, the Combined Cadet Force, took on a different note. On one field exercise, practicing field craft, we came across a decomposing, headless, limbless torso on the old railway embankment, not fifty yards from our school grounds' boundary. It was quite unsettling. At one point, it was seriously being considered to arm the senior boys, which would have made the CCF games very real, and might have caused us to be even more unsettled. Our fellow students, when they left school, went straight in to the real Kenya Regiment, to fight the real Mau Mau in the Aberdare Forest.

Probably the biggest impacts came from some new rules. We were not allowed to use the cross-country shortcut to cycle to the Boma, we had to go almost all the way down into town and back up the hill again. We Catholics were not allowed to walk the mile to St. Austin's Church on Sundays. We had to be driven there and back in the lorry, which re-regulated what had been a welcome weekly escape from school bounds.

The only really welcome change was the abolishment of that legalized form of torture commonly inflicted on schoolboys, known as cross-country.

The problem with boarding school, on a level other than that of the inmates' struggle for survival, was that it cost hard cash. Even the government schools had fees. The family really had not had the chance to build up its resources from the Depression and war time. Furthermore, the population of Wachagga around Kibongoto had been growing very rapidly ever since the war ended. Medicine and hygiene were already beginning to play their roles in detonating the African population bomb. This was happening all over the southern half of the mountain, which included the area directly upwind from Rongai Farm with respect to the rain-bringing southeast trade winds. The deforestation resulting from this population growth was causing a marked year-to-year drop in the rainfall, exactly as our school geography text books were teaching us would happen. Rongai had once enjoyed rainfall in excess of thirty inches per year, which fell like clockwork, in the Trade Winds driven "short rains" and "long rains." We now thought ourselves lucky if we got eighteen inches. We were ecstatic if those eighteen inches fell when we needed them.

Rainfall dominated almost all conversation. Would the short rains come when they were supposed to? Would the long rains fail, the way they had done for the last three years? One of our neighbours got involved in attempts to seed clouds, using a hydrogen-filled balloon which he launched from our front lawn. We were upwind from his place. Neither of us enjoyed any rain from that or any other experiment; rain fell and didn't fall when it pleased.

That neighbour was Ken Ulyate, a friendly man whom we all liked. We used to say of him: "He's All Right!", in effect paying him a high compliment. He brought his balloon already filled, and was telling us: "I filled it only this morning. Did you know, Carl, that the grains of hydrogen are so small that they can escape through the walls of the balloon. If I left it inflated overnight, it'd be flat in the morning."

Unfortunately, I had had some physics, by then, and he had just punched one of my buttons. I started: "Graham's Law states that the relative rates of diffusion of gases is inversely proportional to the square root of their molecular weights. Helium's mol- ... "

For some reason, the conversation changed direction. I don't know if I could have remembered the rest, anyway.

When rain did fall, in however meager amounts, farmers would compare the measurements taken from the rain gauge that each had on the lawn in front of his house. You would have thought that it was parents comparing the achievements of their babies. The "winner" would boast of the amount he had measured, as if, somehow, the luck that he had with rainfall reflected his character or worth. Whatever our worth relative to our neighbours, our crops failed, year after year. Six years in a row, we barely recovered the cost of the seed.

In those years, we watched Dad and other farmers barter crops for services and services for services. One thing you could not barter anything for, especially unharvested crops, was school fees.

Dad had a brilliant idea. Moshi was a growing town and there would be a growing demand for fresh vegetables. They used to say you could buy anything under the sun at Moolji's, why not vegetables? Dad spoke to Mr. Moolji. Moolji said it was a great idea, he could sell all that Dad could produce. Dad set about producing. He planted ten or twelve acres, up near the top of the farm, where the furrow ran full, and each acre produced prodigiously. He produced artichokes, beans, carrots ...jalapenos, kohl-rabi, lima beans, ... rhubarb, spinach, tomatoes, ... and probably yams and zucchini, for good measure. When he was not yet quite in full production he went in to Moolji with some samples. Moolji was surprised. He could sell vegetables, but not *that* many vegetables. And that was just a trickle, compared to the flood that Dad had coming.

We ate a lot of vegetables. Had we had the facilities for canning, we could have said: "We eat what we can and can what we can't!" I've always wanted to say that, but I didn't get the opportunity. Dad got the opportunity to chalk another one up to experience, and, while we moaned volubly about eating all these vegetables, to cry silently, inwardly.

At some point, the old lorry needed some repairs. Dad left it with the Chevrolet agent in Arusha, possibly not accidentally named General Motors Limited, for some poorly specified repairs. When he collected it, they had redone the whole engine, put on a new body and slapped an invoice on it for ten thousand shillings! This was more than the thing was worth, possibly more than the whole farm was worth! After he had recovered his breath and could stand up again, he promised to pay when he got a crop. He needed the transportation. I think he eventually gave up the lorry to them, in part payment of that debt.

While he was without the lorry, Dad bought a bicycle. It was a heavy, upright *Kondoo*. It was, of course, purely for practical reasons that he had the bike. The farm was three miles long and nearly a mile wide. However, he must have felt guilty about having the luxury of wheels. Or, maybe, being who he was, he just couldn't leave anything alone. How would we like to listen to the radio more, how would we like to have some electricity? What did we think of the concept of having a stand for the bicycle, where it could be clamped in the evenings, when it would be otherwise not in use, so that the rear wheel could move a belt which could drive a dynamo which could generate electricity to charge a battery or even light a bulb or two? He might even take a turn, himself.

We must not have thought much of the idea. it never happened. Dad must not have thought much of the bike, eventually, because he didn't ride it much. I learned how to ride a bike on it, before I was even tall enough to straddle it, by sticking one leg through the frame, under the cross bar. When I could straddle it, but still couldn't get my seat on its seat, I rode sitting on the cross bar. Despite the intervention of a cushion thrown across the bar, I went to school once with twelve boils in the region of my anatomy that touched the cross bar.

In some of those bad years, the rains might have been sufficient for some wheat to grow, but what did grow was eaten by flying or crawling creatures that would have made the biblical plagues pale by comparison. The "wheat birds" came in flocks numbering millions and daintily ate the ripe grains of wheat right off the stem. Locusts and "army worms" were not as dainty. They were not patient enough for that. They ate everything, leaves and stems and all, and they ate it long before any grains appeared. Whether the loss was of almost ripe grain, just before the harvest, or of the whole plant, long before the harvest, the end effect was equally disastrous.

Farmers could, and did, fight the birds with petrol bombs, igniting several forty-four gallon drums full of fuel in the areas where the birds conveniently bedded down for the night in their tight flocks. They risked burning whatever the birds hadn't eaten, but it helped. They had no way to fight the locusts and army worms, for these enemies did not stop for the night. The very fact that locusts had appeared meant that the battle had already been lost where it had to be fought, in the hatching grounds of the Sudd.

One year, the rain came at the appointed time, the seed was already in the ground and the wheat germinated nicely. The rain was even heavier than we hoped for, and we began to look forward to a good crop. Then we saw the weeds. We knew these weeds. We called them water weeds, since they seemed to like wet conditions near to the furrows. They seemed to grow five times faster than anything else and they grew in a solid mat that choked the wheat. I saw Dad "hunker down" in his

93

customary position, sitting on his right heel, and start to pull the weeds by hand.

There was nothing unusual in this. It was habit, utterly futile, but utterly instinctive. At every field he ever stopped by, he would hunker down and weed or dig out "cut-worms" or brush off thrips or some other pest. I was young enough to think to myself: 'For goodness' sake Dad, what do you think you're going to gain, doing that? You're pulling out the wheat that you're trying to save with the weeds!' What was unusual this time was his expression. When I saw it, I was glad I'd said nothing. I hunkered down, too, and pulled weeds from a token few square feet.

It had been hard enough to get the fuel for the tractors. It would have been impossible to raise the credit for weed killer, too. Then, even if he could have afforded weed-killer, these weeds were straight-veined plants that were immune to most of the weed-killers that would not have killed wheat.

At that time I had not yet read the Book of Job. When eventually I did, I knew Job's face. I had seen it, on the edge of that wheat field. I cannot claim to have understood, even in a small way, what he must have been going through. I don't think I could honestly make that claim, even now. But it didn't look easy.

Dad never allowed himself to be down for long. He said that you can't beat a man who doesn't know when he's beaten. Crops didn't, or wouldn't grow, but grass did, and we had rights to a few fractions of a cusec[27] of water from the river. Cows need only grass to eat and a little water to drink and they produce milk. Dad had started to build the dairy herd, improving the hardy local cattle by breeding them with an expensive pedigree bull. The first bull had turned out to be sterile but the second worked as advertised. Milk became the chief source of income for the family. It raised enough money for necessities beyond the food that we grew ourselves, but, again, it could not pay for school for five children. Dad obviously had to do something else.

In 1951, he went back to Germany to try to free up some more of his inheritances. It took a long time because his father became ill and died during the visit. During his absence,

---

[27]A cusec is one cubic foot of water per second.

stories went around Moshi that he had abandoned his family. This helped the local Water Board to decide to give some of Rongai's water rights to a neighbour whose property did not border on the river. We wondered who might possibly have started the stories.

Mum, who did not drive, and wouldn't have had a vehicle to drive, anyway, managed the farm for 18 months. The nearest telephone was four miles away in one direction, six in the other. She calmly and competently managed Rongai and a second farm, three or four miles away, that Dad had arranged to lease for one or two years for a percentage of whatever he grew on it, and he had organized the planting of wheat on it. If I remember correctly, that was the one year the crops did not do as poorly as usual and Mum brought in a record crop of wheat.

Dad came back with not much more than some samples of tools and things produced in the newly re-industrializing West Germany, for which he hoped to develop an import market. He also brought an American military jeep which had been lengthened, converted into a station wagon and painted red. The "box body" was one of the first efforts to satisfy the huge German demand for automobiles that could not be satisfied by the not yet rebuilt factories. The former didn't sell and the latter, while it was dismal as a car, was the world's best vacuum cleaner. That there was any dust left on the roads after this vehicle passed over them, even once, is a miracle, or it is a testimony to the inexhaustible supply of dust that is Africa. We could not go half a mile in it without being covered and caked with dust. When we went into town, the first stop was to visit anyone we knew who could survive finding all that dust deposited in her bathroom. Few people we knew were spared this honour. I've been implying that some of Dad's difficulties with some of the British came from his Teutonic stain on their very Britannic image of their beautiful country. It might well have been simply because he had left Sanya Plains dust stains on too many Britannic towels.

The dust came up through the floorboards, which were poorly fitted. The boards fit so poorly that much of the time they were scraped by the hand brake drum at the rear of the transmission. They shrieked in protest, making a frightful noise. If you didn't understand that it was not a life-

95

threatening situation, it was also a frightening noise. We got used to it, though Dad was never comfortable with it. We would be driving to Kibongoto, to go to Christmas or Easter mass, which we did religiously every now and then, and as we came up the last hill to the church, we would be flagged down by some of the faithful, who were running as late as we were and were hoping for a lift up the hill. Dad knew, or felt he should know many of these people, and felt he might be slighting a friend, but with the car sounding so dicey, he didn't dare add any load. He'd slow down (further), lean out of the window and shout: *"Haiwesi! Anakamatana!"* by which he thought to say: "I can't! It is scraping!" but actually was saying something like: "He (or she or it) can't! He (or she) is holding onto themselves!" Anyway, the would-be rider would be confused enough not to feel offense at being left in the little dust that we left uncollected behind us.

Don't let me lead you to think that we stayed away from church. Any time we were reasonably close to church on a Sunday, or had working transportation, and Dad could get anyone to go with him, he went to mass. Once Dad even caused it to be brought to us, when he got Father Joe McGinley to come from Kibongoto to read mass in Rongai. We liked Joe, he was All Right. He was one of the first Americans we got to know at all well. He used the *mvuli* monster as the altar, while Mum's scottie, Feathers, used his foot as a pillow.

One of the things that Dad brought back was a small, two-stroke engine powered, multi-function garden tool. It could till and weed, and it could throw dirt up over rows of root crops, like potatoes, all by changing the things attached to it. If you replaced the blades with wheels, it became a tiny tractor with which you could pull a small trailer. It was simplicity, itself. It had magneto ignition, so it needed no battery and no dynamo, and therefore it had no lights, no wiring and it had few things to go bad. You started it simply by opening the fuel cock and priming the carburetor. You then wrapped a cord around a small pulley and pulled it. Its simplicity appealed to Dad, who had a phobia about what happened to complicated things in Africa.

Most field labour was done by hand, and, while labour was cheap, it was not very productive. The majority of the farmers, i. e. the African farmers could not afford a full sized tractor and were limited to what they could cultivate after working eight hours in their employers fields, or to what their wives could till between having babies and fetching water. Dad knew there was a market, but I think he saw it first as the European farmers, not the Africans. Anyway, he was now the agent for Hako, and dreamt of building a business. It would stay a dream if the Hako never left the farm, for how would anyone get to know about it? We learned later that he had picked out one of the more successful European farmers as his first sales target, and would rely on the references, recommendations and testimonials to take his venture further.

Dad's children discovered the value of the trailer as a transportation device which was even more fun than the stick cars they had built to the plans and specifications of their Chagga friends, and shortly thereafter, they gave the Hako its first public viewing. We decided, one day, after getting bored doing the loop around the lower dam, to do something more adventurous, like taking a drive down to the plains at the bottom of the farm. We went well provisioned. Pauline fixed us some lemonade and we took a can of spare fuel. An African youngster, a *mtoto* younger than all of us, who was hanging around got offered the opportunity to come along on our adventure, which he bravely accepted. Six of us piled onto and into the thing, and we headed down the long hill. It was smooth riding. We went farther than we had ever walked in that direction, and then even farther, even past Paga's hand carved sign board to "Rongai". We were all the way off the farm, maybe by a mile, on the road shared with other farms, when we decided to turn around and go back up the hill towards home. Almost immediately, the small petrol tank ran dry. No problem, we had some spare, and refilled it.

Small, two-stroke engines are simple. They are also simply temperamental. It had enjoyed going downhill, and now it didn't want to carry us all the way back up the hill. It demonstrated its position the only way it could. It would not start again. We broke the pull cord trying. The *mtoto* was no longer amused and demonstrated his displeasure by crying. We felt like joining him, but our upper lips were too stiff, or something. We were pushing the contraption, slowly and painfully, when Ozzie Barratt, a neighbour from the big farm next door but one, came by in his Land-Rover. He stopped and asked us what was up, and we quite obligingly told him what a rotten time we were having, which he could see, and how much trouble the bloody Hako was to get started once it got hot, which was also probably obvious. He didn't have room for the Hako, and we declined the offer of a ride which meant abandoning it there, so he went on, the *mtoto* carried on and we pushed on.

Many hours and more blisters later, we got home. The *mtoto* was silent, not because we found out how to silence him, certainly yelling *"nyumasa"* in his face didn't do it, and not because he was any happier, but from pure exhaustion. We were, none of us, any happier than he was, nor any less exhausted. Dad had been unconcerned about us, safety-wise, for we had been in no danger. He might even have been slightly amused at our toughening experience. However, all signs of amusement evaporated immediately when he heard that Ozzie Barratt had witnessed our distress.

The Hako stayed around for a while, and did some good work for us, but Dad didn't even try to talk about it to Ozzie again. I think it might have done some work on the Moolji vegetable project. For much of the rest of its life with us, its rubber wheels replaced the wooden wheels made from slices of tree trunk, on our un-powered stick cars. They were great. They worked better with a new kind of lubricant, also green and slippery, but which came out of a can, so we were able to move to a higher level of technology. Actually, we felt forced to, to protect the Hako wheels, so we felt better about using scarce, depleting resources instead of the abundant supply of replaceable ones.

Dad obviously had to do more than try to sell a few German tools. He borrowed some money from Paga for a down payment on a brand new, bright blue tractor with a hydraulic power-lift operated, three-point-linkage plough. I know it hurt him to do so, but he undertook to plough fields for the very same Chagga farmers whose land clearing was directly responsible for the failure of the rains. At least, he felt, he could see that the ploughing was done on the contour and not in ways that would cause erosion. Due to some *Schweinerei* in H.M. Customs in Mombasa, the tractor and its attachments at first were delayed terribly. Then, when they arrived, after missing about half of the ploughing season, they proved to be not up to the task of ploughing stone- and stump-filled new land. Soon they were broken more than they were working. That project failed.

One day, Bill and I rode into Moshi on the lorry that came twice daily to fetch the milk and doubled as a *"passinja"*,[28] or bus. Maybe Dad dropped us off and went on somewhere else, because he was not with us. We were going to catch the train to Nairobi and we stopped by to see Paga in his office, hoping to get invited to lunch. We found Paga very animated. The police had been by, looking for Dad. Despite Paga's agitation, we did get lunch and went on to catch our train to school. We heard the rest of the story much later.

In what was obviously an intentional breach of protocol, an African police *askari,* a uniformed constable, appeared at Rongai on a bicycle and served Dad a warrant. The story did not get any better. Dad was taken to court by General Motors Limited for not paying the full cost of the repairs that they had made to the lorry, which debts had not been satisfied by his handing over the lorry. He obviously was intent on defrauding them their rightful due. He had run away to Europe, abandoning his family, without telling anyone where he had gone. And then, when he had disappointed everyone by reappearing, he had the effrontery to be driving a luxury limousine, "the envy of [the attorney 'Akili' Reid's] entire family". And he was buying new tractors. All this, he was doing instead of paying his debts, etc., etc. Dad was not given time to advise his lawyer, a nice, but unassertive man, and was forbidden by the judge to speak on his own behalf in the proceedings. Dad spent two weeks in Kikafu prison at the end of this part of the charade. The only person outside of the family who visited him during his stay was Mr. Babu, the Indian trader who ran the dairy which bought our milk. Babu wanted to know how much cash Dad needed in order to get out; he could call on his friends and bring the cash the same day. Dad told him this was a matter of principle; he would rather fight and get out by winning his case than by buying his way out. He thanked Babu, who didn't understand, and settled down to catch up on his reading. Eventually, Dad was released. The people who didn't like him had managed to score a punch,

---

[28]Pronounced: 'pass-EEN-ja.'

and felt happy about it, never mind that it was below the belt. He declared personal bankruptcy. The jeep, that envy of Akili Reid's entire family, was given up, to nobody's real regret. I wish that I could have seen Akili Reid drive in it once, across the Sanya plains, with his envious family in the back seat.

Dad started to seek redress for his mistrial and wrongful imprisonment. He took it up with the chief magistrate, who at first seemed willing to help him, and with whom he seemed to be making some real, if slow, progress. At one point, the progress got even slower, then the Chief Magistrate advised him to come back in a month or two. A week or two after that, a Goan clerk who knew Dad well, sent him word that this man was leaving Tanganyika for good, within a few days. He thought Dad might just want to know. Dad hurried to Moshi, to find that he had already left for Dar-es-Salaam. He dashed on his motorcycle, his only means of transportation, all the way to Dar, on unpaved roads, only to find that the boat had sailed. Dad took that as a strong indication of the low probability of his obtaining justice, let alone any compensation. Solicitors cost money and the concept of contingency fees was alien. He satisfied himself with verbally composing a few letters to "Her (very new) Britannic Majesty," to advise her of what *schweinerei* was happening in the administration of justice in her name.

I once asked him why he didn't actually send such a letter, after all, at the end of the war he had written to Her Britannic Father on behalf of others in Oldiani, and that had worked to right those wrongs. Simply put, his response was that he was willing to go to any length, including stirring up Buckingham Palace to redress injustice against someone other than himself, but he would not bother the new, young Queen with his own problems.

A short while before this, he had heard from Jack Williamson that The Prudential Insurance Company paid commissions for selling insurance policies. He took a three-day crash course and bought an under-powered motor cycle, the cheapest practical mode of transportation he could think of. Peppy, the donkey he rode in Karatu would have been cheaper, but far from practical. He rode the motorcycle 16,000 miles in his forty seventh year, as he sold insurance door to door, from one end of Tanganyika to the other. He rapidly became one of the leading producers in East Africa. It helped, slightly, that a paved road had been laid from Moshi to Arusha. It might have helped more if more than just twelve miles of a typical trip had been on this road.

A motorcycle may have been uncomfortable on rough roads, even dangerous, but over and above that, it had certain very serious limitations in utility. To avoid getting backaches when he rode, Dad always had to wear a six-inch-wide leather belt, the way weight lifters do. He had two saddle bags on the bike and always carried a rucksack, turned around to rest on the fuel tank, in front of him. All of his portable office went with him this way. With his beret, his goggles and his back-to-front rucksack, he was a sight for sore eyes. "A sicht for sair een," Sims would have said. He might have looked better on Peppy.

"I don't dare fall off," he would joke, patting his rucksack. "Did I ever tell you about the young fellow who accepted a ride with his friend on a motorbike?"

"Yes, Dad, you did." Optimism and truthfulness are traits that will earn you respect and points in the afterlife, even if they don't always get you results in the present life.

"Well, it was cold, you see, so he turned his jacket round, to cut the wind. They rode. A few minutes later, his friend noticed that he was missing, realized he must have fallen off, and went back for him. He came to a place where there was a group of peasants in the road, standing around the passenger, who looked rather limp. He asked them: 'Is he all right?' They replied: 'Well, yes, but he looked a lot more lively before we turned his head around the right way!'"

There was room in the rucksack or the saddle bags for a Thermos flask for hot or warm water to make warm or tepid instant coffee. There was also room for a bar of soap, a hand towel (if Dad's hands were dirty, he felt dirty all over) and a tin of talcum powder. There was room on the pillion seat for Mum or one of his children to accompany him (relying on Dad, not a turned coat, to break the wind).

There was no room for any camping equipment. This meant that he was limited in his trips to the distance he could ride in one day at the slow speed the conditions allowed. We sometimes suspected that he was limited to the distance he could go on a Thermos flask full of hot water.

Despite the limitations, he took more than one trip to Dar-es-Salaam, and one to Mombasa. I know because I went on one of them. The former was six hundred miles and the latter three hundred, one way! The longer trips were broken at Catholic missions, where he was attempting to get all the insurance business with volume rates. He was usually offered their hospitality for a night and a meal or two, while he talked to the Fathers about fleet rates. He was referred anyway to the Father Procurator at the diocese, but that was never before a pleasant, polite interlude.

After a while, the insurance company paid for the installation of a telephone. The wires were strung for six miles, from the General Store cum Post Office at Ngare Nairobi. They had to be something like 15 feet in the air, to avoid being cut every time a giraffe walked by.

Until the telephone came, our only regular contact with the outside world had been the daily *passinja*. One day, we were all home from school and hovering around the house, waiting to be called in for dinner. The milk truck did not go to the *boma* or cattle pen where the milk cans would be waiting, but came, instead, right up to the house. Paga was a passenger on it. He got his suitcase off the truck and announced that he was home to stay. He had retired, at the age of seventy something. From that point on, there was never a dull tool in the toolbox, nor a lock or window in the house that didn't open or close properly. Almost. I do believe that, like a good general, he chose the battles that he would fight; the mvuli front door stayed open. A rose garden appeared in front of the house. Paga was retired, but not tired.

The house at Rongai nestled in a little crease just below the summit of a hill which was about a hundred paces from the front door. There was a certain spot from which you could see in just about every direction. If you turned around and looked back towards the house and a bit to the left of the line of jacarandas, you sometimes could see the snow-covered peak of Kilimanjaro. At sunset, it would be bathed in a pinkish light and look quite unreal. The sunset, itself, often had strange colours in it, my favourite was a luminescent apple green splash that would come and disappear in about five minutes. If you looked straight out to the Northwest, you could see over a hundred miles, past Longido, a view I've already described.

In this direction, in the daylight, you could see a few metal roofs shining in the sun. After dark, you could see not one single light other than grass fires in the dry season, or the headlights of infrequent vehicles down on the plains. You could see the lights of vehicles, after they crossed into Tanganyika from Kenya, as they climbed the long, straight grade out of what used to be the bed of a sea covering the Serengeti and Amboseli plains. You could see them closer to home, too, on the road from Sanya and Moshi. If the lights reappeared in a certain spot, as they usually did, the vehicle was not coming to Rongai. If they didn't reappear, then the vehicle was broken down, stuck, or had taken the turn-off. If the latter, pretty soon the lights would appear in another place, and then, in another five minutes, they would be coming up the drive.

When Dad was away, Mum would like to go at dusk, past the double row of jacarandas, past the sisal plant, past the spot where a wild alium would bloom every year, past a clump of wild jade plants, to sit on a certain tuft of grass on that hill, and look out in that direction. Even if she didn't really expect Dad home that evening, she could admire the sunset.

In 1956, after sixteen months on the motorcycle, Dad had enough confidence in the insurance game that he planned to buy a VW beetle, so he could redouble his efforts. At first, there was not a single car available. Dad reminded the principals of Cooper Motors, the importers, that it was his introduction and recommendation to VW at Wolfsburg, during their 1952 visit to Germany, that got them the agency. A car became available in the very next shipment, but they regretted that it was to be landed in Dar-es-Salaam, and not before a certain date. Dad said he thought was nice of them, since that was where he had his next business to do in Dar, right about the time that the car would land. Before he could thank them further, they advised him that he could pick the car up in Nairobi, at their headquarters, a week after its arrival in Dar. Nothing could change it. The car had to be prepared in the Nairobi workshop, the Dar workshop would not do.

That to get its preparation, the new car first had to be driven seven hundred and fifty miles over unpaved roads, in the rainy season, by an African truck driver hired off the street for the trip, only so it could turn around and go back to Dar, over the same bad roads, defied common sense. It gave Dad something to fume about for a while. I went with him on the 600-mile trip to Dar, which via Nairobi became nearly a thousand mile trip. I was asked if I understood the logic of it. I answered in the negative. My answer must have been wrong. I was asked the same question, three times each hour, for the next few days. My answer was negative as we hitch-hiked to Nairobi and just as negative as we waited for an attendant in the lobby of a small suburban hotel. It was just as negative between the minutes of sleep that we got as we spent the night trying to sleep sitting up on the couch. And it was again negative as we escaped before first light and before any attendant appeared. My answer was negative at dawn, which came as we walked the three miles into town. It was still negative when we were taking a hot bath at another hotel, and as we each paid our two shillings.

To add insult to injury, Cooper Motors asked us to give the driver a ride back to Dar. The driver's presence just reminded Dad of the situation. My answer was still negative, many times negative, as we started to drive through the rain and the mud to Dar, a trip that took two days and two nights. By the time we got to close to Dar, I think I must have started to get the answer right, finally. Practice is supposed to help. Dad stopped asking the question.

At about the time I was starting to improve my answer, Dad was becoming more and more deeply impressed with the ability of the beetle to get through or over mud. As long as you didn't stop, you could keep going. Instead of cussing Cooper Motors, he began singing the praises of the new vehicle. We were able to pass about one hundred other cars stuck in the ditch, up to their axles in mud. Normally, one stopped and helped anyone else in trouble on the road, regardless of race. The cars we passed were all being helped through the mud by crowds of singing, entrepreneurial Africans, and their situation couldn't have benefited from another car stopping and sinking into the mud with them.

The beetle's ability to get about on East African roads became legendary. Dad was proud to have had a small part in its introduction. He often lamented that he hadn't thought of asking for one percent of profits for the first few years for his intervention in Wolfsburg.

104

The beetle opened up vast new possibilities. Dad could now pack a camping stove, two Thermos flasks (even with the stove), tea, instant coffee and instant soup, bread, salami or wurst, tins of sardines and some fruit. (For some reason, he liked bananas, despite their habit of developing a strong smell as they quickly ripened and rotted). He no longer had to fast. Best of all, a couple of camping beds and a canvas ground sheet which he could use as a lean-to roof off one side of the car, could all fit in, along with the talcum powder, the soap, a full sized towel and changes of clothes. Now he could (and did, as I know from personal, direct experience), spend as much as two weeks on the road, never hungry, never without a place to sleep and never feeling unpresentable. More and more of Tanganyika "got a piece of the rock[29]" and slept more securely while Dad and whoever accompanied him earned a small commission and slept on the edge of the road among mosquitoes, native African pedestrian travelers and wild animals.

Actually, that is an exaggeration, for two reasons. First, Dad was frequently invited by his insurance victims to spend the night or was directed by them to a Government rest house. Second, Dad didn't mind trying to sleep among howling hyenas, growling lions or wandering Africans, but he would never sleep among buzzing mosquitoes. If a mosquito wakened him with its hum, he would pack up and move on for miles until he found a site that he thought would be mosquito-free. If the mosquitoes there were not disposed to allow him to fall asleep before dive-bombing him, which was mostly the case, it could mean driving all night.

The motorcycle had placed a hiatus on conversation. The beetle lifted it.

Every vehicle we had driven, up to this point, had been unlikely to allow any plans to be made, let alone be inspired. We'd have been optimistic to plan on arriving where we were headed without some mishap. We drove, or were driven, with one ear tuned to the engine's sounds and the other to the rattles and squeaks of the body. Even as passengers, our eyes

---

[29]The American ad campaign for the Prudential Insurance Company, which Dad represented, is: "Get a piece of the Rock." Their symbol is a stylized picture of the Rock of Gibraltar.

would be on the road ahead, looking for stones, potholes, ant-bear holes, wild animals, cattle or people. We would be conscious of the weather, rain would probably mean getting stuck somewhere inconvenient. Always, but always, we'd be listening to the engine because the only thing that gave us any hope of progressing towards wherever we hoped to arrive, was its continuing sound. When it seemed that it might stall on a steep hill, we'd get ready to jump out to reduce the load, or to push. When it coughed on some dirt in the petrol or misfired on a cylinder, our hearts would miss a beat in sympathy. We traveled with our sympathetic hearts in our mouths. It is an uncomfortable way to travel.

Now, with the new beetle, all those concerns almost melted away. We could go for miles and for days without any of the old problems. We could think as we drove, and with our hearts back where they belonged, we could talk. And it meant Dad could plan. Whoever accompanied Dad was expected to carry one side (usually the light side) of a discussion or help him develop his plans. As the increasing number of miles registered on the counter, one particular plan evolved.

"Wouldn't it be nice to drive into [the Volkswagen factory at] Wolfsburg with one hundred thousand miles on the milometer? I bet you it doesn't happen every day, wha'? Quite good publicity for them, hm? They might even pay for some of the expenses. *Je?* Ay? Hm? Wha'?"

But there were practical things to think about. "I suppose we will have to do it in two cars." And: "I wonder how we will cross the Sahara." Not "if" but "how".

A number of possibilities presented themselves and were given serious consideration. "The sand is soft and you sink in. How do you think wire mesh would work? Mesh could be laid down in front of the vehicle and picked up and put in front, again, as it passes."

An image formed, in his companion's mind, of rolls of chicken wire strapped to the top of the beetle. Perhaps we could keep chickens in the roll in between, for a supply of eggs and fresh meat. His companion was not brave enough to suggest this, perhaps for fear of being thought cheeky, or worse, for fear of being taken seriously. But eventually the companion was able to ask who would be likely to be doing the picking up and putting down of the mesh. That person would land up walking, in the sun and sand, at least three times the distance traveled by the car.

After a few moments of reflection, Dad had a solution: "Well, how do you think it would work with a long, continuous loop of mesh that rolls along with the car inside it?" Which concept brought even more vivid images in to play. That's the stage of development at which the plan stayed for a while.

Another subject that came up fairly frequently was career plans. Sims had warned us "... never go into farming, it is a pure gamble!" We had started out, of course, wanting to be lorry drivers, mechanics or train engine drivers. These plans were never taken seriously, but they always earned us a lecture along the lines: "You don't want to choose a job that any African, Indian or half-caste can do. Choose a profession, not a job." In East Africa, clerks or *duka wallahs,* storekeepers, were Indians, low-ranking government officials, postmasters and station masters, were Goans, train engine drivers were Sikhs and labourers, lorry drivers and mechanics were Africans.

During one of these conversations, I mentioned accounting to Dad, in an offhanded way, thinking of the most boring job possible, so I could come around to a more exciting one.

"If you go into accounting, be a Chartered Accountant. That's the top of the profession. They earn much more, too!"

"How much?"

"Three, maybe as much as three and a half thousand pounds per year."

I had been going to work the conversation around to the then current plan to become a Forestry Officer. The attraction of a government issue Land-Rover, the outside work and the fresh air faded in an instant. Chartered Accountant didn't sound bad, at all. Over three thousand pounds a year! Wow! I should have been more careful not to show the level of my enthusiasm; on the strength of my response Dad dragged me in to meet with a Chartered Accountant, the very next time we were in Moshi, and started asking me when I was going to write to the Institute of Chartered Accountants for information on how to become an Articled Clerk. I did that, and with the help of the forthcoming materials, the plan rapidly lost most of its appeal.

With the enclosed car, we noticed a strange phenomenon. Dad suddenly could not stand a draught. Draughts caused him excruciating sciatica pains, in direct proportion to the level of his anxiety. The same man who could, and did, ride a motorcycle in any weather, could not have the window of the car open, unless it was cool outside. If it was hot, and it gets hot where we were likely to have been driving, the car had to be hermetically sealed. The 1956 VW beetle did not have air conditioning. Traveling with Dad in this state was a mild form of hell. At the time, we thought he was just torturing us, the way adults seem to like to torture their offspring. Now, with the advantage of hindsight and the perspective of our own parenthood, we see that he was only doing it for us. He was conditioning us for the climate in the Congo. Like most parents, Dad would not dream of putting it in terms as hackneyed as "I'm only doing it for your sake!" So, to avoid the cliché, he acquired this pain that made it easy for us to do something for his sake. He was thoughtful, in some ways.

I sound unsympathetic, treating his discomfort so lightly. It is true, I was. He had other symptoms of stress. He had a shorter fuse than ever before, and a more or less chronically distressed stomach. The latter might have dated from his encounter with the killer mushroom, but whatever the original cause, stress could not be helping it. These were just additional nuisances for his children to bear. No one, other than Mum, understood even a fraction of the stress that he lived under, and so we didn't give him the benefit of the doubt.

The school fees were being paid, mostly, but not much was left over. Mum sat on the hill, at dusk, more and more often, as Dad was away on more and more trips.

One of the early trips Dad took in the beetle, he invited me to go along. It was more like a command performance, but 'invited' sounds better. I had no excuse not to go, and despite being sixteen and not yet being licensed, I knew I would get the opportunity to do a lot of driving. In fact, Dad and I met the Superintendent of Police as we were about to head out. Dad happily told him that I was going to be his chauffeur. I cowered under the scowl that Dad didn't seem to notice on the face of the law.

The trip was going to take about two weeks and circle much of Tanganyika in an anti-clockwise direction. We would visit all of the major business offices of the Catholic Church in Tanganyika and try to get all of their vehicle insurance business by offering fleet rates.

The first day out, we drove right by the road to the coffee plantation at Karatu which had been our home for some of the war years. We craned our necks for a glimpse, but hurried on because we wanted to get to the mission before it was too late in the day. We could always see it in the morning. I looked forward to seeing it again, now that I was ten years older, and bigger. I wanted to check out what I remembered of the place. I wanted to see the peach trees that Mum and I sat under, blinded by conjunctivitis, feeling around for peaches to eat. Peaches that were too hard weren't tasty, too soft and we knew they surely had worms in them. Just right tasted just right, and because we couldn't see the worms we ate, we couldn't taste them.

The first night, we failed to get an invitation to stay with our insurance victims, so we left on the next leg, after dark. We had instructions on how to take a short-cut to the Great North Road, the main road south to Dodoma. It meant giving up a chance to see Karatu again, but there'd be another time.

The instructions for the short-cut were imperfect. An ill-defined track petered out totally in a small Mbulu home site, at about midnight. The night was pitch black. The Wambulu live in *tembes*. A *tembe* is a structure that is dug into the side of a hillock, with a mud and wattle front wall and a turf roof. It looks like a hillock or a mound from all directions but the front. At night, the cattle are closed in with the family, for warmth and for protection against wild animals. I found myself shouting at a mound, in Swahili, asking for directions to the main road. The mound answered, very sleepily and most suspiciously, in *kimbulu*, something that I couldn't understand. I felt rather silly, talking to a mound, but there was no one to see my embarrassment, so it didn't matter. After half an hour of my shouting my questions over the rising bleating and lowing of the disturbed animals and trying to hear the consistently unintelligible, but becoming less sleepy responses, I felt we were going to get no light on the matter. We felt our way back along the track, to the original, long way round, and continued until we felt we needed to sleep.

The mosquitoes found us at our first potential campsite,

and at the second, and we went on all night.

Our fourth or fifth day out was a Saturday. We finished our business in Mbeya, which lies close to where the main road from Dar-es-Salaam that comes straight(ish) across the country and joins the Great North Road as it goes through the gap between the lakes, into the Rhodesias, now Zambia and Zimbabwe. The Great North Road was not that great. It probably got its name when some wag said: "That's great! We have a road north!" We were headed for Songea, which was to the south, but on the side of Lake Nyasa that was avoided by the GNR. Songea lies at the end of the road that goes across the country from Lindi, on the coast. Other than the GNR, all major roads in East Africa, all three of them, seemed to head roughly westwards in from the coast, and if they didn't get stopped by a lake, or something, they'd go on into other countries. There was not much traffic between these east-west roads, apparently, not if you looked at the existence of roads as being evidence of traffic, for few major roads go north-south. The link road to Songea was the kind that is drawn in thin lines that are hard to find on the map We got instructions to find the turn-off. Apparently it was as hard to see on the ground as on the map, and we were advised that we should try to find it before nightfall. Having recent experience in the consequences of missing poorly marked turn-offs, we hurried and got there in daylight. We turned off the unpaved major road, on to the even more unpaved minor road which was clearly identified by a three inch wide, hand lettered signboard nailed to a tree on the edge of the road.

We were an hour or more into this road, when the beetle seemed to get tired. Eventually, it lost all power. It couldn't get up what seemed to be a not unusually steep hill.

"Try in reverse!" suggested Dad. "Reverse may be a lower gear than first." 'Yeah,' I thought, 'maybe the hill will think we're going, not coming.' It was the kind of thought that I was beginning to learn to keep to myself. Dad was not always amused. I tried in reverse. If we could just get over this hill, maybe we could go all the way to Songea.

The hill could not be conquered by this trick approach, any more than it could be by the full-frontal attack. It had already sensed that the beetle was fatally weakened and just refused to be taken. The beetle admitted defeat and died. We ran the battery down, completely, trying, hoping, to get the darned thing to start. I fiddled with and took off the distributor cap; I had seen our mechanic, Marcel do this, and it sometimes seemed to resuscitate dead engines. I noticed that the points were not opening, at all, and knew that this was not right. I suggested to Dad that I try to adjust them, so they would open as the cam turned. I had seen Marcel do that, too. All we needed was a screwdriver, and we had one.

Dad asked: "Is it electrical?"

"Yes. Well, not like the rest of the electrical stuff. It's the ignition, it's separate. It's not the kind that burns. My instinct tells me that this is where the problem is."

"Don't touch it! Put it back!"

We obviously both remembered another occasion, perhaps three years earlier, when I had tried to follow Marcel's instructions as to how to treat the jeep, if it acted up.

"If it dies like *that*, bwana Carl, do *this*." The trick involved a matchstick and one or another of the gaps in the relays comprising the voltage regulator. The jeep had died on a drive with Dad, exactly like *that*, with no Marcel in the neighbourhood, and I had done with a matchstick what I thought was exactly *this*. *This* had produced an impressive puff of blue smoke and Dad and I had waited, expectantly for Marcel's magical cure to manifest itself. When the smoke cleared, what was manifest was that an essential component of an expensive part had disappeared, alas without leaving any sign of the desired cure in its place. The jeep had to be repaired in Moshi, at great cost in money, in time and in my loss of face.

So, remembering my imperfect record, I did as I was bid and we slept there that night, mosquitoes or not. And we would sleep there the next night.

Dad had figured out exactly how the lean-to tent was going to work, in theory. This was the first time that it would be tried in practice. We had poles, but no pegs. In much of Africa, there is wood all around you, all the time. Pointless to take pegs with you, when you can cut them where and when you need them. You just take your *panga*, Swahili for machete, or your ax, and cut them, then you hammer them into the soft ground with your mallet. It works best when you have a *panga* or an ax with you, we didn't. I scavenged for sticks that could serve as pegs.

We were at the edge of the road, at the bottom of a dip, so, we couldn't roll or push the beetle out of the way. Roads like this one were made by shoveling off the topsoil and throwing it up on the edge, leaving the road bed a good two feet lower than the surrounding land. The left side of the car was close to the edge of the road, which didn't leave any room for the tent on that side. The tent had to go on the other side of the car, in the roadway. When I tried to drive my blunt pegs (scavenged pegs don't come sharp), using fist-sized stones, Mankind's first tools, which were possibly invented quite close to this same spot (if we didn't have a panga or an ax, do you think we would be likely to have a mallet?), I quickly found that the road surface was too hard to take them. Eventually, the strings were tied to the stone mallets instead of to pegs and the shelter was up. It was up precariously. Autosuggestion probably played a greater part than physics in its remaining up. Rain was highly unlikely; we could see that. Nevertheless, the tent had to be put up; the situation was exactly why we had it with us, and there'd be no point in having it if we didn't use it now.

We slept fitfully in the heat, looking like mummies with our down sleeping bags zipped up to our necks because of the mosquitoes. During one of the rare moments when I was actually asleep, I was wakened by a voice saying, in Swahili: "You are sleeping here!" I acknowledged that we were and complimented the voice on its owner's powers of observation. I do not think I was quite as polite as that makes me sound. Apparently my sarcasm was wasted, it did not discourage the speaker. He spoke on, for a while, but I didn't hear much, being half awake, half asleep.

In the morning, now Sunday, we opened our eyes to find an African, the owner of the voice, sitting on the edge of the road, the bank the perfect height for that purpose, waiting for us to show some signs of life. Dad must have been the first to awaken and was asking him: "Are you from here?"

I saw him think for a moment. This place was nowhere, as anyone could see, but he decided that the question, though silly, should be given a serious answer. You could never be sure, with a *mzungu*. "No, bwana. I'm from back there, *mbali kidogo* - a small distance." He pointed, with his tongue, in the direction in which we wished we were going. "I am traveling in that direction, to visit my sick relatives. It is *mbaaali saaana* - a looong diiistance." His tongue, again, indicated the direction, while the length of his vowels told us just how much farther he had to go compared to how far he had come. "I walk at night, when the sun doesn't burn. I saw you here, and I stayed to watch over you."

Dad, who was not born in Africa, had learned the patience of Africa. He carried on a conversation from his camp bed, as though this was the most natural setting in the world. He found out that there was a Catholic mission not far away, but nothing else in the way of civilization, for dozens of miles. I was sixteen, and, despite being born and raised there, had no patience. I kicked my heels, fumed and fretted. Well, I fumed and fretted while I got out of the sleeping bag, then I kicked my heels. You can't get a good kick at your heels when you're in one of those bags. Dad created some peace for himself by inviting his new friend to show me the way to the mission, but not before he had asked me to find and fetch his novel, and, while I was at it, to put a fresh packet of cigarettes near him.

My companion and I set off along the road, took a sudden turn on to a path into the bush and walked for well over an hour. At the mission, I found no one who could help. I was met by a German brother who had been in the country exactly one week. He, the brother, told me that the padre was off on his motorcycle, to say mass at a remote location. He, the padre, was not mechanically inclined, anyway, and would be of dubious use to me in my predicament.

I was given a roll of mints: "Gut for ze tirst!".

When I and my new friend got back to Dad and the car, it must have been early afternoon. Our friend decided that he would continue on his trip. His curiosity about us had been blunted by the long side trip to the mission, and even with the sun burning the way it was, walking on probably was preferable to waiting long enough for the *mzungu* to get another idea. We thanked him, Dad gave him a pack of cigarettes for his trouble, and we were alone, again. He was the only human we had seen on that road in over twenty hours. This was one of the very few times that I ever stopped in a vehicle in Africa, even in the most uninhabited looking places, without being surrounded by curious people within minutes. Suddenly, I missed him.

Dad was still in his bed, well into his book. "You must be hungry and thirsty after that walk. How would you like a nice boiled egg and some tea?"

113

"I'd love it," I said, "but where did you get the water? We used up just about all of it last night and I didn't think to get any at the mission."

"That's all right," still from his bed, "there must be some around here. Look over in that direction."

I understood. "Thanks, Dad!"

I looked all around, but found only some whitish looking water in a puddle, about fifty feet from the road. The same meager pint of water yielded two boiled eggs, one of them cracked, and some strange looking and stranger tasting tea. We ate and drank. Neither of us died, at least not soon enough for anyone to link cause and effect.

Late that afternoon, the padre appeared on his tiny motor bike, with an African youth clutching on to him with one hand and on to a *kikapu*, a basket, with the other. The *kikapu* contained a ripe papaya and a couple of lemons. The padre cheerfully confirmed that the brother had been right about his mechanical aptitude, gave us the fruit and a benediction and left.

The fruit, I can remember. It was helpful. The warm papaya was even more palatable than the egg-drop tea.

Well, I'm not being fair. Maybe the benediction was helpful, too, for on Monday morning, at about eight, only eighteen hours later, a *passinja* roared around the bend, enveloping us in its cloud of dust as it stopped just short of our tent. As the dust settled, the driver asked us what was the matter. I explained, to the best of my ability. He took off the distributor cap, adjusted the points, snapped the cap back on and yelled for his passengers to get out and push the *mzungu's* car.

Three minutes, ten shillings, a packet of cigarettes and many heartfelt thanks later, we were on our way to Songea. Somewhere, it is written that you pay a price if you do not follow your instincts. Somewhere else it is written that there is one instinct that a smart sixteen-year-old son does not follow. There was no benefit I could possibly expect from saying: "I told you so."

The remainder of that trip was a little less eventful. However, days later, on the complementary northward leg, we were following the "thin line" track north from Lindi to Dar-es Salaam when it appeared to get thinner and thinner the farther we went. Eventually, at about midnight, there is something special about midnight, the track petered out totally in a coconut grove. It was as though the man who drew the map had tried, but failed, to stretch out his last drop of ink to complete the line representing this track, and the field people of the Public Works Department had followed his disappearing line literally. We spent the night there, once again mummified in our sleeping bags against the mosquitoes, under a rudimentary shelter made of coconut fronds that we came across on our fifth attempt to get out of the grove. After daylight, several hours of back-tracking got us back going in the right direction. The patternless, almost frenetic, back-tracking, done with the windows hermetically sealed even as the sun started to heat the air to its usual level of discomfort, made me think about what it must be like to be an insect closed in a heating oven. It reminded Dad of something else.

"This is the way it used to be in the old days. There was no *road* to Nairobi, it was more like a *way* to Nairobi."

My patience was short. I interrupted him. I had heard it before. But Dad was feeling pleased enough with things, now that we were progressing again, the frustration and discomfort forgotten and the mosquitoes left behind. Life was good. My rudeness could be overlooked. In time, I would learn patience, no point in making a lesson of it now. I heard the story about the roads, again. It led to other stories, of course.

"I've told you about how we used to have to make do when we broke down in the bush?"

I might have said: "Yes, Dad." But it wouldn't have helped. Maybe I was already learning this patience thing. But, we had time and I didn't have anywhere else I could go, anyway, so maybe I said something like: "How was that, Dad?"

"Well, you see, when we broke down, we didn't have parts with us. It would take a day to walk to the main road (caught you, Dad, there wasn't a *road*, right?), or some part of one of the tracks where you might have a chance, if you waited for another day, for someone to come along. And then, when you did get a lift it took you a day to get to town. Then, you had to wait a day to get a lift in your direction and two days to get back to the lorry. Or, more likely, the garage wouldn't have the part, so a week was wasted, wasn't it? *Je? Ay?* H'm? So, there was no point in going and nothing to be gained by waiting because there was no one to come along and help you. So we just had to do something ourselves. *Je? Ay?* H'm?" Then there was a short, reflective pause. "Of course, Belinda was a *diesel*, so we didn't have many *ignition* problems. (Don't look at me. I didn't say anything!) If it was just the springs broken, or the drive shaft, or the chassis, we would cut down a branch or a tree, strap it to the broken part with rawhide and drive on, slowly."

Then we came to the Rufiji River, where we had to wait for over an hour for the pontoon to be pulled back by hand across the half mile expanse of water. There was nobody in sight when we stopped. Within five minutes, we were surrounded by children and a few adults. They put their faces against the windows and stared at us as though we were inanimate objects on display.

Dad said: "Why don't we have our lunch now?"

"What? In this fishbowl? Don't you want some privacy? Shoo! *Ondokeni! Nendeni nyumbani!* Go away! Go home!"

Dad said: "They *are* home! Don't let it upset you. You know, your ancestors used to allow the peasants to come and watch them eating. It was a special treat!"

"Special treat for the ancestors and a special torture for the hungry peasants. Or else a treat along the lines of tickets to feeding time at the zoo," I supposed.

I supposed it under my breath; you sometimes can score a point, but not often. Well, I wasn't an ancestor, yet. Perhaps that's why I let it upset me. Dad was on his way to being an ancestor, so he didn't let it upset him; he ate his bread and salami and bananas, and washed it all down with tepid tea from the thermos, every move followed from inches away by the dozens of pairs of eyes.

Later on the trip, or it might have been on another one, Dad heard of a Dutch-made shock absorber that cost a bit more to buy, but was repairable. The typical life of a set of shocks (and tires) on those roads was about 10,000 miles, a somewhat disappointing performance, since at that point you threw them away. On those road surfaces, you needed shock absorbers just to stay on the road. Replacing shock absorbers was a cost you calculated into the cost of running a vehicle. He tried these Konis and became a convert. He bought a set which he nursed through the next two cars that he owned. That meant that everyone he met also heard about these wonderful

116

Koni shocks and how good the VW was in mud, along with the usual repertory.

On another, he met a German woman who had made some canned sauerkraut. She wanted to introduce the product across East Africa. Dad landed up carrying a case of sauerkraut around in the beetle. Some people heard about and were permitted to test the product, though not as many as those who heard about Konis and the beetle's aptitude for getting through mud. Sauerkraut, believe it or not, was further from the immediate everyday interests of most drivers on African roads than were shock absorbers and driving in mud.

On another trip, again, he absentmindedly drove through an intersection that had a stop sign. In most of the country, traffic signs were few and far between because vehicles were few and far between. If there was no stop sign at an intersection, or if there was and one didn't notice it, the result was usually not serious. Besides, a plume of dust usually warned you if another vehicle was coming. However, this incident happened in Nairobi, which has paved streets and more cars than any other part of the country, cars driven by people whose city life rendered them more prone than their more rural countrymen to be harbouring death wishes. It seems that if you have the right of way, there is no reason not to be willing to die exercising it. On this occasion, although Dad was going at his customary snail's pace, the front of the beetle got in the way of, and was totally removed by, a car that had, and took, the right of way through the crossing. The remaining half of the beetle was the more valuable half, but, by itself it was unusable. Despite Dad being in the insurance business, the car was insured. It was replaced with another beetle, a whole one, in fact a new one, which ceremoniously inherited the used Konis and less ceremoniously, the case of sauerkraut and the smell of ripe bananas. It also inherited the plans to "drive into Wolfsburg with one hundred thousand miles." The milometer's fresh start gave us a little breathing room, allowing us time to work on some of the details.

On yet another trip, which preceded the one we just heard about, he was selling insurance to some old friends on a sisal plantation. Between riveting discussions of insurance, VWs, shock absorbers and sauerkraut, his hosts complained of the chronic shortage of labour. Dad was reminded of his twenty-year past activity, made some inquiries and soon found himself in a new undertaking. With Pauline now out of school and in charge of the dairy herd and the rest of us away at school, Dad and Mum packed the necessities into the old beetle and drove to Ruanda-Urundi. History did not record whether or not the sauerkraut went along. Ruanda-Urundi was the name for two African kingdoms then administered by Belgium, but now independent and known, separately, as Rwanda and Burundi. They had a chronic, severe overpopulation problem. The intertribal wars that have been fought there since then, and the associated genocide, have probably not even been enough to alleviate the problem.

The roads were rough and strange to Mum and Dad, and, though the Konis were in good shape, the beetle's tires were worn smooth. One sudden stop on the gravel road surfaces would probably have surprised the life out of one or more tires, and there were many things they would rather spend their small reserves on than new tires. (It was about this time that Flakey had had to step in and bail Bill and me out at Prince o', so things were really rather tight). To his children, Dad's driving style was always painfully slow. It was a good thing that it was his patient wife who went with him, this time. To anyone else, it would have been excruciating. He crept. I was not there, but I'm sure the windows were sealed tight and that, if the diet didn't do it, the Turkish bath conditions probably cost each of them several pounds of their weight.

In Urundi, Mum and Dad went to Kitega to see the *Gouverneur*. After that, they went, very properly, to visit the *Mwami,* or King, of the Warundi. The Belgians were delighted to offer Dad a permit, as long as he kept to their rules, and they had lots of rules. *Mwami* Mwamputsa was delighted to deal with a European whom he could consider his equal, and who came to offer solutions to some pressing problems his people faced, rather than to create more problems. All was arranged. They drove back to Tanganyika, another 1,000 miles on the very tired tires and another few pounds lost.

There followed a few weeks of research into how to carry the most people in a lorry, first, economically and, second, legally. During these weeks, Konis and sauerkraut were forgotten. Dad discussed the details of the design with anyone who would listen and many who would rather not. Dozens of people, all over East Africa, listened with quizzical expressions to expositions on and questions about the ratio of wheel base to rear overhang, the elusive perfect relationship between hip room and leg room and the probable ratio of adults to children in the typical Warundi family. The vehicle also had to be convertible to haul freight on the return trip, in case there were no returning contract labourers. His *modus operandi* was always to talk and gesture his designs and plans into shape, using his unfortunate audiences as a drawing surface, the way an engineer or an architect might use sketches to develop a design. Many verbal sketches were drawn on many a glassy-eyed audience of friends, acquaintances and officials. A design took shape.

A lorry was ordered, with a body on it custom-built to Dad's specifications, which were changing as much as they were exacting. The removable seats were the most salient feature of the body, which, except for the unusual door on the side, looked a bit like a *passinja* from the outside. The seats were made of steel pipe frames spanning the body sideways, with canvas deck chair like seats slung from the frames. Canvas side curtains would keep the rain and wind out. Not all the wind, Dad had always had an interest in breaths of moving air.

Marcel, the Mchagga mechanic who practiced some dark, secret, art or magic to keep our ancient Farmall M tractors running at Rongai, was appointed the driver of this lorry. He named it Polonia, after his sister. We could not guess if this was to describe her or to honour her, until we heard him speak, rhapsodically, about it 'flying like a big white bird.' Anyway, we did not want to eat the lorry, so it didn't bother any of us that it had acquired a name. Garages were hundreds of miles apart in the regions that were to be crossed. Dad thought that Marcel's skills as a mechanic would be invaluable in the venture and would outweigh his shortcomings. He underestimated. As a mechanic, Marcel had few rivals and was worth his weight in gold. As a drinker and a liar, he had many rivals, but few who were his match. Fortunately, he did not let these habits kill any of his charges, but Dad couldn't possibly have foreseen half of the problems he eventually would cause.

The convoy of Dad in the beetle, with Mum or a lucky one of his children on holidays from boarding school, and Marcel

119

in the lorry, carrying about seventy Warundi, made the round trip maybe as many as ten times. A trip would usually last up to five weeks, including the travel time and recruitment.

The pipes that were the frame for the seats, bent and collapsed in the first ten miles of the first trip with passengers. They could just about carry the static load, but not the extra forces due to the bumps in the roads. They needed constant modification and repair.

While the recruiters were about their business, recruiting the candidates, Dad would visit officials and friends and scout up "relations". Believe it or not, he found relatives even in Kivu Province of the Belgian Congo. These were relatives only relatively speaking, of course. Anyone who had a common ancestor with Dad, or whose ancestor might have been married to one of his ancestors, or to one of the children or cousins of one of his ancestors, was a "relation". Being a relation or a friend of Dad elevated one to a very special group. Membership meant that one could count on being visited, without notice, at any time of the day or night, when Dad happened to be in the neighbourhood. In Africa, distances are long and neighbourhoods large. Telephones were few and far between and Dad wouldn't have known where he was going to be far enough in advance to write, if it had occurred to him to write.

Dad developed drop-in visits into an art form. The host would always be allowed to find out that the visitors' alternative to a nice indoors bed with sheets and a warm bath was going to be the "luxurious, private hotel that went with [them] everywhere, (in the trunk of the car) which had its own built in ventilation system (being open on three sides) and with its own kitchen (the camping stove)." He knew how to refuse just long enough for the kind offer not to be withdrawn by the time he reluctantly let the host and hostess prevail and to undertake the extra bother of having a house-servant make up a bed and run a bath.

To be fair, it was not unusual among old hands in Africa to assume hospitality before it was offered. Travel amenities were spread apart, and there were certainly no fast food places and motel chains. In these conditions, a unique hospitality developed among Europeans in Africa. Most drop-in visits turned into invitations to meals or to spend the night. One could not, in good conscience, send a visitor, even an

120

unwelcome one, off into the night if the nearest town was hours away, over unpaved roads of questionable passability.

There were many families all over East Africa, and there were soon to be several in Central Africa, who would express no surprise, at least, not the second time, on waking up in the morning to find Dad and one or more members of his family asleep in their camp beds, in the living room or dining room. When they thought about it, they would remember saying: "Drop in any time" or making some equally rash invitation. Anyone who could not stand that sort of surprise only had to say so, and some did, to be assured of never being bothered in the same way again. There were some very special friends who would have been offended if any of us had been within a few hundred miles and had not stopped by. The Williamsons, who, over the years, lived in different parts of Kenya and the von Kalcksteins, friends during the exile in Oldiani, by this time living in Kenya, had beds permanently made up for us. They and some others were genuinely pleased to be visited in this way. While some of his hosts were happy to get a break from their lonely, farm or plantation routine, Dad loved to be able to address a fresh audience. The eyelids of his wife or child, along on the current trip, would get lower and lower as Dad would sink lower and lower into his adopted armchair, his voice getting deeper and deeper, as he got deeper and deeper into the subject of the discussion. Konis, a new herbicide effective on the scourge of star grass, it didn't matter what the subject was, he would be seemingly unaware that his traveling companion and he, himself, for that matter, had not slept for perhaps forty hours and would desperately love to do so now. Nor would he notice that his hostess had gone off to bed, after midnight, leaving the visitors with the glassy-eyed host and perhaps some sleeping dogs - lucky, sleeping dogs.

Perhaps to prevent the glassy-eye syndrome, Dad would involve his listeners by emphasizing points with what was a trademark of his very own. *"Je?"* -wait for a response - "Ay?" - wait for response - "Hm?" - and sometimes - "Wha'?" (In Swahili, questions are denoted in two ways, first, by intonation and, second, by starting the sentence with "je", pronounced as an abbreviated "jay." "Ay?" was a sort of "Eh? but pronounced like an abbreviated "-igh" as in "high." "Hm?" and Wha'?" were simply for good measure.

121

Many of these "conversations" were in German, some were in French, some in Swahili and some mixed. They were on a wide range of topics, including European politics, colonial politics, tropical agriculture and, increasingly frequently, independence for African countries. The latter became a reality for Ghana in 1957, but was not yet scheduled for the three East African countries, though it was considered inevitable, already. It actually came about within six years. Independence did not have much appeal to the colonials, considering that the Mau Mau Emergency in Kenya was not yet over. The Congo would not go that way for decades, for sure. Why, the Belgians hadn't even educated anyone in the country beyond middle school. The country simply was not ready for independence. Therefore it would not happen. Not for decades and decades.

We were not bothered that we were Europeans in Africa. Our history books had given us glowing stories about the brave and resourceful explorers and missionaries who opened up the "Dark Continent" to Christianity and medicine and stopped the slave trade. Mum and her five children were all born in Africa. We had a right to be there and had never done anyone any harm while we had been there. We were more interested in making a decent living without our future being threatened by upheaval and fighting than we were in avoiding independence.

As we know from the way he got into insurance and labour recruiting, Dad did not only talk, he could listen, too. Some of the people he spoke with were assertive enough to get a word in and, sometimes, even had interesting things to say.

On one of these drop-in visits to someone in Kivu Province, he heard of a section of land being surveyed by the Comité National du Kivu, in the "Watalinga" area, the most remote part of the Province. The CiNKi[30] was one of the monopolies that King Leopold II of Belgium franchised to finance the development, or rape, depending on your viewpoint, of his "domaine privée"[31]. The only way for a European to acquire

---

[30]Pronounced: 'SEE-en-KEY'.
[31]The Domaine was a million square mile stretch of the Congo Basin that Leopold tricked Stanley into opening up for him, under the pretext that the organization he set up was a philanthropic one. He then snatched it for his personal use, before the European powers wakened to his intentions.

undeveloped land in the Province was through the CiNKi. Undeveloped land was the only kind of land that Dad could afford. The land in question was reputed to be good, and, as a good opportunity, it was likely to be snapped up by graduates from the latest class from the agricultural college.

Dad reflected on the grinding routine that was his life. The income was improved, but the price was becoming high. He was lucky if he spent three, maybe four nights out of every five to seven weeks at home. The rest of the time was taken driving back and forth, over one thousand miles in each direction, or waiting for something not normally in his control to happen. He thought about the politics of the three East African countries. He did not have a problem with an African government in Tanganyika, other than the question it raised about the future of land ownership by Europeans. There was always a question about what would happen to free enterprise after independence. He looked at the way he was earning his living. It was nothing like what he would have expected a person of his social position to be doing. He knew, of course, that this was an academic question. Had he stayed in Germany, he would either have had to teach youngsters how to bully little old ladies, harass and kill Jews, or die himself. He thought about his frustrated dream about starting a coffee plantation in Africa, thirty years ago. He knew that, due to a disease in Brazil's coffee trees, the price of coffee was fifty Belgian francs per kilo, at the plantation (about $1/kg, or $0.40/lb.), an astronomical price. Even if this price were to drop a bit, a fortune could be made, and if it dropped a lot, still a good living. The status of a gentleman coffee planter was much more in keeping with his self-image.

He asked three questions about the land: "Does it have water? Does it have fertile soil? Is it mechanizable?" The answer to all three was affirmative, and he made plans to go and see it.

This was the end of 1957. Pauline was already out of school and had taken over the day to day management of the dairy herd at Rongai. She had spelled Mum on a couple of the trips with Dad, who liked company on the lonely job he was doing. Bill and I were just ending our time at the Prince of Wales School in Nairobi. I had used the Higher School Certificate exams to excuse myself from all of the recruiting trips.

123

Ruanda-Urundi and the Congo were all strange to me, except for what I had been told by Pauline, Mum and of course, Dad. John and Richard had been on a trip. They had come back thoroughly impressed by the intelligence of the Belgians. "Even the little kids, you know, two and three year olds, can speak French!" I knew that, sooner or later, I'd have to go.

Nairobi is on the route that Dad followed, and, if it was not in the middle of the night or class time, he would stop and visit when he passed through. The visits were usually short. Marcel would have to be caught up with, or the drive to where he hoped to spend the night, in the one direction, the von Kalcksteins at Njoro, or the Williamsons at Turbo, and in the other direction, home, would still take two or six hours. I don't know if Dad ever thought of putting up his tent in the parking lot or his camp bed in my dormitory. I think I don't want to know. On these visits, we'd sit in his car in the parking lot in the shadow of the clock tower, smell the ripe bananas and talk. Usually, Dad would talk.

On one of these visits, Bill and I heard about the land at Watalinga, and Dad's interest in it. I had completed the university preparatory curriculum, and, ostensibly, university was an option for me. Someone in the Tanganyika Education Department had even told me that I could probably count on receiving a bursary worth a few hundred pounds, if I chose to go, say, to Cambridge. I did not need to be an economics expert to know that a few hundred pounds would not be enough, and that we could not find the remainder. Bill had, at that point, not considered university as an option.

Our Kenya-born school friends knew their future. They were going into the Kenya Regiment, like it or not, to fight the Mau Mau in the Aberdare forest. We were born in a country that was not a British property, therefore we were excused. We could have volunteered, I suppose, but somehow the thought never entered our minds.

Dad was offering us the choice between becoming either an impoverished student and a bank teller, respectively, or wealthy coffee planters. It did not seem to us to be a decision to be taken lightly. We listened. We reflected. We asked at least two questions.

Q: "Can we each develop our own plantations as the first starts to pay off?"

124

A: "Of course, that is understood."

Q: "When do we start?"

About two months later, with the Higher School Certificate exams completed, school was over for me. I left for home on my eighteenth birthday. I no longer had an excuse to stay home from the recruiting trips. In early January, Mum, Dad and I got into the beetle and headed off on what was to be the last one though we didn't know it at the time. The beetle was loaded with all the food, beds, other paraphernalia and ripening bananas, this time for three people. Mum was the smallest of us, and didn't drive, so she chose to sit in the back seat, next to a pile of bags and things that would have fallen down had she not been there to act as a cargo restraining device. We stopped in Njoro to see the von Kalcksteins and in Turbo to see the Williamsons, and then curved around the north side of Lake Victoria, on Dad's established route. On the map, this looks like a long way around, but it was the only road that was passable year-round.

On this trip, though, we would leave the usual track. Instead of turning south around the Western side of Lake Victoria, towards Ruanda-Urundi, we would head due west to cross into the Belgian Congo at Kasindi. We were to visit the Watalinga land for the first time.

In Kampala, we stopped to pick up a coffee drier for a plantation in the Congo. We were told it was not ready to go. It still had to be checked before Gailey and Roberts, the company selling the drier would guarantee it. I think that a mutual dislike had developed, instantly, between the manager of G&R and Dad, or it could have been that Dad did not want to give up the revenue. Most likely it was that Dad had promised to pick this thing up and deliver it and simply would not take no for an answer. He dug his heels in. We were allowed to take the drier, eventually, only if we opened each wooden shipping crate and listed each component, down to the last screw. And then the guarantee was going to be limited to provision of any parts that could be shown to have been missing from our lists. We spent two or three days doing it. During that time, we honoured Father King, Padre of the biggest Catholic church in Kampala, by sleeping on our camp beds in the basement of his church and gave a fright to a good number of the women of his flock going about their churchy

125

business. When we were done, Marcel went on to deliver the poorly re-packed drier, with a long, handwritten list of things like '6 sections of drier drum, 18" pulley, 2" x 36" shaft, 3" x 5/8" bolts with nuts.' We would meet him in Burundi, in a few days. We never heard if the planter who bought the drier really was grateful that we won such a moral victory for him, or if he would have preferred to have a full guarantee instead of an earlier delivery, or if he ever got the thing to work. What mattered to Dad was that he had stuck to his guns, one more time, and won. Damn the consequences.

As we drove through Uganda, I began to feel slightly ill. By the time we reached Beni, late on the first day out of Kampala, I was shivering and sweating and not very good company for Mum and Dad. We did something that was very rare for us, we checked in to the Hotel Ruwenzori. My company did not get any better, even after a whole day which seemed like forever. Someone suggested we visit the American Mission Hospital at Ouisha, about twenty kilometres to the north, on the Bunia road. We went there, and I was diagnosed by Dr. Becker as having malaria. Two days of quinine treatment made me well enough to go on, if not totally comfortable. We would meet Dr. Becker again, sometimes in very strange circumstances, but, thankfully, never again due to our own illnesses.

The road to Watalinga, the only road there, started a few kilometres short of Ouisha, at Mbao. *Mbao* is Swahili for board, as in signboard. That this place had a signboard was sufficiently important as to merit it being its name. Apart from that, there were only two other things of note at Mbao. One was that if you stopped there for two minutes, you'd be surrounded by pygmies wearing a big smile and a G string, one of each for each pygmy, that is, and begging cigarettes. *"Taba! Taba!"* The other, Marcel would find, later. It was a native bar, this one Pope-less.

At Mbao, the road was already in the Ituri forest, which continues all the way to the Atlantic Ocean. A few more kilometres, and the road entered the Parc National Albert. There were traffic signs that advised drivers that elephants have the right of way. Some drivers, we supposed, may need to be told that. A few more kilometres further, the road went down a steep escarpment, the western wall of the Western Rift Valley. The point where the road began to drop would have been extremely interesting to Livingstone and Stanley, only 80 years earlier, for the drop of rain that fell before it would find its way into the Congo River and on to the Atlantic, while the drop which fell on the other side would flow into the Semliki, thence to the Nile and on to the Mediterranean, thousands of miles in another direction. I regret to report that, when we passed the point, hermetically sealed in the beetle, it meant absolutely nothing to me.

The road was reputed to have followed the existing elephant trails, as our friend Joseph would tell us later. It did seem to follow a fairly easy grade, except for a short stretch on the escarpment. The tall trees blocked any view, other than through the tunnel between the trees, so it was not easy to see where we were going. At one point, the road made a sharp right turn and came, abruptly, to the edge of the 100-metre-wide Semliki River. We were lucky to be doing this in the daylight. There might possibly have been some people who might have had occasion to drive along that road, who might not yet have figured out for themselves that elephants had the right of way. For them, signs to advise them of this revolutionary concept were considered to be helpful and necessary. There could not possibly be anyone driving along that road who did not know that there was no bridge over the Semliki, or, more correctly, that it was still under construction. After all, nobody would go down that road. There wasn't a bridge, was there? Therefore no sign was necessary. It's pure logic!

A team of native employees of the Travaux Publiques, working on the bridge, dropped what they were doing and came to our assistance. They guided us onto a platform made of rough-cut timbers laid over a couple of dozen empty oil drums, strapped together with wire. This pontoon was somehow attached to a steel hawser whose ends were anchored on opposite banks. The workers then grabbed the hawser and walked towards the near shore. The reaction of their feet on the pontoon was to make it move away from the shore, into the current of the river. As each man reached the edge of the platform, he let go and ran to the other end to grab the hawser, again, and to repeat the process. This got us to the middle of the stream. The men stopped. The pontoon stopped. Hands came out in the international sign meaning: "Cross my palm with gold or tobacco, if you want to go on from here!"

When palms had been adequately crossed with *taba* and a few francs, we proceeded, with the work accompanied by singing and laughter.

The road continued on the other bank, straight into another dark, green tunnel. A bit farther, we came in to some small villages, the largest of which was Kamango. Here there was a Catholic Mission.

We had been advised to call in on Père Jean Adam, who ran the mission with the help of Père Rombaud. You see the difference between real life and fiction? No night club singers! No white hunters! Not even a world-wise but kindly old nun, let alone a madam! Just a snaggle-toothed priest and his deaf helper.

At the mission, we were welcomed and offered a meal. The meal was memorable for two reasons.

First, I got my first opportunity to practice the French that I had been learning for nine years at school. When I was served a plate of scrambled eggs, I stammered and stuttered. I finally managed: *"D-d-d-danke schön!"*

Second, we were served coffee, which Père Jean proudly told us was locally grown. When he noticed me examining the ring of dissolved metal that the spoon left on the saucer, he elabourated, at the same time sounding slightly apologetic: *"C'est fait noir, par les noirs, pour les noirs!* It is made black, by blacks, [fit] for blacks!" He loved his people, but this example of what now would be considered 'political incorrectness' was tame for the Congo. Had he been overheard saying it three years later, he would have been expelled from the country, immediately. Anyway, the incident gave us something to think about concerning the probable quality of the coffee that we hoped we might one day grow here.

Père Jean's church was made entirely of local materials. It had walls of mud plastered on sticks tied to poles, but they only went halfway up to the thatched roof. This made for excellent, and we later found, necessary ventilation. The floor was packed earth. The communion rail was supported by two magnificent elephant tusks. There was a beautiful Madonna and child, carved out of a whole tusk by a local artist. The use of ivory was totally natural, in that place, at that time. It struck us as beautiful. There was a new church being built out of bricks and it would get a corrugated, galvanized iron roof. It would serve the growing congregation better, but it looked sterile and out of place.

Père Jean told us the names of the chiefs of the two tribes.

We stopped in to see Raphael de Jaeger, a Flemish planter who had been there for six years or so after taking over from his older brother. They had had to walk the entire forty-mile distance from Mutwanga through the forest, when they had first come, spending a night in the trees on the way, because there had been no road from Mbao and no pontoon across the Semliki. Now, his coffee was producing in high gear.

We drank a warm beer with de Jaeger, while he told us things that we would need to know. He told us that the local people would not work. He brought in tribesmen from Bunia, a couple of hundred kilometres away, who would work, and who would sign three-year contracts, too. He told us lots more and wished us luck. The whole time he had an amused look on his face. It must have been his usual expression, for we rarely saw him without it. Or else we were more amusing than we gave ourselves credit for. No matter, he was to become a most useful source of information and, eventually, a friend.

We went on to look for the land that had been described to Dad in Bukavu. We found it. There were five parcels. Three of them which were contiguous, in a block, looked best, and two, across the track to Njadot, had less desirable layouts. We examined the lie of the land. There was a hill overlooking the bulk of the land, from a height of about 70 metres (about 20 stories). The land sloped evenly and gently from the top corner, nearest the Lamia River which formed the northern boundary of the parcels that we liked best and was also the boundary between the Congo and Uganda. There was another, smaller river which cut through the southeastern corner of the same block. The land lent itself perfectly to mechanization and to irrigation. It was covered with a healthy stand of *matete,* assuring us of the fertility of the soil.

We visited Basikania. He was chief of the Nandi tribe which had ceded the land to the CiNKi and which occupied Njadot, the village just above the parcels, and all the land and villages up into the mists of the Ruwenzoris. He was delighted that a European gave him the courtesy of a visit.

"Iko shauri moja! There is one matter!" said Dad, as we were being walked along the boundary we were to share with

his people's territory, by Basikania, himself. "I need to get the land on the top of the hill, to build my house."

Basikania assured Dad that the availability of the hill could be discussed. He also told us that his mud and thatch *gîte* in Njadot would be at our disposal while we built our own house.

We spent that night in the brick *gîte* at Kamango, which gave Dad an opportunity to describe his plans and his ancestry to chef Pascal of the Watalinga and a crowd of his bewildered tribesmen.

We left with Dad totally seduced by the place. Mum was her usual agreeable self, and I think she liked it well enough. I was hardly well enough yet to have cared one way or the other, but must have given my support. Now we just had to get to Bukavu and advise the CiNKi of our interest in the land before they granted it to anyone else.

We might have saved some time by detouring back out into Uganda and down to Goma on the relatively flat bottom of the Rift Valley, I can't remember. We certainly didn't make good time if we stayed in the Congo and took the apparently more direct road through the mountains to Goma. Either way, there was only one way from Goma to Bukavu. It was a drive full of hairpin bends and beautiful views of Lake Kivu. One of my first sights of the lake was a place where lava from an eruption more than ten years earlier had flowed over lava from twenty years ago, to cut off a small bay. The older lava had a few plants growing on it, the newer was sterile. The water in the small lake was bright green. The main lake was blue.

The road took us past old cinchona plantations, which produced quinine before people learned to produce it in a laboratory, and past well-established coffee plantations. And every few miles, a stunning view of the lake and the island in the middle of it, Idjui.

After two or three days in Bukavu, which included day-long visits by Dad with the powers at the CNKi, while his family sat, as usual, in the car, Dad, Mum and Pauline were the designated concessionaires of the three contiguous parcels, the ones that we wanted. If you didn't count Paga, who was 81, Dad, Mum and Pauline were the only ones of us who were over 21 or would be 21 at the next birthday. I and my three brothers would wait to have the opportunity to fund our own plantations from the proceeds of these first ones.

130

We stayed with Irene and Joe Cassel, at Katana, which was only 45 minutes outside Bukavu, for the nights between the long days we sat outside the offices. Pauline had been staying with the Cassels since Dad's last trip. They were always delightful hosts. Rene was a White Russian[32] and had fled the Bolsheviks to Shanghai. Joe was Australian. They had lived in New Guinea, Texas and Moshi, before coming here. Their home was an oasis of civilization in a primitive part of the world and it was an opportunity for us to see a successful plantation. No matter that they grew *arabica* coffee, at an elevation close to six thousand feet and we were going to grow *robusta* at about two thousand feet. This was a chance to study the subject of coffee growing. When Dad couldn't start something right away, he studied it. We would stop often at going plantations, to get the latest ideas and for Dad to discuss his evolving mulching concept. Joe Cassel invited us to visit his second plantation, at Mutwanga, on the southern end of the Ruwenzoris, where he was growing *robusta*. There, we could see something more like what our own operation would be. We should also ask his manager ("my Indian") to show us the house, built in New Guinea style, and to hand over the small motorcycle which Joe gave to Pauline.

Bukavu was a charming little town, nestled on the shores

---

[32]The 'white' in white rhino is really a mistake. Members of one species of rhino have wide mouths, set in rather square jaws. The early German explorers described the species as the *'weit,* (wide)' rhino. English speakers never can get things like that right, so they started saying 'white', even though it's no whiter than the other ones. White hunters got their name the same way, I'm forced to believe, from their propensity to be acted in movies by tough looking actors with wide smiles mounted on rather square jaws. You immediately ask yourself why hippos and crocodiles, which have much wider mouths than any rhino, aren't called white. The answer is, you see, they *all* have wide mouths. There isn't much point in going around talking about wide mouthed hippos than there is in talking about big elephants or small rock hyraxes, is there? When you grow up in Africa, you just know these things. So, what about Rene? Rene sometimes smiled, and though she was tiny, she was tough enough to have a square jaw. But she didn't, and neither her smile nor her mouth were anything other than ideally sized. She never did explain why her Russianship was 'white'. Maybe, if you'd grown up in Russia, you'd just know. For the rest of us, it has to remain a mystery. Or a cocktail.

131

of Lake Kivu. The altitude gave it a very pleasant climate. The Belgians gave it a very European look by using their own Belgian architecture and planting imported trees and shrubs[33]. Half close your eyes (and ignore the pedestrians) and you could think you were not in Africa. The restaurant menus could have been from restaurants in Brussels. The foods in the groceries, even the meats, were all imported. In Kenya, there was a strong local industry in producing foods, to the point that there was a strong export business to Europe. Here, despite 100,000 Europeans living in the Congo, everything was brought in. We would find some answers to this puzzle, later.

We went on to Dad's usual base camp for his recruiting, in a *gîte* in Kayanza, on the one main road through Urundi. There Pascali greeted us with enthusiasm and the first of many meals of stewed chicken and *pommes frites,* his most believable evidence for his claim to be a cook. There, also, another Joseph greeted us with a list of his recruits, but not yet a full booking for the lorry. It would take us a couple of weeks to fill the quotas.

We had bumped into the *gouverneur* at the post office in Usumbura (now Bujumbura) on the way. He had invited us for lunch on Thursday, next week. We went. It took us two hours to be driven to Kitega, where he had his *résidence*, with Pauline and me riding in the back of our *gîte*-host's pick-up truck. Once we were there, it took over an hour for our host to appear. Wearing our usual uniform of khaki shorts and shirts, which uniform and our hair showed clear evidence of our most recent drive, we were shown in to his elegant home by a disdainful Mrundi servant. When our host arrived, we were still uncombed and slightly brown, but we were served a very

---

[33]Drury Pifer describes the town of Elizabethville, which he visited as a twelve year old, in 1945: "The town looked like a French village transplanted onto a Hollywood jungle set. There were surreal sidewalk cafés and good French pastries served under palm and banana trees. It seemed perfectly normal to us, but if a dinosaur had walked out of the jungle, we would probably have made the proper mental adjustment to include that as well. We had grown up among the juxtapositions of impossible things." (Innocents in Africa. Harcourt Brace. New York, 1994).

fine meal, including asparagus in hollandaise sauce, on expensive china, and a very fine red wine, in crystal. There was more to the lunch than that, but that is what I can remember. That and that it seemed important to the good Governor for the meal to be distinctly European, despite the climate, the lack of a single paved road in his capital or any other evidence of high civilization beyond his front door.

Dad caused some consternation and must have torn whatever remained of the little bubble of gentility when, after complimenting the host on his wine, he asked the same Mrundi servant to pour only a short glass of wine and to add water. "Wine in the middle of the day makes me sleepy. This is the way I drank it as a child. I think I even prefer it this way! Very refreshing!" The Governor nodded to the hesitating servant, who rolled his eyes, shrugged and did as Dad asked. What could the rest of us do but follow?

As we drove through Urundi, we noticed that some of the people were very tall, men and women alike. The women wore clothes similar to those of the Baganda women, and had strange, sculptured haircuts. They looked very dignified, even as part of the pedestrian crowd scrambling off the road in the dust of our passing car. Dad told us they were the Tutsi.

"They are like the feudal lords in Europe. They rule the country. The Hutu are like the serfs. The Tutsi moved south into this area a century or two ago, with their Ankole cattle. The cattle are mainly a form of wealth and are bred for the length of their horns. They have beautiful, long horns, but they're practically useless for either beef or milk. The Tutsi still own all the cattle and are kind enough honour the Hutu by letting them look after them. The Hutu know how special the cattle are, with their big, long horns, after all, the Tutsi themselves have told them so, and are delighted that the Tutsi are so generous with this honour, and, over and above that, with taking on the chores of ruling the country. Clever, Wha'? Je? Ai? H'm? Wha'?" There was more than a little admiration in his voice for the creativity of the Tutsi and their ability to get away with it for so long.

He also described the palace that Mwami (King) Mwamputsa lived in. It was basically built of the same materials as every other Mrundi's hut. However, it was on a grand scale and was full of the finest grass weaving you ever

133

saw. Each surface, even each column was covered by intricately woven patterns. When a citizen went to seek audience with the Mwami, he was expected to take a gift. The gift, even if it were no more than a couple of eggs, had to be in a basket. Any one of the baskets could have had a place in a museum in Europe.

One day, Joseph came with the last recruits needed to fill the truck and the required signatures or thumbprints of the village headmen. They had been interviewed and found suitable. The word went out to all of the people concerned: we would be ready to leave at *"jogoo ya kwanza, kesho kutwa,"* literally, "the first rooster's crow, on tomorrow again." In an area that had no telephones, each member of the group had to be visited, in person, by Joseph and his team, on foot and on bicycles, to be given the message. The bachelors would have been ready to climb on the truck, then and there. The government knew that it was easier to recruit bachelors, and since it was a Catholic goverment, they understood that the departure of bachelors didn't do much to reduce the birth rate and alleviate the overpopulation. That is why they gave Dad quotas of seven families for every three bachelors. We had to take the list to the *Chef de Poste,* the colonial official in charge of the area, for his approval.

Pauline said: "I wonder if it is still Boniface. You know, the last time we went there, it was just before Christmas. He rather pointedly told Dad that he preferred Johnny Walker Black, but Red would do! Of course, Dad just looked blank, smiled sweetly, thanked him and we left. I wonder if he'll have the nerve to hold us up because we didn't deliver." He didn't. He must have forgotten.

Pauline and Mum conjectured that Joseph and his helpers actually did a bit of matchmaking in the marketplaces where they did most of their recruiting. We could understand that they needed to, to balance the numbers; it was so much easier to get single men to go than couples or families. We could imagine that when they had a strong prospect of a bachelor, they'd canvass likely young women.

"Are you unmarried? Are you tired of being hungry and crowded and working like a slave at home for nothing? Come to the land of milk and honey! Earn good *posho* and minimum wage! Here, young lady. You, with the basket on your head!

134

Yes, you! Step right up! How would you like to be married to this fine young man?"

Maybe we just imagined it, it sounds so good, but several of the 'couples' we processed really seemed not to know each other well, I mean, to the point of the 'husband' needing to ask his 'wife' her name. Maybe it was to involve her in the process. Maybe it isn't right for a man to speak his wife's name.

It was the ready-made families, not the instant ones, who needed the extra few hours to take their leave before disappearing for three years, and for whom we had to wait the extra day.

Pascali begged to go with us, to see the world. After all, we would be back in two weeks, or so he had just heard us say. Dad agreed.

I imagine the conversation at his home, that night: "Josephina, I'm going to Tanganyika tomorrow."

"Oh! What am I going to eat while you are gone? And the children?"

"No problem. I will return in two weeks, when the *bwana* comes back."

"So? What am I going to eat?"

"Woman! Go to the market, the way you always do!"

"But I don't have any money!"

"I will ask the *mzungu* for two weeks' ration money (about half a dollar) and leave it with you. Now, where is my food?"

Predictably, we left, not at the second dawn, but at about the third sunset. Predictably, we would not come back in two weeks.

Nobody would or could have predicted that we would never come back.

Mum and Pauline were with Dad, in the beetle. I went as co-driver in Polonia, with Marcel. To save a half a day of driving, we took a short cut. One stretch of this road, negotiated in the first night, thankfully at night, was around the side of one of the volcanoes of the region, and was so narrow and steep that they allowed traffic in only one direction at a time, for periods of six hours at a time, and in no direction when the weather was bad. Over the groaning of the engine on the way up and the squealing of the brakes on the way down, Marcel regaled me with stories about his many brushes with death on this mountain. They were due mostly to Polonia's penchant for losing vacuum for her brake servo, for sucking air into her fuel line and for jamming her low-range gears, always on the most dangerous hills and in the sharpest curves. He described, with little modesty, his innumerable heroic deeds, without which he, the passengers, Polonia, Dad's *biashara* and his *heshima,* his business and his honour, and our livelihood would have been at the bottom of the mountain, in a charred heap. Innumerable charred heaps. I wondered if his attention to the telling and his need to make gestures with his hands wouldn't perhaps succeed to send us off the edge where the untrustworthy brakes and steering had so far failed. It was the first night of this part of the trip. I didn't sleep.

Marcel's driving style was simple. There were two possible positions for his right foot: pushing the accelerator to the floorboards or punishing the brakes by standing on them. In Uganda and most of Kenya, where the roads were straighter and fairly well maintained, we made good time. We stopped only to stretch, eat and change drivers.

"Look at them! They're like animals! I've never seen anything like them!" Marcel complained, pointing to a very panicky looking young mother relieving herself at the edge of the road, not ten feet from the truck, and running to scramble back on board. "Do you know, they even pee in the cans that hold their food!" What he did not acknowledge was that this was the first stop in six hours, and when she and other brave or desperate passengers were getting off the truck, he, Marcel would hover round them, like a sheep dog guarding its flock, barking at them to hurry or they'd be left behind. He told me, proudly, that comfort stops like this were going to be limited to three minutes. In three minutes, one could hardly get as far as the edge of the road, do the necessary and hope to make it back. He was certain that his charges would run off, and that he'd be blamed. I wonder what he thought these poor, tired, aching people, who didn't speak any language, other than their own, might think of doing if they ran off in a strange country. Even if they had been given thirty minutes for each comfort stop, which was what they got only twice on the whole journey, for cooking, they wouldn't have dared go farther than the edge of the road, just for fear of being left. He was paranoid, and his way of treating them made me think that if they did run off, it would be to get away from him! Much to Marcel's

136

disappointment and to the accompaniment of his muttering something with a meaning along the lines of 'no way to run a railroad', I took it on myself to cause the stops to be longer, as much as ten minutes.

We got to Tanganyika and delivered our workers to a plantation not far from Oldeani. We were asked to return one family (another Joseph, with wife and children) and two bachelors (Sengerengabo[34] and Sebastian) to Urundi. They hopped on to Polonia and we went home to Rongai, still three or four hours away, to sleep.

The trip had taken two nights and two days. I was sure I had aged ten years.

---

[34]Pronounce the 'Gs'.

CHAPTER THREE

One of the first things that developed on our return to Rongai was that a person with whom Dad had been negotiating a possible sale of the farm decided to make us an offer. For the 750 acres of arable, fertile land, a furrow with year-round water in it, two dams, a well-built *pisé de tèrre*[35] storage building and a five-bedroom stone house, he would pay four thousand pounds, equivalent to ten thousand dollars. This was not at all generous, but no other offers were in sight. Dad discussed it with Paga, who was the owner.

Paga knew the situation. Rongai needed a lot of capital to make it less dependent on rainfall. It would cost time and money build up a better stock of dairy cattle and install some irrigation equipment to cultivate the required fodder. There were other things that could be done, given sufficient money, and even these plans were not without their own set of risks. The truth was, of course, nobody had any money and, because of the history of crop failure on Rongai, the banks were not approachable. Paga was not and had never been afraid of the unknown. If James and Fiona had seen the land in the Congo and had liked it, and there was really plenty of free water, to remove the dependency on Africa's fickle rains, that was good enough. Although he had just turned eighty-one, he was ready to go along.

The offer was accepted. A closing date was set. The farm which had been the family's home for over thirty years, would change hands in September of 1958. This gave us seven months in which to get ready for the expedition into the Congo.

The next recruiting trip to Urundi was canceled. Pascali, Joseph and Sengerengabo had their plans changed. As Paga might have said, quoting his favourite poet, "The best laid plans of mice and men ging aft agley!" They all decided to wait and go with us. In the meantime, they would work for us, for *posho*. The Congo was the neighbouring country to Urundi and getting a ride that far would bring them nearer to home.

---

[35]Pressed earth, or adobe.

Tanganyika also shared a border with Urundi, but that didn't seem to make a difference.

Somewhere in here, we had some discussions about the history of the Belgian Congo and its probable independence in the future.

One of us would ask: "Who's right is it to decide?"

Dad would say: "Brussels."

"How do they have the right to decide the future of another country?" We weren't trying to annoy him, we didn't know the history, and we really wondered. We knew from our Anglo-centric history courses about Clive of India, and that Stanley had presumed to find Livingstone, and all that, but we hadn't gone into the other countries' exploits.

"King Leopold gave the Congo to Belgium."

"What? How could he give a whole country to somebody else?"

"Well, you see, it had been his."

"How's that?"

A little testily: "The European powers gave it to him."

"You mean the European powers gave a million square miles of somebody else's continent to an individual, just for himself?"

"Well, yes!"

"Did they ask the natives?"

"Well! Now you're being silly!"

Dad was a fair man, but he was a monarchist. Monarchists will accept odd manifestations of absolute power being vested in an individual. I'm trying to remember if I got the impression that he approved of the situation. I know he accepted it, I'm not sure it meant that he approved of it. Had he known the truth of the way Leopold ran his country, the extent of the brutality, he would not have been so accepting. We were much more naïve than we were principled, but this history bothered us. Had we known the truth, we would have been much more bothered.

We had some other talks, in which Dad lamented the amount of money that the concessions that Leopold had set up to exploit the resources were taking out of the country, which was high compared to what they put back in for development. That was economics, therefore it had to be boring. We couldn't grasp the importance of that so easily as the more human import of the earlier subject.

The next few months were spent in a flurry of planning and activity. We attended several farm auctions in Tanganyika and Kenya, to see if there was anything better than what we had in the way of tractors or other equipment.

Dad had bought one of our two International Harvester Farmall M tractors from the ill-fated Wheat Scheme, in Tanganyika. It was already eighteen years old. The second one had been acquired, new, while the farm was still producing crops; it was about seven years old. Both were still serviceable, but needed some attention. Along with suspensions and tires, Africa really takes a toll on the cooling system and the electrical system of any motor vehicle and these latter two systems are prone to deteriorate more rapidly than anything else. The two Farmalls that we had were the same model, despite being built more than a decade apart. They worked on a magneto ignition system, which produces the ignition spark without the aid of a battery or generator, and they were hand cranked, therefore, they had no battery, no generator, no starter and no wiring to fail. While it meant relatively trouble-free operation, it also meant no lights. When we ploughed at night, which we had to do each season, we could do it only by moonlight or with an assistant walking ahead of the tractor with a hurricane lantern. Even if the cool night air helped the radiator to avoid boiling as frequently, it didn't do anything for the leaks. The "turn boy" or *tanni boi* still had to make a run to the water drum or the furrow after each turn around the field.

Another peculiarity of the Farmalls was that they ran on kerosene, instead of diesel fuel or petrol. Kerosene was cheaper, probably because it has a drawback. It does not vapourize at normal temperatures, and if it is not vapourized, it will not ignite in the engine. To provide the heat to vapourize the fuel in the carburetor, the exhaust gases are diverted to a chamber that surrounds the air intake manifold, to heat the incoming air. This very ingenious solution works only when the exhaust manifold has been heated to the required temperature. This can be achieved two ways. The first is by running the engine for five minutes, during which time the intake manifold is heated by the exhaust, but it must be started on a fuel which will vapourize at ordinary temperatures, i.e. petrol. The need for this second fuel necessitates a second fuel tank and cocks to switch the petrol supply off and the kerosene on, and a good sense of timing. The second way, equally recommended in the handbook, was to play the flame of a blowtorch on the exhaust manifold, for five minutes. The game with the hand crank and the petrol and kerosene fuel line cocks, while it looked like a Chinese fire drill, was a lot preferable to putting a blowtorch in the hands of the semi-skilled farm hands who were the tractor drivers.

Today, when I smell a hot engine I'm transported back, immediately, to a cold, pitch black night. I'm huddling against the leeward side of a tractor standing in the middle of a field, just where the driver let the kerosene run out. The engine is still slightly warm, warm enough to make a difference in the night wind. And warm enough to smell, but not warm enough to get it going again. The driver decants a bottle of petrol into the appropriate tank. I'm just big enough to be able to turn the crank, and rather proud of it, but I leave it to him to perform the ritual, in his words, to waken the tractor. Half an hour ago he was wakening me, calling outside our window to say that the tractor had died. I'm the lucky one who woke first. The tractor was refusing to wake up, he said, and it had already drunk all of the petrol he had. He, the driver hadn't wanted to siphon a bottle of petrol out of the car's tank on his own, and, now that he had reported the trouble, maybe he should just go to bed and we could waken the tractor in the morning. He was right about siphoning the petrol, and he was wrong about going to bed. On the first point, the dogs would have made a great show of not being kind to any African, even a known employee, who tried to do anything around the house by himself at night. They liked to perpetuate the myth that they watched the place. On the second point, it was always amazing how machines regained control of their bad attitudes and sprang back to work when any member of the *mzungu* family was present, even one of the children. My presence might be enough to shame the tractor back to work, so the ploughing could be done on schedule, so I would have volunteered to walk back to the field with him. So, here I am, trying to keep warm. In another five minutes, much to the driver's surprise, the tractor will be running again. He will not go home and sleep, and I will walk back home alone, through the dark night. I'm not sure who feels worse about it. I know every step of the way by heart, but I know that every step will be watched. I never know what it is, or what they are, but I know it or they is or are there, behind every bush. In the really black-dark night, even ploughed fields have bushes and shapes in them, that loom up and reach out at twelve year olds. It is at least as dangerous as the things that used to be under my bed, when I was just a kid. The night isn't any colder, in fact, the started tractor is beginning to radiate more heat, but I shiver. I wish I had a big stick, or something, but I don't. I shall just try to let the thing know that I know it's there, but that I don't care. It worked for Dad, didn't it? I grit my teeth as I step out of the warmth and the protection that the tractor affords and head home. I'm lucky, my bravado works.

The complications that I have described would seem to work very much against the Farmalls as a choice of equipment to use so far from sources of help, but their indestructibility made up for the fuss about starting. The Farmall M is built like a tank. I could take you, today, to farms not half an hour from where I now live, and show you Farmall Ms that are fifty years old, at work in the fields.

At the auctions we saw several tractors, including some with tracks instead of wheels and some with starters and lights. Few appeared to be more robust and reliable than what we had. To acquire the ones that did would have taken much of the proceeds of the sale of Rongai. We decided to stick with the Farmalls, to bring them up to top condition and to take them with us.

Marcel came in to his own. He had trained as a mechanic under Jock and his employer, who owned the International Harvester dealership in Arusha. He could close his eyes and recite a list of the repairs that should be done to each of the two tractors, in turn, and then give the list of parts, by name, sometimes even by part number, that would be required to accomplish the repairs. I think he could have kept his eyes closed to do the repairs, too! He took Bill and me under his wing, as we stripped the tractors down, totally, and then put them back together again. And then, most importantly, he showed us how to make them start when that was done. The process gave us a great deal of confidence.

We wanted to have the equipment look as valuable as possible. It had to do with the degree of commitment to our

142

enterprise that we were demonstrating to the Belgian authorities, and, possibly, also with collateral value, in the event we had to get a loan. We splurged and bought two gallons of Harvester Red paint and two sets of decals. These tractors were going to look as good as new.

When, months later, we had the tractors back together again, Dad, always wanting action, needing to get things moving, took up a brush and, ceremoniously, started to paint the side of the tractor nearest to him. After about ten minutes, he got a distant look in his eyes, waved the brush towards the general area he had been painting and handed it to me.

He said, magnanimously: "Here, you do some."

I dipped the ceremonial brush and moved to the place he had indicated. The parts that I could see were covered with a nice shiny, new coat of paint. I had to look hard for the areas that Dad could have thought would need to be painted. I found them, right behind and completely blocked by parts covered by his very fresh, very wet paint.

All of the farm equipment that had been collected in thirty-five years of mixed farming was examined, piece by piece, and was assessed as to whether it was going to be useful for opening up new land. If yes, we asked ourselves what had to be done to it to make it worthwhile taking along and to put it into a condition in which it could survive being several hundred miles from the nearest source of parts. If there was any doubt, it would come with us. A reaper-binder would not go; we weren't going to grow wheat. A wheat thresher would go; we might grow something that would need to be threshed, say soybeans. We took all of the "keepers" apart and replaced or repaired missing, worn or broken parts. The missing parts had probably been liberated by the entrepreneurial local blacksmiths, turned skillfully into various tools and, in these new shapes, sold back to us. We did not give this equipment quite the same treatment as the tractors. Certainly, it did not merit the same expensive paint.

On one excursion to find equipment or tools, we were in Nakuru, Kenya, fairly close to the von Kalksteins' home, where we had stayed the night and told them all about the evolving mulching system, how the coffee factory was going to be on a hill so that gravity would help move the beans through the process and much, much more, all of it of vital interest to them.

We were having something done to the VW beetle, at the Cooper Motors' Nakuru garage. Dad saw a used VW pickup in the showroom. He drove it around the block, slammed its doors and kicked its tires and had a little talk with the manager. We continued our trip in the pickup, leaving the now Koni-less beetle in exchange. The pickup would be much more useful on a plantation.

Some of the excursions to look for equipment and for parts were planned. Some were not. One evening, on the way home from a day trip to Arusha, we were about twenty miles from home when a tire blew out. We took a look at the other tires as we put the spare one on. Dad assessed their condition. He concluded that we had better stay on the relatively good roads and go directly to Nairobi, two hundred miles away, to get a replacement tire and to have the remaining ones retreaded, rather than to risk covering, unnecessarily, twice, the distance on the less good roads that lay between us and home. We had no clean clothes, no toothbrush, no bedding. The pickup did have a compartment in which the camp beds were stowed, so at least we had them along with us. We drove for four hours. We ate bread and sardines and we slept on the camp beds, in the pickup, outside the tire retreaders' godown (hotels were, as I have said, not in our vocabulary) where the night watchman had a fire and was used to us. We had our tires retreaded there, very first thing in the morning, while we ate some more bread and sardines. We stopped at a military surplus store for jungle boots and Australian army hats, before heading for home[36]. We arrived home after only forty hours had elapsed from the start of an eight-hour trip. I cannot remember if the phone at home was working or not, such things were in the hands of the gods, the giraffes and the current demand in the native population for copper wire. It was not a big deal, Mum, and anyone else at home, would not have been surprised by our not showing up when expected. If anything, when she heard about

---

[36]There had been a huge buildup of military force in Kenya, to fight the Mau Mau. There were battalions of British soldiers brought in to supplement the Kenya Regiment, and they all had to be supplied. A large market developed in used and surplus military equipment. The volume of materials available to this market picked up as the State of Emergency neared its end in 1959.

the diversion, Mum was surprised that we had managed to come back that soon.

On one trip, Dad, Bill and I were three hundred miles from home, somewhere near Mount Kenya. It was dusk. Normally, if we were finished with our business, we would start for home and drive through the night, but there was going to be an auction starting the next day at sunrise, that had some interesting equipment. The lights of the pickup were not working very well, anyway, so we wouldn't want to drive all night. Dad remembered that the Hunts, friends of the Cassels, (the Cassels who lived near Bukavu, in the Congo), had once said: "Look us up, if you are ever nearby!" Their home was nearby, it was only fifty miles away. We headed off, in their direction, Dad, as usual, letting one of his sons drive. It grew dark. The lights failed. We drove on, with only parking lights, the change in shadows at the side of the road telling us roughly where the road was. Once or twice we saw the headlights of another vehicle coming. We pulled over and let them go by.

One of the major causes of fatal car accidents in East Africa was unmarked, unlighted, reflectorless lorries parked on the edge of the road. They are hard enough to avoid when you have headlights, invisible when you have none. Fortunately, we didn't come across any, they are usually found near a settlement or a *kilabu,* and this was relatively sparsely populated, being the Kenya "White Highlands". Another danger was ant-eater holes. Anthills don't grow grass, so, by *aardvark* logic, where there is no grass, ants are to be found. The unpaved roads of East Africa were very frustrating to the hungry and industrious diggers. Where there are *aardvarks,* there are holes all over the road. If you hit an *aardvark* hole it could take off your wheel. Better than the lorries, though, because if you hit one of them it is likely to take off your head.

By about nine or ten at night, having safely negotiated whatever booby traps there might have been, we pulled in to the Hunt's driveway. They were not there. The houseboy said they were "*safarini,*" or on a trip. No matter, he would feed us whatever we wanted to eat, would make us up beds and light a fire in the guest rooms and "at what time in the morning do the *bwanas* wish me to bring them their tea?" I suppose he later told his *bwana* and *memsabu* (master and mistress) about the visit, but he would not have known to tell them how

145

close they came to hearing more than they ever wanted to know about mulch and gravity. Come to think of it, Dick Hunt might just have been the person who told Dad about a gravity operated factory on his plantation. But it wouldn't have mattered. Even if he had been the sole inventor of the system and held patents on it, it wouldn't have protected him from getting a long lecture on it. We went back to the auction, in the morning, able to drive a little faster in the dawn light.

On one trip, we bought a well-used ten-ton trailer from an Italian owner-operator who was part of a big transportation co-op, based in Nairobi. For well used, read abused. The seller recommended his brother in law's machine shop for the repairs that it needed. Its brakes were designed for operation by the compressed air from the truck's system. We decided not to rebuild the whole system to work with Polonia's vacuum brakes, opting instead for a mechanical system operated by cranking a wheel which tightened a set of cables which pulled on the brakes' actuating levers. The brakes could only be operated by a person riding on the trailer, and it would be possible to use the brakes effectively only when the trailer was standing still or moving very slowly, say behind a tractor. These fine points were not troublesome to us, at this point, for we couldn't have afforded to have them done the other way, anyway.

Dad believed that if he did not stand over the work being done in a garage, he could expect at worst to be cheated and at best to be delayed. We spent three days waiting for the work to be completed, watching over the machinist, ducking his flailing hands and ignoring his resentment, expressed, volubly, verbally and by sign language, both in Italian, at our apparent distrust. An Indian came by and, right under the Italian's nose, tried to recruit our work away from the latter's workshop. I made the mistake of saying something along the lines of maybe it would go quicker if the Indian did some of the work while the Italian did what he was doing. I compounded this mistake by saying it in the Italian's hearing. It took Dad hours of diplomatic effort to restore the peace and have the Italian continue to work on our trailer. When we weren't hovering over the work, we ate bread and sardines for meals and slept in the pickup or in the back of Polonia, parked across the street from the tire retreader's night watchman and his fire, with the tarpaulins up to protect us from the wind and curious eyes. When we went to settle with the seller, he left an indelible impression on us concerning Italian chivalry. He was a scruffy looking, stubbly- and multiply-chinned man, but when he addressed his colleague's wife, whose rear view bore a strong resemblance to a similar view of the trailer we had just bought, he said, with a great flourish, in a sincere tone and with an even more sincere smile: *"Buongiorno, bella signora!"* Such class!

One trailer would not be enough. We took an old chassis that was built like a tank and had it converted into another trailer. The chassis had belonged to Belinda, the diesel truck that had been Mum and Dad's honeymoon getaway vehicle. The workshop in Moshi was run by the Indian dairy owned by Dad's friend Babu, essentially to keep its fleet of milk lorry *passinjas* running. Babu was suffering some economic troubles of his own, at this point, and the dairy owed us some money for several months' supply of milk, so the work was going to be done against our account. In deference to Dad's paranoia about garages and to make sure that our project didn't get put aside for some other work that might be paid for in cash, one or more of us spent every day of two weeks in the workshop, driving back and forth the forty miles between Rongai and Moshi. By that time, this was not too uncomfortable a commute, because, just in the last few months, the road had been paved to within three miles of Rongai. That is not to say that it was safer than it used to be, for the road had not been realigned. It still had the twists and turns in it that developed as the original, informal alignment evolved to avoid anthills, trees and other obstacles, many of which had long since disappeared. But it was paved, so, with the corrugations (the washboard-like ripples in the loose, graveled surface) and the blinding dust gone, one could go at much higher speeds, and most local drivers did. Most drivers were from the Marcel school of driving, the right foot either pressing the accelerator to the floorboards or standing on the brakes. Their motto was "Devil take the slowest!"

During any of these trips, whoever rode with Dad had his mental arithmetic and memory tested. "What was the number for papaïne?"

"Which number for papaïne, Dad?"

"The number per hectare."

147

"I can't remember. Maybe you did it with Bill."

"Well, we can start again. Normally, papaya trees are planted on two and a half metres but we will put them between the coffee trees, which are at three metres. How many less trees does that make per hectare? What percentage?" We'd do the arithmetic. "Now, that is the reduction in production that we can expect from the norm for papaïne, which is umpty ump kilos per hectare per month. Remember that. Now, the price for papaïne today is so many francs per kilo. Say the price drops a little, say by a quarter, the income per hectare is ... what?" We'd do some more arithmetic. "Remember that number. Now, what was the revenue with just papaya, without the coffee? We'll see if the advantage of having the coffee growing the extra year will be worth the drop in papaïne revenues." And so on.

The object of the exercise was to plan how to bring in revenue sooner than the five years that it takes for coffee to produce a crop. Five years is a long time to wait for income, particularly when you know, in advance that your starting capital will be severely limited. We went over papaïne, soybeans, ground nuts (peanuts), cotton and all sorts of things. Why we didn't do it sitting at home, with pad and pencil, I don't know. Maybe it lacked challenge, that way. Maybe it was because Dad couldn't trap us at home, while in the car we were captive.

The exercises resulted in plans to grow several crops between the coffee trees, particularly in the early years, when the coffee trees were small and the crops would not compete for space, water or light. By the time the coffee approached production of its first crop, its cultivation would essentially have been paid for by the other, temporary crops. It was a good concept which was essential to the success of the undertaking, even if the planning exercises were unwelcome to one category of the participants, causing them the kind of pain that only teenagers who have recently completed school can truly comprehend.

Not all of the mental exercises were as painful. "What was that car you were looking at? How much does it cost? With coffee fetching fifty francs per kilo, how many acres' production will it take for each of you to have one?"

With coffee fetching fifty francs a kilo, *papaïne* fetching a hundred and something, we could do lots of exercises without pain.

The only refrigeration we had at Rongai was the tiny Electrolux kerosene 'fridge that Dad's mother had given Mum as a wedding present. It worked reliably, but its freezing compartment could only hold one tray of ice. It would not be adequate in the hotter climate of the Congo. Someone told us that you could take a soft drink cooler, the kind that you used to find at service stations and country stores, the kind in which the bottles stand in water, and if you did not fill the chest with water, it would work as a deep freeze. These were kerosene powered, since half of the service stations and country stores were without electricity. They usually had a large Pepsi-Cola decal on one side. We found and acquired a new one that had not yet had its decal applied, which suited our decor better, and, who knows, by catching it before it had assumed its identity as a drink cooler, we might have made it easier to trick it into freezing instead of cooling. It worked, like a charm.

The wood burning stove at Rongai was not going to be invited to come along with us. We knew there was not much wood on the plantation to fuel it and it was cantankerous. It took considerable skill to light it, it took ages for it to heat up and when it got hot, it was very hot. It was impossible to regulate the heat. Paga had learned how to bake very good bread in it, but it was a struggle. Dad promised Mum a bottled gas stove to replace it. On one trip to Moshi, I was given some money and the instructions as to which model Mum wanted. It was a Saturday, and I got to the KFA (Kenya Farmers' Association) minutes after its noon closing and went home stove-less. Before the next time we came to town, someone gave us a kerosene stove. It seemed to work, it was as easy to light and to adjust as a hurricane lamp. It had an oven. It was easy to find fuel for it, since it was the same fuel as the tractors were going to use, whereas the bottled gas might not be so available in the Congo. It looked as though, partly thanks to my failure to get the gas stove when I was supposed to, the stove problem had been solved, and in a better way. That is what it looked like, then.

We knew that there were going to be large animals on the land. For crop protection, we would need something a little more assertive than Dad's ancient 9 mm rifle and our .22 air gun. We all were skilled shots and had used rifles for years, though mostly on targets rather than game. However, the British Administration imposed such heavy license fees on guns that one tended not to keep many, unless one was in the hunting business or otherwise could justify them. We visited the Moshi gunsmith, a Czech who had earlier owned and operated the Bata Shoe Shop in the same premises. We looked wise and nodded as he told us about muzzle velocities and trajectories and grains of lead and grains of charge. We bought a new, Czech made .404 magnum rifle which could stop a charging cape buffalo or an elephant, but would tear up a smaller animal. For good measure, and to cover the remainder of the spectrum, we bought a 12-gauge shotgun. Dad had once had a 20-gauge, double barreled shotgun. It had been a coming of age gift from his father, who was, at the time, president of the Association of Hunting Clubs of Germany, or some such organization, so this gun had been made, with extra care, to his measurements, by the best gunsmith in Germany. Its blued barrel had been decorated with a beautifully etched hunting scene. That was the gun that went missing from Melile's hut during the Mau Mau troubles, probably to be sawed off with a hacksaw, the better to suit it to its newly intended application. The guns we bought were without frill or extra feature, quite well suited to their intended utilitarian application.

Dad had always maintained a friendship with Chief Pedro Marealle, the High Chief of the Chagga tribe. He often told us that Pedro was very broad minded in that he was willing to treat him, Dad, as an equal. He said it with a smile, more ironic than joking. In colonial Africa, it was normal for the lowest European to see himself as far above the highest African, without ever stopping to think that the African might have a different perspective. This pervasive colonial mind set did not serve to make friends and influence people. It was not meant to. To Africans of standing, however, Dad's open attitude stood out against that background and it earned him much respect. One day we were driving into Moshi, when we saw Chief Marealle standing at the edge of the road, among a group of his people. Dad stopped to talk to his friend and to tell him that he was, alas, forced by the climate to leave the tribe into which so many of his children had been born and to move to a foreign country. After some discussion of the relative climates, the availability of water for irrigation and, doubtless, mulch and gravity assisted processing of coffee, Dad lamented that the people over there knew nothing about irrigation, unlike the Wachagga who seemed to be able to make water go uphill. He was not sure that we would be able to take full advantage of the huge supply of water. The river from which we would have to get it from was steep and it ran fast. It would be rather tricky. It was a pity that there were no Wachagga near to the place. Pedro, who was justly proud of the skill of his tribe with water, and who was quite capable of picking up hints[37], stopped Dad and commanded him to come to see him two weeks before we were to leave. He would appoint a true expert, the best among the Wachagga, to go with us, to stay until our irrigation system was finished.

So we acquired the services, and the membership in our entourage, of an old man whom we heard Marcel and the other Wachagga address as "Meku".[38] If his name was Meku, we naturally would call him "*mzee* Meku". We did that and noticed some smirks on the faces of the Wachagga. *Mzee* (m-zay) is a Swahili word meaning "old" or "old man" and it is a sign of respect to use it as an address to an elder, with or without his name. We all spoke Swahili fairly well, but despite being in Chagga country, we knew very few words in Kichagga. We learned, later that *meku* is Kichagga for *mzee*. We were calling him "Old Man Elder", or, perhaps, "Elder Elder". One *mzee* is a sign of respect. I doubt that with two we gave a double dose of respect. I don't think that any of us ever learned his name in the next two and a half years, and we heard him called "*mzee* Meku", even in the Congo. Since he took on a new life there, he probably thought it was fitting to take on a new name.

Someone, an American missionary, perhaps, showed Dad a book put out by one of the American home magazines, indeed, it was in magazine format, which contained information on about fifty house plans. Since it gave an artist's rendering, a brief but glowing description of each and a plan of each floor, all on a single page, you can imagine that the plans were wanting in detail. We acquired a copy of this

---

[37]Dad called broad hints "Winking with a beam."
[38]MAY-koo.

catalogue and spent some time discussing the merits of some of the designs. Dad kept coming back to a simple design for a small bungalow. The idea that a twelve foot wide by fourteen foot long living room could have a "cassedral ceiling" that soared to nine feet rather intrigued him. We have since recognized the language of the descriptions as Gushing Realtorese, and Dad would be much pleased to learn that any ceiling which slopes with the roof line is a "cathedral ceiling", even if it soars only to nine feet. The ceiling notwithstanding, this bungalow was the favoured design for a temporary home. A much bigger house, whose design seemed to fit the hill site better and to take advantage of the view, was chosen for the permanent home.

The interest, at this stage, in the catalogue and the discussions about housing were brought about by the fact that the Congo property had no usable timber on it, but Rongai had. It occurred to Dad that while we still owned Rongai, we could cut and saw much of the lumber we would need for our new home and have it essentially for the cost of the cutting and transportation. Down at the river there stood a big, old podo tree. It had a trunk about four feet in diameter and went straight up for about thirty feet before major branches began. We walked around it with a *fundi,* an expert at sawing wood. It was decided that the podo would yield lots of lumber. The unfortunate thing must have survived decades, perhaps more than a century, of all kinds of attacks by insects, disease and fire, to survive to this size, but it fell to the *fundis'* axes. A pit was dug underneath it and the *fundis* went to work with their two-man saws, one man up on the trunk, one in the pit, cutting it to usable sizes. The pit was moved to follow the work. The tree wasn't going to move from where it fell.

The wood of the podo was clean and had no rot or insect damage, but, because of the wind or its nature, all of its grain went in a corkscrew, its whole length. Every board had grain running diagonally across, rather than along it. Its cross-grain strength turned out to be minimal and the boards split or broke easily. We had a large pile of timber good only for dunnage or expensive firewood. Oh, well! Perhaps it would be best to see what timber will be available in the Congo, after all. And, since we weren't going to have a cheap supply of dimensioned lumber after all, the plan for the "cassedral ceiling" was dropped. We'd go with thatched huts, instead.

Now that we were so far along as to be planning the house, we thought some more about what we would call the plantation. Various suggestions were made. I can only remember two of them. Mum suggested 'Neu Affenheim'. Dad really looked pained at that. She dropped it. Someone suggested 'Kagando', again, and it stuck.

It became time to pack up the household things. The house had been occupied continuously for nearly three decades, by a family which did not throw things away. A dark room which once had been called the Black Hole of Calcutta, yielded boxes that contained things that had not seen the light of day for as long as anyone could remember. Among these was box which had been left in Dad's care by someone long since departed from this world. It yielded an Imperial German Army officer's helmet, complete with spike and braid and an early muzzle-loaded revolver which had six barrels. In the nearer reaches of the Black Hole, there was a collection of several decades of The Farmer's Weekly, which had survived the pop-gun wars, and which, fortunately, Dad still couldn't do without, so it came with us.

It was time, also, to plan the convoy. Polonia would be loaded with some furniture, personal possessions and some of the farm machinery, broken down into small, manageable sections. She would be carrying a heavy load herself, so she would only be asked to pull the smaller of the trailers, the one that was the reincarnation of Belinda. The newer of the Farmalls was fitted with rubber wheels. It was to pull the large trailer, with a full load of pieces of machinery. The older Farmall would ride on one or another of the trailers or Polonia, perhaps in pieces. The tractor needed kerosene, a fuel not available at your ordinary service station, so, on board there were to be a couple of forty-four gallon drums of "Voco", a can of oil and an essential can of petrol for starting. The trip would take between one and two weeks, so provisions consisting of a couple of bags of *posho*, corn meal, or some rice, was to be thrown on. Bill would ride with the tractor, captaining the crew which would sleep on the trailer's load. To protect crew and load cargo from the weather, a military surplus tarpaulin was flung over the steel pipe frames of the trailer's body. If we worked it out properly with the other vehicles, which could do the trip in two to three days, I could spell Bill long enough for him to be able to take one or two baths during the two weeks. Lucky Bill.

None of our tractor drivers, including Bill and me, were licensed to drive tractors on the roads. The tractors weren't licensed to be driven on the roads, for that matter. We set about getting ourselves licensed and the one tractor legal. Drivers who could turn the monster Farmalls on the proverbial sixpence and plough a line as straight as a ruler, came apart under the glare of Mr. Davies, the Moshi Superintendent of Police, to whom Dad had introduced me as his chauffeur when I was an (unlicensed) sixteen year old. This six-foot three, sixteen stone Welshman, an ex-Regimental Sergeant Major with a bristling mustache and matching demeanour, had reserved for himself the duty of keeping the roads safe by keeping all incompetent drivers off them. He was the only driving examiner. It was well intended, but, in a way that Darwin might have helped to explain, I think that he might have kept off the roads only the timid drivers, the ones who might have had the greatest predilection to drive with caution, while letting all the brave, uninimitable cowboys out to do what they would. It took at least two attempts for all the drivers to pass, but it was done. One, Tsingei, had more trouble than the others, which was odd, because he was technically one of the better drivers. He was showing some reluctance to coming with us to the Congo, because, he said, he couldn't pass the test. But then he did pass it, and he worried that he would be alone because he didn't know anyone over there. We said that we didn't, either, and that we could be alone together, and hadn't he survived coming to Chaggaland from Mbululand? It was not very persuasive, apparently, because the day before we were ready to head off, he disappeared without collecting his pay. Only then did we learn that he had been courting a fellow Mbulu, a woman who brewed the best beer at the *kilabu*, the drinking club, at the village of Sanya Juu. We understood. Nothing should come in the way of true love.

On the licensing trip, we picked up Meku and a nursery sprayer that had been for an extended visit to the radiator *fundi*, or specialist, who was Moshi's best solderer. Someone had sat on the sprayer, at some point in its long history, and it had been squashed almost flat and it had some leaks. Like many other things that we already owned that might possibly be usable, we knew that if we left it, it would turn out to be the one indispensable thing that we hadn't brought. It was not cheap to have the *fundi* beat it back into shape and repair it, but certainly cheaper than to replace it.

When we got home, Dad looked for his prized sprayer and shouted: *"Haki ya Mungu!* God's truth!" Normally this would be followed by: *"Akili ni mali, na wewe ni masikini ya Mungu!* Intelligence is precious and you are among God's poor!" which was not usually meant as a compliment. Because Meku was Pedro Marealle's delegate, Dad swallowed the usually automatic second half of the outburst. We looked at the sprayer. It had been squashed flatter than it had been before the ministrations of the *fundi.* Meku had used it as a seat, in the forty-mile trip in the back of the pickup. With our departure planned for the next days, it was now too late to take the sprayer back for another repair, but I think it had lost its appeal, anyhow, and Meku had already lost some of his halo. Sometimes you just can't win for losing.

We planned for the tractor to be driven day and night, stopping only for long enough to boil some rice or to make some *ugali* out of the *posho*. To make night driving possible, we needed to put lights on the Farmall, one of whose most endearing traits hitherto being that it had no electrical system. The evening that the load was being secured on the trailer and the tractor crew were packing and preparing to board, Marcel was away. I had to finish the installation of the battery, dynamo, voltage regulator and wiring for the lights. The extent of my mechanical abilities was what I had learned from Marcel and practiced on the Farmalls, over the past six months. It could be deduced that these abilities were rather shy on the electrical side, but they had gone beyond pushing match sticks into relays in voltage regulators. In fading light, I had to read and interpret the minimal instructions that came with the components and try to relate them to wiring diagrams for high school physics experiments. It was just about pitch black when we turned the headlights on. They worked. We waved good-bye to the cumbersome mid-twentieth century version of the *voortrekkers' veld schooners* in which the Afrikaners had come, at the turn of the century, to East Africa. We sat on Mum's favourite spot on the hill and watched as the light

155

slowly progressed down the farm road, getting fainter and fainter before eventually disappearing into the *korongo,* the gully between Rongai and the neighbouring farm.

In two or three days, I would follow, with Marcel, in Polonia. We would catch up with the tractor, probably before Nairobi, one hundred and seventy miles away. Bill could plan to be relieved for long enough to take his first bath then. Dad and Pauline would be along in the pickup, starting an undefined number of days behind me, to allow him his second bath.

After months of talking and planning and hard work, followed by more planning and more hard work, we really began to believe that the move was going to happen. Seven of us went to bed while Bill started to turn our dream into reality.

CHAPTER FOUR

Dreams sometimes have a way of not wanting to become reality, at least not without a fight. We had been asleep for no more than a couple of hours, when Bill appeared back at the house, on foot. The lights that we had watched growing fainter from our perch on the hill, had also been watched growing fainter by Bill from his perch on the driver's seat. They were now not working at all. The tractor was only a few miles away, hardly even off the farm, unable to continue safely in the pitch-black night. The African co-drivers spent their first night asleep on the trailer while Bill walked home for help.

In the daylight, we brought the tractor back and went to work to correct the wiring. Something was preventing the battery from receiving any charge. Maybe it needed match sticks, after all. It turned out not to be that complicated and Bill was soon ready to set off, again, this time with a little more faith in the lights. We had tested them for a while. It was late in the day, but as there were going to be many nights on the road, nothing was to be gained by waiting for morning. This time, we decided to follow Bill for the first thirty miles, until he got out onto the Arusha-Nairobi road, beyond Ngare Nanyuki. We were sure that this would be the worst stretch of road between here and the Congo, at least until he got to the road into Watalinga.

The Farmall is a field tractor. It is much more at home pulling a plough in a field than a heavily loaded trailer on the highway. It has five forward gears. The first four are for heavy work and have very close, low ratios, meaning the speed is very slow, the fastest of the four is, perhaps, capable of keeping up with a man, walking. The fifth is designed for moving, relatively rapidly between jobs or back to the barn with little or no load and can get up to twenty kilometres or twelve miles per hour. The tractor's drawbar is intentionally located below its rear axle. This makes the resistance of the load that it is pulling actually help to keep the front wheels down on the ground. This, in turn, helps considerably in steering, which is the technical term for the struggle between the driver, who has

157

some idea about the general direction in which he would like the contraption to proceed, and the mysterious forces that seem to act on Farmalls, that have a set of very different and constantly changing, whimsical ideas about where they will have the tractors go.

I was driving on the stretch towards Ngare Nanyuki, letting Bill rest up, when I discovered the corollary, or the flip side, of the advantage of a low drawbar to steering. If the low drawbar becomes a low pushbar, you have a disadvantage in steering. If your load is pushing you from behind, against a low drawbar, it tends to lift your front wheels. This occurs only if you apply the tractor's brakes before the trailer's brakes, and it matters only if you care where you are going. It adds some excitement to the process, and it introduces some degree of chance in the outcome of the trip if the operation of the trailer's brakes is not dependent on the tractor driver and his application of the tractor's brakes but is dependent, instead, on the actions or reactions of a man sitting on the trailer. It becomes more exciting if the brake man has yet to become alert enough to estimate just when his services are required, and, further, on his reacting in time for the results of his ministrations to take effect.

I had just become comfortable at the fifth gear speed when we came to a sudden, short steep drop combined with a sharp left turn that took the gravel road round a pile of rocks. This second start to the big move came very close to being aborted only ten miles farther along than the first attempt. When I braked, the Farmall's front wheels reared up in the air and bounced down on the gravel, failed to grip, reared again, gripped jut enough to tease me before going skywards again. With the front wheels in the air, the steering wheel moved freely, too freely, and I turned the wheels too far. I had to hang on to the steering for fear of being thrown off, and, fortunately, was not able to keep my foot on the brake. The wheels came down again, just in time and they bit into the gravel just enough to keep us out of the ditch.

When we opened our eyes and our collective hearts stopped pounding, we saw that we were still on the road and in one piece. Never mind, it was, surely, the worst example of that problem between here and the Congo! We kept on going.

Our guardian angel was on duty that night. He did not let

158

that bend be the end of this trip. It would have been a messy end. He chose, instead, a much more passive way of allowing us to protect us from ourselves. He did it with the very next obstacle.

A twin-axled trailer does not put any load on the tractor or truck's rear axle. A full twin-axled trailer can be towed by a truck, if the truck is also well loaded. That is because the weight of the truck's load on its driving wheels allows enough traction to develop. The same trailer can be pulled by a farm tractor on level ground or, as we've seen, sometimes, with help from superior guiding forces, downhill. However, for each given combination of farm tractor, loaded twin-axled trailer and road traction conditions, there is a gradient that is too steep to be climbed. With no load transfer to the tractor's rear wheels, at gradients above that limit, the tractor's wheels will just spin.

There was a hill at Ngare Nanyuki which was probably the worst hill where we would be likely to meet this problem between Rongai and the Congo. Surely, if we could get past the fifty-yard-long bad stretch of that hill, we could go on the rest of the way!

We tried all night, using up half of the life of the tires and destroying the road in the process. If anyone had wanted to see what happens when an invincible force meets an immovable object, all he would have needed was to bring along the invincible force. We had the immovable object. The trailer stopped at exactly the same spot each time we tried. Before long, there was a two-foot-deep trench across the road, at just the point that the tractor's wheels could reach before spinning.

At a dawn council of war, we considered the options. To avoid the hill, we could partially unload the trailer and make two trips up the hill, or go all the way round Mount Meru, which would add about one hundred miles to the trip. We were now all less sure that this was the worst hill between here and the Congo and even less sure that if we could only get over it, the rest would be a breeze. We knew that we couldn't afford to risk letting Bill have too many such experiences, far from home and with essentially no means of communication. Mum, who had been following the trailer with Dad in the pickup and had witnessed the tractor trying to act like a praying mantis, offered her opinion. We listened to reason and decided that

159

discretion was the better part of valour.

We redirected Bill and his obstinate load to Moshi, about fifty miles away. It behaved better for him, and he arrived there without further problems. In Moshi we leased a boxcar from East African Railways and Harbours. We loaded everything into it, including the tractor, which we had to take apart (served it right), but not the trailer.

A few days later, a smaller convoy started for the Congo, from Rongai. Polonia was pulling the large trailer, with a new load. The Warundi who were getting their seven-month delayed ride towards home were piled on top of the load in Polonia. The pickup followed, driven by Dad, who was concerned about the impression we might make on our arrival in the Congo if we were to allow Sengerengabo to continue to wear the Imperial German officer's helmet that had somehow come to grace his head. Some of us thought it was funny, so we didn't do anything about it. By not doing anything, then, we probably allowed a precedent to be set which later allowed the shoe incident to happen.

All of these loads did not take care of everything, so one more trip with Polonia would be necessary. Mum and Paga stayed behind, with all of the pets and the remaining, much reduced pile of matériel. Dad would have to come back, anyway, for the sale of Rongai and would fetch Mum and Paga. During that delay the temporary camp could be built on the hill at the far end. This would work out well, since we did not want Paga, who was eighty-one, to have to sleep in the truck or under canvas. When he actually came to live in the camp, he probably found it less luxurious than any tent might have been, but Paga never once complained about it.

As we drove out through The Portals, I didn't look back. It wasn't that I was not attached to the place. I was. I was too attached. We all were. Mum had asked that one acre be kept, down by the ford, close to where General Earbiter used to hang out, so that she could feel that she wasn't really leaving. We had made ourselves promises that we would be back, somehow. Richard was the first to say that he would earn a lot of money and come back as soon as he could and buy it, so Mum could live there again, forever.

When we were already down on the plain, I looked back, once, to see the whole scene of the farm, tiny against the mass

160

of the mountain. I don't remember what I saw in that glance, but it doesn't matter. I remember every curve in the land and every twist in every footpath. I've convinced myself I can still see every leaf on every tree, every pebble in the road.

I loved the place, as we all did. But the love we showered on it couldn't replace the showers that crops needed to grow. There was no future for us here. Our future was in the Congo, at least it was going to begin there.

I doubt that it was the attraction of that future that made me not want to look back. It was more likely my need to keep control of myself. Don't do something that might make you show your emotions. After that departure, I have found it easier to leave most other places I have lived.

In August, 1958, Dad, Pauline, Bill and I arrived at Watalinga. Some things had not changed in the seven months that had elapsed while we were getting ourselves ready to come. *Matete* still covered the dark black earth and the climate was still steamy hot. The best thing that could be said for Père Jean's coffee was still that it, too was black and hot. De Jaeger's beer, fortunately, was neither as black or as hot as that coffee, but, unfortunately, in all that time it had still not been able to find its way into a refrigerator.

We heard from Père Jean, over his coffee, and again from de Jaeger, over his beer, that the Brazilians had had the cheek to solve some of their disease problems and that the price of coffee was now down from fifty francs per kilo, to thirty eight. Not as good as it had been, but still pretty good.

There were signs that life had gone on. The pontoon over the Semliki had been replaced by the now completed, ninety-six metre long, single lane, concrete bridge. Père Jean's altar rail and Madonna had moved into their new places, in the new, brick church. They looked less at home than they had in the old mud and thatch building. The *gîte* at Njadot was occupied by two graduates of the Agricultural College and Chef Basikania had built another one, slightly below the old one, in the sure knowledge that he had more *wazungu* tenants coming: *Mzee Mbogo* and his family.

There was another change that we learned about over Père Jean's coffee and de Jaeger's beer. This was a change that did not seem, at the time, to be as important as the quality of the mission's coffee, the temperature of de Jaeger's beer or the

161

price of coffee. We could do nothing about it, anyway, any more than we could do anything about any of those problems. The Belgian government had agreed to start talks with some groups in the Congo, concerning a long-term plan to ease the colony into self-rule and eventual independence. The horizon, in the administration's minds, was still measured in decades. I don't know if anyone reported, or cared, what time frame was in the minds of the groups demanding independence.

CHAPTER FIVE

On our first morning we were surrounded by hundreds of Watalinga and Wanandi tribesmen. There was no telephone in the area and no other visible means of communication, but despite that, the word had got around to all villages within two hours' walking distance, that the new *wazungu* had arrived and that they would be hiring workers. Everyone who needed to earn money to pay his personal tax, or for whatever reason, a bunch of people who were just curious and their brothers, cousins and uncles, all showed up at our door. We were not only surrounded, we were mobbed.

The night before, Chef Basikania had come to welcome us and see us settled into his *gîte*. I think his visit lasted late into the night. The novelty of a *mzungu* who was willing to talk to him was an attraction more powerful to him than his sense of self preservation, which was vainly trying to protect him from hearing more than he could assimilate about mulch, gravity and breaths of moving air. As a reward for his fortitude, Basikania got to hear about all of the ancestors of this d'Ysembourg family (giving the name the traditional pronunciation when using French) who had been Belgian or nearly Belgian.

As Chef Basikania was reluctantly taking his leave, Dad had said: *"Iko shauri moja!* There is one matter! I will be needing *travailleurs,* workers, lots of them. Can you send me people who want to work?"

As he dragged himself away, Chef Basikania had promised to send us workers.

On our arrival, Dad had also seen Chef Pascal, of the Watalinga, on our way through his village, Kamango. He had casually dropped the names of the Belgian ancestors of these d'Ysembourgs and had finished with: *"Iko shauri moja!* I need workers."

Chef Pascal had noted that *Mzee* Mbourgo needed workers and promised to send him some.

So, that morning, we looked at the mob and then at each other and smiled at de Jaeger's attitude about these good

163

people. *He* couldn't get workers, but all *we* had to do was to ask the chiefs, nicely, and we were flooded! "Hah! So there, de Jaeger! You know so much!"

We assigned Joseph, the Mrundi who had come up with us from Tanganyika, the job of *"andika*-ing" (writing or signing on) the workers. It took a good part of the morning and considerable discussion.

Each man had a traditional name and a "Christian" name. We would ask, our imagination restricted by our own frame of reference, for the father's name. We knew that surnames do not mean anything, but the father's name might help us to distinguish between several people with the same names. The system in the Nandi tribe for naming children is quite simple, if you understand it. Augustin explained it to us, later. "The first child, if she is a girl, is given the name 'Muhindo'. The same name can be given to the first boy, if there is only one girl before him and she hasn't taken that name. The first child, if he is a boy, is named 'Puluku'. The second...," and so on. I can't remember if the Watalinga had a system. And if they did, the system did not apply when the birth coincided with a noteworthy or interesting event. One poor Mtalinga was called *Kakwisha,* meaning, roughly, "The Finished One." Apparently he was a sickly looking baby and they didn't expect him to live. Another was named *Mpendawatu,* Lover of People, and yet another was *Nyamayabo,* or Their Meat. (My imagination doesn't work as well for me for Mpendawatu as it does for Kakwisha, but I have a great time thinking up the conversation which led to one particular name being given to the new arrival. "Darling, we must discuss what would be the most auspicious name for our little bundle of joy. I know you've always wanted to name your son after his great uncle, the club-footed dwarf with three nostrils, but we won't inherit anything from him. On the other hand, the neighbours have just been hunting ..."). Perhaps because of their system, it seemed that there were only a half dozen names to go around for the whole Nandi population. If you know the system, you can claim to know the system, but you can't claim to be able to distinguish between all these people with the same name. (Picture a suburban playground where dozens of little folk are doing what they do in playgrounds. It is time for some of them to come home and get ready for ballet class or soccer practice.

Mothers come to their doors and shout out: "First Born Daughter! It's time to get tutu-ed!" Or: "First Son Who May or May Not Have an Older Sister, And If He Does, Her Name Isn't First Born Daughter! It's time to ..." It's time to get confused, isn't it, even among the little folk who know each other. Think of the confusion it could cause in a bank, in an army, or even on a plantation!) Obviously, knowing the father's name would add some clarity, right? Obviously! But, first, it helps to clarify the concept of "father". Your biological father's brothers are your father. Anyone who belongs to the same age group as your biological father is your father. Even if you know who your biological father is (and how many of us know that, or care?), you have a lot of people to choose from, at any given moment, to name as your father. It depends so much on where you are and on the context of the inquiry. We discovered some of this after an old renegade, André, had told us he was the father of about fifteen of the conscripts, and we began to doubt him and asked more questions. The concept of brother and sister is just as complicated. Anyone in your age group is your brother or sister. Believe it or not, the concept of mother is not any simpler. If you must know, for whatever obscure reason, the relationship in the way we understand it, between any two people who are introducing themselves as brothers, you have to ask "Do you come from the same belly?" And then "Do you come from the same seed?" And whatever you are told in answer, it is probable that you do not really know the truth, in our sense of the word. Eventually, we realized that we should leave genealogy to Dad. We found out about and then relied on the little *carnets de taxe* that everyone was obliged to carry. Whatever way the Belgian Administration had written the name was good enough. But then a man whom you thought you had figured out was named Albert might easily turn up again as Arobé (aro-BAY) and Lekisanderi (lakey-san-DARE-y) as Alexandre, even when written by the same scribe.

I can joke about it. That's because I'm superior, you see. Our European superiority, our strange systems and our inability or unwillingness to understand theirs sometimes bewildered the Africans, but sometimes it offended them, sometimes with tragic results. While we were still at Prince o', Dr. Leakey came to speak to us. He was one of the few Europeans who came close to understanding the Gikuyu. He

165

was fluent in Kikuyu and had been initiated as a member of the Gikuyu tribe. He wanted to help us to understand some of the things which contributed to the Mau Mau "situation". He covered the whole age group thing, the primacy of the extended family over the nuclear family and the fact that a Gikuyu's name is never supposed to pass his own lips. It was possible for us to see how a bureaucrat wanting to take a census could be driven bananas and to believing that every African was stupid at best, certainly evasive and evidently a congenital liar, but few of the schoolboys who heard Leakey that day could make the connection between the things we heard in that assembly and the things we learned just the day before in History. We could all recite the Ten Causes of the Indian Mutiny, including the seemingly little thing about the Army making sepoys bite the ends of cartridges covered in animal fat. But, you know, that was history. History belongs in books; it has nothing to do with today.

Anyway, the name problem was cooking our brains and the sun was beginning to cook us, so the decision was reached, without too much discussion, to wait until the next morning to start work. "Without too much discussion" is meant in a purely relative sense. Some things are done with a whole lot of discussion, some things are done with much discussion. Nothing is done without discussion.

Dad had set out what we would pay them, which was the going, government-established, rate of twelve and a half francs per day, about twenty-five American cents. We would pay them some of their wages each *siku ya posho,* ration day, Saturday, and we'd settle up for the rest of each completed month on the first *siku ya posho* of the following month, just as was the custom all across the whole country.

The next morning was a mess. Two hundred people milled around waiting to be assigned tasks. Pauline, Bill and I tried to work out where to place the men, with dozens of them crowding round us. We hardly knew where to start, ourselves, and we were supposed to put this crowd to some useful activity! We were hardly the picture of self-assured leaders.

"Iko shauri moja," said Dad, "Meku! Choose two or three men who live up in the mountain, near the river, and go start planning the furrow." Meku asked for four, maybe six volunteers and was followed by ten or fifteen men as he

disappeared up the hill.

A few minutes later: *"Iko shauri moja,* I need some men who have been *capitas,* headmen, before." Several men came forward to accept their assignments. These men were probably more qualified by their gift of persuasion than by their leadership skills, particularly our friend André, but so be it. *Capitas* they became.

Sometime in the middle of that morning, the whole lot of the newly hired work force congregated in a big, sullen looking crowd around Dad. Any crowd of people you don't know can be threatening, even if it is quiet. This one was not quiet.

"We are striking for more money!"

"We are not animals to work in this heat!"

"There are *mbogo,* buffalo in the *pori,* in there;" pointing into the *matete* with their tongues. "We could get hurt!"

"Iko mbogo porini! Shoot one so we can eat meat!"

"Oh, yeah, meat! Meat! We want meat!.."

Dad hunkered down, in his own peculiar way of sitting on the heel of his right foot and leaning his left elbow on his bent left knee. *"Iko shauri moja!"* he said, apparently not in the slightest way intimidated by them. "We agreed on the standard wages. You know the heat better than we do, and even the *Princesse,* here, is working in it, without complaint. As for the buffaloes, we do not have our guns, yet, ..." and so on.

They started looking at each other every time he said *"iko shauri moja."* After a while, they started counting. Then they cheered. They became about as threatening as a bunch of schoolboys who had just made note of their new teacher's quirks and put them away for future use.

They eventually went back to work, quite cheerfully. When they went home at the end of the day, they were able to take pride in having accomplished three things. They had tested us with their strike, they had tested us further by completing only about one quarter of the expected task and they had given Dad his new name: "Shauri Moja." It was much more fun to choose a name for him that had some significance to them, rather than simply to accept the one that he had introduced himself to them with. The name by which he had introduced himself to their chief sounded very much like *"Mzee Mbogo"* which translates as "Elder Buffalo." Such a fine name was obviously a formal name, and therefore it was more respectful to use it

167

to his face, but among themselves he would be *Shauri Moja.* So far, he had said: *"Haki ya Mungu! Akili ni mali na wewe ni masikini ya Mungu!"* only a few times. I think that the people were still trying to figure out what it meant. Certainly, had it been less of a mouthful, or even something they recognized from previous exposure, it would have become another name for Dad to enjoy. I did, in time, hear several people refer to him as *"Haki ya Mungu,"* (God's truth) but it didn't catch on.

Somehow, a telegramme addressed to Prince Isenburg, Watalinga, Belgian Congo, found its way to Beni and thence into Dad's hands. It advised him that the boxcar had arrived in Kasese, where the East African Railways and Harbours' line ended just short of the Ruwenzoris, on the Uganda side. Demurrage charges would begin to accrue for each day it stood there, beyond a date that was either already past or would pass soon.

We left lucky Joseph and all his fellow *capitas* to keep on working the way we had shown them. We dumped some of the stuff from Polonia and the trailer at the mission and some at the end of a path on our parcel. We shoved a couple of helpers on board Polonia, our camp beds into the pickup, and dashed to Kasese to fetch our stuff.

The boxcar was waiting for us on the only siding, by the godown, or warehouse, of Express Transport. This was one of the three buildings that made up the town of Kasese. The other two were the railway station and an Indian *duka*. A Scot who introduced himself as Mrs. Will's little boy, Sandy, was in charge of the affairs of Express Transport from that station. He must have been the only non-Italian in that co-op of owner-operators. Maybe that's why he was based at the end of civilization while they worked out of Nairobi. He recognized the trailer that we had bought from his chivalrous colleague and was nice enough to let us think we had done well with the price we paid for it. Maybe it was because he, too, was so chivalrous, despite not being Italian, that they suffered his membership in the co-op, albeit a membership-at-a-distance.

It took a couple of days of back breaking work to get the equipment off the wagon and loaded into Polonia and the trailer. We slept in Polonia, and when she was full, on the floor of the godown. Mrs. Will's little boy, Sandy, had left with a load for Goma-Kisenyi, and was not at all bothered that we were in and out of his building. Over the next two years, we would occasionally be wakened at customs posts by Mrs. Will's little boy's offer of a hot cup of tea. We'd drink together standing on the dusty road, on the leeward side of his lorry, while we waited for the *douanier* to finish his breakfast and come down to the office to let us through.

We ate lavishly in Kasese, since there was the *duka* so close. We had bread and sardines, of course, but we also had some kind of anchovy paste, out of a tube, and perhaps even baked beans out of a can. We washed it all down with Dad's staples, instant coffee and instant soup.

Kasese had only three buildings, but it must have had a town planner. Where he had an office, I'd be hard pressed to say. There were several streets laid out, some even paved and with signs and all. From the station, you could see the duka, a half mile away, with nothing but brown grass and several street signs to hinder the view.

The backdrop to that view was the Ruwenzori mountains, but in the west, now, instead of the east. The road past the *duka* went straight into a deep valley in the mountain and disappeared. A few miles away, at the end of that road was Kilembe Mines, a town to itself, whose copper was the reason for the railway to exist, or at least, for it to have come that far. We knew of Kilembe, but did not look for it, not that time.

We hurried back to Kagando and the work that was waiting there.

Soon, we settled into the routine of setting out the *kipaniyés* a day or two ahead. This chore had the prerequisite of a master plan, of course, so that we could spread the workers out and have the patchwork pieces all come together in the pattern of alternating thirty metres of clearing and thirty metres of virgin *matete*.

To lay out these swaths, we worked with a small team of men armed with machetes, who cut paths through the *matete*. As markers, we used pickets cut from the inch-thick stems of the grass, itself. We couldn't see more than a few feet in any direction, except along the paths we cut, but we could set out our base lines and keep them straight by sighting back along the line of pickets. We set out the swaths at right angles to the base lines using the three-four-five triangle from trigonometry. It was as easy as pie.

169

Shauri Moja stayed around for a while and handled two or three more strikes. Together, we decided where Pauline would start the coffee tree nursery, chose a rough alignment for the access road to the hill. Then we visited de Jaeger to discuss access to his *coup de bois,* so Bill could start getting the material for the camp, and we asked him, casually, without admitting that he was right about the locals, what he had had to do to get labourers from that tribe in Bunia.

About two weeks after we arrived, Dad left for Rongai, to fetch Mum and Paga. He left us with a promise to return as soon as he could, but probably in three weeks. Three weeks sounded like quite a long time, but he had a lot to do.

We started out in a mild state of shock. The old hollow-in-the-gut feeling appeared, reminding us of our first arrival at Arusha School not ten years earlier, but we soon got over it. We had a lot to do, too, with Dad's instructions as a guide, the Watalinga and Wanandi workers to control, the two Belgian colons to be treated Politely, but Distantly, the camp to be built to Catch Every Breath of Moving Air, and with the buffalo waiting in the *matete* to review our work.

CHAPTER SIX

One hot morning, we trudged the two miles to check out the newly completed camp on Kagando hill.

As we walked, someone asked: "How long have three weeks taken, so far?"

"Six, I think."

"Dad's best intentions haven't helped, have they?"

"Have they ever?"

"I wish they'd just come! I wonder what's keeping them."

Then we saw the buffaloes' calling cards left in the 'living room'. "Do you think that maybe we should move into the camp, before the bloody buffaloes take it over?"

"I think maybe the bloody buffaloes can have the bloody camp! At least they're aware that it's ready and showed up, unlike some people!"

"I don't think the buffaloes want it. They've given us a pretty pointed message as to what they think of it."

"You don't think that's a Maasai-like blessing?"

"That's bull—!"

"I see what you mean. Maybe you're right."

The mild shock of being left had given way, quickly, to the excitement of handling a lot of responsibility, of doing things on our own for the first time and of looking out for ourselves and each other. The excitement had given way, more gradually, to numbness from the hard work and the physical discomfort, and, eventually, as the time dragged on past the three weeks, to concern. The concern was masked, incompletely, by our irritation. Yes, the workers were working, at least, they were showing up, even if productivity was not what we would have liked. Yes, Pauline had got something going in the nursery, the one thing that could slow everything else down. Sure, something was definitely to be seen for our work, because Bill had started the tractor working in the *kipaniyés,* and yes, even I was seeing some progress in laying out the *kipaniyés,* ahead of the workers. But it was not all rosy.

Pauline was doing wonders in feeding us from the supply of locally grown foods, but variety was not a strong feature of the Wanandi or Watalinga diets. We spent half an hour before each meal, picking small chips of stone out of the rice, because if we didn't we could spend half an hour during each meal picking them out of our mouths, along with small chips of teeth. There are only so many ways that you can boil cracked rice and Pauline had tried every one of them. We had boiled rice for breakfast, lunch and dinner, seven days a week. For breakfast, it would be sticky, to mimic porridge. For lunch and dinner, it would do something else, to go with, or substitute for, whatever we were having or wished we were having. Nivari brought a lot of scrawny chickens to an untimely end behind our hut, so that they could help out the rice, but Dagobert lived on.

While it was not enough to make us sick, we each had dozens of small but irritating cuts on our arms and legs from the rows of tiny teeth that turned the edges of the *matete* leaves into sharp saws. We think we know why grass leaves are called blades. We were finding that the cuts turned nasty if we didn't treat them immediately. The iodine and mercurochrome disinfectant that we daubed on the cuts at the end of each day were giving us a cheetah-like camouflage.

The equally inescapable heat and mosquitoes, the lack of creature comforts and the still strange surroundings were not helping to soothe us.

So, that morning we were sounding a little upset that Dad hadn't come back with Mum and Paga when he said he would, and it didn't matter that even if they had come in three weeks the camp would not have been ready. It sounds as though we were being a bit self centred. Actually, despite being absorbed by the hard work and having the freedom to make decisions and to fend for ourselves, we were lonely and, also, not very deep down, quite concerned about Mum, Dad and Paga's progress and even their safety. Remember, we were totally out of touch. The only vehicle we had was the Farmall tractor and we had no telephone, no mail, no radio and not even a newspaper. The jungle telegraph was no substitute. It must have stopped at the edge of the jungle, because it didn't reach far enough into East Africa to bring us any news from Rongai.

Three weeks had turned into six and we wondered how long we were going to have to hold on. We wished that we just knew when they would appear. Knowing would have helped.

Throughout our short lives, each time we had gone anywhere with Dad we had had to spend hours, sitting in the car or lorry, waiting for him to come out of whichever building he'd disappeared into. Sometimes it had seemed like the better part of a day. Sometimes it had seemed like the better part of those short lives. That was chicken feed, compared to this.

Interwoven with our concern over the lack of news, and quite in spite of the visible though small signs of progress, we really felt as though we were barely in control. We worried that we could lose it and everything would dissolve into chaos at any time.

We were making a mistake in that we didn't talk openly and honestly to each other about our concerns. You know, the stiff upper lip, and all that. Had we confessed our worries, we would have helped each other very quickly to reach the conclusion that we had nothing to worry about. It was already chaos. There was no control to lose. It would have been a most reassuring thought.

We hadn't yet learned to talk about that sort of thing so we shrugged, re-stiffened our upper lips, cleaned out the buffalo mess and went about our work.

In the middle of the same morning, we heard someone shouting, excitedly: *"Shauri Moja yuko ngambo.* Shauri Moja is on the other side!" And: "He has brought *Madami,* the other *mzee* and dogs!"

Mum, Paga, Dad and Marcel had left the pickup and Polonia on the other side of the river, in Uganda, as close as they could drive on the poorly defined paths and tracks that led up to the Lamia. They had made it to within about two miles of their destination. There, they had press-ganged some local residents, *"watu ya ngambo,"* as porters and they were walking the rest of the way. Even arriving as they did, unannounced, and from a direction no one expected them to use, it seems that their presence was known before they appeared on the hill. There were ranges and time-frames within which the jungle telegraph did seem to work.

We dropped what we were doing and hurried up the hill to the camp, to find a straggling line of people struggling up the other side of the hill, carrying the cages and crates that our poor animals had traveled in from Rongai. The line included Mum, Paga and Dad, leading our four dogs.

"The animals would probably be a problem at the customs," thought Dad, "so we decided we would deliver them to the back door. Much simpler, this way. *Je?* Ai? H'm? Also, it saves them one more day of traveling."

The equipment and furniture in Polonia were not dutiable, since we were immigrating, otherwise we might easily have found ourselves carrying all sorts of things over that back door river.

The humans didn't need to be carried across, even Paga did it on his own steam, but they did need to be documented as immigrants into the country, so they had no choice, they had to go through customs.

The Customs Post was at Kasindi, on the southern end of the ever cloud-hidden Ruwenzori Mountains. We were on the northern end. We were separated by only about a hundred miles by instrument-qualified crow flight, but by a long half a day's drive. Customs were open day and night for people, but only in normal office hours for things. Since Polonia was full of things and Dad didn't want Mum and Paga to have to sleep on the edge of the road, they had to be at Kasindi in daylight. They had to get away, fast.

Fast is seldom achieved by some people, even more rarely by a certain few than by others. Within an hour or two after their targeted time, they were gone again. Even as we realized that they would not be 'home' that night, our mood was different.

I thought about the buffaloes' message, again, in the light of Mum and Dad's arrival. It was definitely a positive omen: an African welcome and a blessing.

There was no question that they had been there. We had evidence in the form of cats, budgerigars, chickens, a rooster, sundry other birds and a family of ducks, all carefully, separately, caged, and four dogs running around.

There was evidence, too, in our spirits. We were not alone, anymore. Some of the burden of responsibility would be shared. The relief we felt showed.

We set about trying to care for the animals. We opened the cats' cage, to try to give them something to drink and a Siamese cat, Josephine, bolted. Siamese cats are not very calm and you could say that she was an excellent example of the breed. So now there were four dogs and a cat running around. We saw

Josephine, on and off, for a couple of years, but she never came closer than the edge of the clearing. She "walked by herself."

Stinker was long gone, happily hunting avocados in another orchard not of this world. The most noticeable personality of the four new canine inhabitants of Kagando was Mulvaney, a brindled, single-minded, muscular bull terrier. Not all of his muscles were between his ears, a generous portion of them was spread around his frame. He belonged to Pauline, which explains his name, but you wouldn't have known that he did. You see, a long time before, when I had few fixed duties on Rongai, I was once or twice bored at the same time that Vaney was and he invented some games for us to play together. Because he found me so trainable, he adopted me. It started out with him bringing me sticks, then pebbles to throw for him. Then he began bringing me pebbles to shoot from my catapult, (slingshot) and, before we knew it, he taught me exactly where to aim them so that he could catch them in the air. He showed me that if from a range of fifty feet I could shoot a pebble anywhere within three feet of his head, he could catch it, CLACK, in flight. When I took a rest from this instruction, and he wasn't preparing for the next class by chewing on it, he'd bring one of his teaching aids to me to throw for him, and he'd attract my attention by dropping it on my foot. The aid was usually a pebble, sometimes a stone. I was almost always barefoot, so he seldom missed getting my attention. Before long, he had no teeth and I had blue toes. If you haven't met a bull terrier, you don't know the meaning of the word persistent. They were bred either to fight bulls, and to hold on even if they were being battered to death, or to be drill sergeants in the army. The army couldn't figure out how to use them if they couldn't polish brass buckles and leather boots, so the dogs had to settle for bull fighting. It was difficult to get any peace when Vaney wanted to play, which was when he was awake. When he napped, he'd have his nose on my foot and his stone one inch away from his nose. One slight move on my part would waken him and, by the time his eyes were fully open, he'd be on his feet, in his crouch, challenging me to get the stone from his mouth.

Once, sometime later, when he was asleep like that, his head resting on my foot, a panicked *sibiri*, a cane rat, that had lost its way scampered into the living room of the Kagando camp. It hadn't run five feet before Vaney had wakened fully, taken measure of what was going on, bounded across the room and snapped its neck. He did not ever do it to my feet when I moved them, not to the cats, not to the chickens or Dagoberts that strayed into the camp. I like to look for the meaning of things, so I deduce from this that my feet did not look, sound, move or smell like a cane rat. Like a cat, a chicken or a pig, perhaps, but not like a cane rat.

I had to be quite inventive to get any peace from Vaney. He liked to jump for things. I discovered that I could tie his favourite empty Nescafé tin to a branch of Pedro's tree (you'll hear about Pedro in a moment), just high enough to be out of Vaney's reach. After he'd jumped at it for hours, he'd lie down under it, looking at it while he caught his breath. During one of these pauses he must have wondered if he could get better height with a running start. I saw him try it and it worked. After I had let him hang there for five minutes, looking ridiculous with the stupid can and its attached tree in his toothless jaws, I let him down. I felt embarrassed for him, and I preferred to suffer his games rather than to have to explain to Pauline why he had died of suffocation, or eventually, perhaps, of starvation. But I did re-hang the can with a shorter string. That trick gave me weeks of peace and gave him more training than any Olympic high jumper. Alas, the tree didn't come with us to Kagando.

The chickens were not remarkable and they were not named. The rooster was splendidly colourful and was named. He was Pedro, probably named after the man who had given him, at some point, for some reason, to Mum. He had developed the habit, in Rongai, of taking his harem ten feet up into the tree that stood right outside Mum's bedroom window, every evening at dusk. Dad's deep litter chicken coop had fallen into disrepair and offered inadequate security. In the morning, Pedro would crow us all awake and then flutter down to the ground. His weight made his landings quite heavy. The repeated abuse that his landing gear took from the years of crash landings, caused his legs to grow very unusually shaped calluses. It was not only his character, plumage, grotesque legs and name that kept him out of the pot. He was as old as Methuselah, and about as appetizing.

Kagando was settled that night for the first time in the

many decades since Ngando died, by our august advance party of delegates. It should count as settling. A structured social group had come to stay, not just to pass through. Mulvaney, Carrie and the other two dogs came with us to the *gîte,* but Pedro and his women stayed in their cages, on the hill.

If the honour of being the first re-settler was not enough for Pedro, the next day his prestige was enhanced even more when his following was augmented by what was left of the Watalinga chickens, which had been our larder-on-the-hoof at the *gîte,* when they came with Dagobert and the rest of us for the formal, human occupation of the camp. The assimilation of the new harem members appeared to take place with minimal language problems.

The ducks had come all the way from Korogwe, in Tanganyika, where they had been about to be killed and cooked by their owners. Pauline had been in earshot when their sentence was announced and had quickly offered them a new home. They were going to the pot because their home was too far from water, and the owners thought that their quality of life was bad. So there they were, saved from being cooked to save them from their state of water deprivation. I know that, had I understood *kibata,* duckspeak, I would have witnessed, on the top of a waterless hill in the middle of nowhere, in the blistering heat of the equator's sun, the telling and retelling of the saga, of just how lucky they were to have a stranger come along and, in the nick of time, name them just before the pot claimed them. "Look around you!" they would have been saying, "We might have missed all this! From here we can actually *see* water."

While we were able to stay in Kagando, the ducks were cut off from all communication with other ducks. Then, when they did not leave with us, I'm forced to believe that fate caught up with them and that they suffered, very quickly and probably with little ceremony, from severe deprivation of longevity. Probably terminal cases, at that! The ironic duck adventure never made it into the great body of duck oral history and tradition. But then, there is probably not much more of a trace of any of our efforts on Kagando, now, than there is of that duck story in duck oral tradition. The ducks have stopped worrying about it. So should I.

I have worried, and still do, not infrequently, about the

more serious parallel story concerning the Warundi and the Wachagga who came with us. Only a few left with us, on our very disorganized retreat. The rest, for various reasons but at their own choosing, stayed. That was all to be more than two years into the future, at this point

Late on the next day, Polonia appeared on the path that we had cut to the hill and stopped at the little swamp. A good while later, doubtless there had been obligatory stops at Père Jean's and de Jaeger's, Dad drove up with Mum and Paga, in the pickup. Because the swamp was still impassable, everyone had to climb the hill on foot, again, but this time, up Joseph's road.

Walking up the hill was not a real hardship, we had been doing it several times a day. Its height was only the equivalent of a twenty-story building and the distance less than half a mile, but we obviously had to do something about completing the road.

As usual, Dad knew exactly what to do and had, in fact already taken some steps towards solving the problem.

"When I left, I noticed the pontoon lying on the riverbank. Shame to see that material go to waste, like that, what? I stopped in and asked the *Administrateur* if I could have the drums from it. He seemed rather doubtful, but I told him how I could use them. Well, you see, he's a good sort. He understands. He was delighted to make a contribution to the cause. Nice of him! *Je?* Ay? Hm? Wha'? He offered them to me, for the price of taking them away." And to escape from having to listen to much more of the explanations of the ways they could be put to use, and of mulch and gravity, no doubt.

Oil drums are usable and reusable for all manner of things. These ones, some of them, were to have their tops and bottoms cut out so that they could pass their third or thirteenth life as liners of a culvert over which Joseph's road would cross our swamp. Others would suffer similar metamorphic surgery to become the flue in a dryer for the papaïne that we soon would be producing. There were a dozen uses already planned for the treasure trove of drums.

Easier in the planning than in the execution.

"I thought you said the drums were ON the bank, not IN the bank."

"Well, we'll just have to dig them out. We have two hours of sunlight. Can't just give up, can we? *Je?* Ay? Hm?"

178

We had set out, Dad, Pauline, Bill and I, at the end of a day's work, with few helpers and even fewer tools, to throw a few dozen or more empty drums into Polonia and drive back with them.

Ninety minutes of digging with shovels, machetes and hands, in the smelliest, soggiest, blackest mud, freed up four drums which were movable, and uncovered two more. Our feet were in the water and, when we moved them, the mud kept our boots. The mud was holding on to those two drums with a suction that couldn't be broken. The tangled remnants of the steel hawser were helping the mud keep the drums by getting in the way of our work. If we could have cut the hawser and broken the suction, I'm sure we would have found the drums impossible to move, anyway. Being full of water and mud they would each have weighed a quarter of a ton.

The mosquitoes were threatening to fly off with anyone whose feet weren't anchored in the mud. Swatting at the mosquitoes didn't kill enough of them to make a difference and left a smear of foul-smelling mud, but it had a psychological value. Our choice was to be passive about being sucked dry or maintain a semblance of fighting back and getting dirty. Dirty won.

"I think these [SWAT] drums are stuck where they are. [SWAT] We'll never move them by hand." [SWAT]

"Well, try a little longer." Dad was not trying to sleep, so the mosquitoes were not going to be allowed to bother him. Rather, we were not going to be allowed to see that they did.

"Is someone looking out for crocs while I've got my back turned?"

"I don't see any crocs, but there are some hippos out in the middle of the river."

A few minutes but hundreds of swats later, the sun had set and it was getting dark, rapidly. There was a blast that sounded like a train engine letting off steam and a loud rumble from the river.

"That's another of them, just come up for air."

Not long after it, there were more blasts, a louder rumble, then a roar.

"You know," analytically and nonchalantly, "I think that where you're working is right in one of their paths out of the wa ... Look out! It's coming!" No longer quite so calmly, now:

179

"It'll walk right over you!"

It was the first in a line of several large hippos, each weighing several tons and probably a member of the same family (but then, they all look the same to me), and it gave no sign that it was interested in any territorial concessions, or in any negotiation or in any further delay of any kind. It came. They all came.

If we had stood our ground, we would have become planted in the bank as deeply as the drums. We got out of the way and the line of hippos walked right past us, into the grass on the bank. Then it was totally dark. The two uncovered but obstinate drums, and all the other ones that we hadn't even touched, stayed where they were. We didn't need them all that badly.

At dinner we discussed the experience with Mum and Paga.

"Hippos really can only come out of the water to feed at night," Mum explained. "Their skin is very sensitive and they get sunburn."

"Imagine a getting a burn on a skin that big!"

"I didn't know how territorial they are. Those chaps could have gone to any of a dozen paths within fifty yards of where we were, but they wanted the one we were on."

"If you're between anything that big and something it wants, you'd better pay attention and get out of the way on the first growl!"

"Imagine letting a belly that big get hungry! You'd pay attention and feed it on the first growl, no matter what's in the way!"

With the smell of the warm Semliki mud removed by a session in our own icy river-bath, our appetites were back, in force. Mum had brought with her supplies that included things other than stony rice. We paid attention to feeding our own bellies.

The next day, we had Joseph's team scoop out the muck of the swamp where the road was to cross it. We took the four drums, cut the ends open, and set them in place in two rows of two. We back-filled with earth from the bank. We called everyone within earshot to walk and stomp, back and forth, over the new causeway, to tamp down the soft earth. When Joseph pronounced it ready, we had him put on another few layers and tamp them down. Then we drove the pickup across, a couple of times, for good measure.

We could have left Polonia at the bottom of the hill, but there were things on her that were destined for the top. There were household things and some furniture. And there was asbestos cement roofing. Dad had given in to his urge to save the cost of transportation on the materials for our permanent house. He had stopped at Tororo, just inside Uganda, near the Kenya border, where there was a cement factory that made asbestos cement roofing. Well, if we couldn't save on the cost of the lumber for our future house, we would save on the transportation of the roofing.

Marcel was occupied with the tractors, so I decided to take the inaugural drive up the hill. We crossed our fingers, hoping that Polonia's temperamental batteries would start her engine; for if they didn't, we'd have to push-start her. That worked, but only just, so we kept our fingers crossed, hoping that the culvert would be able to carry her weight. That didn't work. An axle-deep hole opened up to swallow the front wheels when the first row of drums flattened under the load. With finger-crossing out of order, at least temporarily, I left Polonia's engine running for the rest of the day, while we dug her out. If the batteries failed to start her she'd have stayed there a long time, with her nose buried in the swamp.

A day later, we had recovered Polonia with the help of a tractor and the culvert was somewhat repaired and fortified.

Marcel announced: "*Bwana* Carl, this time I'll drive Polonia. I'll show you how to do this. You must accelerate across, as fast as you can go. Top speed! Before the drums feel the weight, Polonia will already be across." He placed little stock in crossing fingers, and even less in Newtonian physics.

Two more feet of earth and the fact that we had taken part of the load off the truck might have played a greater part than the physics, or metaphysics, of Marcel's theory. But Polonia did get across, successfully, if not gracefully, thereby validating Marcel's theory for him for all time. The presence of speed as a factor would have given unquestionable validity to any theory in Marcel's book.

Success was short lived. Polonia got to the first of Joseph's two hairpin bends. The combination of the sharp turn and the steep grade were too much for her. She stalled.

181

Marcel displayed his considerable skills as a driver. He was able to start the engine by rolling backwards, change back into first gear and continue. It was a tricky maneuver, involving slipping the clutch a lot and some hair-raising antics with wheel chocks by a quick-witted and fast-footed Sengerengabo, as Marcel lurched Polonia forwards in two foot increments. I didn't tell anyone, but I was glad that the culvert had stopped me on my attempt.

Coming down was simpler, in case you were worried. But the lorry's clutch and the spectators' constitutions could not take a repeat of the trip up. We had to find another route up the hill.

Rongai's Black Hole of Calcutta had yielded a surveyor's level. I was able to find it in the mass of unloaded and still unorganized things and to attach it to a home-made tripod. With the help of a staff with some marks on it, a measuring tape and *matete* stalks as markers, I traced out an alternative route, up the back side of the hill. I tried for a gradient of less than one-foot rise in ten feet of travel, which de Jaeger said was more than the steepest of any public road, and I was surprised at how much easier it looked than Joseph's slope.

Joseph went to work to build the road, following my markers rather than his nose, or whatever it was that he had been accustomed to using, shaking his head. "Maybe, if Polonia had tried a few more times, she would have overcome that hill! Perhaps she wasn't well."

We hadn't yet started to work on any part of the land away from the Njadot road. Just before Joseph began on the new alignment, I had asked him to cut a path from one side of the swamp to the other, so I could bring a tractor over without losing it in a trap. He had done this task and had told me it was ready for me. He had decided that the thick vegetation on the flat land hid too many traps, so he had gone around the swamp by going above it, just on the edge of the hill. Since he was the expert on roads, I started out on the path without first walking its length, even though we'd already seen that his skills were, in some ways, lacking. Some people just do not seem to learn quickly.

I was driving the tractor and had a turn boy riding on the big hillside plough. I think it was the first time this particular chap had ridden on a machine. We came to the edge of the swamp and the cleared path turned up the hill. Tractors are made to go all sorts of places, and I'd seen them on slopes like this one, so it was certainly better to tackle the hill than lose it in the swamp. This was no problem.

It remained no problem for at least ten yards, at which point the path turned to go across the slope instead of up it. It continued to be no problem for another thirty seconds, or so, which is when the uphill wheel of the tractor left the ground and allowed two or three of its steel teeth to cut some grass instead of propelling us forwards. The wheel came back down again, and we proceeded for a couple of seconds. I made a quick, reflex decision, the wrong one, to go on rather than turn back. Stopping and figuring out the best thing to do would have been smarter than either of those choices. Who's smart when he's eighteen? The tractors that I had seen on slopes this steep were fitted with rubber tires, which tires were filled with water and acted as counterweights. It is really useful to remember things like that at times like this. It is even better to remember them sooner.

Within a few more yards, the wheel left the ground again, and meant it. Before I knew it, I was thrown through the air, down the hill. It would have been fine, if the tractor hadn't decided to follow me. It's not true that you see your life flash before your eyes, or maybe it's only when you're going to die. What I saw flashing before my eyes, within inches of my eyes, was lots of red-painted steel wheel spikes. If any one of the spikes had wanted me, it could have had me, because I couldn't control where I was thrown or where I rolled.

I had just about stopped rolling when I heard an "Oomph!" from the turn boy. I scrambled up the slope and found him pinned under the plough, with the sharp edge of one of the disks resting against the soft part of his stomach. Something about *his* life flashed before my eyes and somewhere in the region of *my* stomach. But he seemed to be in one piece. I grabbed the frame of the plough and lifted it. It is true that in an emergency, and when you are very frightened, you find strength you didn't know you had. The young fellow slid out of the jaws of the plough and stood up. I examined him, quickly. He had a gray scuff mark where the blade had taken his measure, and he was another shade of gray all over, and he was shaking, but other than that, he was all right.

183

We left the tractor standing upside down and walked to Joseph's first road up the hill and sat down on the edge of it. At least I did, to hold my head in my hands and to reflect on how lucky I was to be alive. I think the turn boy went off for some medicinal *pombe,* to help him not to think about how lucky he was to be alive. A short while later, not ten minutes, Dad came by with Mum, in the pickup. They had been in Kiesegeta, about ten miles away. They had heard, already, that *bwana* Carl and the tractor had fallen. They didn't know any more than that, but that was already a lot to know. I had spoken to no one and the vanished turn boy was the only witness that I knew of.

Dad saw that I was unhurt and immediately asked about the tractor. I told him I'd seen some drips of gear oil coming out of the gear shift lever mounting. On the "Don't just sit there thinking you're lucky to be alive while the precious oil that we can't replace here is pouring out of the tractor do something!" principle, he sent me at once back to the scene, with a worker who had been with him in the pickup, to make sure that whatever oil might be spilling was collected.

I remembered a similar situation. About four years earlier, Dad had suggested I try his new motorcycle. At that point, I was not an experienced driver, and the strangeness of the hand throttle, hand clutch and foot operated gear shift caused me some confusion. I tried to get into a lower gear, with low revs, to slow the bike down as I approached the plank over the furrow. Somehow I got in to a high gear, at high revs, which propelled the bike and me with it, across the furrow, into the air and then down the hill, at a frightening speed. It *was* frightening. I was so scared that I bellowed at the top of my lungs.

I yelled something carefully designed to undo the mistake and put everything back under control. Something really useful, like: "NO! NO-O-O-O!"

The roar of the bike engine and my screams brought out a crowd to see what was going on. It brought the milkers running from the cattle *boma,* it brought the workers more reluctantly out of their daily line to collect their *posho,* and it even brought all of the passengers of the milk lorry, even the world-weary driver, at a more sedate pace, befitting his status, to see what was going on. This sounded like it could be the most exciting event of the week, they wouldn't want to miss it, any of them. It also brought Dad running down the hill from the house, motivated by a very different concern, just in time to see me pull myself out of a large pile of dry brush that had snagged the manned missile out of the air as it was about to go ballistic.

In one glance Dad saw that I could stand on my own legs, my own wobbly, scratched, rubber legs, so he showed his concern by asking: "Is the bike all right?" The bike's ability to carry Dad around Tanganyika was the only thing between us and total poverty, so it was not an inexplainable concern.

Anyway, such was the tractor's state of balance, or imbalance, on Kagando Hill, that the two of us, one again with rubber legs, were able to roll it back upright. It was easier to do that than it would have been to find something to catch the oil in.

I myself supervised the cutting of a new path before I drove the tractor out. I may learn slowly, but I learn. The once and never again turn boy took up another calling.

While Joseph's team was creating the new road, which meant digging soil from the uphill side of the line of pickets and pushing it to the downhill side, to create a ledge the width of the track made by Polonia's wheels, we had some interesting talks.

"*Bwana Kallo,* do you know why people always move away from you when you come near to them?"

I had noticed this behaviour. I had some theories, mostly to do with the different culture and the relative novelty of *wazungu* in this area. Maybe to them I had an unpleasant smell. I said: "No. Why?"

"It is because of your stick. They fear that you will beat them with it. The *Wabelji* beat people a lot. Don't carry a stick! The people will not fear you if you leave your stick. Then if you come close to them, they will not move away."

My stick was a carved walking cane that André had produced and given to me the day he had been appointed a headman. It was a nice piece of handiwork. I liked it for the help it gave in pushing through the *matete* and I liked its heft in my hand. I had developed a swagger, as I walked with it, that would have put a big city dandy to shame. Apart from the fact that I liked my cane, Joseph had unwittingly given me another reason not to be immediately inclined to go along with his

185

suggestion. It was hot. The work that the men were doing was dirty and very sweaty, so they tended to wear their oldest clothes and those old clothes smelled. Given that when they did use soap it was likely to be a locally made brand that was so strongly and pungently scented that you could smell it a mile away, it is unkind, but to some extent true, to say that I did not look on it as a disadvantage that they moved away a little when I approached.

Joseph was in a talkative mood. "One *Belge* in the *Travaux,* you know, where I learned how to make roads so well, used to beat people. He beat us very badly. Even if we stopped work only because we were tired, he would beat us and beat us."

A pause, then: "He's not there anymore."

I said: "That is one *mzungu* you must be happy to see go back to Europe."

"He didn't go to *bulaya.* One day the workers led him into the forest." The sharp points of his filed teeth showed through his smile.

"What happened?"

The experience now seemed to have been less firsthand. "It was a long time ago. Maybe it was in the time of my father."

"So, what happened?"

"As I said, it was a long time ago. Nobody knows. *Wanasema walipiga ye!*" Kinguana, the local version of Swahili, is an economical language. The word *piga* means both 'beat' and 'boil.' It is quite possible that he meant: "It is said they beat him!"

I dropped both the subject and the habit of carrying my fancy cane, or any cane.

CHAPTER SEVEN

The nights were cooler and the mosquitoes didn't bite as much. It could be that mosquitoes do not fly to the top of seventy metre hills. It could be because we were catching every breath of moving air. It probably was that the family was now back together, again, and the basic cause of our discomfort, our insecurity, was gone and we simply didn't notice the heat and the mozzies.

We each happily took on and went about our own set of duties. Fairly happily. Life settled into a routine.

Every morning, at some ungodly hour, Pedro would come and stand on the half-door to the half of the hut that we boys shared, and he would crow. It is a hell of a way to wake up! Pedro's reveille was immediately effective in two ways and had a slightly indirect effect in another. It wakened us, immediately, and it developed, immediately, a very special relationship between Pedro and Bill, who, at the ripe age of seventeen, cherished his sleep even more than the rest of us did. It could not get us moving immediately out of bed. A few minutes later, though, Dad's cough from a lifetime of smoking, having been stirred by Pedro's call, would kick in to action. "COUGH ... COUGH ... Cough ... Cough ... cough ... cough! W H E E E E Z E! gasp! COUGH ... COUGH ... etc. ... W H E E Z E! Ach! Gott!" Before the second or third gasp for breath, we moved. Fast. We would be at the breakfast table before Dad, or we would regret it. If we showed a lack of enthusiasm to get to work, Dad would let us know, with a total lack of subtlety, that we were letting the side down. It was good to get a lot of work done before the sun got very hot and we knew it. But bed was so much better! Stealing a few more minutes was worth risking Dad's displeasure.

Mum ran the household. When John and Richard were home from St. Mary's, there were eight of us, so Mum was running a minor hotel rather than a home. She provided us with three cooked meals every day, with lunch often staggered through the afternoon.

Breakfast had always consisted of *"mealies,"* or maize

187

meal, porridge. It was good stuff, it stuck to your ribs and let you keep working until late in the day. In Kagando, we did not yet have a source to replenish the supply that had come up from Rongai. We had had enough rice, for a while, so Mum made wheat porridge from flour grown and given to us by the von Kalcksteins. Wheat porridge was not as satisfying as the *mealies,* but it would do. Paga was using the same flour to make bread.

At some point, I noticed that my eyes were doing funny things. I had difficulty focusing and my eyes were sensitive to the sunlight. Mostly, the problem started a short time after I got down to the fields and ended by midday. I was worried that it had to do with the harsh sun, but the effect was worst when the sun was not yet at its strongest. A funny sensation in my stomach gave me the idea that it was something I was eating, but no one else was being bothered in the same way. I skipped porridge, one day. The problem was gone. Days that I ate the porridge again, the problem came back and it was worse if I also had bread. I talked to Mum about it. She remembered that Inge von Kalckstein had said that the Kenya Farmers' Association had not wanted her wheat because it had "a bit" of *dattura* in it. *Dattura* is a plant that was grown extensively, before the war, for its properties as an antihistamine. It had become a prolific weed everywhere in East Africa, avoidable in a wheat crop only by expensive spraying with herbicide. The *dattura* in the wheat flour was dilating my pupils. I don't know just how much "a bit" of *dattura* is. I stopped eating the porridge and cured my problem.

The stove in Mum's new kitchen was a two-wick kerosene thing that, when it worked well, belched black smoke. With two burners, you could boil two pots at one time. The oven consisted of a box that sat on the two burners. If the oven was being used, nothing else could be cooked. When the stove was only smoking, at least it wasn't dangerous. Every now and then, for reasons it alone understood, instead of smoke, it belched flames that licked towards the thatch roof. Mum and Pascali became experts at snuffing out the flames with a large pan. They never dared leave the thing unattended. To supplement the efforts of the stove, a fire was usually going between three stones, outside.

Apart from being a Lieutenant in Mum's Fire Brigade,

Pascali spent a good part of the day going about a quarter of a mile to the river with *debes,* four gallon cans, on his head, for there was no water on the hill. He also carried and heated bath water for us all, on the three stones, and he did the laundry and the dishes.

Baths were taken in an old galvanized tub. It had been the laundry tub, in Rongai, but was promoted after the move. The tub was set up in Pauline's bedroom, which was about the only place with a bit of floor space and it was the room closest to Pascali's three-stone fire. Pauline couldn't go to bed until everyone had had a bath, but, since the tub was simply emptied out onto her floor, she had the benefit of having the least dusty floor of the camp, and therefore the fewest fleas.

An important part of running the household was the operation of a small, informal dispensary or clinic. Every Mtalinga and Mnandi within walking distance, and sometimes within carrying distance, came to Mum for treatment of everything imaginable. Most usual was *"nyoka tumboni",* snakes in the tummy. The *nyoka* were usually treated with Epsom salts. Sometimes, though, they would be all over the body, climbing from the stomach, round the side and up the back, to the neck, biting as they went. Those snakes were very difficult to treat, but somehow, Mum found a pill, potion or lotion, something, that might have some power over them. A change in diet and lifestyle, not to mention sleeping in a bed rather than on the ground probably would have done more for all of the complaints than any of our pills could. What they really wanted, of course, was for Mum to give them an injection. Any medicine that hurt the way a needle did had to be effective medicine. Of course, the corollary was that if medicine does not hurt as much as a needle, it cannot be as effective. Anything short of an injection would have to be looked on as a stop gap, until the patient could find a *"mganga,"* a "doctor" with a syringe. Anyone with a syringe and a needle could make a good living, pumping something, anything, into his patients. If the patient got well, despite the treatment, it just proved how effective it had been. If he died, well, life was short, his time had come and he wouldn't be around to discourage other patients, anyway. Nothing you could say would convince the people that these injections could be lethal. Didn't they see the *daktari ya wazungu* giving

189

them, all the time? The more we tried to teach them, the more they suspected us of just not wanting to share the benefit of our powerful medicine with them.

Mum was most careful to be serious with her patients. She hadn't always been. Several decades earlier, as she changed a dressing on a woman's badly septic big toe, she had joked about what would be the most effective treatment. The woman had not come back again for a new dressing, which was not unusual. She eventually did come back, days or weeks later, and proudly showed off her foot. The septic wound was gone. She said, happily: "See, *Memsabu!* I did just what you said. You were right, now it is all cured. Only my husband had to help me cut it off with his ax."

Some of the cases that came to Mum were very sad. The local Africans cooked on wood fires between three stones, usually inside their huts. The huts had no windows and the only light was from the fire. Children crawling around in the dark, or in the little pool of light from the fire, while their mothers cooked, were very susceptible to falling into the fire or pulling pots full of boiling water over themselves. The burns were terrible and there was not much Mum could do for them, other than to dress them and send them on to Ernesto, the medic at the government run clinic, down by the mission.

Sometimes, Mum was asked to help with a difficult childbirth. During a typical delivery, the womenfolk would gather around the mother and assist her by wailing and carrying on in a way that was supposed to show sympathy and support, telling her how much pain she must be in and how much more horrible it could still get to be. It probably only helped her to get really tense, which I'm told is not the best way to be for that particular procedure. Mum's prescription for that was a slug of whisky or rum. If Dad was not out of his medicinal rum, or Paga wasn't guarding his last half bottle of carefully rationed Dimple Haig, she'd swipe a "tot" of the most accessible one of the two and send it off with instructions for use. She was careful to say that it was most effective when chugged by the mother-to-be, rather than by the helpers. They could go on doing the wailing, let her do the chugging. The sudden calming and relaxing effect of the unaccustomed hard liquor usually produced results. A day or two later Mum would be introduced to the new member of the family and would be given a few eggs or some other gift.

Once, though, we were wakened, at about three in the morning, well before Pedro's time. A Mnandi who did not know us had braved the dogs to come and shout in through the door of the hut of the strange *wazungu:* "Bwana! Bwana! Please help me!"

Sleepily: "Who is it?"

A name was given and not recognized. "I'm from up in the mountain."

"What is it?"

Very distressed: "It's my wife. She's having a baby."

Still sleepily: "That's OK. Happens all the time."

"But, *bwana,* it has taken four days!"

Less sleepily, now: "Oh!"

"And, *bwana,* the body is out, but the head refuses to come out!"

Not at all sleepily: "Where is she?"

"Here, on the hill. We carried her here. She is very sick."

Bill volunteered: "Put her in the pickup, we'll take her to the dispensary."

We didn't know what else to do. The mother was put in the back of the pickup, with whatever they could find to make her more comfortable, and Bill drove her down to Ernesto. Ernesto was in a drunken stupour and could not be wakened. Bill did the next best thing he could, which was to drive her, gingerly, the fifty miles to the American mission hospital at Ouisha, near Mbao.

When he got there at dawn, she was dead.

Paga undertook to make the camp livable. There were no locks, doors, windows or plumbing fixtures to repair, but he found an endless stream of things that needed attention and he kept them in good working order. Dad had a large library of books, packed away in trunks, that Paga would bring out and examine. If it was necessary, he'd repair the bindings. He read or skimmed each book as he worked on it. He was a very self-sufficient person and could keep himself entertained. In the two and a half years that we were there, he left the hill only a few times, but I don't think he was bored once.

It was Paga's self-appointed task to light the Tilley kerosene pressure lamps. This involved a ritual and marked the end of the day. The lamps had to be filled with fuel, using

191

a tin funnel. The pre-heating element, which was kept in a jar of methylated spirits, or "meths," was clamped to the stem of the lamp and lit. While the meths was burning, Paga would pump up the pressure in the tank until the little button-gauge showed that the pressure was right. The pump made sounds something like the noises that we boys could make in our armpits, but more mechanical, quite distinctive, really. The sounds could be heard throughout the camp, as they had been within a hundred yards of the Rongai house. The sounds signaled the start of the time when the whole family gathered together, to read, eat and talk. It brought us in as surely as the sound of any monastery bell ever brought in its monks to prayer. By the time the meths was about to give out, the mantle and the vapourizer would be about hot enough for the kerosene to vapourize. Paga's quick twist on the valve would cause a "pop" and there would be a flood of bright, white light. Several times during the evening, the light would dim a little as the pressure decreased or some dirt blocked the jet. Somebody would get up, give the pump a few strokes, burp the lamp and sit down again. This maintenance was not so definitely claimed as Paga's territory. There were several hurricane lamps, *fanusis,* which could light the way to King's Club, or between huts, but only the two pressure lamps gave enough light to read by. It would have been more convenient for us to have more, but it also would have made it easier for us all to go our own ways and a daily communal time would have had no reason to happen. I am glad that during our search for equipment for the move we never found any more lamps.

One of Paga's pleasures was the card game, cribbage. Back in Rongai, somebody would play a couple of games with him, in the light of his lamp, almost any time he suggested it. Sometimes there was a game each night for weeks on end. Mostly, the game was serious business and anyone holding it up would be nudged and told to keep his mind on the game. Sometimes, Paga would reminisce about his childhood in Scotland, his youth in South Africa and the early years on Rongai. No one ever suggested that he should keep his mind on the game. We wouldn't have needed to. Even when he was in the middle of his stories, he seldom lost. If there were too many volunteers, we played in teams. In one such game, one of us made an embarrassing sound and we all tried to ignore it

192

because we were still a bit in awe of Paga. But Paga reminded him, very quickly, that there was not supposed to be any communication between team members. A lot of the awe dissolved that night, in the laughter.

In one of his stories, he was underneath his lorry, adjusting its brakes, or something, when a passing Maasai *moran*, a warrior, stopped to stare at him. Paga was a patient man, about some things, but he didn't like people seeming to have nothing to do. Staring at him was not an acceptably productive activity, besides, he hated being stared at. He didn't speak *kimaasai*, his "Shoo!" didn't get the desired result, so he resorted to magic. He allowed his false teeth to drop onto his tongue which he then stuck out at the *moran*. It had exactly the effect Paga wanted. The man bolted. Paga congratulated himself. He had found a new weapon with which to protect his privacy.

The very next day, Paga was busy doing whatever he was doing, when the same *moran* appeared. He was accompanied by twenty other *morani*, probably his entire age group, each carrying spears and a *simi*, the Maasai double edged sword. They were all very excited and it took a concerned Paga a few moments to understand what was going on. Finally, it dawned on him what his friend from yesterday needed him to do. He obliged. He demonstrated his trick with his teeth. It did wonders for the enhancement of his friend's prestige, but did nothing for the future of his own privacy.

At times like these, we could sometimes get Mum to tell us, again, about spending one of the first nights of her honeymoon, in Belinda, stuck on the railway tracks, with a train coming. There was not much suspense in the story, it always ended happily, but we loved to visualize the scene. We could as good as see the African cook running back along the track towards the train, wildly waving his blanket. We could imagine the engine driver seeing this and wondering if it was a native from the bush, excited at the sight of his first train, a drunk or the village idiot. We imagined what would have happened had he not played it safe and brought his wood-burning, smoke-belching monster to a hissing, screeching stop, just in time. We could see the passengers get out to stretch and to see what was wrong, this time, and then good-naturedly helping to push the lorry off the tracks before getting back on and continuing their trip.

193

Or, we might get her to tell us about the night Dad saved the chickens, in Rongai. The chickens were going to lay eggs that would supplement the income from the cows. They were housed in a coop just beyond the line of jacarandas. To protect them from any two-legged marauders, they were only about fifty yards from the house. The four-footed kind were, Dad hoped, going to be kept out by the wire mesh. One night, Dad had gone to bed in his usual pajamas, his birthday suit, and was reading a few more pages in his book, or The Farmers' Weekly, before turning off the Tilley lamp for the night. When he heard an awful noise from the chicken coop, he jumped out of bed and threw his dressing gown over his shoulders. In one he hand grabbed the lamp and in the other the first thing that he could lay his hands on, a riding crop that had hung on the same hook on the back of the door for ever, and dashed out to the chicken coop. Through the dust and the flying feathers, he saw the animal that had torn the wire and was killing chickens. He whacked it across the rump with the riding crop and watched it jump through the hole in the wire and run away, maybe more surprised and confused than frightened. He stalked back to bed, his hands full and unable to prevent his untied robe from blowing back from his shoulders, giving him part of the look, but none of the macho swagger, of a Maasai warrior. Mum's question he answered, calmly: "It was just a leopard!" As he said it, he realized what he had just done and his calm vanished.

A neighbour had had half of his face bitten off and his shoulder badly mauled by a leopard. Like a real *mzungu,* the neighbour had been armed with more than a riding crop, and had been fully clad, too. Perhaps that was his mistake. Maybe the Maasai dress code has something to do with their legendary prowess in hand to hand combat with big cats.

The Maasai dress code might work against wild animals, but it didn't help against wild Scotswomen. Mum would tell us about when Sims is saw a *moran* leading a calf. The calf didn't want to go where the *moran* wanted to take it, so there was a bit of a tug-of-war going on, with the calf's leg looking like it would be the loser no matter who won. The calf was protesting in pain. Sims asked the man to stop hurting the calf. The man was a foot or two taller than Sims and was probably carrying two spears and a *simi*. He looked at her blankly, not

194

understanding her. If he could have understood what she was saying, he wouldn't have understood why, or what concern it was of hers. She repeated her request. He ignored her and hurt the calf again by yanking on the rope.

At this, Sims grabbed the unsuspecting Maasai by the leg, up ended him and dragged him for a few feet, saying: "Therrre, see how you like being trrreated like that!" We wondered if the chap saw the light and went off to join the RSPCA. Probably.

We could get Dad to tell us about how he stopped the Adler touring car he drove for a while, literally with its nose under the belly of a giraffe. And he could be got to tell about the time he was riding Peppy, the donkey, in Karatu, when he awoke from a daydream, to find himself in the middle of a herd of grazing elephants. We didn't mind hearing, again, how he had left Belinda in Nairobi, to be fixed, leaving a turn-boy there to sleep on the lorry, as a watchman. Dad was supposed to get a telegramme when it was ready. The first thing he knew about it being ready was when the turn-boy walked up to the front door at Rongai, to report that he needed fuel. No one could understand why he needed fuel, so he explained that he had run out, down on the plain near Longido. They couldn't understand that, either, until he explained that he would have driven Belinda all the way home, but for this mishap. He had never driven in his life before, possibly never even sat in the driver's seat. Which explained why it took everyone so long to grasp the situation. Also why he had with him on the truck, a part of the garage building that he had acquired as he negotiated the exit from the garage.

In Rongai we were young and the stories were an important part of the evenings. On Kagando, we were much older and of course much more sophisticated. The stories were less important, but the light still brought us all together in the "living room" for reading and conversation. Paga still could count on someone to give him a game of cribbage. He could still count on winning.

A habit that Paga had had as long as we had known him was to listen to the BBC World News. It was very clear to us that that was really the only reason to have a radio and the only use to which it ever should be put. Our radio was an old Philips that ran on a six-volt car battery. In Rongai, Jock had once rigged a battery to a wind-powered generator, so the battery was constantly recharged. Jock wasn't there, with us, and nor was his genius with things mechanical. We had to resort to the crude solution of borrowing the battery out of the pickup, or one of the two in Polonia, each night and putting it back in the morning. We made sure that whichever vehicle was lending us its battery was parked on a slope. If delivering the news to Paga drained too much out of the battery, a short roll down the slope would kick the engine into life. Actually, we always parked on a slope, if we had the choice. Batteries had a way of waking up dead in the morning, news or no news.

Pauline was in charge of the *pipinière*, the nursery. She had received a crash course from Joe and Rene Cassel, which she supplemented by a visit to de Jaeger, and she knew what to do to get from seed to healthy, field-ready plants in eighteen months. She had the patience to tend to the details. The males were much less prone to see that work through. Give us the slashing, cutting and tractor related work, any day, even if it meant a lot of walking.

Pauline was lucky, we assured her, that she could have Kakwisha, the "Finished One," the one who hadn't had the energy to die when he was born. He was so well suited to the type of work she would be doing, you see. With Kakwisha, Izidori, who had lost some of his toes to jiggers, or some other such thing, and a couple of other specimens, she could fulfill her need to take in strays and lame ducks, lame anything, while preparing for planting about an acre of land that Bill had plowed for her. It was close to a small spring and swamp, for access to water. She made beds and built stick frames over them. On the frames, she laid cut *matete* to create partial shade. On the surface of the shaded beds, she placed the coffee seeds touching each other, in rows about two inches apart. Then, several times a day, until they sprouted and grew to about two inches, she would water them. At that point, she pulled the little plants out and replanted them in another bed, no more than four inches apart. In this second bed, she watered them a little less frequently, but still paid them a lot of attention. Some weeks later, she would move them, again. This time, they would have no shade and would stay put until they went into the field, at eighteen months. To the rest of us, it looked like an awful lot of fuss, but she knew what she was doing.

196

"It really is less work like this. It means that I don't need to shade and water such a big area. And, I think it makes for tougher plants."

Bill and I could understand all of that, but we were thankful she was there to figure it all out and to fuss with it. We would have gone crazy with the finicky work and the hours of bending over. And dealing with Kakwisha and Izidori.

Some of the *matete* was so dense that nothing we tried to do with the tractors made much of an impression. The tractor would knock over the tall stems and the disks of the plough would just ride over them, unable to bite into the soil. Some of those areas were left for the workers to cut down and clear by hand, some were treated with the tractor knocking down the *matete* and workers clearing a break along the edges before setting a fire. On much of the land, there was a mixture of *matete* and its junior cousin, *mnyasi*. The latter was much shorter and had much thinner stems. It was, in fact, what we had used for thatch on the camp. In these areas, the plough had a better chance to bite through the flattened grass and it was worth sending the tractor in before the men.

Bill enjoyed working with the tractors and spent most of each day with them. Before he had been at it two days, he asked us the question: "What is the difference between an elephant and a Farmall?"

To which question one of the answers was: "An elephant is too smart to fall into a Farmall trap!"

The engineers of International Harvester knew about prairie gopher holes. They didn't have much exposure to the pitfalls, so to speak, of working in a country shared by elephants and Watalinga tribesmen with an appetite for elephant meat. The narrow spacing of the front wheels of the Farmall was designed so they could fit at least reasonably well between crop rows, where, incidentally, the occasional gopher hole could be easily seen and dodged, though it posed little danger. In fact, coincidentally, the narrow spacing of the wheels fit perfectly into the elephant traps, which were designed to be quite invisible in the *matete*.

Frustrated from spending several hours each time to get a tractor out of a trap, Bill worked out a system that was simple but effective. A worker walked ahead, on foot, with a long stick. He would probe for and mark traps in the path of the tractor.

197

He could stay ahead of the tractor, which had to be in a low gear. After one or two runs around the *kipaniyé*, hurdling the fallen *matete*, he would be exhausted so he would be spelled by someone who had rested. Effective as the system was, it did slow down the work. Bill often was in the field until it got too dark to see.

We all worked, all day, every day. We had no friends and left the plantation only to go Mass at the mission. We began to feel cut off from the world.

One day, Bill said: "I don't even know what's on Hit Parade! I used to know all the tunes."

It was just the three of us talking, we got quite bold. "What would happen if we tuned in to Hit Parade on Paga's wireless?"

"We're not going to get the sack, or anything"

"Well, they can take it out of our pay!"

"They can have *all* of *my* pay!" We weren't being paid. Did I tell you that?

"Let's do it this Sunday!

On that Sunday, while Bill was finishing up some ploughing, Pauline and I set up Polonia's battery half an hour earlier than necessary for Paga's news, and tuned in. Hit Parade was carried on Cable and Wireless, Nairobi, at 5:30 and it ended at 6:00 p.m., when Paga's BBC news came on. It was still light at that time of day. Bill would have to remember to stop before the darkness stopped him. From the hill, we could see the whole plantation, but we didn't need to look. We could hear that Bill was still ploughing, and Hit Parade was coming on in a few minutes. He was two long miles away, on foot. There was no way that he would make it in time. He was going to miss it, for another whole week, and we didn't know how brave we'd be, next week.

Joe and Rene Cassel had given Pauline a 125 cc motorcycle, the smallest one BSA made. She couldn't ride it, at that point, which was fine with me, because I got to use it. With the bike, Bill was only two short miles away. The distance could be covered in minutes. I dashed down, on the bike, to where Bill was working, caught up with him at the end of one of his passes, and signaled to him to stop. He looked at the sun, understood my signals, parked the tractor and hopped onto the metal rack of the bike. I opened the throttle wide and we zoomed towards the hill as fast as the tiny motor could take us.

The air temperature, the load and the unseemly haste were a combination that was just made for trouble. The bike had only one seat for the sole purpose of limiting the load to one person. Small two-stroke engines do not like being overloaded. They register their disapproval by overheating and going on strike. This one was true to type. It struck. We pushed the bike home from the spot, a few feet up from the bottom of the hill, where it finally told us that it had had enough. Breathless, tired, hot and dirty, we caught the last notes of the BBC signature tune at the end of Paga's news.

In itself, this little adventure was unimportant. We had other chances to hear the Hit Parade, which was, after all, not the most important thing in our lives. Trivial as it was, it does illustrate the frustrations that our plantation life gave us, every day, at all levels, particularly with respect to our personal and social needs and wants. For the most part, our social life outside of the family was limited to Sundays, after Mass, sharing a cup of bad coffee and smiles with Père Jean while Dad shared bad coffee and politics with him, or, an hour later on the way home, sharing a warm beer and smiles with de Jaeger while Dad shared warm beer and coffee prices, techniques for harvesting and drying papaïne, mulching and gravity powered processing of coffee harvests with him.

A gratification as simple as listening to a half hour of pop music on the radio, once in the week, didn't seem like much to ask for. Little as it was, it was hard to come by. We wondered, among ourselves, about what life outside in the real world of Nairobi might be like.

The prospect of our own plantation was sometimes enough to put the frustrations in their proper perspective and to save us from getting too sorry for ourselves.

"When my place is up and running, maybe in five years," ten was more likely, but it was too long a time for me even to comprehend, "I'm going to ... er, I want to ...What am I going to do in this place, anyway? Invite some Greek shopkeeper's daughter to come look at the *matete* grow?"

Dad, an accomplished dreamer himself, was not one to let a dream go undeveloped, or to puncture anyone else's fantasies. He offered: "When your own place is in production you don't need to be here all the time. You could get a manager to run the place. I think you can hire one for one hundred thousand francs per year."

That was about two thousand dollars, a lot of money, to our ears, but not difficult for a successful plantation to afford. The mention of that kind of money turned our imaginations loose.

"I'm going to have a small plane and fly in and out whenever I want to. Maybe the manager can run the place while I live in Mombasa ..."

"Lamu!" said Pauline.

" ... and we could have a radio for emergencies. The bottom stripe of *matete* would be a good landing strip."

"Kiesegeta [where there was land that Bill and I were mentally reserving for ourselves] looks like it could have a good one, too."

For a while, the dreams worked to keep order in the ranks.

Dad didn't discourage any of them, in fact, as you've seen, he often helped them along. In his youth Dad had seen, if not himself enjoyed, great wealth, but he had very simple dreams. He wished only for a good future for his children, a future in keeping with their heritage, for a comfortable old age with Mum and for "security for Mum after I'm gone." Visits to Europe with the family would be nice: they would help to keep us in touch with our "relations and connections." He had nothing against Greek traders, or even Flemish planters, but he thought it would be good for us "to meet our own kind."

I said his dreams were simple. That is not completely true. They were simple until you heard the details. The trips to Europe were not to be as mundane as getting on a plane in Nairobi and getting off in Frankfurt. First, we would find a suitable diesel truck chassis. We already were examining every chassis we saw. Then we would build a caravan on it. We were already looking for designs. There must be magazines with caravan designs in them, the same as there are for houses with "cassedral" ceilings; all we have to do is write to America. The design would include a kitchen with a fridge and a deep freeze and a "douche" with running water, heated, why not, by solar power. There would be a built-in generator for the fridge, freezer and lighting. Don't forget that underneath there would be storage for the gear that would be needed for the trans-Sahara part of the trip. It might be worthwhile having four-wheel drive for that part of the trip, despite the cost in higher fuel consumption. Balloon tires would be best for the sand, and maybe would make wire mesh rolls unnecessary. Maybe we'd need snow tires for the winter; they could be carried underneath, too. Maybe we should avoid the winter in Europe, Paga shouldn't be subjected to that. But there would be plenty of mud between here and the Sahara, for the snow tires to be needed, anyway. They say that there is no road through the southern Sudan. ... ...

Well, as I said, there was no television.

Sometimes we heard about Mum's dreams and not very deeply hidden desires. "I wish I had a real kitchen. It would be even better if it had running water."

At the beginning, I was mostly concerned with setting out the work for the next day. With a team of men armed with *machetes* and Joseph, Augustin or someone else who could read numbers on the far end of some measuring tapes, I laid out miles of lines crisscrossing the *matete*. I used to look at one of our neighbours, setting out his clear-cut fields with a surveyor's transit, capable of measuring fractions of a degree. Whether I was feeling superior over his obvious lack of imagination, or envious of his investment in the right tools, I can't remember. The fact is, his coffee trees seemed to snap to attention and salute, row by row, as you moved past them, in a way that would have made a drill sergeant in the Marines proud. Our fields never looked tidy. Some of that was because we had the mulch strips. Much of it was that the method and the tools that I used hadn't given my lines much of a chance to start out straight, let alone remain so. If it was the fault of my tools, I must have been a bad workman.

Saturdays, the men who worked tended to start early. When they were done, everyone would congregate on the top of the hill and wait for money for *posho,* or rations. Ostensibly, they would then go to the market for the week's supply of food, cooking oil and other necessities. *Pombe* was a necessity, as much of it as you could physically get down your gullet. Some of the more experienced women met their men folk as they collected the money. The ones who didn't probably got stories more often than money.

It was one of my duties to do this *posho* distribution. It was a simple enough duty, but I found it quite stressful. For a while I would get stomach cramps every Saturday morning. They'd last until the process was over. I had a box full of money, openly, in front of two hundred *machete* armed, rough men. That part didn't make me the slightest bit nervous. If the wind had blown any money away, it all would have been brought back. It was just the overall tension that affected me. For instance, every week, when I got to one particular guy, I just knew what to expect. He'd been one of the most vocal, all along. He probably had led the strikes in the first week.

Bukanula Kayumba would pick up the money and, without even looking at it, turn to hold it up for everyone to see. "Is this all I get for five days of sweat?" and so on.

I would go through the whole thing, each time. "No. You are being given the traditional advance for *posho*. At the end of the month you will be paid the remaining amount. It will be the amount set by the *état,* the government." Then, at the end of the month, I'd be saying: "No. You have already been paid three *posho* advances out of your wages that are set by the *état.*" Each time I would be shown a face just full of disbelief and pain, designed to melt the hardest of hearts. How could I take advantage of this poor, weak man? A weak man who could have picked me up and thrown me ten feet, with one hand tied behind his back. His acting prowess was notable, but it went un-rewarded. My capitalistic heart must have been too hard. I used to give him the opportunity, along with everyone else who had a question about the way their money was calculated, to wait until the end, so the others would not be delayed from their marketing. He stayed the first time and saw there was no audience left. Everyone else was happy to be paid and to go find the beer. He didn't stay again for this private audience, but neither did he let his turn to collect his money pass quietly.

The pay was not much. Adults got twelve and a half francs, about a quarter of a dollar, for a full day of physical work in high heat and humidity. The climate was, to us, most unfriendly. To them, it was normal. Half a franc could buy a kilo of local rice, with the stone chips thrown in for free. The daily wage could buy them food for the week. The weekly wage could buy them a suit of clothes. In that climate, food grew within a few weeks after you threw seeds on the ground and clothes were unnecessary for survival. If a man didn't want to walk to work from home, each day, and some of them had a two hour walk, he could build a hut on a designated spot on the plantation, move his family in, plant some food in a little *shamba* and live, rent free. Mum treated all of their minor medical complaints. What Mum couldn't treat, the government clinic in Kamango would cover, at no charge. Larger, well established plantations would have clinics, schools and sports fields, but we were still a long way from that.

I have since read that the colonial governments imposed poll taxes or head taxes on the natives, in order to force them into a cheap labour pool. I am not surprised that they had that amount of forethought, even cunning. I would be surprised, though, if those governments or the writers ever found evidence that the tax was the reason anyone went to work. We never could find anything that could incline anyone in that area to work if he had the slightest disinclination. Also, it seemed plain to us that if the economy were left to drive the wages, they would be lower than the government's set minimum. Certainly, wages higher than the minimum could not easily be supported by our commodity crops. Coffee took five years before it yielded the first harvest. The harvest had to be picked, processed, dried, bagged and taken to the transportation depot, in our case, Beni. From there, it had to be transported over a thousand miles, by road, river, rail and river, again, to the port where it would be transshipped to ocean freighters and taken to the markets halfway round the world. Except for times when problems in Brazil's crop caused world coffee prices to rise, the price at the plantation was not high. Higher wages for our workers would not have meant a better standard of living for them, it would have meant no work and no wages.

Enough apology. We believed that we were working towards the goal of making a good living for ourselves while priming the local economy and giving our employees a significant improvement in their standard of living and life expectancy. In fact, without us, there was quite a sound little entrepreneurial economy going. There were large open-air food markets on Saturdays. There were smaller, informal ones every day. Many villagers had coffee, cotton, rice and other products to sell to the *wazungu*-managed but native owned co-ops which traded in those commodities. African tailors sewed clothes in shops and under trees. Native owned trucks went, weekly, sometimes daily, to Beni and back, carrying people, bananas, rice, chickens, pigs, you name it. There were the ubiquitous *kilabus*. There was plenty of cash around and when someone had no cash, barter worked just fine. We never exerted pressure on anyone to work for us. We had no pressure to exert.

The cheapness of the labour had an interesting, counterintuitive effect. It meant that we could not, yes, not, afford any small luxuries. Can you imagine buying a beer and drinking it for a few minutes of pleasure when you know it cost as much as a man day in the field? Or a Coca-Cola, which cost twice as much? Now, drinking a beer that de Jaeger bought, that was something else. That's quite intuitive!

The routine, the hard physical work and the climate, and to some extent the total lack of social life, wore on us. It became harder and harder to get ourselves up in the morning.

Pedro had to crow louder and longer to get any signs of life from us. Every time he did his duty, Bill would invite him to go crow somewhere else, "- or else!" Pedro didn't take it seriously. He was cock o' the roost! He was not accustomed to being spoken to like that!

One morning, his crowing was interrupted by a deafening bang. It woke me up more effectively than Pedro ever had done, me and everyone within a mile of the place. When the smoke cleared and feathers and dust settled, I saw Bill prop the shotgun against the wall, roll over and pull his sheet over his head, muttering: "I warned you!"

Now, with Pedro out of action, we had to rely solely on Dad's cough to get us up.

I honestly don't believe that there was a connection between the Pedro event and the next one. Dad was aware that he coughed and he was probably aware that his cough was not silent. I'm sure that he didn't know that his cough was our alarm clock.

The cough had been getting worse. One morning, a little after Pedro's demise, it seemed to last longer, and the usual litany ended with a particularly emphatic "ACH! GOTT!" Ten seconds later, Dad stomped into our room, threw all his remaining cigarettes at Bill, who smoked, too, and said: "Here! You kill yourself with these damn things, if you want! I'm stopping!"

Dad never smoked another cigarette.

204

His cough got better, so we had to find other ways of waking up in time to be at breakfast before Dad.

Pedro was not eaten. If there were no sentimental reasons, and there were some strong ones (and he had a name, didn't he?), there was a very practical one. He was too full of buckshot.

CHAPTER EIGHT

Africa has an infinite number of distinct characters. As you go the short forty miles from Moshi to Ngare Nairobi, you go from a plain at an elevation of two thousand feet to a plateau at nearly six thousand feet. You can imagine that as you move a thousand miles across the continent, the landscape, the vegetation, the wild and domestic animals change and even the smell of the earth changes. The sun beats down on you differently, the air feels different. Where it does rain, the rain behaves in new ways and leaves new sensations on your skin. It is not surprising that the inhabitants reflect this variety, in their appearance, in their dress and in their personalities. It was not possible to be in a new place and not be reminded by these differences of the fact that you are in a new place.

Around Rongai, there were several tribes who refused to accept westernized clothing styles. Most exotic among them were the nomadic Maasai and their relatives, the Maasai Wannabes.[39] The warrior age groups of the men of these tribes wore nothing more than a small sheet of cloth, knotted at one shoulder, a beaded belt which carried a *simi*, a double edged, flat sword. Sometimes, they wore thonged sandals made of rawhide. Their hair was decorated with colourful beads, treated with animal fat mixed with *ol-kariya*, a red clay, (did ochre come from the same root?), and braided into fanciful shapes. When they became elders, their heads were shaved and they got to wear blankets. The women wore animal skins and very ornately beaded accessories. Women had their heads shaved. Men and women pierced their ear lobes and wore fanciful earrings that stretched the holes to enormous sizes. They lived with their livestock, which meant that they lived with flies. The animal fat in their cosmetics did nothing to repel the flies from their persons, or to make them welcome in a crowded marketplace or *passinja*.

Most other tribes had given in to about half a century of missionary work and affected shorts and shirts for the men,

---

[39]I apologize for this, wannabes, as in 'I wanna be a Maasai.'

simple dresses and head scarves for the women. Doubtless they were rewarded by reduced sentences in purgatory for doing so. The Muslim men often wore *kanzus,* white, ankle length robes. Their women wore colourful *kanga* prints and covered their heads with black shawls.

When we left for the Congo, we left behind the familiar faces and appearances of the peoples we had become used to. It was more than "become used to". As children, we had played with Mbulu and Chagga children and had eaten their food. We had learned some of their words, folk tales and songs. They had taught us how to make our own toys out of whatever was available, and to amuse ourselves without the help of modern technology. We would have to "get used to" some big changes.

Our little enclave in Watalinga was a minor United Nations. There were two tribes who called the area home, the Watalinga, themselves, and the Wanandi[40]. The Watalinga had no more claim over the area than the Wanandi did, it was named that way, for expediency or out of laziness, by the Belgian colonial administration. Some Pygmies, the BaMbuti, lived in the forest, but though the forest was in the area, the BaMbuti made a distinction between the forest and the villages, and never would have thought of what we called Watalinga as home. Since they were not really considered people by either major tribe, any claim to the area on their part would have been ridiculed. In fact, we were told that many real people kept some pygmies, almost as pets. They were very useful, you see, for a little bit of *taba* and being allowed to come close to the fire, they would steal for you, an activity for which they seemed to have a strong affinity, and they could harvest honey and catch animals in the forest and do all sorts of other useful things.[41]

---

[40]I think I've told you that they called themselves the Batalinga and Banandi. We knew better, of course, and said Watalinga and Wanandi. Remember, technically, that refers to the people of the tribes. The tribes are the Talinga and the Nandi, so we were not any more correct than they were. Not that it matters, they, themselves, might not have recognized the subtleties.

[41]Colin Turnbull, an English-born anthropologist, was Assistant Curator of African Ethnology at the American Museum of Natural History when he wrote a book "The Forest People'" (published by Simon and Schuster,

There were people who were related to both the Watalinga and the Wanandi, who lived *ngambo,* in Uganda, but I think they gave themselves other names.

The interlopers were the half dozen Indian trader families, who lived *ngambo,* in the little village of Bundibugyo, the few European settlers on the Congo side of the Lamia and the people we brought in with us. The Europeans were: the two Belgian priests, both French speaking Walloons, then de Jaeger and the other two Belgian *colons,* settlers, who were all Flemish and, finally, our family of eight. We were a combination of Scots, Dad and Scots-Dad mixture. Dad described himself as European Mongrel. I guess that meant that most European countries were represented in some small way, by us. The people we Europeans brought with us were the workers that de Jaeger imported from Bunia, the Wachagga, who had moved with us from Tanganyika and the Warundi, who were ostensibly on their way back to Urundi.

The Watalinga lived down on the floor of the Rift Valley, in and on the edge of the great Ituri forest. They shared the forest with the Pygmies and a good number of them had stature and facial features reminiscent of their diminutive neighbours. They were friendly and open people, even if we were exasperated when we found that the work ethic to which they subscribed was quite dissimilar to our own.

The Watalinga villages were small clusters of grass huts, scattered along a network of footpaths that were invisible from a few feet away. The villages and the paths were physically in the forest, but they were not part of it, they were reclaimed from it. The huts in a village were not set in any kind of order. The life of a hut was short; termites, other insects, fire and poor workmanship limited it. Because a hut was expected to last a short time, it was built rather shabbily. That made for an untidy look and usually helped to guarantee that the builder's expectations were met. The smoke from the cooking fires in the huts stained the thatch roofs and perhaps served to disinfect them, too. There was an appearance of disarray.

New York, in 1962), based on the three years that he lived among the BaMbuti. Those three years were just ending as we moved to the area. It is a good read.

However, when you looked closer, you saw that the beaten earth around the huts and in the common area was always swept very clean. On the outskirts of each village there were small *shambas* of maize, manioc (cassava or arrowroot) and plantains. Some had a few coffee trees and fields growing cotton and rice. The *état,* sometimes known as *l'état* (pronounced "lay-TA"), or the *gouvernement,* in one manifestation of the paternalistic workings of its collective mind, ordered each village to plant manioc in common fields. This starchy root crop can stay stable for a couple of years after it matures, even if, or rather, particularly if it is left in the ground. If the crop is rotated and maintained, and if the animals are kept out of it, it is an excellent reserve against famine in years that other crops fail. We heard that some years later, when *l'état* had ceased to exist, for all intents and purposes, and there was no one left to tell the villagers to plant, or, since they were, by that time, free and didn't have to listen to despised outsiders, or for whatever reason, they didn't plant. In an area where things grew despite your efforts, famine came and people suffered.

Some villages had never been visited by a motor vehicle, while others were on the edge of the road. Even for the villages on the road, the passing of a motor vehicle was an event. When they heard the sound of an approaching vehicle, children and young adults would run out, line the edge of the road and wave. Older adults would come to attention and salute. If they recognized the people in the vehicle, they'd shout out the names. I heard *"Shauri Mo-o-o-ja-a-a-a-a-a!"* and *"Bwana Ka-a-a-llo-o-o-o!"* every time we went through. The vehicles had distinctive sounds and were recognized even in the dark. We would hear the cheers even when we couldn't see the hand waves and salutes. We enjoyed the friendliness and would wave back. At night we would acknowledge them with a tap on the horn.

You know, already, that children were sometimes named for events. I was told that many Watalinga born after we appeared were named after some of us. If you come across a *"Bwana Billo!"* or a *"Bwana Kallo"* in that area, you should avoid jumping to conclusions. Our comings and goings were events, but not that kind of event.

Each village had a *capita,* or headman. He might hold a

209

hereditary position or have it at the pleasure of Pascal, the government appointed *Chef des Watalinga*.

Pascal had replaced a hereditary sort-of-chief who had not suited the government's needs. He was paid a salary which was apparently enough for him to buy a *camionette*, a two-ton lorry. It was obviously not enough for him to support two great thirsts, his own and his lorry's. While he had his vehicle working, which was for at least a few months after he acquired it, he cut a dashing figure and made many friends in all the local markets and *kilabus*. When it died, or when he couldn't get any more credit, his figure cut considerably less dashingly and his ability to win friends and influence people suffered. His love for his fellow man seemed to suffer with it. He had been an amusing oaf. He became a slightly laughable oaf, but an embittered one. In two years, he would get even and he would have the last laugh. It would be the laugh of a buffoon who doesn't realize that he, himself, is the butt of the joke.

The Wanandi lived on the mountain. They had different appearance and a different language. They said they were the same tribe as the Wanandi in the hills around Butembo, a hundred miles away. They liked being above the Watalinga, both in altitude and in attitude. They were as friendly as their lowland neighbours. They came by to talk, to sell eggs or chickens and to buy tobacco, and, of course, for medicine. Despite being on traditionally Nandi land, we saw less of them than of their neighbours because we were just on the edge of their territory, whereas we had to cross through the whole width of Watalinga territory.

Nandi homes were not clustered as noticeably into villages. They were not surrounded by the alien forest, the way the Watalinga were. There were huts and small farms clinging to the sides of the hills in every direction. There were two main villages, Njadot and another one, whose name I've forgotten. The latter was a good two-hour walk, straight up the mountain. It was Basikania's seat of government, but, understandably, for convenience, he kept a small court, a house, a wife and some chickens at Njadot, which was as far as a vehicle could go.

The Wanandi and Watalinga men wore khaki shorts and shirts. Shoes were not common, they were expensive and anyway were not made to fit feet that had walked without them for many years. I once had a local tailor sew me a pair of khaki shorts. He measured me, very professionally, then proceeded to cut out the material, by eye, without the help of a pattern or of transferring the measurements to the cloth. In half a day, the shorts were ready and I was able to pick them up. I was just able to get them on. What I gained in individual attention and rapid delivery, I lost in comfort. They say you must walk in a man's shoes, to understand him. They don't say much, if anything, about the understanding that you can develop from walking in a people's shorts. Had I been able to wear their shorts more, would I have been able to understand the people better?

The women liked a two-piece fashion. The top was short and had a short, flaring ruffle and puffy sleeves. The tailoring was at least as precise as that of my shorts. The top was perfectly fitted for any torso that would fit, which usually meant torsos that were very young and hadn't nursed. The skirt was a separate piece of cloth, usually of the same bold, colourful print, wrapped low around the waist, leaving the midriff bare, the midriff and anything else that wouldn't fit under the top or into the skirt. The ingenuity of the style was that only one dimension was important, that was the circumference under the armpits. This style allowed the tailor to economize greatly on unnecessary steps, such as taking or using measurements. Mum and Pauline were impressed at the cleverness of the design. The same outfit would fit the owner through a whole pregnancy, or several pregnancies. It must have been cool, too. A piece of the same material would be used as a turban. The fancier the wearer and the fancier the occasion, the bigger the turban.

Among the Watalinga, both men and women sported decorative scars on their faces. Dad had the theory that they originated from the slave trade. Scarred faces and bodies were less likely to fetch a good price in Arabia, so the practice of intentional scarring caught on and it evolved into a form of ritual and into an art.

Many of the older men walked around in a haze of smoke that had a distinct non-tobacco smell. The haze that was also in their eyes and in their minds suggested to Mum that they were smoking *bangi, bhang, hasheesh,* all names for marijuana, or the best local alternative from the forest.

211

European style tobacco was too expensive and was disappointing in that its kick was inversely proportional to its price. There was a local brand of manufactured cigarettes that was almost acceptable: Militaires. They were made of black, smoke-cured tobacco, along the lines of the French Gauloise Caporales. I tried one, once and nearly lost the ability to speak for an hour or two. Even the women, particularly the women, liked a good smoke, and the only way to get one was to eliminate the annoying capacity of the cigarette itself to filter the good stuff out of the smoke before it even got into your mouth. You could do this by turning the cigarette round and putting the lit end in your mouth and drawing in the unattenuated smoke. The mule kick in the throat resulting from one drag this way on a fag rolled with that tobacco is enough to kill the infirm. It took practice, to keep the glowing end from burning tongues and other things that lurk in mouths. It is hard enough to avoid burns with a full-length cigarette smoked that way, but a *Mtalinga* woman could smoke a butt down to less than a half inch, and do it while walking along with a pig or a goat on a rope, a child on her back and an infant on her breast. Maybe the occasional burn just was not serious, compared to life's other little challenges.

There were other burns that the Watalinga had to watch out for. One day we heard that a man was struck by lightning, while he was standing right in his very own doorway.

Augustin, the philosopher, said: "He was a thief!"

Mum asked: "Did you know him, then, a Mtalinga, living down there?"

"No. But it wouldn't have happened if he wasn't a thief. That's what happens to thieves." Case closed.

The *watu ya ngambo* in Uganda were a faster lot than the Congolese. They wore cleaner, newer clothes and seemed a little more world-wise. They had had a road into their area for much longer, and Indian traders had set up shop there decades before the Semliki bridge finally opened up the Watalinga. If you walked through their settlements, *ngambo*, you could see a *mwalimu*, a teacher, clad in his white *kanzu*, sitting in the shade of a mango tree, listening to classes of young boys reciting passages from the Koran. The *waalimu* had also been there generations longer than Père Jean had been in his mission. There were some Protestant and Roman Catholic

212

things going on, too, but less visibly. The *watu ya ngambo* shared a mutual distrust with their neighbours in the Congo.

The Wachagga were very clannish, at first. They were very much out of their highland element, in a strange, low, hot land inhabited by smelly savages. They were all specialists, mechanics, drivers or hydraulic magicians, and had little in common with the unsophisticated natives. The Swahili that was spoken here was very different from the classical Swahili of Tanganyika, and then the foreign influence was Belgian and French, as opposed to English. They built a camp for themselves, apart from the others. After a short while, their physical needs became strong enough to overcome their defenses. They bashfully adjusted their standards, just a little, and only enough to address the most basic of all human needs. Around the hut of each of the better paid ones, would soon be seen a woman, not a local savage, but a *maradadi,* fancy import from Beni or Butembo; there are limits to how far one lets one's self go native. A version of 'polite but distant' was working for them, too, but convention be damned, someone has to cook the food and brew the beer, and so on. Before much longer, the arrangement was quite domestic and developed an air of permanence, as much permanence as anything ever got around there.

The Warundi had an easier adjustment to make. They seemed to learn the local languages with little difficulty. They were a thousand miles closer to home than the Wachagga. Pascal, too, succumbed to the siren call and installed a Seraphina, or someone like a Seraphina, in his camp. Josephina and the children in Kayanza were probably more than a memory, but we have to be realistic and practical about these things. It had become nearly a year since he had left for his two-week trip.

The *Belges* who were our neighbours (other than pères Adam and Rombaud, at the mission) were all Flemish. Van der Zichelen (or v. d. Stichelen?) had the lower, flatter land of the two immediate neighbours. His first name escapes me. John and Richard, who I think were related to Jock, called him van der Stick 'Em Up, so I'm lucky I remember anything of his last name. He chose to build a stone house, off the road, close to the river and to some swampy, mosquito-breeding vegetation. It probably fit best on his orthogonal map at that point.

Everything on his land was laid out with a theodolite. He was going to marry, soon, and it was important to him to have a more permanent house ready quickly for his bride to move into. Poor girl, we thought. Remy Paepe had taken the hilly lot next to ours and was building himself a thatched camp right at the ford on the road to Njadot. Paepe was not as much a stickler as his colleague (I'm sure there's a pun lurking in there, but I'll pass over it). His plantation and his life were much less orderly. He succumbed to urges more similar to those of the Wachagga, rather than those of his neighbour, and we soon saw *kangas* hanging from the wash line outside his house. Mrs. v. d. Zichelen was going to suffer a surprise, a disappointment, or both. Poor girl!

Poor girl! We pitied her, coming to this out of the way place, where she would have no friends, really no company of any sort, and come to think of it, no life. Pauline and Mum pitied her, too. Perhaps they pitied her more than the rest of us did, we didn't notice It didn't occur to any of u, possibly including themselves, s to feel sorry for Pauline or Mum. After all, they were used to this, and they had us, didn't they?

Raphael de Jaeger's brother had started his place, ten years earlier, when there had been no road. He had had to walk in, sleeping in a tree at night, to avoid some of the larger animals. When he married, he went on to open up another plantation where there was a road, leaving Raphael to continue this one and to suffer the rigours. De Jaeger was a no-nonsense farmer. He had already built himself a couple of brick buildings, but each one was planned in a way that it would serve multiple purposes. His first house was now the storehouse and office, as planned. His new house was going to be something else, in the future. It meant that, while he overlooked a valley which had the Ruwenzoris as a backdrop, he had no view in that direction. He didn't even have a window looking in that direction. Then, he didn't have the time to spend looking out of a window in that or any direction.

I learned a bit more about de J after Dad hit on a creative way to repay Chef Basikania for his hospitality. Old B had appeared one day with an itemized bill for x nights at y francs, for the six weeks that we had stayed in his *gîte*. It was quite reasonable, concept, really, come to think of it. But Dad didn't think of it. Instead, he asked Paga to make a sign for Njadot, which made the latter happy to have something new to do. He asked me to walk over to de J's place, with the sign, and ask him if he had a good wooden post to hang it on, and I wasn't unhappy to get out of the *matete*. De J was supposed to be pleased to be a part of this project, for the public relations aspect, and so on, besides, we didn't have a good post. And B was supposed to like his sign, the only one this side of Mbao, so much that he would forget the bill. You appreciate how creative the plan was when you count the amount of physical work actually done by Dad, himself.

I arrived, hot and sweaty, even though I had an Albert (or an *Arobé*) to carry the sign, to explain the mission to de J, in my improving French.

"*Pot verloorie! Qu'est ce qu'il pense, ton père?* A sign? To Njadot? How much time has he spent making this sign? How much have you paid this *macaque* to carry it over here? What do you think it is worth to humour that old clown Basikania? *Nom d'un nom!*" I beat a retreat. Albert and I cut a pole from the edge of de J's property, making him a de facto, if unwilling, part of the scheme. We nailed the sign on to the post, stuck it in the ground and went back home. (Basikania loved his sign, but he didn't come and ask for his bill back).

De J was single-minded about life. He never could see how or why Dad could spend so much energy in so many directions, at one time.

In a later conversation, yes a conversation, not a confrontation, he asked me: "*Got verniaarde!* What does *le Prince* find to do in Bukavu, Butembo and Bunia, or wherever it is this time? How much *essence* has he burned this week, then?"

It was too complicated to explain the things Dad was bringing back to plant in his 'tastes'. De J was sticking to the tried and true, papaïne for the short term, coffee for the long. His products had developed markets. While we tested, he sold. He was successful. It is hard to argue with success.

When we talked with long-time *colons* about our Père Jean Adam, whom, of course we politely called and referred to as 'Père Adam', they often, for some unfathomable reason, confused him with another padre, their Père Adam. I met this other guy a couple of times, and, apart from the fashions they both affected, they bore not the slightest resemblance to each

215

other. Père Adam looked like a fictional friar, less the tonsure, that is, well fed and healthy. On the other hand, Père Adam was a small man with a scraggly beard, scraggly teeth and a big heart. He must have had good legs under that cassock, despite his small stature. He, also, had first come to Watalinga before the road came, and it was not until a while after we arrived that he allowed himself, for the first time, the luxury of wheels. He bought a Citroën Deux Cheveux, an 'ugly duckling', which he apologetically called "*un moto avec parapluie,* a motorcycle with an umbrella." We worried with him that it might get lost in a pothole or an elephant footprint. And it did. Once, on the way home from delivering a load of coffee, we came upon his car, abandoned in the middle of the road, in the forest of the Parc Albert. With three or four men, we threw it onto Polonia, picked up its loose wheel and delivered both to him at the mission. He was not at all surprised that it showed up that way. It was quite normal for a lorry to drive up and for four men to get out and lift down to the ground your car that you'd left on the jungle track some days before. Happens every day. Just the colonial Lost and Found Office at work.

Père Jean (we'll call him that so you don't confuse him with the other guy, who doesn't come into the story again, anyway, so you really shouldn't have any trouble) was a good observer of people, particularly his own flock, and later, with his network of missions a great source of information on the developing political situation. We attended his second mass most Sundays, and always stopped in afterwards for a chat and bad coffee.

When we showed up for mass for the first time, Père Jean had a little talk with Joseph Kwambuga, the *sous-chef* from Kiesegeta. From then on, Joseph came to the earlier mass, so we could sit on the wooden chairs in front of the communion rail, rather than on the planks resting on bricks, that the populace sat on in the nave. Yes, there is segregation by race and by class even in God's house in the jungle. If I were Joseph, I might have resented that usurpation. If he did, he never let us know it. For Père Jean it was normal. He couldn't have dreamt of letting us sit down among those tightly packed, sweaty bodies and crying, runny-nosed babies.

Père Jean's assistant, Père Rombaud, was an older man. He was almost deaf. Mum was sure that it was because he had taken quinine against malaria for most of his life. It is a fact that quinine puts a shrill whistle in your ears. Tintinabulation is great sounding word for a maddeningly annoying sound. We experienced it, from time to time, and didn't doubt that it could eventually deafen you. It was a nice treat, every now and then, to have Père Rombaud chant the Latin mass. His voice was deep and rich and, despite his hearing problem, his pitch was perfect. Perhaps because of his deafness, he never said much. It may have explained Père Jean's happiness to see us each time we came by. The first half hour with Dad could make up for the past week of conversation deficit. The extra hour or more, he put in the bank for future weeks, or for a month of rainy days.

CHAPTER NINE

John and Richard came home from St. Mary's, not on the infamous Tanganyika train anymore, but on the longer but kinder Uganda train, which took them in the opposite direction, and on which they stayed all the way to its end. Mum and Dad went to pick them up in Kasese, and in the process, met the Cleggs, who lived 12 miles away in Kilembe Mines and whose son Mike was at Saints. That seemed like a good reason to visit Kilembe Mines, and there they discovered a source of goodies unknown in the Congo. The Mines had a grocery store filled with good East African things. We laughed at the Belgians for being so dependent on their strange stuff that they were used to and which they had to import from Belgium. It was totally natural, and we felt not at all defensive about it, for us to look forward to shopping at Kilembe to get things that we were used to. Things like Kenya Highland Blue cheese and Upland Bacon.

Mum and Dad came home with John and Richard and a whole 20 lb. wheel of blue cheese. John and Richard were at least as welcome as the cheese, but we tried not to let them know it. They went to work like everyone else. John went into the *kipaniyés* to supervise some of the teams of Watalinga and Wanandi, while Richard gave himself the task of clearing the top of the hill, around the camp, and trying to establish a vegetable garden.

At some point, Dad had acquired some dynamite to flatten the top of the hill to make a place for the future permanent house. John and Richard did much of that work. The hole for the dynamite was made, I can't say drilled, with a large steel bar and an even larger hammer. The process was not without its exciting moments, and it gave Dad several opportunities to tell us about his attempt to prospect for gold in the Namanga Hills.

John and Richard both pitched in on the plantation and wherever else their help was needed, including attacking the cheese. After a month at home, too soon for them, I'm sure, they would head back for another three months at Saints. They did this for two full years.

On one of the trips across the border, John and Richard were with Polonia, and there were some things on Polonia which had to go through customs. The arrived at Kasindi after dark. Things and lorries meant waiting for the office to open. There was a *gîte* there, beside the road, for the use of Europeans caught in this predicament. They tried to sleep in it, on the floor, wrapped in Polonia's tarpaulins. They didn't sleep much, instead they spent the night trying to dissuade mice and rats from running over their faces and eating their toes and fingers.

Pauline's *pipinière* was coming along. The rains hadn't come, yet, nor had Meku's furrow, so she had bucket brigades going between the little spring and the beds.

Bill was with the tractors, most of the time, trying to keep them out of the traps. He succeeded most of the time.

I kept on with the *kipaniyés*. The Plantation was about a mile and a half wide and a mile deep. If I wanted to see what was happening in each area at least twice each day and to stay ahead of the men with the layout, I had an awful lot of walking to do. From time to time I'd use either Dad's old Francis Barnett motor bike or Pauline's BSA to get from one side of the place to the other.

The bikes saved miles of trudging through the heat each day, and I was thankful for them. What was even more important to me, though, was that I could cheat the climate. The air down in the *matete* on the flat land stubbornly refused to move. In the direct sun it was so hot that you'd sweat if you were lying down and doing nothing. Fanning yourself was counterproductive because of the effort it took and the heat that the effort generated. The air wouldn't move past me, but on a bike I could move through it. The feeling was unbelievably pleasant, almost intoxicating. It made it possible to forget the discomfort of the heat, the itching, the scratching and the cutting of the *matete* blades. The faster the bike went, the better the feeling and the better the forgetting. Some of the things It helped me forget weren't anything to do with the heat or my heat related discomfort. One time, I was riding along the lower boundary road, my shirt mostly open for the artificial breeze. My eyes were mostly closed against the same breeze and the bugs it carried, because I wasn't wearing goggles. The foam rubber on Dad's goggles had reacted badly to the same

219

heat and humidity and had melted, so if I put the goggles on, I couldn't easily take them off. So I rarely wore them on short trips and rode, instead, with my eyes shut except for quick glimpses to see where I was going. I really hated the way the fat, juicy, local bugs burst when they hit my eyeballs, or when I hit them with my eyeballs. That usually hurt so badly that I couldn't even keep my eyes partly open, and I'd have to hope I could stay on the track until I was able to stop. Some of the tracks were made by people and were twisty and more of a challenge. I couldn't have gone very fast on these tracks if I had wanted to, so I could ride with my eyes open. Some tracks were made by vehicles and were actually two parallel, beaten dirt tracks in grass that was kept down to about a foot in height by the passing vehicles. These tracks were straighter. I knew all of the tracks well, so I was convinced that my system of navigation by quick glimpses was perfectly safe. Besides, I hadn't forgotten that I was a teenager, and teenagers just don't get hurt, themselves, it just happens to other people. But I had forgotten why Joseph had left one of his trademark kinks in the otherwise straight lower boundary road. I had been around long enough to know that there is not always a reason for kinks in roads or tracks in Africa, but usually there is, or there has been. I was reminded when the tree stump that was hidden in the grass in one such kink caught the toe of my right boot. It ripped off the whole sole of my army boot, the kind of boot that you swear is made of cast iron not leather. Had the stump been half an inch taller, or had my toes dragged a little lower, I would no longer have a right foot.

For a while I couldn't walk, so the bikes were even more important. I rode a little more than I usually did, I rode a bit more slowly and carefully and I rode with my eyes open. For a while.

We had been buying the kerosene fuel for the tractors, that had the trade name Voco, by the drum. We had to get it in Kasese, there was none in the Congo. Each time anyone went to Kasese, a couple of drums of Voco had to be brought back. This was not very often and also not very satisfactory. The fuel was more expensive this way than in bulk, there was the bother of looking for and the expense of buying the drums. There was the bother of having to be at the depot when it was open for business. It was usually Dad who went on these (or any) trips, and on Dad's trips, one was never there when anything was open for business. On one of the trips, he hit on a solution to all of the problems. He ordered and paid for five thousand litres of Voco, a small tanker truck load, to be delivered in bulk to Kagando, as soon as possible. I may have heard about it. I probably heard the discussion of how one day we would have our fuel in a tank on the hill, with gravity feed to the fueling point for the tractors, even, perhaps, for Polonia and the cars. I probably took it as an adjunct to the distant future gravity fed coffee factory or as just another trip to Europe across the Sahara. Whatever I heard or understood I had soon had forgotten in the daily routine. I next was aware of the plan when the tanker arrived at the little culvert in the swamp. The driver decided that he couldn't take his lorry across it, and he was unsure about the hill on the other side of it. He wanted to know where to deliver this load of Voco. Where was our tank? Had he not stopped before the culvert, he would have given us our tank, unwittingly, but it would have been in the wrong place for a gravity fed system.

Some quick calculations told us we needed about thirty drums; we had fewer than twenty, and some of them were not empty. I don't claim that we equaled the miracle of the loaves and the fishes, but we somehow stretched our inadequate resources by begging, borrowing, stealing and commandeering empty diesel fuel drums from de Jaeger, palm oil drums from the shop of Milingos, the Greek, empty *debes* (four gallon oil tins) that Pascal used for fetching water, in short, anything that could hold any amount of liquid. About the only things we didn't use were the cooking pots and the galvanized bathtub; we would have had to fight Mum for them. When the tanker left, the better part of a day behind his schedule, he had a dry tank and we were swimming in Voco.

The tanker had stopped at the swamp and that is where our new fuel depot was planted. It didn't matter that this track, which was our first attempt at an access road to the camp on Kagando hill, was now almost never used. Actually, it almost looked intentional, having the fuel drums there, because they were among a whole bunch of machines and equipment that had come up from Rongai. The latter was there for much the same reasons, namely that that was as far as Polonia was able to get on her first trip, and since no one had had any use for

221

any of it since, therefore no reason to move it, it was still there. Some of us made notes to ourselves that, maybe, just maybe, there would be a better place for the fuel, gravity or no gravity.

A few weeks later, we knew that we were right.

The *kipaniyés* were being cleared by a combination of methods. Where the *matete* was thickest, and that meant that you couldn't even walk through it, the plough just bounced over it, never able to touch the soil, let alone dig into it. The only way to get the *matete* out was by hand, and that was a slow process. Bill was investigating a slightly quicker way, which involved knocking the twelve feet high stalks flat by running over them with the tractor and the plough, letting them dry out a bit in the sun, clearing a firebreak around each strip, burning the leaves off and then clearing the reduced bulk by hand. This meant that there was fire around, much of the time. Fire was a natural phenomenon in the area, anyway. It was an annual event in the dry season, and this was the dry season, so we were doing nothing very different.

At the end of one long, hot day we were looking out from our verandah, admiring the view and how much we could see of the results of our work in the developing pattern of cultivation and mulch strips, or just enjoying some breaths of moving air.

Mum pointed and asked: "Is that fire heading for the Voco?"

A burning leaf had been carried by the wind, or else the fire had crept out of the controlled area of a nearby strip, unseen, and the grass was burning only yards from the fuel stockpile. We ran down the hill, covering about a quarter of a mile in what seemed like two hours, and beat out the small flames, before they got close enough to be a real danger. If you remember, one of the normally less endearing traits of Voco is its inability to vapourize at ordinary temperatures. We rethought that, even as we ran; it was suddenly a much more endearing trait. But we also knew that if the fire did reach the drums and heated enough Voco to make it burn, or if it found any spillage on some grass, we'd have a pretty mess. Our knees shook. It wasn't only from the scare. If you've ever run downhill as fast as your legs can carry you, you know that we were due to ache for days. You use a whole different set of muscles going straight downhill than you do walking.

222

I don't think that we ever moved the drums. There was no other place on the property that would be any safer, and this place at least was in our view from Kagando Hill. We cleared the area around the fuel, a little, and we watched the fires in that side of the plantation a little more closely.

The grass was getting drier and drier. The sun was hot. It hadn't rained for weeks and the next rains were weeks away. It bore watching.

Before long, it was December and the sun was hot and getting hotter, the grass was dry and getting drier. While other parts of the world were heading into winter, we were roasting. We had all read about white Christmases, and dreamt about one with Bing Crosby and Bob Hope, but Dad was the only one who had seen one. He was the only one of us who had experienced snow in this century. White Christmases were as far from our minds as we could imagine.

On Christmas Eve, we drove past de Jaeger's oldest stand of coffee and saw our first white Christmas. We were totally surprised by our first sight of *robusta* coffee in bloom. Coffee has white blossoms and robusta has a lot of them, massed along the branches. It looked just the way I would have imagined snow would look on the branches of trees. It was magical. It was a beautiful sight, but more than that, it was a promise of a crop. Of course, it was also a tease. The flowers would turn in to berries that wouldn't be picked until nearly a year later, and those particular ones were going to be picked by de Jaeger, not us. We could not possibly be in a position to be admiring our own blossoms for another four years, and not to be picking them until a year after that. Still, it was beautiful, and if we had to dream to imagine our own crop, it was only another part of the dream that had brought us there.

In Rongai, on Christmas Eve we would have made an expedition to the top of the farm, just above where the Moolji vegetable garden had been, to cut our Christmas trees. One should have been enough, but life isn't that simple. At about the time we were growing enough vegetables to feed all of Moshi and some of Arusha, perhaps some of the rest of the Northern Province, Dad thought it would be neat to have some real Christmas trees, too. There's some logic there. If you're doing intensive cultivation of one kind on twelve acres, it is easy to do a little more on, say, an extra quarter of an acre. So we put in a quarter acre of Christmas tree seeds, which turned into Christmas tree plantlets, which grew well and looked good while they were small and had room to grow. Long before they should have been thinned out, Moolji had pulled the plug on the future of the vegetables. We had lost interest in, or forgotten the trees, until Christmas, a couple of years later. The trees were something like puppies and piglets, cute when they were small, but then they got big. Trees that grow within six inches of other trees tend not to grow well. Only the ones on the edge know that they are supposed to have, or are brave enough to try to have branches, the rest don't even want to think of it. The only way we could have an esthetically acceptable tree was to cut down five or more of these lopsided, stunted things from the edge of the forgotten nursery, and strap them together so that the single, vertical row of branches on each tree, that looked like the teeth of a very coarse comb, radiated outwards from the centre, to give us a full, three dimensional tree. We developed an eye for how they'd go together and created some pretty impressive trees.

After this engineering, we'd decorate the tree, with glass ornaments dating from before we were born, with ornaments we'd made as children (from the lead or tin foil that was used, way back, in Karatu, to protect the lowest six inches of young coffee plants from a parasite), with lametta and real candles. We'd light the candles, and then watch like hawks, lest they set the tree, and with it our house, on fire.

While all the Africans from the farm came and crowded round the always open *mvuli* door and gaped at the spectacle, we'd sing carols. We weren't good singers, but we could manage a few carols at Christmas. The Williamsons, who were often there for Christmas, were singers, and they could carry parts. I don't know why we weren't big on singing; Dad had a rather good though untrained bass voice.

In this current stage of my life, every Christmas is, somehow, every other Christmas that I ever experienced. Every time I sing *"Stille Nacht"*, even if it's called "Silent Night", I hear Dad sing it, and I cry. I did, even before he died. About the only way I can survive a service of lessons and carols is to be silent and to think of something sufficiently distracting, say an ingrown toenail, or something.

In the Congo, we had no Christmas tree nursery. I can't

even remember what, if anything, we did about a tree.

That first Congo Christmas Eve evening, Paepe, the *colon* who had needed a hammer, appeared on Kagando in clean clothes and with his hair still damp and combed. He never said what he had come for, but it soon became evident. His friend had gone to Bukavu to be with his fiancée over the holidays, and Paepe was left alone. De Jaeger probably was in Butembo with his brother's family. The padres at the mission were probably busy, it being a busy sort of season for those in the religious professions. To Paepe, the prospect of sitting in the *gîte* alone on Christmas Eve was probably even more daunting than that of inviting himself to the holiday dinner with these relative strangers who spoke poor French and no Flemish. The meek may eventually inherit the earth, but they probably miss a few Christmas dinners while they are waiting. And nobody ever called Paepe meek. Another, equally valid, reason for him to be there could have been a heartily meant invitation, given but soon forgotten by Dad.

So, nine out of the eleven Europeans within a fifty-mile radius were going to sit down to Mum's Christmas feast. It was not a traditional Christmas feast. There was no Yule log. There was no turkey, no stuffing, none of the accoutrements and condiments that you'd expect. We had, instead, buffalo steaks that Mum had cut thin, drizzled with the latex from a green papaya to soften them chemically, pounded with a wooden mallet to beat the remaining toughness out of them physically, then fried thoroughly over the kerosene flame thrower to discourage and disarrange any parasites or other beasties that might lurk in them. The steaks were very tasty, though, despite the two tenderizing treatments, as tough as shoe leather. Think what they could have been like without any treatment! There were sweet potatoes, rice, green vegetables and gravy. There was enough of it all to be passed around more than twice.

The first time I offered Paepe another helping, he tried his English and said: "Tanks!" and seemed disappointed when I immediately passed the plate on.

Sorry, old chap! I thought "Tanks!" meant "No, tanks!" not "Yes, tanks!" I understood better when, just for form, I passed him the plate the third time. He supplemented his unexpanded verbal vocabulary with some body language. It had only been minutes, so we can forgive him for not having learned any

225

more English words. So, before it could move out of his reach, he grabbed the plate with both hands, and said his "tanks!" only after he had another couple of steaks safely on his plate.

We had no drinks before dinner, no beer or wine with dinner. We drank water carried from the river on Pascal's head, perhaps turned into lemonade with fresh lemons bought from *watu ya ngambo*, perhaps turned into milk with the help of Klim powdered milk from Kilembe, and probably some very black, locally grown, spoon dissolving coffee. Paepe's presence was strange, but not a damper. Somehow, he was included in the conversation, and we had a noisy, teasing, laughing time. We had few if any presents for each other, anyway, so he wasn't even excluded when we had none for him. He left, eventually, with a slightly bemused look, but probably quite tankful that he had got up the nerve to come rather than stare at the mud wall of his *gîte*. We were glad that he had come; it made the occasion enough different to add to its specialness.

CHAPTER TEN

After Christmas the heat continued. Nothing new here, the heat always continued. The rain continued to stay away. Perhaps it did us a favour; staying away, it kept the humidity down. But you know how people are, we were anxious for it to begin. The heat was drying out the *matete,* increasing the discomfort of working in the long grass and increasing the danger of fires getting out of control. Since the dry grass came up the hill to within a few yards of our dry grass buildings, we were not disinterested in what was burning down on the flat land. Richard took note and cleared some more of the area around the camp, before he and John went back to Saints.

We were anxious for the rain for the reasons that every farmer looks forward to its coming. Rain starts everything. It starts the growing, which is everything. We weren't there for the views, anthropological observations or for fun. We weren't even there to cut and be cut by *matete*, or to be sucked dry by mosquitoes. We were there to grow things, particularly coffee. If the rain began, we'd feel that our new life could begin. And it might just cool things off, a bit.

We asked Augustin: "When does the rain start?"

Augustin, the amateur meteorologist, looked thoughtful for a moment, then said: "On the fifteenth of January, but not before noon. Maybe in the seventh hour."

We said, to ourselves: "Yeah, Sure! At thirteen hundred hours, like on a railway schedule!"

On January the fourteenth, the sun was just as hot. It was still sunny at about eleven, though a dark cloud appeared away in the distance up the Rift Valley, over Lake Albert. It came closer, but we didn't lose our sun.

On the fifteenth, the sun was still shining at noon, and the cloud appeared again, in the same place. This time, the cloud came closer and became bigger. At one o'clock, just like on a railway schedule, it was overhead. There was a clap of thunder and a strong gust of wind. The bottom of the cloud opened and the rain fell in big, warm drops, then in sheets.

The first few days of this short rainy season, the rain was

227

like clockwork. One of those days, we were in the camp, I suppose we had learned to be closer to home when the rain was scheduled, not that it was uncomfortable to be rained on, it was just inconvenient to get so utterly wet. Some of the workers were standing in the lee of the big building for shelter. The wind that accompanied or preceded the rain on that day was a bit more violent than usual, and the drops stung.

I had an irreverent thought. "Every breath of air is moving today. I wonder just how many of them we're catching!"

Too many, I think. Three minutes later we had all of the men scrambling to hold the house up against the wind. Some of them ran to get the poles that had been left over from the construction, to buttress the walls. If the men hadn't been there, or if the poles had been used to heat bath water, we would have watched the whole building sail off the hill to join the buffaloes in the swamp.

I had been so proud of the lightness and airiness of the main building's structure. It had clear spans in the dining room and only one pole in the middle of the verandah. The other uprights had been buried in partitions. When we were laying it out, I had told Augustin, the planner, and all the other experts who had crowded around to supervise the construction, that we wanted an open, airy construction which would allow us a view of their beautiful country, and to catch Every Breath of Moving Air. We were *wazungu*, therefore quite mad. Though they felt a need to make a nod towards their perceived obligation to protect us from ourselves, in the last analysis we were paying for it so we could demand whatever we wanted. What we demanded was quite different from their usual small, windowless huts with doors so low that one had to stoop to enter. They rose to the occasion, even got a bit excited about it. We had to have a clear span in the dining room because of a table that was going to come there, one at which all eight of us were going to be able to sit at one time and, if we had guests, which could be extended further to sit fourteen. None of them had seen such a table, it had to be one from *Ulaya*. Indeed, such a wonderful table had to have a special place and that justified taking special measures and stretching building technology and the materials to their limits.

None of us knew what those limits were, so it was easy.

The dining room was spanned by a pole laid horizontally as a beam, which supported a king post to hold up the ridge pole. Everything had been measured out, carefully, with strings, a spirit level and the eye of Augustin, the master builder, before the parts were cut to size. When the skeleton was up, before the thatch went on, we had stepped back to check out its appearance to be sure that it was properly proportioned and dimensioned. Other than a slight dip towards the rear, over the kitchen, it had looked passable. The better materials had been used first up front, the kitchen had been framed with the smaller, thinner poles. Correcting the problem would have necessitated another trip to the fire-ant protected *coup de bois*. After that thought, it looked even more passable. After we had got the workers started on the thatch, we went off to do the daily rounds of supervising the work. From the lower land, the advancing building looked different, but it was hard to know what it would look like, with the foreshortening of our unusual perspective and the thatch not being complete and all. When we next came up on to the hill, towards the end of the day, the dining room beam had sagged as it took the load of the thatch, but only by a foot or so. It gave the roof line a slight dip over the dining room. The sag brought it in line with the roof over the kitchen area, so it almost looked intentional. But it was a pity, the house now looked rather sad from its rear, sort of the way a beached humpback whale might look, not that I knew what that would look like. We didn't want to undo everything, we didn't feel we had the authority to waste that kind of money on mere esthetics, so we let it be. Over the next few weeks, the materials had sagged a little more as they dried out and insects started to bore into and weaken them, but we were used to it by then, and the sag looked quite normal.

When the big wind came, it found a much-reduced profile to beat against, but it found enough of one to have a big effect.

After the storm blew away, we quickly added some poles to support the dining room beam. It meant we had a couple of extra uprights to dodge, and Paga had to eat with a pole at his elbow, but we had a greater feeling of security to make up for that. Dad also suggested some strategic replacement of a few wall posts that had looked a little too willing to fall over. In the process of replacing poles we saw where the workers had

229

decided that six inches was as much as anyone should be expected to have to dig into the decomposing rock that they found at that depth. We had not checked each hole. We hadn't thought we'd have to.

Well, overall, the camp did meet the primary criterion of its design, didn't it? With a vengeance!

The start of the rains brought changes to our routine.

Dad had been occupying himself with everything. When he was home, he checked up on every one's activities. He was concerned about getting some fields far enough along to start some annual crops that could be grown and harvested in the same space that the coffee would be coming along in. Papaïne was a good candidate, it produced revenue within nine months. It was a standard procedure to grow papaya trees for papaïne. All our plans included it. Dad went further, investigating crops like soy, ground nuts (peanuts) and cotton. He would go into Beni on Fridays, in case there was mail or to visit the bank. Sometimes he would disappear for a few days or a week at a time, to meet with the powers that be in the CiNKi in Bukavu, or someone else somewhere else. Sometimes he went with Mum, sometimes with one or another of us, seldom did he go by himself

Dad always came back from these trips with new ideas, often with new seeds. The next time it rained, everything we were doing stopped. We would leave our workers doing their tasks and go with him to the *kipaniyé* that he decided would be the one to get the trial crop, the "taste". We'd spend the day planting the seeds. If it was not yet the rainy season, Dad's patience would be sorely tried and usually found slightly wanting. We'd find ourselves carrying water from the small swamp or hurrying Meku to finish the furrow to bring water to the test field.

At a certain point, Dad realized that buying field-ready coffee plants from de Jaeger would cut the time we had to wait for our first crop from five years to three and a half. Pauline's nursery would not produce field-ready plants for another year or so. Pauline's plants would be cheaper, but the wait would be expensive in opportunity cost.

From this point on, each time it rained, and now it rained most days, seeds or no seeds, everyone within shouting distance was conscripted to plant coffee plants in the fields.

This made sense. It was what we were here for. Everything else, soybeans, cotton, whatever, was a means, not an end. Then, when the prepared land had coffee plants in place, and we were waiting for more to be ready, the other crops were put in.

Every time Dad passed the first *kipaniyé* that we had planted with coffee, he would stop, hunker down, sitting on his right heel, and weed around the first few trees. He'd rake the soil with his fingers into a nice basin to collect rainwater around each plant and place some mulch around it.

Every Sunday, now, after mass, the bad coffee, the warm beer and the discussions of political developments and agricultural methods, we'd stop for a while in the fields to watch the coffee grow, before going up the hill for lunch. Dad would stop at his usual place and perform his ritual. A little less than two years later, the ten coffee plants in that row repaid him for the personal attention he gave them by being the first ones, out of the thousands planted the same week, to produce blossoms. They were the only flowers we were to enjoy on our own coffee trees.

The attention was personal, but by no means exclusive. During that time the coffee trees shared his attention with the nearest plants in their respective rows of all the interim cash crops. The behaviour of these other plants was similar. The healthiest ones were always nicely ranged on the ends of the rows, nearest to the road. It served to show us that everything needed a lot of attention. Nothing really took care of itself, even in the best climate for growing things. A climate even mildly good for any useful plant was bound to be very good for weeds. Some weeds, particularly the *matete,* if there was so much as a scrap of a root left, grew back six inches overnight. The competition that our crops suffered from the weeds was formidable.

The crops suffered concurrently from another adversary. The buffaloes had moved off in the first few weeks of our messing about in their area, but after a while, when the maize and some of the other crops sprouted, they were attracted back. Young maize plants contain a sugar in their sap and the stalks taste like slightly watered down sugar cane. You might not have known it until I told you, but buffaloes know it. I'll tell you more about that, later.

Papaïne was the cash crop of choice for planters looking for

231

a source of income pending the maturation of their coffee. Papaya was known to grow well in the climate, it started producing in the first year, it produced for about two to three years and there was a ready market for the product. The trees grow to about six feet in the first year, and only produce fruit on the new growth. That means that the business part of the plant gets higher and higher as it gets older. There comes a point when it is too tall for its own good and it can't pull enough water up to the fruits and they get smaller and smaller. At that point, the tree can be cut down and some shoots come out of the stump. By selective pruning, one shoot can be encouraged to pretend that it is a tree, and this deception can stretch the useful life by about one year. At three years, the coffee is fairly tall, and perhaps getting close enough to its own productive life that you don't want to give it any competition, so the papaya is removed.

We put about a third of the coffee planted area under papaya.

Unlike most plants, the papaya plant is not hermaphroditic. If you leave nature to itself you land up with half of your plantation occupied by male plants, many more than you need, and that is not good for productivity. The ideal ratio is about one male to ten females. This may sound good to the one male, but nine males have to bite the dust during the social engineering that brings about this ideal. Tough luck for the nine! You have to plant a whole bunch of seeds where you want one tree, then, when they have germinated and have grown to a few inches in height, you reduce the number to four. If you don't know your papayas, you wait until they start bearing flowers, then you can tell the sex of each plant by the sex of the flower. You weed out all but the strongest looking female in most of the positions, leaving a male in every tenth one. If you know your papayas, you can tell the sex before the buds appear. There is something about the shape of the leaf stem of the male plant, where it joins the trunk. If you don't know about this, or if you can't discern the difference, you wait. We knew nothing about this early sign, until Pauline's teenage friend Tina Schultz, from Sanya Juu, near Rongai, came to spend one holiday with us. Tina's trick that she had learned by direct observation on her father's small plantation, was accurate, and when we had learned it, we allowed our plants to grow much faster by removing the competing plants weeks sooner.

Old man Schultz had a small farm, which he worked himself. He had it planted with coffee and papaya and had some lemon trees. It was right on the edge of the main road that went through Sanya Juu to Moshi, and it was one of the stops that Dad made every time we went past, particularly after Mrs. Schultz had died. Schultz, as Dad called him, had a gravelly, deep, voice, deeper than Dad's, and the sound of the two of them arguing or just talking (I trust that they could tell the difference, it was in German, so I couldn't), late into the evening, usually put me to sleep as I sat on the bearskin carross on Schultz's couch, waiting for the rumble to stop and we could go on home. Sometimes, when Tina was home from school, Pauline would invite her to stay with us in Rongai. They both got girl company, good even if there were five years between their ages, the rest of us liked her, and Tina got some company in her own generation.

Now we were in the Congo, Pauline invited her to come for one of the holidays, which she did, one time, riding the same train as John and Richard. She was the only "old" friend from East Africa to visit us.

For all of the scientific stuff that the Agricultural College taught the three Belgian planters, who in turn had trained the worker pool in the area, it took a schoolgirl to come in and teach us something as simple as sexing papaya plants. Perhaps it was an unknown or an unimportant detail to the professors, but to us it was it a treat to discover one of nature's little secrets, and even more of a treat to have learned it that way.

The papaya fruit is delicious, but it is soft and can't really be transported when it's ripe. If you see it in the shops, you can pay three dollars for one fist-sized, not really ripe papaya that has been flown in from Hawaii. We weren't growing it for fruit. We wanted the latex that is produced in the fruit before it ripens. In fact, once the fruit ripens, it produces no more latex and is useless, it gets thrown away. There were dozens of papaya fruits from each of a thousand plants on each of hundreds of hectares, each fruit the size of a rugby football, and each eventually allowed to rot on the ground. It seems like a waste, but once the fruit has been tapped for its latex, it doesn't taste good, anyway.

233

The latex is harvested by cutting the skin of the fruit with a razor blade inserted in the end of a long stick. It dribbles out and falls into a cloth butterfly-like contraption that the worker clamps to the trunk. The latex curdles on contact with the air and is collected and dried over a low heat. The method of choice for drying was over near-horizontal flues made of our old friends, empty oil drums, with chimneys at one end sucking the heat along from wood fires at the far end. This, as were most systems for doing anything, was an imprecise, unpredictable process. It required constant watching to prevent burning. A few minutes too long, and the papaïne turned brown. A slight brown tinge in a batch knocked it down several quality grades and cut the price to a fraction. In its dry form, the papaïne was sold for cash in Beni, then transported to Europe for use in meat tenderizer and synthetics.

The maize, known as *mahindi*, as in Indian corn, grew well, once we discouraged the buffaloes from eating the baby plants.

One day, I was going through the fields where the *mahindi* was maturing and I noticed something that made me very indignant. Someone had had the cheek to pick some ears, light a fire, cook himself a meal and not even bother to hide the evidence. And this was right where he would have been seen by anyone passing.

I vented my indignation to Augustin, volubly, even with no bananas at hand. What kind of dirty, thieving, no good sons of blankety-blanks were there in this country, anyway?

He was surprised that I felt that way, but was careful not to anger me further. He was a diplomat, that's why he was Basikania's ambassador to the *wazungu*. He explained, and I had the idea that he was watching me and timing his speech to the rate of the settling of my hackles: "Bwana Carl, you are right, of course, to be upset. But think of it like this: when a man is traveling, he does not always have food with him. If he gets hungry, it is only natural that he must eat. So we have the custom that a traveler can eat from any one's *shamba*, any one's field, as long as he cooks it on the spot. If he cooks it and eats it right there, that is not stealing. If he takes it away, it is stealing. It works in every one's favour, for we all travel away from home at some time or another. Someone is hungry and eats something from my *shamba*, today, some other day I will be traveling and feel hunger and eat from another man's *shamba*."

I lost my indignation, but slowly. Even slowly, I had plenty of time to lose it all by the time he had finished. It isn't a bad system, if it isn't abused. I mean the 'help yourself' custom as well as Augustin's calming, hypnotic language trick.

When the *mahindi* was ripe, we started to harvest it. There wasn't anywhere to put it, immediately. That would have required planning of a different nature than that which Dad would have done. So we handled it in the traditional African way, we tied back some of the husks in a loop, strung the ears on poles and put the poles on racks made of shorter, forked, poles. This kept them in the sun, to complete their drying, and off the ground, so if it rained, the sun would dry them right out again, and also to keep them out of the reach of rodents and insects. The racks were on the slope of the hill, just in front of the verandah, under the watchful eyes of Paga and Mulvaney, which we thought would keep the crop out of the reach of Watalinga. We started on a thatched barn to store the crop, sending Samweli, one of the Chagga tractor drivers, on a quick visit to de Jaeger's *coup de bois* for the materials.

In a week or so after the racks were filled, and before the barn was complete, we heard the husks rustle. The rustling grew quite loud, and we thought to ourselves: "It's the husks drying in the sun."

Then we noticed that the husks were rustling when the sun wasn't shining. And we noticed, further, that it didn't really sound like rustling, anymore, maybe more like chomping. We took a look and found that it was just like chomping. Weevils had not bothered to ask why the poles were up off the ground, or anything, and had attacked the crop in masses. There was not one single grain of corn that did not have a weevil hole in its germ, which meant that not one grain of our crop had any value.

The maize had grown well, but the crop was worthless. Some of the other crops that Dad got us involved with, in experimental or test amounts, "tastes," he pronounced it, were groundnuts (peanuts), Soya and cotton. The groundnuts and the Soya were not big crops and we hadn't found a ready market. The cotton produced interesting results, though we saw at once that we would need to treat against boll weevils, and it was labour intensive.

Wouldn't anything other than the papaïne work?

Dad came home from one of his trips with "the answer to a maiden's prayer". In a town named Mambasa, between Bunia and Stanleyville, he had met and talked to a man who worked for BAT, the British American Tobacco Company. This man's job was to get the Africans to grow tobacco from seed provided by the company, to harvest and cure it according to his directions and then he would buy it from them. He trained African representatives, each of whom would be sent into a different area and be the teacher, trainer, quality controller, hand holder and general factotum. Dad volunteered to be the spearhead of an effort to introduce the crop to the Watalinga area. It would be a good cash crop for the local population and for us, and the buying and transporting might become a paying activity for us, all of which were important considerations.

Before long, we had a tobacco *pipinière* going next to or in among Pauline's coffee seedlings. Before much longer, we had tobacco planted out in the coffee strips. We would spend an hour or two extra on each trip that we went on to Beni or beyond, stopping at the edge of the road to track down Dad's new colleague and friend, the tobacco *capita*. If we found him, we'd be off on foot along a path into the forest to find a crop growing in a clearing beside a village, to admire it and to agree with the *capita* and ourselves that tobacco grew well in Watalinga. We would spend an extra hour on the way home from Church on Sundays, after abbreviated bad, black coffee and warm beer breaks, to weed and feed the tobacco plants and to agree among ourselves that tobacco grew well in between young coffee trees

Now we lived in fear of hail. A minor hailstorm would rip the leaves to shreds. We looked out for clouds that threatened to produce as much wind as the one that wanted to take the house. We got both, but not too badly. We watched for black spots on the leaves and clucked over brown ones. We went into the rows, periodically. to pinch off the flowers before they went to seed and sapped the strength of the plant. We weeded. We waited.

In a while, actually before the crop was totally ripe, we sent Elias (Samweli wouldn't go) to de Jaeger's *coup de bois* (we never did get our own), to get some long poles to build a curing barn. This type of tobacco has huge, heavy leaves, the joke among the workers was that you could sew a pair of pants from

236

two of them, and it is cured in smoke. It yields a cured tobacco that goes into the *Militaire* cigarettes that mimic the *Gauloise Caporales,* the smoke that separates the men from the boys and the Watalinga women from all other more weakly constituted species.

We harvested some of the crop and cured it. Dad sorted through it, his face long. He had been lectured long about the quality that the company was looking for. BAT would pay little for poor quality, in fact, it just didn't want poor quality. Compared to the standards that Dad remembered, this looked too thin, or it looked too pale, or the darned brown spots had worn through to make the leaves look as though Bill had mistaken them for Pedro. We packed one bale and pressed it with the screw press that BAT had loaned us and found that we didn't have enough. Reluctantly, Dad told us to put in the leaves that he had selected out, to make up the bale. Dad was eager to find out how it had turned out and probably dreading finding out that it was not well. We needed to get this first quarter ton bale to BAT in Stanleyville. We could take it to Beni and consign it to the weekly red mail truck, but that would take too long; Dad would have turned blue holding his breath that long. Our pickup was out of action, so we borrowed de Jaeger's truck and I drove it down to Stanleyville the same night that we packed it.

Sometime later, we heard that the tobacco was excellent. We had a good crop, which had a good market and which required no capital investment to speak of. Good things could and did happen.

However, this was later in our second full year there, and I was getting involved in Mutwanga, so I'm not sure when if ever the second bale got to the market.

A much earlier trip to the Bunia area had produced some cattle. Dad liked cattle. The idea of introducing milk cows to our new home intrigued him, for there was no fresh milk to be had. The closest excuse for it was canned milk or powdered milk.

He went with the intention of finding and bringing cattle, so he went with Polonia. The half dozen cattle arrived in bad shape. They hadn't enjoyed the trip at all. One of the steers was even dead on arrival.

The remaining ones soon demonstrated to us why no one

had cattle there. There were black flies that just sat on the poor beasts and bit them so continuously that they barely ate. The animals stayed thin as rakes. They were obviously not going to be milk cows and, in this state, were useless as beef cattle. No one slaughtered them and they refused to die. We had them around for a long time, hoping, maybe, that they would get accustomed to the flies. They didn't.

Here was a partial answer to the question about Belgians liking to import their food.

CHAPTER ELEVEN

The half a million Belgian Congo francs we started with were only ten thousand dollars, or only four thousand pounds. Some of that had already been spent on the preparations for the move. However frugal we were with the rest of it, it would not be enough to develop a thousand acres of coffee. We paid ourselves no salaries. We didn't buy beer or sodas; a beer cost as much as a man's pay for the whole day! We never went to the flicks. We spent no money, to speak of, on ourselves, but the money was going fast.

One of the ways that we hoped to make a little money while we waited for our first cash crop was to run a little company store, so to speak. We bought cigarettes (the famous *Militaires*), sugar, tea, shoes and all sorts of things we thought the men couldn't do without. We paid wholesale prices and charged the going retail. It was quite fair, really, the money would have been spent anyway at Milingos' or Ernesto's shops, and it meant that we could stretch our meager cash.

This enterprise started fairly soon after we got there. Mum and Dad's bedroom was where the medicines were kept, so the inventory for the shop was put there, too, and so, fairly naturally, the Dutch door to that room became the dispensary and shop counter. Most afternoons there would be a small line of people out there, waiting for medicine or to buy something.

"*Bwana*, I want some sugar."

"You mean, '*Please*, may I buy some sugar'."

"Yes."

"OK, here it is. One quarter kilo of sugar. That'll be 15 francs."

Manners are relative. Why should I presume that mine were better than his? He would never dream of being so rude as to reach out with only one hand to accept what I passed to him, rather off-handedly, in one hand. He would carefully hold out his right hand cupped in his left hand, for that is the proper, polite way to offer and to accept. And he'd never dream of not thanking me, even as I seemed not to understand his real needs.

239

"*Akisanti, Bwana!* But where are its leaves? I need its leaves."

"Oh, I'm sorry, here they are. One hundred grams of tea leaves. That will be another ten francs." (I'm guessing at the prices, I can't remember them).

"Why don't you just *andika* them, write them down." Then, while it was being *andika*'d: "I'm going to be happy tonight. Just put all this in a pot with a little bit of water, boil it all up and drink it."

"Isn't it too sweet like that?"

"That's why I drink it. Sweet is good!"

"Oh! All right! Go well. Who's next?"

"*Bwana*, I want some shoes. Do you have any of the kind that cry out while you're walking?"

"I don't know. Usually people don't want them to make any noise."

"Bwana! To wear shoes and feel that pain and not have anyone know that I have them? That's silly! When I wear them, I want everyone in every village I walk through to know that I have shoes on! They will even come out of their houses to see me walk by!"

"OK. Wait a few minutes and I'll look. Next."

"Give me one cigarette."

"You mean: '*Please* sell me one cigarette'."

"Yes. Give me one cigarette."

Whoever was available to tend to the shop did so, except Paga. No one asked him. We *andika*'d most of these sales. We started out with scraps of paper and then got a pad. We didn't ask for a signature, it was a meaningless concept in the context. The scraps of paper and the pad stayed in the black steel box that held our money, an army surplus ammunition box that Paga had adapted.

One day, several months into our time there, someone asked Dad a question about money.

He said: "Ask Carl. He's the accountant. He should be keeping the books."

That was news to me. I had heard that accountants kept books, but what books, I had no idea. I didn't even know what one of their books looked like, let alone what should be written in it. Mum looked around and found an old book with some red and green lines on its pages. She thought that that might

240

help. It had the word "Journal" on its cover. So I spent the next three months, or so it seemed, copying the information from scraps of paper and lists that said 'Izidori - 25f' and 'Seng. - cigs, 10f' and so on, into the book. I gave each employee a page, I thought that would be clever. I entered them in alphabetical order, I thought that was fairly clever, too. Then, when it came around to pay day, all I had to do was to go to each man's page, draw a line across the bottom, add up the numbers and deduct the amount from the pay. Bookkeeping wasn't all that difficult! It shouldn't intimidate anybody with half a brain.

If the same person did all of the entries, such a system might work. It would help if the names would stay still, too. If Alexandre came and charged something and his name couldn't be found, his name would be written in on the first clean page at the end, right after Zidori. If he was already in the book, as Lekisanderi, the way he usually pronounced it, he would now be in twice. Mpendawatu could be Pendawatu. He could also be Mpendawatu and Mpendawatu, once in the 'Ms', again in the non-alphabetical section, and perhaps yet again, farther in the back, for no good reason. You're beginning to guess that it didn't work smoothly.

By the time I got it organized well enough to start deducting the charges, some of the chaps had run up quite a tab. When pay day came, there was weeping and gnashing of teeth. Remember Bukanula? I won't go into it all, just close your eyes and imagine it.

Many of the *watu ya ngambo* had run up more debt than they were due in pay. They listened incredulously, as I itemized their charges and told them that they owed me money, rather than having something due to them today. They put on a bit of a show for me, and left not with pay, but with a slip of paper telling them how much they had to work off. It was the last day any of them were seen on our plantation.

In my new-found duties as accountant, I cleared off Dad's big *mvuli* desk, the same one, made in Karatu by Voigt, and opened some old mail. I found a check for about ninety thousand francs, from Ernesto, the medic at the clinic in Kamango. He had inherited some money from his father, how, no one knows - I mean, I know how he inherited it, I just don't know how his father had any money to leave him - and he had opened a bank account. He had started a *magazin,* a shop, beside his clinic. He had persuaded Dad to buy some of his supplies for him in Beni over a month or two, on credit, and he had paid for everything at one time, with this check. When I found it, the check was dangerously close to its ninety-day expiration, if not past it.

The next time Dad was in Beni, he presented it to the bank.

"We are *desolés*, M. le Prince. Zere are not sufficient funds in 'eez account! Of course, eef you 'ad presented eet when 'ee wrote eet, eet would 'ave been *tout à fait en ordre,* but now, [shrug] zere eez nossing we can do!"

When we told Ernesto the sad news, and asked him what he would do about it, he was just as *desolé,* though I can't say surprised. However, he went further than the bank did in offering a solution; he magnanimously offered to write us another check.

The inventory was long gone, of course, as were the proceeds, and as was nearly one fifth of our capital.

The tobacco concept was patterned on a system well developed and used by a co-operative society of native coffee growers, by COTONCO, a corporation which bought and ginned native grown cotton, and by a rice marketing company, whose name I forget. The natives would be instructed in the cultivation and harvesting, and the co-op or the company would buy and market the crop.

Early on, Dad had seen the coffee co-op as a source of revenue. There was the tiny commission, about five dollars for each ton, which they offered for the work of purchasing the coffee, handful by handful, kilo by kilo, and there was the transportation to Beni, which actually was a paying proposition, particularly if the wages for the person doing it were zero.

So, Dad paid a M. Poncelet, the European manager of the co-op, a visit in his Butembo home and all was arranged. We became the official representative of the co-op in the Watalinga area. Which made us, in a way, the employees of some of our employees, or of their wives and aunts. Not that we let them appreciate it.

This put some of our underutilized assets to work: Polonia was not doing much, and there were several young people in the house out of whom some more useful work could be got. I was the only non-Dad, non-Marcel driver of Polonia, so after

Dad did the buying a couple of times, I won uncontested rights to the rest of the season.

Why me rather than Marcel? There were two reasons, one purely practical and the other bordering on theoretical physics. First, Marcel could keep the tractors going when I couldn't; his constant availability on the plantation more valuable than was mine. Second, there is phenomenon that has to do with an area of study, as yet incomplete, concerning relativity. Marcel could and always did drive much faster than I ever dared, yet trips which he made at a high speed to Beni with coffee, or to the COTONCO gin, sometimes took a day longer than the ones that I made at a much lower speed. And he always came back looking as though he had been to war, and sometimes even Polonia looked the worse for the adventure. The answer lay, perhaps in the fact that we were so close to the Equator or to the magnetic field disturbance caused by the mountains. Or, perhaps it lay in the frequency distribution or the scatter pattern of the network of sources of the acoustic disturbances produced by John Bosco's works played on wind-up gramophones, partly muted by thatched roofs and partly covered by the voices of men and women discussing the things they are wont to discuss when they meet in those surroundings. Whatever the reasons for the Marcel factor, it was better for our peace of mind, for our productivity and for Polonia's longevity that I drove.

Besides, Marcel had taught me, one more time: "Bwana Carl, if she does *THAT* to you, do *THIS*." *THAT* was when Polonia allowed the gear lever to select both reverse and second gear simultaneously. It was a thing you just felt her do, as it was happening. It was sort of the way you feel when you see that you're grabbing some nettles or poison ivy with a handful of weeds, but you don't stop your hand in time. For a moment you can hope you didn't touch anything, but soon you'll know. With Polonia's gears, you wouldn't really know until you let out the clutch and either the gear box would be ruined, or the engine would stall. The first was a major problem. The second was only a minor inconvenience, unless the batteries happened to be weak and you weren't stopped on a hill. It was a major inconvenience if the batteries were dead and you hadn't thought to bring a hill along with you. The only way to avoid either of these two results was to do *THIS*. *THIS* was to keep your foot on the clutch while reaching back behind the line of the seat, down to floor level, behind the hot engine cowling, with your left hand, to remove the cotter pin from the gear shift lever pivot pin, then to press the gear lever down so you could remove the pivot pin, then remove the pin, then remove the lever, then reach behind the seat to pick up the tire iron that had to be kept within reach for just this purpose, insert the tire iron in the hole and feel around in the slots and notches, de-select reverse gear, de-select second gear and, finally, free up the thing called the gate. Only at this point could you unwind yourself from the contortions and let out the clutch. Then all you had to do was to put the lever and its pins back, select a gear and go on. With this knowledge, and the knowledge that the vacuum for the brake servo and the power steering could fail at any time, probably on steep hills, I had as good a chance as had Marcel of surviving a game of Polonia roulette. A ten-dollar expenditure on a new gate would have fixed the gear problem. We didn't see any reason to spend that kind of money when we both knew how to get out of the problem. The brake and steering problems were just *shauri ya Mungu*, fate, literally God's concern. We couldn't control that.

And, Marcel had given me a dry run. My first run to Mutwanga with cotton was with Marcel. As we passed the place where *Papa ya Roma* held his audiences, Marcel remembered that he had some pressing business to transact behind the row of banana trees. He took an advance on his *posho* money for the week, told me that I would find him right there on my way back, and disappeared towards the sounds of John Bosco. I knew that the term 'dry run' was already inappropriate as I drove on towards Mutwanga. Everything went just fine, for ten miles. At that point, Polonia sensed that she could test the boundaries with her new, inexperienced boss. She quit. I hitched a ride back to town, asked the Pope to call Marcel out. I got instructions as to how to bleed air out of the diesel fuel line. I hitched a ride back to Polonia, did what Marcel told me to do and continued. Three more times, I bled the line, before I got back to ask the Pope to call Marcel out again, to go home. Marcel was not fit to drive home, but that couldn't stop him. Neither could I. He punished Polonia all the way home. We survived her punishment, but barely.

During the season, every *siku ya kazi mbili,* Kinguana for

the second day of work, or Tuesday, Joseph (the Mrundi) and I would heft Paga's steel box and the weighing balance into Polonia and go to the village that we had announced on the previous buying day. There we would set up the box, hang the balance from a rafter of the thatched shelter built for the purpose and buy coffee until we dropped. Each co-op member had a little booklet into which we entered the number of kilos of coffee purchased, the amount paid and the date. Week by week, or whenever the mails could find us, we adjusted the price to whatever M. Poncelet told us. Later, after the coffee had been marketed, there would be a distribution of the profit, with settlement made against these entries. It would take some time, the coffee had to go to Beni, thence to Stanleyville, both by truck, and then on by river, train, by river again, truck again and God knows what else, down to Matadi or Boma, at the mouth of the Congo river, where it would be put on a ship to the markets in Europe.

The little books were very valuable, for in fact they were almost like cash. They were treasured, so they were kept jealously, close to the owner. They were kept close to the owner's body, in 100-degree heat and 100-percent humidity, while the owner trudged ten or more miles to the market with a load of coffee on her head. The books were valuable and they were very ripe. But, for each one I handled, I earned our enterprise almost one whole US cent.

The coffee that we bought was, because of our own buying activities, a form of hard currency. The Africans could prevent theft of their crops by witchcraft, but our deterrents were much less powerful, being only guns and dogs, so we wanted to keep the coffee under our eyes. The only place we had was the verandah of the main camp building. Joseph and a couple of helpers would make it up into ninety kilo lots in jute gunny bags which they would sew shut with sisal twine. Every now and then, when we had enough to make a five-ton load, we'd put it on Polonia and I'd make the trip to Beni.

Mulvaney took to lying on the pile of bags, I think because he liked the view from the verandah. With his beady little bull terrier's eyes, he would watch the bagging. He started sleeping there at night. We joked that he was the coffee *capita,* on guard duty.

Bad joke. He woke up one morning very sick. In a few

hours he was dead. Mum thought that only poison could have done him in that suddenly.

Cotton was a slightly different story. The *bwana Coton* would do his own buying and would store his purchases in thatched structures in the villages. We got a deal to carry the cotton to his gin beyond Mutwanga, on the other end of the mountains, almost all the way to the border at Kasindi, at so many francs a ton kilometer. Cotton looks light and fluffy and quite benign. We had no machines or tools load it with, and it was a little like loading leaves onto a truck by hand. Eventually, we developed a bit of a system with some tarpaulins or sacking to make manageable bundles. We had thought of putting Polonia's side tarpaulins up to stop the cotton from going through the airy slats. We expected that to get a full load, we would have to stamp it down with our feet, but we found that the roof got in the way of that operation, so, before the second trip, we took it off. The stamping made loading take nearly a whole day, and it showed us the less benign nature of cotton. The seeds have a small, sharp protrusion, which, in large numbers, eventually work a bit like sandpaper on your skin. Then, too, the fluffy stuff is full of dust and lint. Never mind, it didn't kill anybody.

The coffee trips to Beni were easy, I could load five tons of those sacks with one helper (and I've the bad back to show for it) and get to Beni and back before nightfall. Polonia was officially a seven-ton lorry, but she had a hard enough time getting the smaller load up the escarpment. The trips were mostly in the dry season. They only came every couple of weeks.

A cotton trip started out with the loading, which wouldn't be complete until late afternoon. I'd get going as soon as it was done, needing to get up the escarpment before dark or before it rained. The escarpment had a stretch of about a hundred metres which was really too steep for Polonia at her age and in her state of health, and it came after a mile of increasing gradient which killed any momentum that might have helped her over it. We could only get up that stretch by lurching forwards in two and three metre steps, with a lot of clutch-slipping and with Sengerengabo dancing behind the rear wheels with chocks. It was better to do this in the light and impossible to do it in the wet. We'd get to our destination quite

246

late in the evening. I'd back up against the building and, if it wasn't raining, I'd sleep on top of the load. If it was, I'd curl up in the cab. COTONCO would have only a couple of men there in the morning, so we'd do much of the unloading ourselves, to speed our turnaround.

If it hadn't rained during the night, I'd be home for a meal and a bath, and to turn round to do it again. If it had rained, and it often did, I slept on Polonia, among the mosquitoes and the animals in the park at the place that she usually sank to her axles and refused to go any further. If I dug and pushed and cursed and fretted, I could move along about one more mile, but it would take all night and into the morning, until the sun had had a chance to dry the road out, usually by about ten in the morning, and then, finally we'd get unmired and going again.

Once, tired of this routine, I pulled over to the edge of the road at the last settlement before the park, told Sengerengabo to buy a chicken, which he boiled at the edge of the road, using some of Pauline's favourite pilipilis. We ate, surrendered ourselves to the mosquitoes and waited for the sun to come up, which it eventually did in its own sweet time. We watched the vapour come up off the surface of the road and from time to time checked the consistency of the mud. When we were satisfied, we set out again. At ten, as we drove past the place where we had always stuck, Polonia thanked me for not having again wasted thousands of miles of her life.

This went on for some weeks.

On most trips, I took some sandwiches with me, and washed them down with Mum's lemonade, if *watu ya ngambo* had recently supplied us with lemons, or coffee or tea out of Dad's old Thermos. Sometimes I stopped in at the Greek grocer's and bought canned sterilized milk, though at eight francs I worried that this was a bit of an extravagance. Once I met de Jaeger and he suggested we repair to the other European hotel for lunch. I ate the three or four course *prix fixé* meal, including artichoke and veal. It was good. De Jaeger got the bill and I made the right noises about sharing it. I needn't have worried, he intended just that. I nearly died when he told me my share. It was ninety-five francs! Nearly two dollars! That was two weeks of wages for a worker in the fields! I hadn't imagined that food could be that expensive. De Jaeger didn't mind commenting about Dad's spending a few francs on a sign for the "old goat in Njadot", but he could casually spend ten times as much on a meal! For me, it was back to Mum's sandwiches and water and the occasional pilipili chicken, but my guilt complex permitted me fewer treats of canned milk.

Polonia usually took her refreshment at the Semliki river. It was one of several places where we'd stop because there was water near to the road. We'd stop and scoop a *debe* of brown water and fill her radiator. On one of these stops, I watched an elephant wade out into the water from our bank, about a hundred yards upstream from us. I thought that I was going to see it take a bath, and certainly, it swished its trunk in the water and splashed, but just a little, and not playfully. It looked very purposeful, and kept going, until its back had disappeared under the surface. Then I could see only the tip of its trunk out of the water, and I followed it farther into the current. Half a minute later, its back started to appear again, and then the whole elephant, as it came up the slope of the far bank of the river. It walked serenely into the forest. I was rather impressed. I never had thought about it much, but I'm sure I had been living with the idea that the river was a barrier that divided distinctly separate populations of non-amphibious animals.

That particular elephant was of the old school. It didn't like modern technology. They weren't all like that. Dad and I were coming home one night in the pickup and we came face to rear with a couple of elephants who were crossing the river on the new bridge, in front of us. They took their time. The VW pickup has its front seat occupants sitting over the front wheels, with not much between them and an elephant. It looked like we were dealing with a mother and child, and I was not interested in finding out the limit to the mother's tolerance. I wanted Dad to back off the bridge and not disturb them. He wouldn't, instead he inched forwards little by little, as they ambled on. He wasn't impatient, he just wasn't frightened. After a little while, we tried turning off the lights, to see if that helped them see better to move on. We couldn't tell if it helped.

Eventually, we reminded ourselves that there were signs posted at the beginning of the park, 'Elephants have the right of way,' and that of one of the lessons that Africa teaches best is patience.

There was a joke going around, over twenty years ago.

Question: "How many bananas do you let an 800 lb. gorilla take?"

Answer: "As many as he wants!"

New question, along the same lines: "How long do you let an elephant take to get out of your way?"

CHAPTER TWELVE

Mum's suggestion of *Neu Affenheim* as the name for our new place was prescient.

A few months after we settled in, Pauline was minding her own business in the camp. A stranger came up onto the hill, carrying a young colobus monkey.

He offered it to Pauline: "What? You don't want to buy this monkey?"

She confirmed the implied conclusion: "Yes, it's true. I don't want to buy it."

She went on: "You can't sell it, because it isn't yours to sell. Why did you take it from its mother? Where is its mother? What did you do to its mother?"

"*Akisanti, madamwazeli!* Thank you, mademoiselle! I will cook, it even if it is very small. There is little meat on this baby, but it will be sweeter than its mother was."

That is how Jakopo came to live with us. He got the immediate protection of a name, though he didn't really need that protection from us. We would eat lots of things, but our line was drawn well this side of colobus monkeys.

Jakopo was tiny. We didn't have a rubber teat to feed him his milk, nor, for that matter, the milk to deliver through it if we had one. Pauline was never put off by considerations of a purely practical nature. She had and still seems to have an almost magical way with these things. She worked out a way to feed him food she invented for him. Through her ministrations Jakopo became very tame and would lie asleep, curled on a lap, or would hang on to the shirt of anyone who let him, the way he'd seen wild baby monkeys cling to their mothers' fur.

Jakopo spent the rest of his life, or much of it, with the verandah attached to him via a leash hooked to a dog collar around his waist. Our waists are designed to hold up trousers and therefore are able to hold belts. Colobus genes have not had the same driving forces in their evolution, so their waists are quite useless for our purpose, a waste you could say. The periods of his life that Jakopo spent untethered were through no lack of our trying to have it otherwise, they could be attributed directly to his genetic deficiency aided by his Houdini-esque escape skills. He frequently slipped out of his collar-belt to swing about in the rafters. A favourite place to sit was above the dining room table.

I can only remember one time that someone commented on the need for an umbrella indoors. We took it to mean that he must have liked us, most of the time.

Dad had had a previous experience with a pet monkey, in Rongai, and was not very amused when Jakopo appeared. Dad had been the person who usually put that earlier monkey in its cage, or maybe he had only done it once. Whatever the evil that he had perpetrated, it was enough that the monkey took an intense dislike to him. Apparently monkeys, like elephants, never forget. From then on, every time it escaped, it would go for the rafters (Rongai started without a ceiling, too) and try to relieve itself on him. It once got hold of Dad's only pair of gold cufflinks, which, though they were about as useful to Dad as they were to the monkey, were a keepsake from home and of sentimental value. It put them in the pouch that monkeys have in their cheeks. Using monkey-style psychological warfare, it would add insult to injury by taking out the cufflinks when Dad was around and examining them, ostentatiously, turning them this way and that, all the time being sure to stay just out of Dad's reach. And if Dad forgot and came too close ... Well, as I said, Dad didn't have pleasant memories.

Jakopo grew, but never got very big. At least once, some part of him grew far more than nature intended, almost too much for what she had allowed as safety margins in her design. Paga used to bake bread in the old exploding kerosene stove, using sourdough. Part of the ritual involved putting the dough in a nice sunny spot for it to rise. The verandah had many suitable places. The same verandah was Jakopo's territory. Once, Jakopo got to the rising dough and helped himself to a large amount of it, in fact, he ate as much as he was physically able, then looked for his own sunny spot to take his usual nap. When the sun had done its job on the yeast and the yeast its job on the dough, the dough did a job on Jakopo's stomach. It nearly ripped him apart.

He lay there, wailing: "Weh-eh-eh-eh! WEH-EH-eh-eh!" There was nothing we knew to do to help him, so he just suffered through the night.

251

He survived and contributed to the lore of the family. Anyone who has eaten too much sooner or later mentions Jakopo or utters a pale imitation of the pitiful "Weh-eh-eh-eh!" Everyone else understands, even if no one is able to duplicate the same truly heart-rending, compassion generating cry of Jakopo's original performance.

An African gray parrot came to us in a similar way. Doubtless it got a name, too, probably Kasuku, Swahili for parrot.

Kasuku survived a brush with schizophrenia to entertain us for hours at a time. The first lesson in whistling that he got from my siblings was "The Happy Whistler." When he had learned the first three bars, not even the first full line, he was given a rest from that complicated tune full of staccato eighth and sixteenth notes and allowed to relax with a simpler but more subtle phrase. He appreciated the gesture, but totally misunderstood the intent. From then on, The Happy Whistler always ended in the fourth bar, which consisted of a raucously lecherous wolf whistle that would have put a New York construction worker to shame.

As we added to the entourage, we also, sadly, saw some departures. You've heard about the shyness of Josephine, the Siamese cat, about the untimely end of my shadow, Mulvaney, and the abrupt, unceremonious passing of poor old Pedro.

Carrie was a miniature dachshund. Her parents were named Bus and Taxi, respectively, so she was named Caravan, of course, Carrie for short. She was Mum's dog, and a favourite. She'd always been happy to stay at home. She had not been a traveler until she came to Kagando. One day, for some unremembered reason, she rode in Polonia. Perhaps she was given a ride home, with Mum or Pauline, to save them all from a hot, exhausting mid-afternoon climb up the hill. For Carrie, particularly, with her short legs, the hill was a mountain. However it happened, she rode in the front and got a taste of life in the fast lane. On a later occasion she was given another ride and was asked to go in the back because she was just too active to be in front. She did not like this demotion, at all. She jerked free of whatever hands were restraining her in the back, jumped to the ground, a distance about eight times her own height, and tried to make her way to the front. Unfortunately, the way to the front was along the track. Even more unfortunately, I already had Polonia moving along the track and didn't know what was happening until too late.

Half an hour later, I had the sad duty of telling Mum that we'd just buried her favourite dog at the edge of a *kipaniyé*, down on the plain.

CHAPTER THIRTEEN

How fortuitous that this turned out to be Chapter 13, it might heighten the effect of a warning. **The faint of heart or stomach and anyone who has not been a Catholic priest should skip this chapter.** It is not pretty. It gags on truly disgusting subject matter and, if that weren't enough, it listens to a grown man making sniveling *mea culpa* noises about things he did when he was a youth. Each of these things by itself would be enough to turn the strongest stomach. Together they could be lethal, except, I suspect, to priests, whose work experience may have hardened them enough to survive at least the latter. I like to think that there is some benefit from all that training. The rest of you simply don't have the equipment to handle either part and are at the mercy of this chapter. Well, it seems you are ignoring the warning. Read on, if you must, but be prepared.

Late on a day in our first April, I was on my way back from buying coffee, or some other such errand in Polonia. I saw several Watalinga women coming in the opposite direction, staggering along the road under huge baskets. There was a smell in the air that seemed a little familiar. That was the only thing little about it. The heat-smell of Polonia's engine couldn't mask it. It was the biggest and the worst smell I have ever met, ever, on a jungle road or anywhere! The smell was always even worse just after I had passed one of the women; it didn't get better anywhere, it just got worse.

After we passed about the sixth group of baskets I was close to admitting that I recognized the smell when Joseph, who was riding with me, said: *"Nyama ya tembo!* Elephant meat!"

I had been hoping that it wasn't what I thought it was, but I wouldn't have been willing to bet on it. We were six miles away from the real origin of the smell, so I could be excused for my slowness. Joseph's brevity and certainty left little hope that I had misunderstood him. The knowledge and my suspicion as to the root of his certainty only made the smell even worse.

The day before, I had been with Joseph and several of the

Watalinga workers, hacking our way through the *matete,* laying out the base line between two of the parcels of land, from which line the *kipaniyés* would later be projected. In one spot, there had been a little more smell than usual, and it had a different note to it. I had taken no notice, there are lots of smells in a hot climate. As I moved on to the far end of the tape and waited for them to catch up, a couple of the men had disappeared into the grass, as we all did from time to time to attend to our personal comfort. We had gone all the way to the end of the line and were heading back home along the way we had come, when Joseph decided to let me in on the secret of which by then I alone was ignorant. He pulled me into the *matete.* Not ten paces from where, a while ago, I had stood for several minutes perfecting a 3-4-5 triangle, was an elephant carcass. The skin was dry and crusty looking, but intact all around. Joseph wanted me to promise him the tusks, or at least a share in what they brought. I hardly heard him. My attention rather taken up by this sight. I made no commitment; the tusks weren't mine to give. I didn't have them, anyway, they were gone. Still not paying much attention, I didn't wonder why the discussion about tusks if there were none. Then I saw that there was stuff oozing out of the tusk holes. Some of the stuff oozed while other stuff wriggled out of the holes. Obviously, the tusks had only recently been removed. I learned later that they had moved only ten feet, and that Joseph knew exactly where they were, but that is incidental.

That night I told everyone at home about it and offered to show the sight. Predictably, no one wanted to come and see it. We talked about how long it had been since we last had seen elephants in the area.

We had been in Kagando only a few months, it was November and we had arrived in August, when we saw some elephants in the valley of the small river that ran through the south west corner of our property, the same one which acted as our water supply and bath. The animals were less than half a mile from the house. Bill and I took the rifles out, went down our hill towards them, and, from our vantage point on the hill and across the river, fired a couple of rounds in their general direction. They climbed with surprising speed out of the valley and disappeared into the *matete* on the flat land. Even from our spot on the hill, we couldn't see their backs in the tall grass, though from the camp we might have. When we went back up to the top of the hill, we were able to see that they had left our property. It was the last time we saw elephants anywhere close to it. We congratulated ourselves, because we really didn't want them there; if they stayed around we might have had to deal with them in ways we had no desire to get caught up in.

After talking about it briefly that April night, we thought no more about the carcass, being used to hyenas and vultures of the East African plains cleaning everything up within a few days, forgetting that they didn't exist here. Perhaps that's why we didn't make the leap of logic that if we had seen no elephants after November, the carcass may have been dead even then.

After Joseph confirmed the provenance of the aroma of the Watalinga women's baskets, I had to fight down the rising sick feeling I got from the dawning realization of their intentions towards the meat that had been lying ripening in the heat for at least five months. The thick skin had kept it together all that time, rather like a Camembert cheese. Now it was heading, oozing, towards scores of Watalinga cooking fires. Ugh!

That night hundreds of Watalinga ate it and relished it. And they lived! At least it wasn't wasted. Ugh!, all the same.

Did I warn you?

We had been taught how to handle and use guns, and I can say we even liked them. We were respectable shots; I was the captain of Prince o's shooting team and, a few years later, joined the rifle team at my university. None of this meant that we enjoyed using the weapons on living creatures. We were brought up in a hunting society, but on the whole we were ambivalent about the so-called sport.

When I was seven or eight, I witnessed a massacre. We had not yet come into the period when the rains failed every year, just some years. The crops were at least growing. When they grew, herds of Thompson's Gazelles, Tommies, moved in. One night, when the beans were just getting their third or fourth pair of leaves, getting big, but still juicy, I went down to the fields with Dad and half a dozen workers in the back of the lorry. The African driver drove, Dad stood in the back, with his shotgun and a box of ammo.

As Dad shot, I kept my eyes shut. Most of the time. Try as

I would, I couldn't all of the time. I saw one poor Tommy standing on three legs, one leg dangling grotesquely over its shoulder. It was wagging its little tail constantly, the way they always do, even when they are wounded, even with one leg blown off. I saw the African workers jump off the lorry, run up to it and cut its throat, to make its meat clean under Islam. I watched them throw it on to the lorry beside me, quite dead, but still warm, its warm blood still dripping. It was a cool night, but I was absolutely shivering.

We came back home with a dozen or more dead Tommies in the lorry. Dad was obviously not pleased with or proud of his work. I was terrified and horrified. You couldn't say that the workers were unmoved, either. They were ecstatic.

Despite this incident, I continued my relationship with weapons, including firearms.

I graduated from the harmless pop guns to equally harmless home-made bows and arrows. I became a good shot with a catapult (slingshot), an air gun and a .22 rifle. I could hit tin cans and other targets with them more often than I missed them. The fun was in learning the skill and using it. I sometimes aimed at birds with my catapult, and was quite surprised, even disappointed, when I knocked one down. The problem was that a catapult rarely killed even a small bird and I would have to complete the job by hand. You cannot feel detached from the action of wringing a wounded creature's neck. If you were going to aim at birds, the air gun and the .22 rifle were better in that they did the job more thoroughly.

When I was taken along by well-meaning friends and relatives to hunt, I went willingly; I knew I would get a chance to use another gun. When I got a turn, I would take the shot, but I'd aim at a rock or tuft of grass rather than at a gazelle. I didn't mind if my reputation as a shot suffered as long as I had the opportunity to try out the rifle and as long as *I* knew that I'd hit *my* target.

I speak for myself, but while I didn't mind eating game meat, I was quite squeamish about killing. I never killed even a lowly mouse bird without feeling sorry for it, even as my sympathy for them was greatly tempered by the fact that these birds ate the fruit in our garden. We were taught not to kill for killing's sake and not to waste; we ate what we killed, even mouse birds.

257

Up to the time we left Rongai, only Dad had ever killed anything bigger than a guinea fowl.

Such was our hunting experience when we arrived in the Congo.

One day, not long after we arrived, a young Mnandi carrying a spear came to tell me he could lead me to where there were buffalo, not far from where Pauline was preparing her nursery. His name was Puluku, or Mbuluku, take your choice, which told me immediately that he didn't have an older sister named Puluku. (Now do you begin to see how useful such a naming system is? Or was that Muhindo?) Puluku was a hunter, he said. If I could use a *bunduki*, a rifle, we could all eat meat that night. It must have been before Dad had returned with Mum and Paga, because I seem to remember first, that I felt, somehow obliged to try to hunt the buffalo, you know, to show I was made out of the right stuff, and all that, and second, that I didn't have the use of one of our own weapons. I went to Rémy Paepe to borrow his rifle. It was a .30-06 calibre U. S. Army rifle. It had a number stamped on the barrel: "1918". I don't think it was a serial number and it wasn't the calibre. It had an idiosyncrasy, Paepe told me: to eject the spent shell, I should turn the rifle over, shake it and slap the bottom of the magazine. Other than that, it was in good condition and accurate, at least at close range, he said. At least I think he said that.

I followed Puluku and his spear into the *matete*. We went for several hundred yards, following tracks that had been made in the night. Soon the tracks became fresher, and then even fresher. My knees began to do funny things, then my tummy. I stiffened my upper lip to compensate for what my lower lip wanted to do, and followed.

Puluku stopped, very still. Then, motioning to me to follow, he dropped to his hands and knees to get through a thicket of *matete*. I followed.

He motioned me to come up alongside him. I did.

He motioned to me to go in front of him, the while putting his finger to his lips, in the international sign language for "do not yell for your mother now, or we'll both get hurt!" I went.

My bladder joined my knees and my tummy in trying to communicate with the part of me that was taking them all, along with me, ever deeper into that situation. Urgent and clamorous as they were, apparently none of the appeals got through to the right destination. Whatever part of me it was, it just kept on taking all of us forwards, reluctant as we were.

Matete is always fairly difficult to get through. Here, near the swamp it was thicker and interlaced with stalks that had been in a fire which had curled the stalks up into a tangle that only a tractor or a buffalo could force its way through. Puluku was indicating to me that I must get to the other side of the tangle in front of me, without upsetting the buffalo, though he didn't seem to mind if I upset myself, and that the only way to do it was to lie on my tummy and pull myself along, slowly and utterly silently. (It's an amazing thing how subtle sign language can be. It is context sensitive, you know, which helps).

Paepe's rifle was not going to be much use to me if it was behind me, so it went in front. It occurred to me that if it got excited and couldn't restrain itself, it couldn't hit me if it was in front of me. This was probably also Puluku's logic with respect to me when he sent me ahead. I had to figure all of that out myself; sign language does have its limitations. As I moved, the tricky magazine was inches from my face. I must have hesitated as I thought about Paepe's reloading instructions. Puluku nudged me on. I looked at the muzzle collecting stuff as I pushed it forwards. That was not ideal, but I couldn't get up and shake it out. I thought: "Oh, well, if I do fire a shot, I probably won't live to worry about ejecting the spent cartridge, or about the pain and inconvenience of being trampled by a charging buffalo!" That reassuring thought and Puluku's next nudge got me moving again, but I watched the muzzle more carefully.

In about ten yards, which seemed to take an hour to cover, in other words, it was over too soon, I got to where I felt the light increasing over my head. I took that to mean that I could soon stand up again, but just then my nose came to within about three inches of a fresh, steaming pile of buffalo droppings. Funny, the places they keep popping up. My sweat glands must have sprayed an aerosol warning to the animal that was almost standing over me, because I heard a snort and a crashing, thundering departure that shook the *matete* that was holding me down. While I was thinking how lucky I was that the beast had chosen to run away from rather than over me, Puluku came over the tangle and dragged me to my feet. We set off after our quarry, running at first, slowing down when we thought they had stopped.

Three or four more times we got almost, but never again quite as close, and always with similar results: disappointing to Puluku, welcome to me. Then it became dark and I could give up the hunt honourably - honourably and very, very willingly.

Puluku came back some time later, it was when our own weapons were available, but it was before van der Zichelen had cleared much of his land. Puluku had set a trap that had caught a buffalo. He wanted me to go along and help him finish it off. I went along, for no reason other than to help put a trapped, hurt animal out of its misery in a humane way, rather than to think of it being hacked to pieces with machetes. He led me to a place in the road to Njadot where it looked as though a tractor had gone into the *matete*. There was a wide swath of the grass laid flat and pointing towards the river, a little below van der Z's planned house.

I asked where the buffalo was. Puluku pointed along the swath.

I asked where the trap was. Puluku told me it was with the buffalo, around its neck. The trap consisted of a wire noose attached to a log. The log would drag against the animal's movement through the brush, slowing it and tiring it. The hunters would wait for it to weaken and move in to kill it, if it hadn't effectively hung itself by then. I felt even more compassion for the beast. That seemed like a rotten way to go.

For several hours we followed the eight feet wide path that the poor creature had flattened. We came close several times, but it heard or smelled us and crashed away before we could see it. It obviously was very alert and not tiring quickly.

Once more, it became too dark to continue. Despite feeling sorry for the buffalo, I stopped and turned back for home, suggesting that the job be continued in the daylight. I didn't like the idea of leaving that animal overnight, probably in pain, but nor was I willing to sacrifice myself to it. Sorry goes only so far. East Africa's Cape buffalo are wily; they set ambushes, turning the tables on hunters. I was not yet used to the difference. I didn't know it yet, but these buffalo were more like cows than Cape buffalo.

Puluku didn't come back for my help in the morning, he must have been unhappy with the quality of my services. In one respect, didn't mind. I didn't want the role of slaughterer for every would-be meat eater in the region.

Reluctant hunters as we were, there came a time when we forgot ourselves and became almost bloodthirsty.

We watched the maize that we planted between the coffee rows germinate and grow. This was a familiar crop; we'd grown it every year in Rongai. Its familiarity was rather reassuring in this still strange place, with its strange people who spoke strange languages, with its strange animals, crops and plants. Beyond its familiarity and its obvious economic value to us, we had some other attachments to it. We had each of us, personally, taken part in its planting. We watched what would be our first crop sprout and shoot up, as though it rashly wanted to compete with the *matete*, inches overnight. We went to look at it almost every day. We were very happy with it.

It got to be about a foot high and was winning against the *matete*. One morning, on a routine visit, we found that the buffaloes had discovered it. They had come out of the swamp at the foot of our hill, at night. With what seemed to us to be a perverted pleasure, or at least a systematic destructiveness, they each had taken a row and, starting at the beginning, taken a bite out of each plant, all the way to the far end. The bite included the succulent growing tip of the plant, without which it would never develop into anything but a stump with leaves. And, to add insult to injury, they had stepped on hundreds of the still delicate coffee plants.

We took this personally. This meant war!

Bill and I laid out an excellent plan. After work we built a skeleton platform in a tree that was right over where the tracks had come out of the *matete*. It was one of the few trees on the place. We would wait for the enemy to come out again and attack as the troops passed under us. That night we spent several uncomfortable hours balanced in the tree. We had no torches in working order, so we sat in the pitch dark, listening for the buffalo to announce themselves under our tree. It was a good plan, as far as it went, but it was an incomplete one. We heard mosquito noises, other insect noises, leaf noises, rustling and some muffled shuffling noises, but nothing we could identify as buffalo noises. We didn't know what buffalo noises were, but we knew we would recognize them when we heard them. After hours of discomfort, we must have realized that what we were doing made as much sense as hunting by Braille. We gave up and went home. In the morning we saw tracks coming out at a spot a few yards away from our tree, and that another part of the maize crop had become dessert for the sweet-toothed buffaloes. The slight shuffling that we had heard in the whole spectrum of sound had probably been their only noise.

If the enemy wouldn't come to us, we'd go to it. We scrounged around and found some insulated wire, probably part of a box of scraps picked up at one of the auctions. We took off one of Polonia's headlights and experimented with it. We could attach the wires to Polonia's battery terminals and hold the other ends to the appropriate places on the lamp reflector and bulb to make a searchlight, but when we didn't hold the wire correctly, we got poor light and burned our fingers. Polonia had a twelve-volt system, with two big, heavy, six-volt batteries, wired end to end. If it had been one twelve-volt battery it would have weighed over a hundred pounds and no one could have lifted it into or out of its cradle. One battery alone gave a weak glow in the bulb. We needed both. We put them both in a box. We realized that we couldn't carry both the box and the guns in our hands. We slung the box on a pole. We planned to carry the pole on our shoulders. We would do this ourselves, thinking we might be better able to control the situation if there were fewer people around. We would go down into the cultivated strips, wander around with our searchlight off. When we heard the buffalo, we'd put down the pole and whoever was carrying the lamp would put the wires together to 'turn on' the light. He'd shine it around to spot the buffalo while the other got the rifle ready to aim and shoot. We would do this for several nights, until the buffalo got the idea that they were not welcome. Simple. Now, *this* was an excellent plan!

When it was completely dark, we hefted the pole onto our left shoulders, took our rifles in our right hands and started down the hill. We were not one tenth of the way down when we had to stop to move the load to the other shoulder. The next stop, to switch back, came even sooner. By the time we were near the maize, our shoulders were raw and sore and we were exhausted. The buffalo didn't make any noise near us, but we shone the light, anyway, for good measure. If the buffalo were not making a noise, neither were they making an appearance.

It is possible we were obstinate enough to carry the batteries all the way back up that same night, despite our raw shoulders. If we had done it, I'd remember it, and I don't. Maybe Sengerengabo and some other lucky guy had that pleasure reserved for them to enjoy in the morning.

To heck with plans! We tried again, wandering around in the fields at night, without the light. On the fourth or fifth try, we had some success. On a night as black as a coal cellar at midnight, we startled a buffalo and Bill shot at the sound. The bullet entered just under the tail and hit no bones on the way to the heart. To get even for this undignified way of treating one of their number, the buffalo herd stayed around and wrecked some more of the crops and coffee plants for many weeks longer.

One afternoon, we had just harvested some ground nut plants. We had them in a pile and were wondering how to protect them for the night, not so much from hungry buffalo as hungry neighbours. We would separate the pods from the plants the next day, it was getting too late to do it immediately.

As we considered the problem, a strange looking person showed up. He was very muscular and wore tattered clothes that had never been introduced to soap. He carried a couple of spears. He had a helper, and the two of them moved in what seemed to be a bubble of aroma that you could cut with a knife, perhaps that's why he had one.

Augustin introduced him as Kamabo. He was a Mnandi, but lived *ngambo*. He was a hunter, a professional hunter, and he could give us better success with the buffalo. Why not try right now? We could go right away. Now! That was to say, as long as Bill and I were absolutely, positively certain that we had not slept with a woman recently. Bill and I racked our minds, we couldn't think of any women, let alone any that we might have spent any time with, today, yesterday, or ever, so there was nothing major to stop us from going along, only the ground nuts. Kamabo took one spear from his helper, stuck it in the ground near the pile of harvested plants and tied a small talisman onto its shaft. He beckoned us to follow him. We looked at the ground nuts and at Augustin.

263

Augustin said: "If anyone goes past Kamabo's *dawa* and touches the *arachides,* he will be sick and will die!" We looked concerned. "Well, he will at least be very sick." That was better.

We followed Kamabo. Perhaps we took a detour to get the rifles, perhaps Augustin the planner had set this all up and had suggested we have them along, just in case. I suspect he had a hand in Kamabo's visit.

Before sundown, we had shot three buffaloes between our cultivation and the Lamia river. Kamabo put another of his spells on the site and we all went home. Bill and I to sleep, others first to plan the retrieval and distribution of the meat, then to sleep.

Augustin the security advisor told us that if one of us were present when the buffaloes were to be cut up, it would help to maintain some discipline and avoid people fighting over the meat. Though it would never be necessary to use it, the additional presence of a *bunduki* would guarantee order. I went along. While the carvers were waiting for him to remove his spell, Kamabo insisted on going through a little routine. The animals had been dead overnight. Their mouths were already fly-blown and their bellies had been still for some time, collecting gas A bovine belly is a prodigious gas generator. Kamabo led me to a carefully chosen spot near to one of the animals and told me to stand there, quite still. Before I knew what he was up too, he poked his spear between the ribs to let out all of the pressurized gas in a strong jet that hit me in the face. Then he bent down and put his mouth over the hole to breath it in. It lasted only a few dozen seconds, but I thought I would die.

When it stopped, Kamabo said: "This makes you brave in the face of danger. If you can make yourself do this, you will not run away if the animal charges you. You will think only of killing it."

I had a thought: "If I ever do this again, I will not be in any condition to look for danger!"

Kamabo had two more bellies to puncture. A nineteen-year-old who has had his upper lip stiffened in a boarding school and who does not want to be seen as a sissy in a new life in a new place, goes along and finds a way to fake it. I did the other two with Kamabo. While he held his face over the jet, I held my breath and had a couple more thoughts: "Now I know

264

why K smells so ripe!", and "His whole women thing must be sour grapes! None of them would want to be touched by him?" He approved of my being able to stand still and of my not vomiting on him, but I think he misinterpreted my smile.

Thus was I inducted into Kamabo's cell of an ancient order of hunters. Or was that 'enveloped by Kamabo's smell, the rancid odour of the hunted'?

Augustin the chief of protocol had two of the three carcasses quartered and brought up onto the hill. He told me: "The tradition is that the chief of the land on which a kill is made gets one hind leg of the animal, even if it is as small as a *sibiri*, the tracker gets one hind leg and the hunter gets the rest. With three animals, one goes to the hunter, one to the tracker and one to the chief. In this case, the kills were near the border, but within Basikania's territory, so he must get his rightful share. Now, since Bwana Billo and you have spent your money on bullets, it is right that we sell the meat of one animal to pay for them. Kamabo already has his one animal, it went home with him. I, Augustin should get one. Let's see, that leaves ... Wait! Kamabo gets one, you Bwanas get one between you and if Augustin is to have any, what happens to old uncle B? Maybe he won't notice and will be satisfied with one leg, after all, it was near the border, and they could have run a few more steps and been out of his land. Yes! That's right! Kamabo has one, the Bwanas have one to eat and I, Augustin, will sell the meat of the third one to pay for the bullets. I will save one hind leg of my one and carry it to my chief. He will be pleased with me."

Some of the meat of one beast actually made its way into Mum's deep freeze, as Augustin the organizer set about taking care of the rest.

Augustin the salesman got caught up in the selling, impaling lumps of meat on the hook of the coffee scales, sliding the weight back and forth on the beam with a flourish, shouting out a price, wiping his sweaty brow, shoving fistfuls of limp money into his soon bulging pockets. Before long, a kilo or two at a time, the meat was gone, except for what was on that one leg, over there, Basikania's leg. The temptation was too great. The leg lost a kilo here and a kilo there. Old Basikania wouldn't notice. Just as one more chunk was cut off, Basikania appeared, leading an entourage big enough to carry his whole animal. Augustin, just about to pocket the francs that

265

he held wadded up in his hand, saw his uncle and, without hesitation, pressed the sticky money into my hand, and, as though oblivious of the remaining line of would-be meat purchasers trying to push more money into his hand, proudly picked up and presented the leg bone to his chief.

Basikania had come hungry for meat. He had probably thought about nothing else since the echoes of the shots had died down and the bush telegraph had spread the news. On the way down from his high village, he and his carriers had already chewed and swallowed each mouthful twice, or thrice, sucked every bone and wiped every dribble of fat from their chins and then licked their fingers. The feast that would be held that night was already becoming a legend. Ahh! What glory! A chief who can bring this kind of bounty home is really somebody! They were already relishing the future memory!

And now this! All that anticipation for a moth-eaten looking bone! This was a terrible breach of protocol and an insult to him. He showed his disappointment, but he was a gentleman.

He said: "Bwana Kallo, by our tradition, one whole animal is mine. You offer me one bone with no meat left on it. It is not correct. You did not know this, so I do not blame you. There are people here who do know the right way and I am sure they are at fault for not advising you properly." Augustin was trying to look inconspicuous. Basikania went on: "I do not accept this. I cannot take it to my family and to my village without shame. I will wait for the next time." He turned to Augustin, , and said: "We will have a little discussion about this, sometime soon, won't we?" and walked away with his followers.

Months later, Augustin got a chance to redeem himself, in a big way.

On several days in a row some African farmers in a small community on the mountain came to ask me to shoot some elephants that were destroying their crops. When I didn't seem responsive, Augustin the concerned interlocutor came to me and begged on their behalf. The people would go hungry, wives and children would starve, villages would become ghost towns. Each time I refused.

About a week later, Kamabo appeared and said that tomorrow we would go up there and hunt, unless I had been with a woman within the last week, of course, or had lost my courage. I was not disqualified, at least not on the first count, and I suppose his power of persuasion was irresistible. I said oh, all right, just this once, I would go. Yes, I would bring the big *bunduki*. Not that I planned to kill anything, mind, the animals were not hurting *my* crops. I would use it to make just enough noise to chase the elephants from the *shambas*. I did not want the starvation of hundreds of Wanandi on my conscience. Yes, tomorrow I would go with him.

His set a time and a place to meet and departed, admonishing me not to forget my obligations by making the terrible mistake of allowing my behaviour with women that night to jeopardize the hunt. I promised I wouldn't.

We met at the appointed time and place. After he received the correct answer to the foremost question on his mind, we set off and walked for hours, up and up into the mountain. The path went across the Lamia river, into Uganda and back again. It took us into the clouds that were always there, but which were heavier and lower with the rain. The weather was probably the reason that the elephants had left their higher forest range and come down to the edge of the populated area. It must be tough to climb up and down wet and slippery slopes of about forty-five degrees when you weigh several tons.

We came to the place where the elephants had spent the week. The banana trees were flattened, the maize pulled up and coffee trees broken, up to within a few feet of the huts. Nothing much would be harvested from that place that year. I could understand the concern of the residents. My first thought was that I should be doing the right thing for these people, if I were to chase the elephants away.

My second thought, which wasted no time in coming, was that I was not sure why I had said I would come and that I was even less certain as to why I actually had come.

I said: "What a pity it is so misty and rainy here. I can't see. Maybe we should come back another day."

Kamabo kept me moving along. "Just across this dip. They are there. I saw them yesterday, and the people say they have not gone. Listen!"

I could hear things, cracking things, and rumbling things, but I wasn't sure what. As we moved onwards, the mist parted and I saw that the dip was a valley only fifty paces wide.

Yikes! That close!

Both slopes were covered in my old friend, *matete*.

My knees started to do the traditional dance they do when presented with the prospect of having to carry me away at speed. My bladder started to send its usual message to the knees: "You'll be sorry if you don't let him take care of me, first!"

Kamabo didn't notice. He just kept one eye looking into the mist and the other on the ground. I needed both eyes on the ground and could have used more; we were following elephant footsteps. The elephants' passage had made stair-like steps in the muddy slope, each footprint with a little pool of water in it. The steps were spread four to five feet apart and had a slippery slope between them. It was difficult to stay upright. The rifle in my hands, the shaking of my knees and the calls of my bladder didn't make it any easier.

I thought: "If I just go off into the *matete* now for a pee, maybe they'll go away before I get back."

You know how it is, when you're just about to creep up on a herd of elephants and surprise them, and you're hoping that they're pointing the other way so when they run they don't step on you, and, suddenly, you remember some things that happened nearly three quarters of your life ago? Odd, isn't it?

There I was, trying to stay on my feet on the elephants' trail, and my mind saw flashes of two long past and long forgotten events.

One: I'm five or younger. On one of our Moshi trips, we have been taken by Paga to see a movie, The Thief of Baghdad. The movie is showing in a large room with chairs in it, that serves as Moshi's cinema. Sabu, the young hero, is taken on a trip through the air by his giant genie friend, and rides on his bare shoulder. There is nothing much to hold on to, so Sabu slips off, saving himself only by catching and hanging on to the genie's braided hair. My tummy starts to ache. Sabu spends a lifetime hanging from the braid, a mile or so above the ground. I don't know it yet, but I am not comfortable with heights. This is my first movie, or among the very first, and I also have yet to learn that the good guys rarely get hurt and certainly don't perish. I can't stand the suspense. My tummy is cramping and I think I'm going to wet my pants. Or die. Or both. I tell Mum that I have to go to the bathroom. Really, really! She has to leave the film to take me. I dawdle, and when I have drawn out

268

the time as long as I possibly can, I won't go back in until I've peeked around the door to make sure that Sabu is on the ground.

Two: I'm maybe six or seven. Mum is teaching Pauline and me at home, in Rongai, from The Correspondence Course materials. Mum is reading a story set in the time when Oliver Cromwell and his Roundheads are fighting the royalists, the Cavaliers. The story is probably intended for Pauline's level, but since we're both at the same table in the living room, we each get to hear all the stories. The hero and heroine are a young boy and girl. They are on a mission to carry some vital information to people on their side, or are the only people to survive an attack, or something. The fate of the King rests on their getting where they're going. This excitement and suspense have already got my tummy in cramps and my bladder screaming. The heroes are running, at night, and have flung themselves into a ditch, just in time to avoid being seen by approaching horsemen who might just be (shiver!!) Roundheads. By the time the hoof beats are only a few feet away, and even as the heroes are still pressing themselves lower in the ditch, I am already on my way to King's Club. I pause in the dining room to hear through the door that the silhouettes against the stars reveal that the riders are, indeed, very sinister and purposeful Roundheads, and I'm gone. I don't come back into the room and take my place until I'm absolutely certain that the silence isn't just a pause, or worse, Mum waiting for me to come back before continuing.

That is how well I used to deal with suspense. I was not doing much better, now.

I didn't have time to think for long, for just then the mists parted again and Kamabo was back at my side, I don't know how he moved that fast. He pointed. I saw a great, gray shape, thirty paces away, partially obscured by the *matete* and the mist and moving along the opposite slope at a walking pace. I'd missed my chance to duck away.

The shape came into sharp focus and I aimed and fired, instinctively. The sights were set for a hundred yards. I knew the shot went high, over the neck. I reloaded, reminded myself to aim lower on the neck, just behind and below the ear hole. I fired again.

The kick of the rifle knocked me down into one of the

footprint-puddles. I picked myself up and put another round in the breech. Kamabo was pointing, again, at the animal which was now running along the slope, and fairly clearly visible through the mist. I was a bit shaken by my fall, forgot to aim low, fired and missed, reloaded and fired again, and found myself sitting in the puddle again.

The magazine held only three of the big, fat rounds and I had had one in the breech, that made four. I had used four. I didn't want it empty if the elephant came my way, so I paid attention to reloading the magazine, even while I tried to get to my feet.

When I was on my feet again, Kamabo was still at my shoulder, still pointing, but now shouting: "There! There! Shoot it!"

I was thinking: "Shut up, Kamabo! Let me take a pee before we do any more of this!" But I fired and the elephant stopped running.

"Finally!" I thought.

I, who didn't like to kill and didn't want to do any more here than make a noise to chase away the marauders, had actually shot to kill several times and all I could feel was disappointment that I had missed so many times. Now I had hit one, and it had stopped. I began to feel a bit sick, both at having hurt the animal, and at my lack of control.

I steadied myself, took careful aim for the neck, four to six inches behind and below the ear hole, and dropped it. It was my first 'professional' shot of the day.

Kamabo shouted at me to fire at the rest of the herd, now clearly visible as they stampeded away, around the hill. I thought I had done enough damage, to the elephants in general, to one in particular and to my own self opinion. I declined.

He dashed off, shouting to me to follow. I followed, much more slowly, thinking I might have to finish off a wounded animal, already sick at what I had done and sicker at what I might still have to do. Wringing a stunned pigeon's neck is bad enough. This could be really bad.

I came upon the elephant much sooner than I expected, but the hills and the mist may have thrown off my perspective and sense of direction. It was very dead, with a bullet hole exactly where I had aimed, inches behind the ear hole, where

270

the bullet would sever the spinal cord and kill, instantly. I was looking for the wound that had stopped the animal running, when Kamabo called from further along the trail.

I followed and found him standing beside a second dead elephant, closer to where I thought I would find the one I had hit. It, too, had one bullet hole, just behind the ear.

I was just beginning to take in what I was seeing, when Kamabo called again, from even further along the trail. He was standing beside a third elephant. This one had a wounded shoulder and a second bullet hole in the neck, just behind the ear. I hoped, desperately that Kamabo didn't want to run farther along the trail. He did, but came back to say there was no blood or other sign, though he thought we should follow the herd. I didn't.

I was extremely flushed and agitated and excited and sad. And when I saw that the last elephant to die was still emptying its bladder, I wanted to cry.

It was getting dark and Kamabo said we could leave them 'til morning, which we did, under the protection of another one of his spells.

I got home after dark. Paga was the first to see me and asked how it had gone. I mumbled that I had had some success.

He asked more questions and I finally told him: "Three."

He frowned and said: "That's too much! Much too much!" and turned his back on me and walked away.

That evening, after a bath and a change of clothes, without the evidence of the number of times I'd been knocked down on my tail in the mud, I suppose I sounded quite full of myself, because before long, despite Paga's frown, I was describing the action in some detail. That kind of telling, particularly if one leaves out the sissy stuff, can sound boastful. I wasn't sure I recognized myself in some of what I heard myself saying, but it must have reflected a side of me that existed, one I didn't, and still don't, feel comfortable with.

On the way down the mountain, Augustin the fast thinker had caught up with me and told me what tradition dictated in the event that someone killed three elephants in one afternoon in a certain chief's territory. He also told me that with this much meat around, it was my bounden duty to be there with my rifle to keep order, otherwise people would surely die. So,

271

the next morning I set off up into the mountain again, my rifle on my shoulder. I didn't want to take any risks. I think it was empty.

Basikania was to have all of the meat of one elephant, Augustin the brash somehow got away with assigning him the smallest one. Kamabo had already claimed the one he wanted and I was to have the third one and all of the tusks. Lucky me! Doubly lucky me, Augustin the helpful would see to its disposal for me, I wouldn't have to bother. Yes, I still had to go there, with the rifle, but I would not have to do anything, that is, anything other than look serious and be seen often, with my *bunduki*, near each of the three carcasses in turn.

He hadn't checked with Kamabo before making me that promise. I had survived the buffalo test by holding my breath for about half a minute at a time. My lungs were not big enough to let me cheat on the elephant test. I turned blue, until I had to take a breath, then I turned green. But I stood still for about three minutes that seemed like fifteen but could have been a week, for each deflation.

When that ceremony was over, I ducked out of the way of the mob of people with knives and *machetes* who poured on to the carcasses. At one point, I heard a whole lot of screams and had a momentary fear that I might have to go in and stop somebody from being killed. Rats! The last time I tried to stop a dog fight, I got bitten worse than either dog. Then a young woman ran past, trying to keep something out of the reach of the fifty screaming women and girls chasing her. Augustin, the knowing, smiled at my apparent concern and explained that they were scrambling for the gonads one of the male elephants. "*Dawa* to make them have many babies! Listen! They are not fighting, they are singing!" I might have been quite embarrassed if I'd put myself in the middle of *that* "fight" before Augustin's explanation came.

Other than that, there were no incidents. The August one pressed a few hundred francs into my hand, "to pay for the bullets," probably just enough to do so. Basikania had no complaints, I think he even thanked me.

Kamabo had made me pay a major form of penance for taking those lives, but obviously could not grant me absolution. I wish that the gas penance could have made me feel better about that episode. It hasn't.

It doesn't help me to know that this was a drop in the ocean with respect to the fate of the elephant species. This happened a decade before the elephant population in some parts of Africa exploded. It was also some time before the mutinying armies of the new African states went berserk with their automatic weapons, and before poachers were armed and organized by politicians and their cronies to slaughter elephants for the ivory trade.

It really doesn't help. That is all rationalization. I killed three elephants when I had not intended to do anything but scare them away.

I knew that I was capable of handling a weapon and quite certain, even convinced of my maturity. I demonstrated that I could handle the weapon, devastatingly. But I didn't demonstrate that I was mature. I guess if you put a machine of destruction in the hands of an immature person, whether he's immature at nineteen or twenty-nine or fifty-nine, sooner or later you will get destruction. The more certain the person is of his maturity, perhaps the stronger the reason to expect the destruction.

I didn't know elephants at all, then, and still I don't know them well enough now. But I do know that they are compassionate, caring animals who look after their sick and wounded and grieve for their dead. I sometimes think they are more compassionate than we are. They would not have gone out of their way to hurt me or any other human.

They died because they needed to eat. They were away from home and hungry, but the open invitation that is in the African code of hospitality, "eat from my field if you're hungry, but eat here," does not extend to animals. Not to Tommies. Not to buffaloes. Not to elephants.

I feel terrible about this incident. Nothing will make me feel better about it, not even this confession. So I'll stop.

No, not yet.

With the benefit of a separation of thousands of miles and several decades from the immediacy of those situations, I have the luxury of harbouring some fairly strong opinions about the future of mankind on this planet, I should say lack of future, if we don't preserve the forests and the animals.

Do I condone people "down there" cutting down tropical rain forests to plant crops?

No. I don't.

Do I condone people anywhere killing wild animals to protect those or any crops?

No. I don't.

Do I understand the people who do both?

Well, I - Uh! Yes. As someone who has "been there", I guess I have to say I do. Or I did.

So? Do I think there is hope that the "Third World" will come around and stop the burning and killing, and thereby give the human race a chance to survive another millennium, or two? Or century, or two?

Yes, I do. There is hope. It will happen right after the Industrial Nations, which I guess means you and me, replant the forests that *we* and our parents and grandparents have cut down, stop burning fossil fuels and give up air conditioning and hairspray. And, I suppose, right after the world convinces the Third World nations that it is in their best interest to reverse their population explosions and offers them some realistic alternative methods with which to employ and feed their existing hungry masses. That's all it will take.

I'm sorry, but I did warn you, and you've gone and read the chapter, anyway! I can't trust you to use your judgment. Next time, I think I'll leave it out.

PART TWO

CHAPTER FOURTEEN

Life went on. Work progressed. The view from the hill was no longer of a sea of *matete*. We could see that something was going on in the plantation as the strips of clearing and then cultivation pushed their way into the grass. The Mulching System was making its mark.

The hill itself was showing some marks. John and Richard's work with the dynamite was beginning to be visible. It had been our original intent not to start before we got in our first revenue from a crop, any crop, but Dad had become impatient. I think he felt badly that Paga was living in a grass hut at his age. Anyway, he wanted to build, and to do so he needed a flat area for the foundation, so got it started it even before the bricks were ready.

Bricks? He had hired a whole team of men to make bricks down near to the mission, in Kamango, in the forest, where there was clay that was almost suitable. We didn't have the brick equivalent of the *coup de bois*, yet, but it didn't bother him, we'd sort that out in Bukavu, sometime in the future. For that matter, we didn't really have the money to be making bricks. In that context, the timing of the application for a permit was a minor consideration.

There were trips to Bukavu, for this and other purposes, that would take Dad away for a week or so at a time, usually with Mum or someone else for company. On one of them, Mum met a group of American missionaries. She was greatly impressed by the devotion to their calling of these kind and hospitable people. However, she was intrigued to hear the lament, sighed in a twang that you could bottle, that, due to the influence of French, the Africans were learning their English with the oddest "ecksayunt". Just as intriguing was the question of the value of the English language, with or without accent, to the African residents of this officially French speaking country. We met one of the charming ladies from that

275

group on the road near Beni, months later, with a flat tire. We helped her. Chatting as we worked, she learned of my then more than casual interest in attending university in the United States. Without hesitation, she whipped out her check book (it was an American one) and made one out for the amount that she said I'd need for something called the SATs, Scholastic Aptitude Tests, that are required by all American institutions of higher learning. She wrote down the name and address of the American Consul in Leopoldville and suggested I ask him for information. I did all that, but that becomes another story.

There were trips to Butembo, eighty or more kilometres south of Beni, to see M. Poncelet of the coffee co-op, but they were only for a day. On one such trip, I went with Dad to see a plantation which reportedly had a world-wide reputation for perfection. Reputedly, the quality was always so good that the whole crop was sold before it was harvested. That coffee was *arabica*, a variety that likes cool, mountain air, yields very subtly flavoured coffees and commands higher prices. We were growing *robusta*, which, as its name implies is tougher, less exotic, and, as we know, is capable of yielding Père Jean's *café noir,* and for which reasons, commands much lower prices. No matter, you always can learn something. What I learned was that we were a long way away from being able to pay the attention to detail that perfection requires. It is sometimes inspiring, to see such good work being done. It is often intimidating.

If you were in Butembo, anything that needed to be done to the VW pickup had to be taken care of. There was no other VW garage in the area, unless you wanted to go to George's, in Bunia, two hundred kilometres to the north.

We heard of one traveler on his way through to Bunia, who had some work done on the transmission of his VW van in that Butembo garage. The engine and transmission of the VW van, pickup and beetle are identical, except that the crown wheel of the differential of the van and pickup fits on the opposite side to that of the beetle, to compensate for an extra reduction gear. The garage put it in wrong, an easy mistake, but one you can't hide with a lick of paint, or anything; it has the result that the vehicle goes backwards in forward gears and vice versa. The story goes that the man, already impatient from having had to wait for days for the parts to come in the first place, was so upset by this time that he wouldn't let them touch it again. He drove all the way to Bunia, backwards, to let George do it. Probably took himself to the chiropractor to get his neck straightened while George straightened out the transmission.

On a trip through Kampala, Dad found a VW camper or caravan. Though used, it was in very respectable shape. It would make his travels much more dignified. It came home with him, and did, indeed add dignity and style to his peregrinations.

It added another dimension to the planning for the future trip to Europe. It did very little to enhance our cash position.

On one trip to Bunia, perhaps to do with tobacco, perhaps to do with getting the pickup fixed, I went with Dad. We followed the usual plan. We set out at night, drove to our destination, parked and slept in our sleeping bags, on the camp beds, in the pickup. I think George's garage was our campsite. A 200-kilometer trip is a fairly long one, when the roads are not paved and are strange to the driver. There is something surreal about driving on and on, for hours on end, into a small patch of weak, flickering light that seems to be about to lose the fight to keep the tall trees and the darkness pushed just far enough back to allow you to move ahead at your tentative pace. For all you can see, the world falls away on either side of this little patch of road, into nothingness. Or maybe it rises up around you, on both sides and in front and behind, closing together overhead, and you are moving in this little bubble, hanging on to a scratch on a surface which has no beginning and no end. It gets particularly strange when it gets to be well past midnight, when a teenaged brain begins to demand sleep. More so when there is silence for a few hours, which, with Dad along, was a rare thing.

I don't remember where my thoughts were, or where they had been after hours of hypnotizing, silent driving, when Dad gave me a clue where his had been. Here we were, alone, time for a man to man talk, and I was nineteen, after all. He spoke, out of the blue, so to speak, to give me his only spoken Lessons In Life. He didn't claim them to be from his own wisdom or experience. He was just passing them on.

"Papa told me, when I came to Africa, that if I ever took an African woman into my home, I should be sure to make her leave before morning."

277

"Oh?"

"Yes. If she wakes up in the house, she will expect to stay."

There was a short silence, while I pondered that. My grandfather had never been to Africa, nor ever contemplated going there. I wondered where this strange bit of wisdom had come from. I wondered how it might ever apply to me.

Then: "He also said that if I ever slept with a woman, I should not think that that obliged me to marry her."

I could think of nothing appropriate to say.

After a few more minutes: "Papa also always told me that you must always take people for what they are, not for what you want them to be; you can never change them." This one I had heard before, but he threw it in for free.

"Those are the only things Papa told me about life before I left home! I have not been in a position to need either of the first two lessons. The third one, frequently, but the other two, never." End of lecture. Back to the unusual silence.

The silence gave me time to compare these things to the only other "lesson" I had been given.

Jock's instruction a little before my departure for Prince o' had been: "When an older boy asks you your name, give it at once, and do NOT say '... and what's yours?'"

Jock's lesson I had used within weeks of first hearing it. It was eminently more practical than any of Dad's.

A short while later, I went to Bunia with de Jaeger. It might have been to collect a part, or something we'd left for George to repair, an engine, or something. The driving was less silent, but not by much. I certainly didn't hear anything in the line of philosophy or the meaning of life that became etched in my memory. I did learn some new words. De Jaeger was a bachelor and a farmer. I'm sure he thought himself very modern, his language sounded full of swearwords. But he had an old-fashioned streak in him; if you listened carefully, the words were fakes, close approximations of some colourful Flemish epithets. They may have been almost safe if overheard by the delicate ears of old ladies, or almost risky in school corridors in the presence of cloth-covered ears of nuns, but they left no doubt as to their purpose. I heard a selection of them, to add to the ones Arobé and I heard as we discussed signboards with him.

One thing I was sure to have heard was the question he

asked me every time we met without Dad: *"Eh b'en, Carl, où est ton Père maintenant? Combien d'essence at il brulé cette semaine?"*

We got to Bunia well after dinner. In a very conspiratorial voice, de Jaeger told me to stay in his camionette while he went into the hotel. He came out about half an hour later and told me to wait a few minutes and then come to the window of his room, which I would recognize because he'd switch the light on and off a few times. He would let me in. No need to let these people charge their exorbitant prices for a second person in the room. They'd be getting quite enough from him.[42]

He had brought a couple of bottles of beer from the bar. It was nothing unusual, I suppose, for a Belgian *colon* to take beer to bed with him. We drank our beers and I slept on the floor or in the chair. He woke me before daylight, so I could get out without being seen and wait in the camionette while he checked out.

And there were trips to Mutwanga, where Roger and Denise de Poerck had a plantation. De Poerck's first appeal was that Dad discovered that he, de Poerck shared Dad's faith in mulch, and had, in fact, laid out much of his plantation in strips. He also was experimenting with different cash crops. He had a whole field of castor plants (castor as in oil). Over and above being so wise, the de Poercks were very well educated and genteel, and they took an avid interest in the political situation. Dad found himself talking politics as much as coffee and mulch. De Poerck was tuned in a bit more than many planters to what was developing in Belgium and the rest of the world. There had been some talk of independence. A delegation of Africans had even gone to Belgium to demand it, or had sent a petition, but of course it was silly to think of it. Nobody was ready for it, least of all the Africans who wanted it.

Independence was far in the future, obviously, everybody knew that, but it began to be the main topic of conversation. There were some Europeans, probably in Leopoldville, who thought that it might be a good idea to form a political party

---

[42]Belgian hotels charge a much higher rate for a room when it is occupied by two members of the same sex. I don't know if this prejudice is morally or economically driven.

for both Africans and Europeans. It might be helpful to keep a dialogue open, and to have a channel for information in both directions. It might provide some experienced leadership to the Africans in the process of learning politics and it also might just keep things from getting out of control. It was to be called the *Partie Nationale Politique,* or the PNP. The European founders were hoping to attract some African membership.

CHAPTER FIFTEEN

We took these trips, or some of us did, but we weren't the only people traveling. We were visited, in turn, by an odd assortment of people.

One day a young Australian, Wes, appeared on Kagando hill on foot, carrying a knapsack. He was walking across Africa and had come, quite unofficially, across the Lamia river, from *ngambo.* I think we said come in and sit down, he certainly made himself at home. Two days later, Pascal came to us and pleaded that we get rid of him. Wes was taking advantage of the stop to catch up on his laundry. All the water was still coming up the hill on Pascali's head, which head was beginning to show a flat spot after the tenth trip of the day just for Wes. Pascali normally made three trips a day for the whole family's needs. We suggested to Wes that we would appreciate his doing his laundry in the river, the way ours was done, rather than in carried and heated water on the hill. I don't think we offended him, his laundry was already done, but he left soon afterwards, headed for the Ituri Forest and the Atlantic Ocean.

I was filling Polonia's tanks at Germain's blue pumps, when a white woman rode up on a Vespa motor scooter. Vespas have small wheels which are fine on macadam in town, but they are almost unable to travel on the corrugations of the unpaved roads. She was a twenty-two-year-old American. She wanted to know the way to Mbao, where the pygmies were. I was going in that direction, so I offered her a ride in Polonia. I gave her a bunch of advice about traveling that way, advice that she considered worth every penny she paid for it. She was alone, on a vehicle that was not road-worthy, in a country that had roads that were not vehicle-worthy. Her fuel consumption rate was wonderfully frugal, but I was not sure that the tankful could get her from pump to pump. She did not speak French or any native African language. She was a disaster waiting to happen. I salved my conscience by dropping her off at the *Chef de Poste,* hoping he'd expel her from the country, or something, for her own protection. She had planned to go on across the Congo, but I don't know if she got to try. I hope she didn't. Not long afterwards, a group of Frenchmen tried to canoe down the Lualaba and Congo Rivers, along Stanley's route, and disappeared.

Sometime later, I was not at home, I was spending some time in Mutwanga, a Land-Rover appeared on Kagando, from the Congo side. There were four young men in it. Two Germans and two East African Brits. One German was very quiet, the other not. The latter was an industrial psychologist in Nairobi. They had taken the opportunity to see the Congo before independence, now that there was talk of it. Who knows how long the opportunity would exist. Comforting! When they left, Dad gave them instructions on how to find me in Mutwanga. They succeeded. I remember the occasion, they were the only non-family visitors I had there in eight months, and they could consume whole pieces of my little wrapped processed cheeses in one mouthful. I could make one of those laughing cows last for three slices of bread! Three of the four kept turning up in our lives, two of them for years. I landed up working with one of them, five years later. I attended his wedding. Then I crossed paths with him again, in correspondence dealing with the Philadelphia Flower Show, in 1990. It *is* a small world.

I'm going to get ahead of myself, if I'm not careful. On a trip home from Mutwanga, on the flat stretch before the Semlilki, I saw a VW beetle parked at the edge of the road. It was not one of the usual two or three vehicles that I might have expected to see on that road. I stopped behind it and saw the silent German from the group I've just mentioned, walking rather aimlessly around the car, not sure what he was doing. It was already quite dark, I can't remember how late, and there was no reason in the world to be stopped there, other than that a car refusing to move. It was in the middle of the Parc National Albert, big game - I mean elephants and buffalo - and big mosquito country. But the car didn't seem to be arguing with him, he was just - well, aimless. When I stopped and got out of the thing I was driving, he recognized me.

I asked him if he was okay. Yes, he was. I asked him if he needed help. No, he didn't. I asked him if he had a place to stay that night. Well, yes, he was going to camp right there. I said that was silly, he'd be eaten alive. He could go on a little and stay at our place. He wasn't sure but I was, so he followed me on home.

I stayed part of the next day and left to go back to my duties in Mutwanga.

Weeks later, Mum and Dad visited me in Mutwanga. They told me that the young fellow had hung around there for days, still aimless, almost shell-shocked, not seeming to know what he was doing or why he was there. Eventually, Dad had said to him, rather pointedly, but kindly, that he ought to be thinking of moving on. He had done so. Some days later, a letter had come from the other German in the group. The young guy in question was wanted by Interpol. Apparently, he had robbed his grandmother to finance his *safari* to Africa. It had been fun, until he was about to head home, when it struck him that he'd have to face the music. He had panicked and bolted. He remembered the road to Watalinga and had headed there. It was two or three very long days' drive from Nairobi, and perhaps the most remote place he knew in the world. What he had planned to do there, or whatever eventually happened to him, I don't know.

Not everyone who came our way was strange. Or, maybe I mean that not everyone who came was as strange. A Norwegian anthropologist affiliated with Makerere College in Kampala, Uganda, showed up. He was writing his thesis for his doctorate from the University of Oslo and had chosen to do it on the Nandi tribe. We guessed that Fiji and Tahiti had already been done, and the world was running out of isolated tribes, but heck, *some*body had to do the Wanandi. The Wanandi were fairly isolated, but they could hardly be called untainted. We overheard conversations which included the comment: "No, he's not a Christian, he's Catholic!" and we witnessed Lekisanderi singing the hymn *"Damu ya kondoo,* The blood of the Lamb" as he walked along the hills of Nandiland. Neither of these would be likely to be products of the aboriginal Nandi traditions.

Pauline remembers that the Wanandi called their student *Isse (or Issa) Musoke.* We can't remember what that means, nor can we remember the name his Mum and Dad gave him. It might have been Arnie, or maybe Bengt. Bengt is a nice Norwegian name. It is too obvious, sort of like calling him 'Hank' if he had been American.

Arnie wanted to leave his Land-Rover parked on our hill, which was the closest civilized place to his destination. He

283

would be gone for a few weeks, so he covered his tires with sacking, to protect them from the ultra-violet rays, a novel concept to all of us, spent the night with us - John and Richard's beds were empty - and headed off into the mountain the next morning with his tummy full of mealies. Every now and then, he'd reappear, spend the night in a real bed, hop into his Land-Rover and head off to Kampala for a week or two. Then he'd be back. He didn't notice any damage from the ultra-violet rays, so his sacking must have worked, at least as long as it stayed on his tires. He was a bit disappointed to notice that some paint was missing from his front mud-guard. He studied it for a while. The mystery was solved when he saw Dagobert scratching his back against the bare patch. 'AAAHHH! Just a little lower, just a little more .. There! Yes! Ohhh, yesss! Hog heaven!' Or as close as you can get, if there isn't a mud hole!

Arnie had an open invitation to come for a meal or for the night. There was no way he could warn us ahead if he was coming, but it didn't bother us. He was pleasant, if serious, and very easy to get along with. We were amused that someone in academia, somewhere, would be interested enough in "our" Wanandi to pay this man a stipend to study them. However, we thought that we'd finally find out about the Puluku/Muhindo thing, so there was a keen interest in at least a part of his work.

He soon got an opportunity to return the hospitality.

I was in the middle of a cotton season, and was going back and forth with Polonia, about every day. On one trip, I got as far as the edge closest to us of the Parc Albert, with a full load on board, when I heard a slight tapping sound. I thought at first it was just a new thing Polonia was going to do that week, but it soon turned into a horrendous knocking. I stopped, borrowed a bicycle from someone I knew and started to ride home on it. The frame was bent, the wheels were figures of eight, the chain was loose, the bearings needed grease, the saddle was hard as nails. I couldn't ride it. I got to the next village and abandoned it with someone who knew the owner; I'd rather walk the ten miles than ride that instrument of torture anymore. I got home, got out one of the drivers and sent him down with a tractor to pull Polonia home.

Marcel listened to the engine for ten seconds and pronounced that the big-end bearings were shot. Nothing to do but to strip down the engine and see.

It happened that Arnie was going home to Kampala the next day. We knew that there were no places we could get Austin parts this side of Kampala, certainly not in Belgian territory, so I begged a ride with him, and he agreed to wait for me. We dropped the engine out and took out the crankshaft and the bearings. We found the bearings well-worn and one of them destroyed, as Marcel had predicted. We worked into the night, by the light of one of Paga's Tilley lamps, and into the next day, in order to get this done. We left for Kampala late and got there later. It was about two hundred and fifty miles if you had to be official and go through customs, as Arnie did, which meant going all the way round the mountain. It was a seven-hour trip on those roads.

Mrs. Arnie got a surprise house guest for a few days in her small graduate student's cottage, while I scouted out a small Indian-owned machine shop that would rebuild and regrind the crankshaft. Three or four days after I arrived, with the crankshaft renewed and replacement bearings bought, I found an African taxi service which took me to Fort Portal. Ugandans were never very friendly towards Europeans. The owner of this service, who was also the driver, resented me because, as a *mzungu*, I would not be likely to accept, meekly, his putting (illegally) four people across the front seat of his Peugeot. In fact, totally contrary to his instincts, he let me have the whole front passenger seat to myself; though to compensate partially for it, the rear seat was forced to take five large passengers. In Fort Portal, I found one of the Indian traders from Bundibugyo who was returning home. There I found someone to help me carry the crankshaft and parts across the Lamia and home.

I was home with 200 pounds of parts, everything we needed to get Polonia going again. All except for the little thing that Marcel discovered while I was away. He had found the cause of the original failure; the oil pressure relief valve was doing its job too assiduously, relieving all of the oil pressure, not just the over-pressure. It's not often that one would find fault with something doing more than is required of it, but here we had a good example. I had driven Polonia for a few miles with no oil getting to the bearings, and that was enough to ruin them. Had we put it all back together without fixing this thing, this half inch steel ball pressed by a spring into a round washer

285

like seat, we'd have had the same problem all over again, probably even before Polonia got to Kamango.

The next morning I carried Pauline's motorbike across the Lamia and rode it along the footpaths to Bundibugyo and on to the road to Fort Portal. I thought that such a small part would be available there and I'd be home that night, so I took no change of clothes. It wasn't. Another African taxi ride brought me to Mrs. Arnie's boarding house at Makerere, only thirty-six hours after I'd last left it.

The part was not available in Kampala, either, but the Austin agent's service manager told me that all I needed to do was to " ... take this little round thing here (the seat), push it out, turn it around, press it back in to use the side that isn't worn and Bob's your uncle!" He did it for me, and it appeared that Bob would be my uncle.

Bob remained my uncle for a whole day.

I got home, needing no help to carry the eight-ounce part that was in my dirty pocket. I handed the culprit to Marcel, who by this time had some of the engine back together. It wasn't all done, though, and he asked me if I wanted to tighten the bolts on the big ends of the connecting rods. I did, so I did. I must have been overly enthusiastic in my tightening, because I snapped one of the bolts in the process. These are hardened steel bolts, they don't snap easily. It was probably damaged in the few minutes of knocking that had demolished the crankshaft bearings and it was probably a good thing that it broke then, not in the engine, under full power. That could have been messy.

Be thankful for small mercies, Carl. Or, always look on the bright side of life.

The next morning, I lugged the bike over the river for another trip to Fort Portal, this time with my toothbrush and a clean shirt. The shirt wasn't necessary. Claude, the service manager of the only garage helped me find a bolt. It wasn't an authorized Austin part and it was about a quarter of an inch shorter than my sample, but it fit and was made of the right type of hardened steel. It would do. As Paga would say, "A man running for his life wouldn't notice!" Marcel gave me some coaching on just how tight was tight enough for various applications, particularly the one at hand. The new bolt seemed to work and Polonia never once complained, not about that, anyway.

Polonia's contacts with Fort Portal were to become more direct. We were there overnight, for some reason or another, with Marcel in Polonia and Dad and me in the VW pickup. Dad and I spent the night in our camp beds in the dining room of a young German couple who were doctor and nurse at a mission hospital there. The poor things had not heard the one about letting the camel put its nose under the tent and had once invited Dad for dinner. In the morning, we were headed into town when we saw Polonia on the edge of the road, at a driveway access to an African *hoteli*. Her whole front was smashed in. Marcel had been coming out of the drive and had misjudged the distance of an approaching vehicle, or had not seen it, and PRANG! No suggestions were made as to what Polonia was doing coming out of a drink shop's drive, or what Marcel was doing in the drink shop. No further explanation was offered, no remorse shown, just: "There it is!"

Despite Dad having been in the insurance business a while back, Polonia's insurance had not expired. Our friend Claude at Western Motors was not an Austin agent, but he could do the repair, if he only had the parts. He made a list of what he'd need to do the job, and would be happy to order them from Kampala, or if they didn't have them there, from Nairobi. It might take four days if they were in Kampala, two weeks if they had to go to Nairobi for them, or six months if they had to be imported. We didn't like the idea of waiting, so we took his list to Kampala, one hundred and fifty miles away. They had less than half of the parts, so on to Nairobi with the list. Four days later, still in the same clothes, we had the parts in Fort Portal.

After a day or two, I think Dad went on home with Marcel, leaving me to supervise the completion of the job. Dad had already chosen to have Polonia painted blue, to make the effects of Marcel's rough kind of loving less visible. When Marcel saw the results, a couple of weeks later, he almost cried. What had we gone and done to his beautiful white bird?

While I was in Fort Portal, working with Claude's men on the repair, I slept on the couch in Claude's flat above the workshop. I was treated just like one of the family. I stayed over a weekend, possibly two. The Rassouls liked to take an occasional drive. I was invited, and not being sensitive to any need for them not to have me along, I accepted. We got into Claude's small Ford Prefect. We drove to Mbarara, up in the

287

hills, like a bat - no, three bats - out of hell, which was at the highest possible speed for that car on those roads, scattering chickens in the villages and Uganda Cob antelopes in the game park. We turned around in front of the Mbarara post office and drove back again at the same speed. It wasn't my presence, at least I didn't sense that it was, but there was no conversation, just the very purposeful drive, there and back. When it was done, as though we had taken care of a pressing duty, we went into the flat and chatted comfortably over a cup of tea.

Claude Rassoul and his wife were a young couple, just starting their family. They had no reason to be nice to Europeans, for though they were of mostly European stock themselves, under the British system, as Seychellese they were second class citizens. I think they would have to use the toilets designated for Asians and would not be welcome at European hotels and restaurants. Claude's salary was probably half or a third of what a European would have made in a similar position. Never mind, they were bigger than that, they were hospitable and nice. Mum had knitted baby things for their little Roger when he was on the way, because she liked them and because she liked to do it.

If you're halfway decent to people, you get paid back a hundred-fold.

Speaking of decency ... A visitor of a different kind (I don't want to start out by prejudicing you, at this point I only mean to say he wasn't a tourist), came to spend a night or two at de Jaeger's place. I think his name was Janovic or something equally exotic. Dad met him there and decided that he was a "relation"; he must have found that they had a common knot in their family trees, or something.

This happened just as Dad had managed to free up the last bit of inheritance from an estate in Paris. It was worth about half a million Congo Belge francs at official rates (about ten thousand dollars). We had completely exhausted the proceeds from the sale of Rongai and a loan of about one hundred thousand francs from the bank in Beni and we had run up some credit at various suppliers in Beni. Papaïne was bringing in some money, but not enough. Coffee revenues were a long way off, and prices were now down to somewhere in the low twenties per kilo. If we were going to make a go of this plantation, we'd need that "French money". And, if we got that amount in, about half of it would be gone, immediately, to pay the bank loan and the other lines of credit.

Due to the talk of independence, there was a black market developing. East African shillings were normally worth seven francs, they now fetched up to ten francs from the Greek traders in Beni. We knew, because some of our shop sales were to *watu ya ngambo*, who paid in shillings. If we could take advantage of the black market, the French money would be worth more, perhaps enough to counteract the debt. It was risky to bring it in, just before independence, with all the uncertainty that that brought with it, but we had already risked everything and were in Africa for the long haul. Dad had made up his mind to bring the money in. The only question was when and how. He could go to the bank and get the money in at the official rates, but that would be a waste of an opportunity to augment it that the other market offered.

Janovic was in business, I don't know exactly of what nature, but he moved money back and forth in his business. Dad decided to talk to him about exchanging the money. Janovic would benefit from having the ability to move some money out of the Congo for hard currency in Europe, an opportunity not available every day and therefore worth some consideration. Dad would benefit from having the money where he needed it, and from a better rate.

Dad invited Janovic to come over from de Jaeger's for breakfast the next morning. Wanting to give an impression as to the level of our industriousness, he made the invitation for half an hour sooner than we ever got up. The impression was doubtless modified somewhat by the generally poor showing of the backside view of our sway-backed, thatched, main camp building and the ever present, ever busy zoo led by Dagobert. When our visitor sat down with some obviously sleepy and grumpy youths, he was offered not the sophisticated continental breakfast of rolls and coffee, perhaps with cheese, cold meats and jams, but some barbaric mess that looked like polenta gone wrong!

Dad probably pussy-footed around the delicate issue of the rate of exchange that might be feasible, given the circumstances, and left it to his almost cousin's good judgment and sense of honour as to what would be equitable, given the mutual benefit, and so on.

289

You always let yourself be some one's patsy, Dad! Weeks and weeks later, the draught came through the bank, for exactly the official rate, less service charges.

Now you can form your own impression. Dad did. He shared it with us. We didn't even need to ask him.

CHAPTER SIXTEEN

In January of 1960, quite suddenly, the Belgian government agreed to grant independence to the Congo. Power was to be transferred at midnight on June 30, not six months away.

People have judged the Belgians very harshly on this. They say things like: "There was no planning."

I say that is a cheap shot! I say it is an unfair criticism! I will defend the Belgians on this point! How can you say there was no planning, when not only the hour, nor even only the minute, nay, when the very second of the event was precisely known, more than five months ahead? They were so certain that they even went on the record with their prediction, announcing it to the world, so everyone could see that they had been wrong and the Belgians could have the last laugh. We must give them every shred of the credit that they are due!

The country went into a bit of a frenzy. I suppose, if you think about it for a minute or two, you can understand. Dad often said that Europeans hadn't yet managed to run democracies even passably well in the centuries of trying since the Magna Carta. The Congolese didn't even yet have what could pass for political parties; the poor devils didn't stand a chance to get very far in five months.

Handicapped as they were, it didn't take them long to figure out how to run election campaigns.

The workers started asking us about what they were hearing in the markets. People from Province Orientale, whose capital was Stanleyville, even then usually referred to by its African name, Kisangani, were showing up at local *sokos,* markets, and saying some amazing things. They were talking about this new thing called *"dipandan",* pronounced with a French nasality. Our workers needed help in understanding some of it. Some were bold enough to say that things would be different. A few were bewildered, but most understood perfectly and were happy to share with us what they had understood.

We learned that Patrice Lumumba had survived many

assassination attempts by the *wazungu* and their partners in crime, the PNP. He, Lumumba, had *dawa*, magic, that turned white men's bullets into water. The proof was that he was still there, alive and well, and still a thorn in the *wazungu's* collective side!

We heard also that the citizens of the new country would never have to work again in their lives. Before the *wazungu* left, Lumumba would take away from them the machine in Leopoldville that made money. Every Saturday every man would drive his new *camionette*, his small lorry, up to the Post Office to collect ten thousand francs of *posho* money, tool on down to the *soko* and fill his *camionette* with bananas, *pombe* and women. Then he'd drive around all week, and then repeat the process.

We must have been slow to grasp some of these points, for we asked them who would run the Post Office and hand out the cash, if no one was to work anymore. It caused a short pause before another, better, promise was remembered and repeated. It was not nice to spoil their anticipation, but we thought we ought to say something. It was a vain idea.

We heard lots of rhetoric about the evil PNP that was trying to prevent the good things from happening. The new pejorative was: *"Wewe PNP!* You PNP!" It was just words, at this point, not nearly as serious as calling someone a commie in America in the fifties, or a calling someone German in an Amsterdam bar during a World Cup final between Germany and Holland. It soon would be just as serious. People would soon kill over such words.

Still, at this point when we drove by, men, women and children would wave to us and call out our names.

Dad had a spot in the park where he liked to stop. It was a small African settlement cut into the wall of trees. The family that lived there usually had a bunch of the small sweet bananas he liked, and perhaps some eggs, and he'd buy them. After some of the initial talk of independence, Dad noticed a screen made of *matete* had been built all the way round the settlement, fields and all, shutting it off from the road. He stopped to negotiate a purchase and asked the people what the fence was for; it was pointless against monkeys, too high to be against antelopes and too flimsy to be effective against elephants.

The answer was simple: "We're hearing about this new thing called *dipandan*. Some people say that it is good, then we hear that it is bad. Perhaps it could be very bad. We don't want it to come into our houses. Maybe, with this fence here, it will pass by."

For once Dad couldn't think of anything to say, at least not immediately.

We talked about it later. Dad kept shaking his head and saying, about the coming independence: "How can these poor children possibly survive? They have no idea! *Je*? Ai? Hm? This is totally unfair, to do this to them! It's criminal!"

Basikania was asked to run for the Senate. He agreed to do so and won the seat. De Jaeger and Père Jean said that he was put up to it by people who wanted a puppet. They may not have had much practice in democracy, but some of these people already had sharp survival skills. Not knowing the way things would go, they did not want to be too visible themselves. It was probably wise. I think Mobutu is the only one of the first wave of leaders who lived more than a few years, and that's more because he had the military behind him than anything else.

De Jaeger and Père Jean didn't give Basikania much credit, but we had found him to be very statesmanlike and concerned with doing things the proper way, traits that might be valuable in a Senate. He was very pleased with his election. We heard that he got himself a new, younger wife from the city, one more in keeping with his new status. He left his chiefdom in the care of Apollo and departed for Leopoldville. We rarely saw him again.

The elections came. Lumumba won in Province Orientale. It was proper that he should; his campaigners made by far the best promises. The PNP crowd, evil people who wanted to rob the Congolais of their future, made bland statements about hard work, co-operation and keeping the Belgians around for a long time. Lumumba became the Prime Minister elect for the whole Congo. It shouldn't have mattered to us, we were in Kivu Province.

It mattered. We were much nearer to Stanleyville, the capital of Orientale than to Bukavu, the capital of Kivu, and the Orientale border came very close to our area. These were all good reasons for it to matter.

On one of Dad's visits, Roger de Poerck said he was going

293

to take Denise and the three children to her home, Bruges, in Belgium. Pepino, the son (it was a nickname), was being tutored at home, by a retired Belgian who lived on their plantation. The twin girls were going to need schooling soon. With the hint of a possibility that the transition to independence might not be totally smooth, it was a good time for the family to take this step. It would take a few weeks, and there was the troubling question of what to do about his two plantations during that time.

Before the evening was over, it had been decided that I would live there as manager of the plantations. I should start in April or so.

I would be paid a salary. The salary would help our effort in Kagando and it would also replace the contribution that I made there in my work and in the coffee and cotton transport.

The help was also sorely needed. The "French money" was already gone. We were, again, in that stomach-wrenching state of knowing that we could barely keep the income coming in faster than the money was going out.

Dad came home and described the plan to me. It sounded fine.

In April or so, I went to live at the Plantations Talya, named for the river that ran through it. Dad dropped me off and took my first month's salary home with him. For a couple of weeks de Poerck showed me the ropes. Once or twice we all went to the tourist hotel run by M. Ingels, the elder. I think it was called the Ruwenzori Hotel, to differentiate it from the Hotel Ruwenzori in Beni. There, for a few minutes, we made an attempt to keep a tennis ball inside the fence. We gave up. It was much easier to sip a Campari and soda or a lemonade on the verandah and look out along the Rift Valley at sunset.

People lived like this?

I got used to the layout of the house and of the plantation and was shown what I needed to know about the work.

The house was built of stone right out of the river and had cement floors. It had an idiosyncrasy. The rooms were all in a row; there was no way to get from one end of the house to the other if you didn't want to go through each of the bedrooms, unless you went outside. Passing through each other's rooms didn't matter to the de Poercks, they were all one family. A twenty-year-old male guest felt odd and opted for the outside.

You got to the house over a precarious, temporary looking, bouncy, wooden foot bridge across the Talya. I thought: "How cute, they've got this nice, bouncy, wooden foot bridge across the river! Why didn't they build the house on this side of the river?"

They had running water in the house as well as in the river. De Poerck solved the mystery of the bridge for me when he explained the working of the water system, knowledge of which might be useful to me while I lived there. Bath water had been simple when the house was built. There was a manual pump that had taken water right from the river to fill an old oil drum, high on stilts behind the house. The house servant would keep the tank full by pushing the handle for a few minutes each day. The tank provided cold running water to the two bathrooms and flushing toilets. Hot water was done on the Pascali three-stone method. The river hadn't liked the intrusion of the pump and had moved away from it during one particularly heavy rain up in the mountain. It had moved from the far side of the house, through the house, to its present alignment on the near side, hence the bridge. For a few hours, the term "running water in the house" had had a new meaning. The pump was still set in the now dry old bed and was useless. When I looked at the five feet deep cut that the river had made for itself in its new alignment, I could understand that they were not too keen to upset it again by following it with the pump. Meanwhile, the servant carried *debes* of water up a ladder to fill the drum.

There was a diesel-powered electric generator in a small room at the back of the house, which provided light. It had stayed where it was put. Unlike the river, it was man-made, tame, and had no mind to break free of the bolts that held it to its foundation and to wander around. Unaffected by the river's move, it continued to work. I learned how to crank it up. The lights that the generator lit up in that house were the only lights I ever saw from the house in the eight months I was there, other than three or four times when I saw Dad's headlights come up the drive. If there was no visible sign of human habitation at night, there was often, particularly on Saturday and Sunday nights, audible evidence that I was not the only human in the province. I could hear drums and voices, even over the thump-thump of the diesel. But I'm getting ahead, again.

De Poerck showed me his two rifles, light weapons compared to ours, I think there was a .22" long rifle and a post 1918 model .3006", and he showed me where the ammunition was hidden. He showed me where the account books were, and in so doing, came across reams of leaflets and pamphlets describing the PNP. He said something wistful about that effort and its futility.

He introduced me to Jacques Ingels, the son of M. Ingels of the hotel. Jacques was married and had a young son of his own, aged five or six. He had an established plantation and a nice house, just at the turn-off to Talya. The house looked like something you would expect to see in a Belgian suburb, with no concessions to its proximity to the Equator.

Jacques would come to see me every Wednesday, late morning, and stay for lunch while we went over what I had done during the previous week and what I should do during the coming week. It was no reflection on me, Jacques had the experience and new what had to be done. That was fine with me, I could look forward to and count on another European's company that often. Jacques would also do all the banking and Mme. Ingels might do my grocery shopping for me. I would not need to use the car, though the keys would be there, just in case. That was a small shame, it was a 1956 Ford station wagon, but it had a Thunderbird V-8 engine in it. I had read enough in Popular Mechanics to know that it wasn't a popular brand of vegetable juice. Well, with any luck, some cases of need would arise.

Two or three weeks later, the de Poercks left for Belgium, via Kampala. Roger would settle Denise and the children and come back. It would probably take until sometime in July, just after independence, but he would be back. You could expect me to be skeptical about any promise to be back in a few weeks, but I wasn't.

When I started, the work was straight forward. There was some new ground being cleared in the forest, for coffee. This yielded firewood. Firewood was needed for drying the papaïne, which was harvested continuously, in an already familiar process, and for the coming coffee harvest. The wood was cut with axes and *machetes*, each labourer expected to do a cord of two cubic metres for a day's pay. I'd never heard of a chain saw. I soon came to look on a file as worth its weight in gold and understood why de Poerck bought them by the box.

At home, we skimped on the cost of files. All our men shared a couple of smooth old things that were useless. The decrease in efficiency was much more costly than new files would have been.

While the new was being wrested from Talya forest, the old was to be protected from being retaken by it. All existing plantings had to be cultivated every three weeks or so, to keep down the weeds which competed ferociously with the foreign, interloping plants. The cultivation was done by tractor and by hand. The papaya stands were cultivated by tractor. If the coffee was young and small, or if it had been pruned or was not bearing heavily, the tractors could get in without damaging the trees. Even if the tractor could go in, the last few square feet by each plant were done by hand hoe.

The work would become a little more complicated when the harvest had to be brought in. The harvest season would require every man woman and child on the place and in the surrounding habitations to come out to pick coffee berries. Harvesting of the ripe berries is strictly hand work, no machine can do it. Coffee has an odd habit of carrying flowers, green berries and ripe berries, all mixed on the same branch. Right after the harvest, the trees are pruned to maximize the yield of the next crop. Only new growth flowers and carries berries. This pruning process can make or break the next crop. I shouldn't worry, though, de Poerck would be back in time for both of these functions.

All of these processes required manual labour. Plantations Talya had about one hundred labourers, about twenty specialists, including headmen, two tractor drivers, a clerk and two-house servants. About half of the labourers had been recruited in Bunia, from a tribe whose people had a reputation of being good workers, but also of being as hard as nails. They were the kind of people who worked hard, drank hard when they weren't working and got ugly when they drank. Fortunately, they kept pretty much to themselves. Mum had a theory that the tribes who drank maize beer were always fighting drunks, while those who drank millet beer were usually happier drunks. The Bunia tribe brewed a thick, almost porridgy maize beer. They could get into thick fights.

I had supervised my share of the rabble at Kagando, so I

was not completely intimidated by this crowd, even with the harder, less familiar Bunia element. I noticed a big difference between our Kagando workers and the Talya crew. De Poerck's clerk, Thomas, and the headmen all were skilled in their work and needed little prompting or supervision. If things were normal, the place could just about run by itself. My chief function was to let everyone know that there was still some authority behind the headmen, even in the *bwana mkubwa's*, the big boss's absence, and, if anything abnormal came up, to take action or find Jacques. The difference was not accidental. It came from the planning and organization that de Poerck had put into his place. He was a trained agriculturist, an astute businessman and a very practical man. People had been chosen for their aptitudes, trained to do the required work, given a responsibility and then expected to perform.

Be that as it may, it was a fairly daunting to a lad of twenty to be the man on the spot for all of this organization and all the work to be done on a pair of plantations totaling four hundred hectares (a thousand acres). This was the size that Kagando was going to be when we finished developing it.

I had been a little worried about our long-term future at Kagando. Although we had some successes, most of our efforts seemed to come up short. It was a little bit like swimming against the tide. Seeing the success at Talya it began to dawn on me that those little nagging worries were very well founded. We had heart, we had determination, we had commitment, we had a desire to do well. We had it when we started out. We had a lot of what it takes to succeed, but we didn't have some very important ingredients. We were pitifully under-capitalized; never would we be able to do it right the first time, or to survive to correct it if we did it wrong. We were laughably unorganized; Dad had lots of experience, but was not an organized person. Certainly, he could 'organize' people to do something, in the way that it is usually meant, but he couldn't teach them how to do it in a consistently organized manner. He had a tremendous resource in his children who were very willing to work, but he almost seemed to expect us to know what to do naturally because we were his children and because we were clever. I think he believed he didn't have to tell us what to do, so we learned more by our mistakes than by instruction. We tried, but we were only just out of high school when we began, and, while school may actually teach you some desirable things among the undesirable, it doesn't turn you into a seasoned small business manager.

Pauline, Bill and I had learned to talk a little more openly with each other. We were making the same observations about our chances for success, given the handicaps we were working under, and given our record of few successes so far. We openly admitted to each other that we would be happy to be somewhere else, given the opportunity or a release from the obligation we felt to carrying on with what we'd started.

I saw the stint at de Poerck's as a break from Kagando, for which sentiment I harboured a tinge of guilt. But I also saw that the experience would be another education for me, which would make me more valuable to the effort, perhaps thereby bringing earlier success and earlier freedom. Which made me think about college once again, and about how valuable a formal education might just be, after all.

CHAPTER SEVENTEEN

For several weeks' things were quite normal. Every morning, I'd follow de Poerck's pattern. I'd be present at the dawn muster of the workers by Thomas and the other *capitas,* then I'd make the rounds of the different work locations and walk home for the breakfast that had been set out by Arobé, sometimes known as Albert. For the rest of the morning, I'd take care of specific things that needed my attention, make more rounds of the work and, sometimes, if there was one tractor driver sick or away, do some of the cultivation. I'd walk home for lunch, usually a hot meal, and go back out into the fields again. If it was Wednesday, Jacques would be there at about ten, he'd go over the whole plantation with me and we'd have Arobé's lunch together. We'd talk about the work and plan the next week's activities. Then he'd leave. At the end of the workday, usually mid-afternoon, I'd go over Thomas's accounts (he did them, I just checked them), and take care of mechanical problems. Then I could do whatever I wanted.

I was the only young European in the area, forty miles from the nearest apology for a town, with a car available only for certain emergencies, with no radio, no gramophone, and I didn't know what television was, let alone have one. I went through de Poerck's library. I found lots of reference books in French, some Simenon and other novels in French and two books in English. The latter were: "The High Speed Diesel Engine" and a book on marriage. I read some of the novels, the language making them last a while, and found that diesels proved to be the more exciting of the two subjects that I could read about at a normal pace, in English, since they had more relevance to my situation.

I gave myself lessons in drawing, supplemented by copying etchings of art works from various museums that were in a couple of ancient books. The books dated from an era when they still found it more economical to pay someone to etch a copper plate by hand rather than to use a photographic process. The subjects were the typical classical things including lots of chubby angels and chubby mythological characters, remarkably characterless characters, I noticed. Then I found one American novel set in a college. For no good reason, perhaps in an atlas, there was also a small scale road map of the United States, and I followed the characters of the novel around in it as they went one whole inch from Cambridge, Massachusetts, to Ithaca, New York, and back.

Sometimes, I'd take the tractor out for an afternoon or early evening shift in the fields. It was quite lonely work, de Poerck's more modern tractors had hydraulically operated lifting hitches and didn't need a turn boy. It would have been lonely enough even with a turn boy. It would have been lonely if I'd stayed in the house. On one of these evenings, I saw the Ruwenzoris without their cloud cover. I just stopped the tractor and stared until it got dark, all of half an hour. The sight made me think I'd like to try photography.

I started with an old Kodak folding camera that Mum had given me. It had a fairly wide-angled lens, which tended to make things look small in the picture unless I got close. I could buy the chemicals and paper in small packages, and one of the armoires served as a darkroom. I didn't need an enlarger, I made contact prints from the size 120 film. It used up a lot of time.

Some of the Africans wanted their pictures taken. I was happy to oblige, it gave me something to do. I was offered money, apparently there were some entrepreneurs doing this, and there was an established rate at about four days' wages per snapshot. Because free snaps would have inundated me with business, I accepted enough to pay for my supplies. Maybe I could have gone into business with an old hypodermic syringe, too, but that wasn't my kind of thing.

When Mum heard that I was taking pictures, including some of Africans, she hoped, audibly, that my subjects were keeping their clothes on. Not that she was a prude, mind, it was just that a photographic book had been published in the recent past, with the title *"Venus Noire,"* and it was in every body's office and living room, everywhere we went. Its subject was, unabashedly, African women's bare breasts. Give a book a title like Venus Something and, lo! It is Art! I assured Mum that my subjects would have their modesty preserved.

Some of my time I spent keeping the two other vehicles running. De Poerck had a Chevy pickup and a Chevy three-ton lorry, both about seven-years-old. Mechanically, they were in fair shape. The main problem was their brakes, so I should say that I spent time keeping the vehicles stopping. Every time you went anywhere, on the plantation or off it, you had to cross the Talya at least once in each direction. This meant that the vehicles' undersides never really dried out. The undersides are where the brake lines dwell. Where it is hot and wet you get corrosion. The brake lines all had corrosion, to the point that every now and then, when you stepped on the brakes, a fountain of fluid would come from one of the lines and there would be no brakes. It might have occurred to someone else to replace all of the lines. I wasn't someone else, and it didn't occur to me. I patched them with solder, very ineffectively, I might add, until I knew I could patch no more. Then, while I waited for a chance to go to town, or for Jacques' next trip, to get a replacement part, I'd block off the offending line or lines, killing the brakes to one or more wheels at a time.

The corrosion had given the pickup another idiosyncrasy. The floor of its load bed had rotted and rusted out. De Poerck had put a sheet of steel down on top of the crumbling cross members, as a temporary solution. It was a good solution, some of the time, if there was a load on it, and if you weren't going uphill. A load helped to keep the sheet from bouncing and clattering and making a noise that would wake the dead, and from catching the slipstream and flying off. Going uphill would allow the load to slip on the smooth steel sheet and slide off the back of the vehicle. Going uphill would also allow the sheet itself to slide off the back of the vehicle. A tail gate might have helped, but that was lost.

I got help in keeping the various machines and vehicles running - and stopping - from Emanuel, or Manoélé, de Poerck's version of Marcel. We spent hours with our heads in the engine rooms of various vehicles and machines.

I was offered other help by Manoélé, an offer of the kind that led me to believe that he had never been a serious hunter. After independence he started telling me that it was not right for a young man like me to be without a woman. He, himself was negotiating the purchase of one, but it would take him a long time. I, with my resources, could have one immediately. He knew several very suitable ones. Not local ones, but very evoluée ones, *maradadi*, fancy ones from Butembo. He had started a savings account with me for his planned purchase of a woman. I kept his money in the cash box for him. At least every time he made a deposit he'd repeat his offer of mediation. As often as he made it, I'd decline.

One day he told me that a friend of his wanted to have a picture taken. I made an appointment for late afternoon, after work was finished. His friend was a prodigiously endowed woman in a very *maradadi kanga*. It might have been two *kangas*, she was nearly as wide as she was tall. A *kabambi ya mwanamuke*. High praise - no, large praise - in *kinguana*.

The next day Manoélé asked me: "Well? What did you think?"

That told me what had been the real purpose of the appointment. I thanked him, again for his concern, and repeated my rejection of his pure, unselfish efforts.

CHAPTER EIGHTEEN

Independence was coming closer and closer. I didn't notice very much difference in the day to day life of the plantation. The routines continued.

In the towns, people met people and could share stories. Some of them filtered through to me, via Jacques and Dad, who came by from time to time. I think Dad made a one hundred kilometre detour to see me each time he was out of the Watalinga area. Some of the stories seemed imaginative and some pure imagination. They tended to make people a little more uncertain about the immediate future, and to contribute to the jumpiness.

Dad and Mum told me, on one of their visits, that de Jaeger had been driving along towards Beni when he had an accident. A two-year-old African child had pulled free from his mother and run into the road, right under his wheels, and he had run into the ditch in his futile attempt to avoid it. De Jaeger saw a few people running up, didn't like the feel of the situation, and ran off into the plantation at the edge of the road. He made his way to the *Administrateur* and reported the event. He was told that he was lucky that he had the presence of mind to get away. He had done exactly the right thing. Crowds like that were now exacting their own justice. He would have been killed on the spot.

On one of his days with me, Jacques saw the pile of PNP materials and nearly had a fit. He told me to burn them. Better wait until dark, *then* burn them, *if* nobody was looking. Couldn't let anyone find those things in my possession. I'd be in serious trouble, just like the Belgian colon in someplace else who had been beaten to death for being PNP.

The Congolese Government-elect issued a statement, it couldn't have been a law, yet, requiring all Europeans to hand in all their weapons, immediately after Independence, preferably before it. This act would benefit all citizens and would promote peace and harmony. It would not be right if there were one faction that was well armed while the rest of the citizenry was not. On my own, without Jacques' intervention,

I disassembled de Poerck's two puny weapons and hid them in the ceiling. I felt better having them, though they would be useless to me in an emergency.

The settlers and the traders tried even harder to get money out of the country. The market in East African shillings went to double the official rate.

On one of Dad's trips, he showed me a Coca-Cola bottle full of gold nuggets. He had been approached by a Congolese while he was at Germain's pumps. The man was furtive and secretive as he showed Dad his contraband. They negotiated a price, which Dad paid in cases of *Militaires* and other goods.

We knew there was gold around. The Congo was rich in minerals. Augustin the tribal historian and geologist, told us that there was gold in the mountains behind Kagando. The then chief, possibly Basikania's father, had cut a tree down over the place to mark it and said it was for the tribe, not for any one person, and no one was to touch it. That ruling would be obeyed by everyone in the tribe. I had often thought of it and would have loved to see it out of curiosity, but I would have honoured the chief's wish and wouldn't have done anything about it. I never did see it.

Gold was officially fifty francs a gramme. In the present conditions, it was worth a bit more. Dad was a law-abiding citizen, his main wish was only to keep our enterprise afloat. The Belgian administration was abandoning us, in a way, saying that they were going to jump ship in a few weeks, devil take the hindmost. Dad succumbed to the temptation of a few thousand quick francs or shillings from gold.

So did I.

Manoélé came to me one day, it was still a little while before independence. He told me that a young man, Michel, needed to see me. I had met Michel through de Poerck. He was headman on a plantation which belonged to an elderly friend of de Poerck, and which I was later to check on from time to time. Michel had once worked for de Poerck, when he was fresh out of the mission school, and as a favour, de Poerck had sent Michel to help his friend.

"M'sieu! Michel has something to talk to you about."

"What is it?"

"It's just something."

"It wouldn't hurt to tell me."

Looking around and lowering his voice: *"L'oro."*

"What?"

"Il a de l'or! He has gold!" This was important enough to say it in French rather than in Swahili or Kinguana.

I didn't have cash for a Johnny Walker bottle full of gold nuggets, in fact I didn't have any cash, so I wrote Michel an IOU. I wrote *"Bon pour F20,000,* Good for F20,000" (about four hundred dollars) on a slip of paper, signed it and gave it to Michel. I took the bottle and hid it.

Dad came by again, and we talked about this thing. I had obviously paid a higher price than he had, but time had passed, and I did get more than he did, and on credit, too. I offered to go to the Indians in Bundibugyo, *ngambo,* and see what they could do. I took leave from Talya for a long weekend, and went home with Dad, carrying my Johnny Walker with me.

I decided to start with the Coca-Cola gold. Mum and Pauline helped me sew a crude, cloth belt.

I made a short ride on the motor bike to Bundibugyo. The nuggets were hiding in a slight bulge round my middle, under my shirt. They dug into me. I saw a couple of Uganda Police constables, the first time I had seen them on this stretch. It must have been obvious that I had come across the river, an illegal act. The bulge felt huge and the nuggets dug deeper. I waved to the *askaris,* and they waved back to me.

The Indian trader was not sure what to do. He asked me to wait a minute. He came back with another Indian. They both asked me to wait a minute. They talked in Hindi.

It was getting dark. They would go to Port Portal, early tomorrow, and try to see what to do there. I should go with them. I could stay the night so we could leave early.

They sat me down to eat with them, with the men, that is, the women never appeared, though I could hear their voices in the next room and food which was prepared by them came and went.

"Mister, you want pork?"

That's very hospitable, I thought. They don't eat pork, but they are willing to serve it to a barbarian. I said: "No thanks. This chicken curry is good."

"You sure? Here," handing me a fork, "you want, you use, not want, you eat with pingers like us! We had pingers before we had porks, you see. We say it tastes better with pingers."

He was right. It was delicious. It was "pinger-lickin' good!"

We were in Fort Portal quite early, but it was noon before it was decided that we really couldn't do anything there. It was necessary to go to Kampala.

By late afternoon, we were in Kampala. We went straight to the Indian bazaar and stopped in front of a goldsmith's shop. The goldsmith was sitting in the doorway, working some gold on a little anvil. While a flood of Hindi was being exchanged, he took my belt, opened it, took out a nugget. He rubbed it against a stone, making a mark, and then fished around in his cupboard for some little glass vials of something. Glass droppers measured two drops of this one and one drop of that one on the stone. The gold mark turned black.

The goldsmith frowned. He fished out another nugget, did the same and got the same result. He uttered a whole lot of something in Hindi and the expression on the faces of my companions turned as black as the "gold."

"Mister, this is not gold. Gold will not be black in acid, you see. Gold is wery heavy. This much gold is wery heavy. This is not heavy like gold, you see. This is wery bad."

I spent that night in Kampala, as the guest of the family of one of my companions. They didn't feel so bad that they would forget to be hospitable. Hospitality consisted of putting me in a room by myself, with a tumbler wery full of neat scotch (ironically, it was probably Johnny Valker) and leaving me alone while they discussed something wolubly, in the next room in Hindi. I didn't know anybody who could handle a whole tumbler of scotch, with neither water nor ice, but I drank a sip or two, politely. I would have been happier and would have drunk all of their offering had it been tea, or the other even more ironical drink that they could have chosen, Coca-Cola, even without ice. Never mind. In the morning, we dashed back to Bundibugyo, lamenting the waste of time, the cost of the trip, not only to Fort Portal, but all the way To Kampala, a useless trip, because shopping at the wholesalers had just been done and wasn't due for a while and ... They also lamented, though a little a little less wolubly, that I had been tricked. They did not think for a moment that I was tricking them, but what a bad, bad world we lived in.

Dad was about as pleased as they were, but took it much more philosophically.

I took my Johnny Walker bottle back to Mutwanga.

"Michel, I have decided that I can't do this deal. Here is your stuff back."

Michel was not anywhere near as philosophical as Dad had been.

Before he even had it in his hands, he shouted: "You have robbed me! You have exchanged my gold for brass. Look!" He grabbed the bottle and turned it around in his hands. "Look at this piece here, it isn't at all like the gold I handed you. I don't recognize these pieces as mine, at all! It looks just like brass that has been melted and poured on the ground! I refuse to take it back."

Manoélé just hung around in the background, looking a bit sheepish.

I asked Michel for my *bon pour*. He declined to give it to me. He left.

By this time, it was after independence. De Poerck came back not long after. I told him the story. He laughed, even though he knew I didn't think it all that amusing. He summoned Michel, who came blustering in, perhaps expecting to press what he thought was his advantage.

De Poerck said: "Shame on you, Michel! I didn't expect you, a good mission boy to try to do this to a friend of mine. Shame! Give me the *bon pour* and we'll say no more."

Michel didn't hand it over, he said he didn't have it with him. He left, with his Johnny Walker bottle, muttering. I heard no more, though I must say I was not at all sure that I would not, one day, be reminded of that IOU, perhaps under a new system of justice less friendly to *wazungu*. Even explaining its existence could have put me in deep trouble.

The spirit of entrepreneurship had not suffered in the changes leading to independence. For the last three months before independence, and for long after it, there was not one brass tap, door handle or brazing rod, not any item made of brass, to be found in any shop across the whole Congo. Europeans were quick to repeat stories about other Europeans who had been beaten, raped or killed, but we never heard about anybody who had been duped. When I found that I'd been tricked, I didn't exactly stand in the centre of town and shout: "Don't buy gold the way I did. It's brass!" We all had to learn on our own, which kept a fresh stream of customers

308

falling into the same trap. Possibly the same Johnny Walker bottle went round and round, but I don't think many other buyers were lucky enough have their transaction rescinded.

Manoélé, after he realized that I didn't hold it against him, was able to face me across a cylinder head or under a chassis as though nothing had happened.

PART THREE

CHAPTER NINETEEN

When it came, independence was not noticed, at least, not for a few days. At the stroke of midnight on Thursday, June 30, 1960, just as predicted five months earlier, some flags went down and some new ones went up, in a place a thousand miles from where we were. There still was no television and no radio, so by the time independence had any impact on us, people in Europe and America had already seen it on the newsreels and it was old news.

Belgian colonial administrators moved their things down the halls to smaller offices. Africans who had been clerks in the different departments were nominated by the parties that won the provincial elections and moved into the big offices. The Belgians prepared the papers that fueled the government of the country and brought them in to the big offices for newly practiced, flourishy signatures and some satisfyingly physical rubber stamps. This clever new arrangement for governing the country was supposed to last until the new Congolese administrators had learned where to sign and stamp the different forms, from which point onwards they could go it on their own. It worked very smoothly, for a couple of whole days. Let's see, Friday was a holiday to celebrate Independence, so offices were closed, Saturday and Sunday nothing was open - yes, in Kivu Province it worked smoothly for three days, perhaps even part of the way into the fourth day. It might have lasted longer, but for a blunder in planning the transition for the armed forces.

Unfortunately, the *Force Publique,* the army, hadn't been smart enough to move the European officers down the hall, the way the Civil Administration had done it. As a result, in the Army, things stopped working smoothly in less than twenty-four hours, in fact, the first mutiny occurred on Independence Day. The army became the biggest contributor to, in fact was the origin of the unrest in the first week, which unrest precipitated a crisis. Even removing the Europeans and promoting every man in the army by one whole rank didn't make up for the first blunder, that of leaving the European officers in charge.

It had been an easy mistake to make. After all, can you imagine the criticism that would have had to be endured if there had not been separate transition plans for the Army and for the Administration? They would have mocked the transition planners for having a lack of imagination, and for having to fall back on a 'one size fits all' planning approach. And if you don't think that what 'they' think or say is important, ask yourself why independence was granted so precipitously in the first place.

All this went on at a great enough distance from us that we were unaware of it at Talya for a week.

On Saturday the 9th of July, after one full week of independence, I was sleeping late. On Saturdays, I didn't have to get up as early as on other days. It must have been six or six-thirty when Arobé came into my room, totally out of breath.

"*Bwana! Bwana!* (gasp) *Wamitoroka, wote!* Boss! They've run away, all of them!"

"Who?"

"Everybody! All the *wazungu*! --- Even *bwana* Jacques! I was going to market and --- they told me and I didn't believe it and --- I ran to Bwana Jacques house --- to see if it is true and it is true and they --- have all gone! They got in their cars and went, vroom, like that, --- one after the other all together."

I threw on some clothes and we drove to Jacques house together. I took the station wagon, this seemed like an 'in case' to me, and it was about three miles. As we went, I noticed the Africans walking on the roads and standing in their yards looking a bit edgy, or was I looking for things? We did get some glances, though a day earlier a servant riding with a *mzungu* in a car would not have caused any stir.

At Jacques' house, I found only the house servant. He confirmed that Jacques was away. Last night some other *bwana* had come with his *madami,* and they had gone, all of them to the *hoteli,* and then they had come back and then they had all left, with the *madami* and his child and a whole bunch more *wazungu*. They said they were going to Uganda. *Bwana* Jacques had said he would be back, in a few days, probably by

311

Monday, in time to start the work. If he isn't back on Monday, the men should start themselves.

We went on to the town of Mutwanga, which consisted of three shops and a Post Office. Oh yes, and the hotel. The only other European around was M. Ingels, senior, Jacques' father, in his empty hotel. He told me that there had been a scare about something in Stanleyville, and that the men wanted to take their women and children to safety in Uganda, in case the trouble spread. He, M. Ingels had not wanted to abandon his hotel for any length of time, but his wife had gone.

There was nothing to be learned and nothing else to do, there, so I went back to Talya. I had my breakfast and went down to see that Thomas was doing the *posho* the way he was supposed to. He was. The workers on the plantation seemed to have nothing unusual on their minds I went back to the house.

In the mid-afternoon, Mum and Dad came. They had been in Beni and heard all kinds of rumours. The main point seemed to be that Lumumba's soldiers in Province Orientale had mutinied. They had gone on a rampage, looting shops, raping nuns and killing doctors. Mum and Dad had seen that nearly all the Belgians in Beni had left, including the ex-Administrateur. A few Greek traders were left. Mum and Dad wanted to check up on me.

Mum said she had overheard an African comment, when he saw them parking in town: "What? They haven't run away with all the others?"

To which another retorted: "No, of course not! They're not Belges, they're Princes!"

Something of Dad's lectures on his genealogy must have sunk into some of his audiences. This story tickled Dad, and it gave us to think that we had little to fear. We were respected as fair and decent people, and we had no historical baggage to carry, the way the Belgian *colons* did. If we showed our commitment to staying and showed no fear, we would be left alone.

They stayed the night. We discussed the situation into the evening. Dad had spoken to all sorts of people who had heard that something was happening somewhere else, but to no one who had actually seen anything happen, nor even to anyone who had talked to someone who had seen something happen. He wondered if the tales weren't spread to justify the panicked exodus. That explanation made sense, everything was calm, here, with the local natives. Later, much later, we found out that Europeans had indeed been killed, but we didn't know it then.

We assured each other that we were staying in the Congo. We didn't yet have anything to run away from. We didn't say it, and I don't think we even thought about it, but we didn't have anything to run away to, either.

On Sunday they went home.

After they were gone, it must have been mid-afternoon, I went to Mutwanga again. Again, I found nobody there. I went back to Talya. In the evening I heard, probably from Arobé, that some *wazungu* were at the hotel. I went to check it out. There were a half dozen Belgians, one of them a woman, all looking a little frazzled and all crouched around a short-wave radio, listening to scratchy static and whistling, atmospheric sounds that every now and then barely let a human voice crackle through. They had been to Uganda and had left their women and children and had come back, but they had obviously left their hearts in Uganda too. They had come back here, but they were looking over their shoulders, so to speak.

They were already skittish and the radio was playing to their fears. They were tuned to an amateur operator in Bunia. I couldn't really understand a word and I think that the others only caught a few. But it sounded bad. The young woman present was the recent bride of one of the men. He had been in the colonial service and had decided to become a *colon* instead, and they had been opening up their plantation for less than a year. He had taken her to Uganda, along with all the other women, but she hadn't wanted to be left there. Besides, they had no children to look out for, so she had come back. In gaps in the radio reception they told me all this, interrupting the story whenever the static yielded a few more words from Bunia.

M. Ingels must have had his bar open, because we all were having beers.

After a while, I picked up the gist of what was being said. Maybe the beer improved the reception, if not the news that came through. "... it is very bad, ... no food ... -ty women and chil- ..., all togeth ... one roo ... need medicine ... we can't last without help ... Please, please send ... ... low ammun-... My god! They're coming for us now. We have to get out while we can! Leave if you can! ..."

The young husband picked up his revolver from the table beside him, spun the cylinder, looked sweetly at his wife and said: "Don't worry, my darling! They won't get you alive! I'll save one for you!" Honest!

Bunia was five or six hours away. We never found out who was broadcasting, or who was coming. After a while, even with free beer, I'd had enough, I went back to Talya. I passed Jacques' place on the way. He wasn't back yet.

A day later, after the work was over, I went back to the hotel. The nerves were no less tense than they had been the night before. No one seemed to have slept or even bathed. The radio was whistling and scratching, again, or still. The bar was open again, or still. There was talk of another trip to Uganda, to check on the women. It had been thirty-six hours since they had been left there, all alone in a hotel in Katwe. I think a convoy did leave, that night or the next day.

This time I saw Jacques. He looked a bit sheepish when I asked him what had happened, and if he had thought that maybe I might have been a little surprised to find myself, for all I knew, the only European in the country. Well, he had thought about telling me that everyone was leaving, of course, only to take their wives and children to safety, but he thought that it might unduly upset me. Besides, his father was here all along, and he, Jacques, was back wasn't he?

Over the next six months, everybody left again in big convoys, at great speed and in great clouds of dust, to trickle back some days later in ones and twos, only to dash away, again, in a few weeks or days. Each time fewer returned.

I spent a few evenings at the hotel. This was not exactly fun, but I thought I ought to know if and when I was going to be abandoned again, and at first it was much more entertaining than sitting alone at Talya. Besides, someone always seemed to be getting beer out, or making omelets to feed the crowd. That was just fine. Then I realized that the less I knew about what was happening in a distant, troubled province the calmer I felt, and the fewer times I heard Lover-Boy promise his bride a bullet the fewer times I felt as though I'd be sick. So I stayed at Talya.

Dad came by every other week or so. In those

circumstances, that was fairly frequently. Often he came with Mum. Sometimes they'd spend the night. Other than when, for a short while, de Poerck came back, those visits and Jacques' provided the only non-African company I got for five of the next six months.

The dust had settled and the local Belgian population had gone and come back, and gone again and come back again a few times, when de Poerck came back.

He came back in time to check that everything was going smoothly, to prepare me for the upcoming harvest and to tell me that he had found a job in the United Nations Food and Agricultural Organization, the FAO, in Rome, and therefore he would be leaving again. Would I like to continue at Talya indefinitely?

I supposed so, and we talked it over with Dad. It was arranged.

In a few weeks, after the harvest had been started, de Poerck left to take up his post in Rome. I think he was reluctant to leave his successful plantation, but it was obviously less important to him than his family. Dad and I drove him to Entebbe, Uganda, in his own car.

Before getting on the plane, he asked me to promise him that if there was a life-threatening situation, I would leave immediately and not try to play the hero. I said I would.

The next months were strange. The individual days and the evenings seemed long. The hours after work dragged, but the months went by very rapidly.

CHAPTER TWENTY

In preparation for the coffee harvest, de Poerck and I had gone over the machinery with Manoélé and found that the water pump's propeller shaft bushing was badly worn. Not being designed to operate by gravity, this factory needed a pump. There was no way we could get a replacement part. Dad, who still visited frequently, had the idea of going to Kilembe, where our friends the Cleggs might be able to help. The mine might possibly have a part to fit, but failing that, father Clegg was the chief fitter for the mine, which meant that he had at his disposal all manner of machines and tools. I made a quick overnight trip to Kilembe. Barry Clegg, who was assistant to his father, did a few hours of work on a lathe. I did a few hours of work in return on Barry's pet project, his Jeep shooting brake. I came back with a shiny new, made to order bushing. I had taken only the worn part, not the shaft that it had to fit. Barry had guessed at some of the dimensions, guessing what part of the oddness of the dimensions was due to wear and what might be due to the original perhaps having been in metric measure, so he left a little more clearance than he thought necessary, so it would fit. When I tried it, it fit. In fact, it fit a little too easily. Because it was a bit loose, we had to tighten the packing a bit more than usual, but it seemed to work well enough.

When we were not quite finished with the harvest, it was clear that, having started a little too loose, the new bushing had worn quickly and it now had too much wear to be compensated for by the packing, and it leaked too much to maintain the water pressure that was needed to do the job. I hitch hiked back to Kilembe and imposed on my friends, one more time. While I was there, Barry suggested that I might like to come to the New Year's dance at the club. It was only a little over a month away. I made plans to go.

Meanwhile, we were harvesting papaïne, an activity that went on all year. Jacques had told me that the temperature in the dryer was too high, or that the product was being left in too long, because some of it was turning brown and the buyer in

Beni was dropping the quality to second grade. This meant a big drop in price.

Dad came by, shortly after this advice, this time with Bill. When I told him about it, he wanted to see the papaïne. I showed him. He immediately called for a drying rack to be brought, and for some women workers to be called out. He spread the offending product on the rack and showed everyone how to pick out the brownest grains, each smaller than a rice grain, and to collect them in a separate container. With Dad, Bill and me getting in the way, ten women turned the mess into two batches, one, first grade papaïne which could be sold at the full price, made up of ninety five percent of the original batch, the other, second grade, consisting of the much smaller balance.

Dad had a practical solution, even though he wasn't a seasoned papaïne producer. I don't think Jacques liked the idea much, but he didn't have to. I watched our drying process much more carefully, but was never again going to accept the second grade price lying down.

On one of my few visits to Beni, I stopped at the hotel that we'd stayed in the first time we visited the town. I had to wait there for Jacques, or something. I sat on the verandah for hours, watching the now very changed activity. Where there had been *colons* and their staid wives sipping cups of "French press" coffee and watching occasional fashion shows (Bill used to amuse us by mimicking the models' mincing strut and the way they slithered their hands down their hips and over their bottoms as they turned at the end of their "runway"), now there was a young African woman trying to interest somebody, anybody, in a game of ping pong. Her fancy headdress and tightly wrapped *kanga* were not exactly designed for athletics, not that kind of athletics, but that didn't matter. Ping pong was totally new to her, and maybe it would be a break from drinking Primus, the queen of beers, while she waited there for her beau to come, perhaps any body's beau to come.

In the evening, a beau came. He was driving the big, yellow Mercury sedan that I recognized as having belonged to the Belgian agricultural officer. Some of the departing administration officials had had the decency to explain to their replacements that part of the badge of office was the big American car that they were driving, which, for a small price, the new incumbent could have and enjoy. That helped me to recognize the beau as the new Congolese area agricultural officer. If the deterioration of both the car and the driver were any indication, the department must already have been in a pitiful state, even in that short time. He had a couple of beers with the *kanga* and the headdress, and they weren't the first beers of the day for either of them, by any means, and, as it got dark, they got into the car together. He sprayed the hotel with gravel as he drove off, only to make the power brakes screech in terror as he came to a stop just before hitting the nearest lamp post. He was either using the lamps as navigation aids or he was playing with them. He'd stand on the accelerator, aiming the car straight at one of them until he got really close, then, when the lamp was cringing, he'd slide to a stop by standing on the brake. Sort of a game of chicken. See who gives up and ducks first. The front of the car carried evidence that the lamp poles were better at dodging the big, slower, weekly, red Berliets than at dodging the aptly named darting Mercury.

One day, I drove the lorry over the back road to Joe Cassel's plantation in Mutwanga, to collect a piece of machinery, or something. On the way back, I drove into a torrential rainstorm. The road consisted of a gap between the trees with parallel tracks, just about visible in the vegetation, one for each wheel. The already poor visibility was made worse by a cloud of steam coming up in front of me, which I attributed to the wet grass throwing water onto the hot exhaust manifold.

Wrong!

When the smell told me something was wrong, I stopped. The cloud of steam was from the radiator hose spilling water on the hot exhaust manifold. We were only a few hundred yards from the plantation of an acquaintance, so I walked there through the rain. I had to walk across another ford in the Talya to get there. The acquaintance had been a garage owner in Belgium. I knew he would have tools and be happy to help me get going. He would be happier to help me when the rain stopped, so I waited at his place for that to happen. Eventually, after waiting patiently for over an hour I became impatient. I set out for the lorry before the rain had stopped, armed with some tape and wire in my pocket.

In that hour, the Talya had swollen to the top of its bank. What was usually clear, slow, friendly water less than a foot deep was now murky brown, fast moving, angry and about eight feet deep. It had branches and other debris whizzing by in it. I couldn't get any wetter, so I waited for a big limb or a small tree to go by and swam the fifty feet across.

I wired and taped the radiator hose together, found no problem in locating a source of water to refill the radiator, and drove home to Talya.

While we were driving, Manoélé told me that the river was fierce. Did I know that it used to run on the other side of de Poerck's house?

Yes I knew that.

Did I know that the day it changed its course it left the carcass of a young elephant on the grass behind the house, which load it had carried down from way up in the forest?

I had forgotten that.

Lumumba's province included Bunia, the home of many of the Talya workers. These Bunia people were never the easiest to manage, and after independence they became no easier. One particularly troublesome man was reprimanded several times for not showing up to work, or coming to work drunk, and was fired. A few days later, I received a *convocation,* a summons from Lumumba's party's headquarters in Mutwanga. I forget their initials. They could have been the PDP, *Partie Democratiqe Populaire,* or something like that. The notice was written in pencil on a page torn out of a school exercise book. It was signed by someone with a title like Chef du Bureau Mutwanga. I was commanded to present myself to the PDP, PDQ, *immédiatement,* or sooner, etc., etc.

I was quite indignant about this. I decided that I would go, but I would go on my own terms. I would take the offensive, but I would be very dignified. Dad had always got away with things when he took the offensive. And he always thought he was dignified. I decided to wait a day or two and drove there in the pickup. When I rattled up the main road through Mutwanga, the sheet of metal flew out and failed to decapitate anyone. I tried to brake to pick it up, only to find that the brakes were gone. It was uphill, so I could coast to a stop. Using the engine as a brake, I backed down the hill to where the sheet was, and, because the parking brake was also useless, I backed into the ditch to stop. Whoever was my turn-boy picked up the sheet and put it in place, sat on it to hold it down, and we continued. That is why one has turn-boys. If you've ever seen the antics of the Land-Rover in the movie 'The Gods Must Be Crazy', you know how dignified I was as I drove that pick up to confront the new powers in the land.

When I arrived at the office, I didn't present myself, I asked for the man who had signed the summons. A small man came forward. I lit into him.

"Who do you think you are, commanding me to come here? You have been in control for six weeks and people in my family line have ruled for a thousand years. You call me here about a drunkard who never comes to work, and when he does come, he fights and spoils the work of others. You aren't even the government. You are a political party! You don't even know what your job should be in the six weeks you've been at it. You are offending me and my lineage, and I resent it!" That's what I was saying. Never mind that my family had nothing to do with the situation, nor had the length of his tenure.

I had heard Dad use a Swahili word, *mlango,* for line, as in family lineage. I had never needed the word myself, so I had never tried to find another word. It might be the right term, I still don't know. In plain, everyday, non-Dad Swahili, *mlango* means 'door'.

So, put yourself in the position of the party hack who had just taken on this job. 'There's so much new weight to be thrown around and so little time! Here is a young *mzungu,* whom you hear not only ranting about the new government's short tenure, but also about some ancient door that he has, which he claims can do a better job than you can. You're missing something, here. You've got two choices: throw some more weight, or put your efforts where they will be more immediately gratifying. The easiest one is to follow the ancient African tradition of humouring idiots. And you can find somebody else to bully.'

"M'sieu! Pardon! I'm sorry! I just wanted to know your side of the matter. This man lodged a complaint about you. No problem."

I stomped out and never heard from them again. I don't think I would try that again, anywhere. I certainly wouldn't have tried it with an armed man.

I was to get my first introduction to armed soldiers before long.

A break in the lonely routines occurred when I bumped into an American family who ran a mission in the far end of Mutwanga. They must have been hiding somewhere before I found them, because I had no inkling that they were there. They hadn't hidden themselves well enough to escape Dad, it turned out that he had visited them, once. I visited them two or three times and got introduced to the Sears catalog and to a most ingenious power generator. They had a Pelton wheel, an open turbine driven by waterpower, under gravity, no less, which drove a generator to provide electricity for the station. I was impressed. Dad had talked about Pelton wheels in our future. Here was someone who *had* one.

They had a teenage son, I suppose he was only four years younger than I was, but that was too young to be a friend. Nevertheless, I went by a couple of times, to chat and to keep up on what was going on. They were in radio contact with their organization. And I thought I could learn something about colleges in the United States.

On one of the first trips to visit them, I drove the pickup, whose brakes were not yet repaired. I had the same experience with the steel sheet.

The following week, I spent the afternoons trying to fix the brakes and ripping out the rotten floor members, to see what I could do about the floor. The brakes may or may not have been fixed, but it didn't matter. The rotten body cross members, once I took them off, could not be put back, without several new parts and all new bolts. The body stayed off. The pickup became almost totally useless, rather than just difficult to use.

The next time I went, I drove the three-ton lorry. At this point, its brakes were gone, too. Its cable-operated parking brake worked, and, if the lorry wasn't loaded, that was usually enough to make do.

I had passed through Mutwanga and was on the track that led to the mission when a man in a uniform and with a rifle slung across one shoulder, lurched out into the road, holding me up with one hand, holding himself up by hanging on to the strap of his rifle with the other hand. I stopped.

"I will check your *camion!*" He walked around it.

"I will check your brakes!" He moved, or flowed, to the middle of the road about thirty feet in front of the lorry and motioned me to drive towards him.

321

I did. When I was a few paces away from him, he shot his right hand into the air, signaling me to stop. I resisted the obvious, strong temptation, reached down, yanked on the parking brake, and made the lorry stop about ten feet from him.

"*Maint'nant en arrière! Plus vite!*"

I drove in reverse, a little faster since I was going away from him. His hand shot up, I braked, the lorry stopped.

"*Allez! En avant! Encore plus vite!*"

I put the lorry in low gear and revved up the engine, fiercely, and made it lurch forwards, all to appear to be going *beaucoup plus vite*. I yanked the brake again, making the rear wheels skid. I had to do it two or three times more, while he considered what other tricks he could make me do for him.

He got in beside me. "Now drive me to the *Poste Militaire.*"

I drove him to his barracks and he got out and went to bed. After all, it was Sunday noon and it had been a long, hard Saturday night.

I went back to continue to try to make my visit. I had forgotten that on Sundays missionaries get preoccupied. My friends were true to form. I went back to Talya.

I told my story at home, the next time I was there, or to Mum and Dad on their next visit. I heard that John had had a similar experience.

He went into Beni in Polonia when Marcel took in a load of the co-op coffee. Having a *mzungu* along tended to speed up the trips by a day or so and reduce the wear and tear on Polonia. They were going along the main street when a uniformed, armed soldier flagged them down.

Marcel stopped. He was asked something by the soldier and referred him to John, who preferred to sit on the load in the back to sharing a seat right on top of Polonia's hot engine.

The soldier wanted to know who he was, what he was doing here, where were his papers, where were the papers for the *camion?* John tried to satisfy him, all in *kinguana* because he wasn't fluent in French - and neither was the soldier - but the soldier wasn't going to be satisfied.

"You are under arrest! *Sortez!* Get out! Come with me to the poste!"

John suggested that they all ride to the poste. The soldier thought that was a good idea. John suggested that he climb up

322

onto the back, with him. The soldier tried, but with his hands occupied with his rifle, he had trouble.

The soldier said: "Here, hold that for me," and passed John the rifle.

He got in, retrieved his rifle and they drove to the poste. By the time they reached the destination, two miles away, John had him stripping down his weapon to show him how it worked.

John spent some hours 'under arrest'. He was probably no more bewildered than the typical African who had been detained by the *wazungu* before *dipandan*. The difference was that the confusion was on both sides now. Before it would have been only on the arrestee's side.

At closing time, the African clerk, who might have recognized him as one of those 'not Belgians', said to John: "if you can get hold of Marcel, go home, now! Quick! The soldiers keep office hours too, and the *barrière* is open now!" Marcel was dug out of the nearest bar and they came home.

As the Talya coffee was processed and dried and bagged, I had to get it off the plantation. It was supposed to go to Beni, to the coffee broker. I delivered one lorry full and got a receipt. It would be paid for by bank draught sometime in the future. With everything uncertain, I wondered when that future might be and what the price might be in that future. The Beni price was now below twenty francs, and still dropping. De Jaeger was shaking his head and saying that it cost eighteen and a half francs to produce.

Being Dad's son, I thought of other ways of doing things. There was a coffee market across the Lamia, *ngambo* from Kagando. It paid cash, in shillings. Shillings were worth twice as much as francs, if you took advantage of the black market. I sold the next two loads to some of my Indian friends in Bundibugyo. It was a bit odd, taking coffee into the Watalinga area, I was usually taking it the other way. But, hey, change is good!

An added bonus of this process was that I got to visit home a couple of times, and from there, to visit Fort Portal to collect the cash. In Fort Portal, in my friend Claude's garage, I met an American woman who lived in Johannesburg. She was traveling with three of her daughters, and her car had broken down. I learned that her oldest daughter was in an American college, on a scholarship. Now I knew of someone who had actually gone to college with no money, who was not just talking about it. It made the idea more real.

On the way back to Mutwanga after the first such coffee trip, our old friend Apollo rode with me. He was going to announce to the part of the Wanandi tribe that lived on the Mutwanga end of the mountain, that he, Apollo, now all of 17, was the acting chief of Basikania's part of the tribe while his father went to Leopoldville to be a senator. They truly, desperately, needed to know this.

I couldn't refute their need for this information. I think I was also expected to accept that all of the people he needed to tell it to were to be found in the *hotelis* along the road. I could have argued the point, but what was the point? I behaved. Every dog has his day, and this was Apollo's day.

He had a keen eye for *hotelis*. He could spot a *hoteli* as we passed, sometimes even before we passed it, even after I tried to distract him. I don't think he missed any on the first half of the trip. I stopped when he said: "Stop here!" and I backed up when he said: "Let's go back," and I sat in the lorry while he went into the thatched huts to tell his people the good news. It took half an hour at the first stop. It took longer at each new place, and Apollo came out with less and less interim-chiefly bearing as the afternoon wore on. Obviously, telling this type of news takes a toll. Eventually, his powers of perception had been blunted by all of the delivering of the news. We missed many of the remaining *hotelis,* otherwise we might still be on that road.

When we arrived at Talya, it was dark. I did not want to set the precedent of inviting Apollo into the de Poercks' house. Arobé fed him in the kitchen, looking down his wrinkled nose at him. Apollo sat on a stool and ate an omelet balanced on a windowsill, while I ate at the dining room table. We talked, after a fashion, through the open door. Arobé found him a place in the African camp to marinate overnight.

Describing it now, it sounds like a strange thing to have done. I had been invited and had eaten at Africans' houses with them. I had eaten at Indians' houses with them. I didn't consider myself prejudiced, but I couldn't invite this youth, even an acting chief, to eat with me at my table. I think mostly, it was the fact that it wasn't *my* table. Then, on top of that, that he was in a worsening, stinking stupour. But a significant part was the colonial thing of keeping the distance, still, even after independence. Had I made the gesture of inviting him in, I know that Arobé would have walked out. He would not have seen it as a symbol of the advancement of his people to a new equality. To him it would have been wrong, plain wrong. His body language told me that he was barely suffering Apollo being in his kitchen. At that point, Arobé himself was more comfortable that the social gap was being kept. It maintained the familiar frame of reference.

CHAPTER TWENTY-ONE

I made one trip home with coffee at Christmas.

Bill had set up a ram pump a small way down the hill, to push some of Meku's water up to the top. It was at the highest point that could be reached by the furrow. Ram pumps use no external power, they convert the energy of a lot of water falling a few feet to push a little water up a lot of feet. An empty oil drum served as a cistern, and there was now running cold water in a new bathhouse. Pascali carried no more water, but he still heated it over three stones. Maybe Bill knew what he was doing, but he was flirting with fate by bringing so much civilization so close. The family had lived in Rongai for thirty-five years while there were no paved roads, only to leave a few months after the road was paved.

Everyone at Kagando was in good spirits, despite all of the bad news and rumours that were flying around. Province de Kivu had been taken over by Province Orientale. It didn't mean much in the day to day living, but it led to uncertainties about the future.

Never mind, we were in a backwater and would be little affected by all that. We'd just lie low and let it pass.

I had to store some of de Poerck's coffee in the boys' bedroom overnight, and a few of the workers had helped. Mpendawatu, the lover of people, was one of them. I noticed him dallying behind in the room each time he went in with a bag. Mpenda was one of the more precocious ones of his tribe. He wanted to learn English, so he hung around us a bit more than the others did. We taught him a few phrases. He could say 'Gedda-bladdy-moofon' and other useful things. I'm a trusting sort. I thought he was intrigued by how the *wazungu* live.

We went in two vehicles to attend midnight mass with Père Jean. I was driving the VW pickup, with some other members of the family as passengers. The others were in the caravan.

As we left the church and entered the forest, gravel hit the window. I stopped immediately, jumped out and shouted: "Who did that?" There was no answer.

I shouted: "Are you afraid of me? If you have something to

326

say to me, come and say it! Do not be a coward! You are a coward, hiding in the dark!"

Silence.

I had no torch to look for anyone, and it was pitch dark.

"Come out and show who you are!"

Silence.

I got back in the pickup and drove home. I asked myself: "Why did I do that?" I didn't get an answer. I don't think I'd have done it if I'd thought about it first, and I'm not likely to do it again.

This was a new experience in that place. We still thought the people were friendly. We still got some waves and salutes, though fewer. The perpetrators were probably just children, but children here had always been polite. The influence of the Stanleyville people was coming to the surface.

For the first time, we wondered if we could believe that we would not be caught up in the hatred for whites in general.

I think I went back to Mutwanga after Dad's birthday, Boxing Day, which fell on a Wednesday.

When I went to pack, I found that the bag that I had shoved under my bed with a wad of shillings in it had been moved. Sure enough, a whole lot of the money was missing. I asked around. Joseph told me that Mpendawatu had been seen *ngambo*, exchanging shillings for francs. Mpendawatu was nowhere to be seen. I couldn't have proven anything, even if I could have found him. I doubted that he wanted to make it easy for me to find him. I chalked it up to experience and headed back to Mutwanga.

On the weekend, I drove to Kilembe in de Poerk's station wagon. Manoélé wanted to come along, I think to have *bonani* (*bonne année*, Happy New Year) there. He couldn't have had much fun, he slept in the car. Still, it made him an international traveler, that was good for something. He could tell his grandchildren about having to change his watch by an hour when he crossed the border, and that *les Anglais* drive on the wrong side of the road. I introduced him to Bwana Barry.

Barry Clegg took me to the New Year's dance at the mine's clubhouse. I went with Barry and drank a couple of beers with him, but I danced with the girls. Yes, there were even two girls there, a rare commodity, rarer even in that they spoke English. I had a moving conversation with one of them, all about how

327

her family was moving to Rhodesia in a couple of months.

The dance must have been on Saturday night. I drove back on Sunday, the day before New Year's Eve.

A few days later I was wakened before dawn by a familiar voice calling to me through the window. It was a Mtalinga from Kagando. He had a letter from Dad, and he had spent a day and a night in the forest, bringing it to me.

I no longer have it, I think it was left at Talya. It said something like:

"Dear Carl,

How nice it was to have you home over the Holiday. Here are a few things happening which are a little unusual but maybe they don't mean anything. We have taken in some more tobacco and are curing it and the quality seems to be all right. Yesterday I was with de Jaeger and we talked about the situation and he is a little unsure about the future. Well we will see. We will just continue and see what the future brings.

[Change of pen here].

We wish you a good New Year and we look forward to seeing you again soon. Be careful there at Talya. Things are changing. We will see what happens but we must take care.

Salaams from all, Love, Dad."

Then, in another pen, on the back of the sealed envelope:

"I am giving this to - [I've forgotten the man's name] - to bring to you.

IT IS FINISHED. GET OUT WHILE YOU STILL CAN"

Well, that is enough to spoil your breakfast, to say nothing of the whole morning!

After work I drove to the American mission, where I had planned to go anyway. I hoped, now, also to find out if they had heard anything, and just to have someone to share this rather upsetting development with. I wanted to see if they were still planning to go into Uganda, for that offered the option of another route to Watalinga that did not go through the Congo.

On the way to the mission, I was flagged down by another familiar person. I recognized him as a *mzee,* an elder of Basikania's tribe who was also a trustee of the coffee co-op. He and I were both out of context here in Mutwanga, hut he recognized me. It should have been easy even with me in the strange vehicle. The road limited my speed to no more than

328

twenty kilometers per hour and there were very few white faces around by this time.

"Bwana Kallo! What's going on?"

"I don't know. Can you tell me?"

"Where is Shauri Moja?"

"I think he is at home."

"Shauri Moja has left. He has taken the box and he has gone *ngambo*. I am here to report it to the authorities."

"I saw Shauri Moja at Christmas. He was home."

"He was gone yesterday. And he took the box with the coffee co-op's money. I am here to report to the *Tribunal*."

Mutwanga was no closer to home than Beni, and more than a day's hike on foot through the forest. He probably chose to come this way to talk to his own tribal elders, rather than go to the foreigners in Beni. He must have been quite fired up to undertake the trip.

I was not surprised that Dad might want to put the cash box out of reach of any mob, perhaps even making a big display of moving it away. Any reduction of temptation would be wise.

The *mzee* went on his way, and I on mine.

The Americans said that they had heard that there was some trouble. But that was just rumours, you know. Nobody had been there, the road to Watalinga had been blocked. Sure, they were going to Uganda on Friday, and would be happy to drop me off in Kilembe.

The Cleggs were surprised to see me again, less than a week since I last left. Barry said that he had just visited my family, only a few days before, from the Uganda side. How odd that I should turn up again. Just after I left, the week before, he had decided that some contact with the outside world might be nice for those poor people all caught up in that Congo mess he was hearing about on the radio. He had the day off and had driven his Jeep shooting brake down there, loaded with some supplies that he thought they might need (they told me later, it was mainly a case of beer) and walked them across the river. Everything was okay. Everybody in my family was fit.

I thanked him for the news, but asked if I could borrow his Jeep to go there to see them and to see for myself. It was not a problem.

The next morning, Saturday, it must have been the fifth of January, I set out early. I drove around the mountain in an anti-clockwise direction, through Fort Portal and on to the dirt road that led down to Bundibugyo. Despite its growing familiarity, the road which clung to the escarpment by some mysterious force, was still intimidating.

I was not halfway between Fort Portal and Bundibugyo, just before the escarpment, when something happened under the Jeep's bonnet. Oil sprayed onto the windscreen. I stopped and looked. An oil line had sprung a leak. Barry's nice clean Jeep was being given a bath in dirty oil. Worse, this was using up oil that was needed for something else. I would not make it to Bundibugyo and back up the escarpment like that.

I turned around and limped into Fort Portal. I disturbed my friend Claude at Western Motors. He helped me by doing something to make the Jeep drivable twenty miles to return it to its owner. He topped up the oil, but suggested that I postpone my trip to Bundibugyo until the right part could be found, or I'd certainly ruin the engine. This took until Saturday evening.

Barry had seen my family only a few days ago, and they were all right. Claude knew of nothing going on down that way. Rumours were easy to come by those days and were often wrong. If I listened to every tenth rumour, or believed every hundredth one, I'd go crazy. I suffered a bit from the oldest son syndrome; I had a job to do at Talya, with quite a lot of responsibility, and I didn't want to let the side down. If I left my post, de Poerck's investment could be lost, and it would have happened on my shift, so to speak.

I gave Barry Clegg back his car, apologized for the mess, asked if I might try again the next week and caught the ride back on Sunday, with the American missionaries. Dad's cryptic message on the outside of the envelope bothered me less now that I had decided that he was just concerned for my safety. Since I knew I was safe, he was worrying about me unnecessarily, and I needn't worry too much about his message.

Of course, where there is smoke there is fire. Even as I turned around, both smoke and fire were very much in evidence already, at Kagando, but I didn't know it. Kagando was round the corner of the mountain and out of my sight. Harried as I thought I was, my situation was blissfully calm compared to what the family was already going through.

Back at Talya, I put the men to work, right on time on

Monday morning, the seventh of January. I spent the afternoons and evenings trying to get word about what had happened or was happening in Watalinga.

There were fewer people around to ask. By the people I did see, I was told that the road to Watalinga was not safe, not to try it under any circumstances. That usually meant that soldiers and various other entrepreneurs had set up roadblocks. If you stopped at a roadblock, you would be robbed and possibly killed. If you didn't stop, you were gunned down by machine gun, for refusing to stop at a roadblock. This had been happening a lot in Province Orientale, but not yet here. Now we had the same people here, it stood to reason that we could expect the same tricks.

It was better to stop at these roadblocks, your chances of survival were better if you did. The trouble was that it was impossible to know what was a roadblock and what was just a jungle vine lying across the road. Smart people knew that jungle vines didn't fall across the road. They usually got there by being put.

I heard that the situation was a little rough everywhere, but that nothing bad had happened in Watalinga. Butembo, yes! A Belgian had been beaten to death in the main street. His cries had been heard over the whole town. Everyone had left Butembo. Watalinga, (shrug) is probably all right, I mean, it's nowhere. But don't go down that road!

On Saturday, the twelfth of January, 1961, I had Manoélé drive me down to the back road intersection with the main road to Kasindi and Uganda. I had packed a small suitcase that Paga had lent me, months ago, to take my few things to Mutwanga. I packed for one, maybe two nights, but I included a book that I had been given as a prize at Prince o', simply because I kept it in the suitcase. My clothes were being laundered, so I was wearing a pair of ill-fitting khaki shorts that belonged to de Poerck, and I think the boots were his, too.

I had looked for Jacques, he was not home. I think he was on one of his frequent absences, so I hadn't been able to tell him of my weekend plans. I had told the men that I was going to visit my parents, and that I planned to be back on Monday morning, just like last time, though possibly not in time for roll call. If by some chance I was delayed, they should go on as usual.

It should just be a weekend trip, just like last time.

331

CHAPTER TWENTY-TWO

Manoélé waited with me for nearly an hour until the first car came along. We sat on the roof of the lorry, chatting about whatever crossed our minds, a couple of his friends who had come along for the ride sat under and behind us. For the benefit of these friends, Manoélé made sure that the conversation came around to include the place that was to be my first stop, and the fact that he had visited it.

When we heard the car coming, we jumped down and waved to stop it. The two Belgians in it were going to catch the train at Kasese and were willing to give me a ride.

Manoélé wished me a safe trip, asked to be remembered to Bwana Barry and returned to Talya.

The approach to the Kasindi *Poste de Douanes* was up a long, slow hill. There were several hulks of cars on it, among them that of M. de Bré, Pepino's erstwhile tutor. If a fleeing family's car died there, perhaps if it even only used up its last spare tire, or its last drop of fuel, it was abandoned in the hurry and panic to get to Uganda and presumed safety.

Down at the bottom of the hill is the Semliki river, a little smaller here than where we crossed it in our forest and cutting through savanna rather than tall forest. This was a national park. The land held lots of animals and the river was full of hippos. Within the same view archeologists would discover, thirty years later, barbed hunting and fishing tools, designed and made by "anatomically modern humans", *homo sapiens sapiens*. They were obviously quite effective. They were found in piles of giant catfish bones. They are 90,000 to 173,000 years old, far older than the next earliest known barbed points, found in Europe, which are only 14,000 years old.

We saw an anatomically modern soldier a few yards off the road, disentangling himself from some bushes. We commented to ourselves that he looked as though he must have been unsuccessful in his hunt, too darned bad. The FN semiautomatic rifle carried casually over his shoulder had not served him as well as the carved giraffe bones had served their users, so long ago. We were past him before he waved to us to stop, and the driver could easily pretend that he hadn't seen him, so he ignored him. There was no room for another passenger in their sedan, and we'd soon be out of the country, anyway.

In about three minutes, we were at the customs post.

As I got out of the car, I saw about a dozen white women sitting on their luggage in the middle of the wide, dusty approach to the barrier, where normally lorries would wait to be processed through customs. Some of the women were holding babies, others were calling to young children, trying to keep them a little under control. Only a few of the children though it was fun. The smaller ones certainly didn't, a couple of them were crying.

It was about noon and we were a mile south of the Equator. The sun was rather strong. I couldn't stay half an hour in that sun without getting a ferocious headache, if I didn't have my hat. I was concerned for the women and children. I heard them speaking in English, sounding decidedly American, and by now, I had adopted all Americans. I asked one of them what was going on.

"Our husbands have gone back to Beni to get passes. We didn't know that we need them to get through."

"How long have you been here?"

"Since first thing this morning."

"Don't you want to get out of the sun?"

"We were told to stay right here. We had to take our things out of the cars and stay with them, right here, in the road. They've been a little inflexible. We don't want to upset them. We're okay, really. The men will be back soon, and we'll be outta here." Then, after a short pause: "What's this pass we need?"

"I don't know. I've never needed one, and I came through here only last week."

The women were trying to be very patient, but their nerves were on edge. Things were not very comfortable, particularly for their babies. I tried to cheer them up, just talking with them, trying to calculate with them how soon their men might be back, trying to work out if we knew anyone in common from the other missions, and so on. My Belgian traveling companions were being searched, as was their luggage. Their toothpaste was being squeezed out of the tubes and every inch

333

of the car was being searched. I had time to talk and to try to do something for the state of mind of these harassed people. I knew the *douanier*, a Mtutsi from Urundi. I think his name was Ferdinand or Fréderique. Mum and Dad had even run errands for him as they went through to Uganda, or down to Bukavu through his poste, even while he was just the clerk, under a Belgian. I hadn't reported to him yet, but he'd only take a minute to process me. Last week he had simply stamped my passport as he asked after Mum and Dad and waved me through.

The American women were beginning to relax a little. I said something I thought was funny. I laughed at my own joke as I looked up just in time to catch the eye of the soldier whom we had left on the hill. One or two of the women laughed, too, just as they turned to see what I was looking at.

The soldier was not going to be the butt of any *mzungu's* joke. Particularly a mzungu who left him in the dust at the edge of the road. Particularly after he had failed to kill some meat.

He came over, his scowl as black as his sun-burnt skin.

"Où est ton laissez passer? Where is your pass?" pointedly using the familiar form.

I didn't have one.

"What? WHAT? NO LAISSEZ PASSER?" He demonstrated his parade ground voice, "EVERYBODY MUST HAVE A LAISSEZ PASSER TO GO ANYWHERE, DO YOU HEAR?"

With that, he hit me on the side of my head. It was with his open hand, I think, but it was hard.

I put my hands in my pockets, quickly, thinking that if I raised them to protect myself it might look like a threatening motion. He had a gun, I didn't. Then I thought he'd think I was reaching for something. I put my hands by my sides.

"WHERE ARE YOU GOING?"

"To Uganda."

"STAND THERE!" He pointed to a spot two feet from where I was. I moved there.

"NON! IMBÉCILE! THERE!" I moved to the new 'there', only a foot away.

With this fuss, Ferdinand/Fréderique came out of his office. He looked gray, and as if he hadn't slept for days. He was under stress. He saw me. He came up to the soldier and said something in his ear. The soldier looked a little unsure, for the first time.

Ferdinand motioned to me, and I followed him into the office. He looked at my face, which was still red, still smarted and felt slightly swollen.

He apologized to me. "*C'est pas normale, ici.* Things are not normal, here. I have been joined by these *militaires*, and cannot do things my way anymore. However, I have told that *soldat* that you are not Belgian. You are a son of the Prince. I told him I know you, and you are not trying to escape. I told him you would come back.

He handed me my passport. "*Bon voyage, M. le Prince.*"

The Belgians who were giving me the ride had been processed and had thrown their things into the car. Having witnessed my interview with the soldier, they were in a hurry to get out of range of his rage. They decided not to try to re-pack their toothpaste. They were ready to go.

I said something to the American women, whose state of mind, when all was said and done, I had done very little to improve.

We drove off.

CHAPTER TWENTY-THREE

My ride ended at the Kasese station. The Belgians were by now worried that they'd missed the only train for two days, and didn't want to stop, even to let me out.

As we drove down the street leading to the station, I saw a familiar looking vehicle near the single Indian *duka*. There was a VW camper, the same colour as Dad's, parked there. I had to look over my shoulder, out of the rear window, so I was not certain. It had to be a coincidence, though it would be a rare one. To be there, Dad would have had to drive past Mutwanga, for that was the only existing road, and he wouldn't have done that without stopping in to see me. Or he would have had to come over the mountain or the over the river, impossible and highly unlikely, respectively.

I took my little suitcase and walked the half mile back to the *duka*.

It was Dad's camper. Mum and Dad were in the shop.

It's not quite every day that family members bump into each other in a *duka* in a foreign country, on the wrong side of a mountain range, while their home country is in an upheaval, and they've each heard rumours about the others' demise.

We were not expecting to see each other there, of all places, so we allowed ourselves to be a little emotional. "Hello, Mum. Hello, Dad. How'd you get here, I'm on my way to Bundibugyo to try to see you."

"Oh, hello, Carl! What are you doing here? We're on our way to try to find *you!*"

And we got even more emotional than that, but I'll spare you. Anyway, we fell on each other's necks. We remarked on our good luck that Dad hadn't parked out of sight, or that we hadn't passed each other on the road, and so on.

We started to exchange our stories. You know mine. I can tell you a little of what I can remember of Dad's story, his would have come first, then Mum will tell you hers.

Dad told me what happened at Kagando, between Christmas 1960 and the second weekend in January, 1961.

"Well, you see, Pascal [Chef Pascal] was being quite silly.

336

He was misbehaving. Ona [Mum] and I came to de Jaeger's in the caravan, and there was Pascal, before me, blocking the way, with a whole crowd of his people. He stood in front of the car, like this, ... " Dad stuck his chest out and acted out Pascal's strutting as best he could while driving ... "Well, he was quite drunk, they were all drunk, and he was showing off for his people. He tried to stop me from going. He said: 'You *wazungu* came here with nothing, just a *valise*, now you all have radios and brick houses with *manzanza* [corrugated iron] roofs and drive cars and *camionettes*. It is all from our sweat, so rightfully it all belongs to us. We have come to collect what is ours. Get out of the car! It is now mine!'

"Wha'? Can you believe that? *Je? Ai?* Hm? Well, you can imagine, I was not going to let Mum get out of the car with all those people there, who had been drinking all night. So I told him: 'I am going back to my hill. Let anyone who wants to come to claim anything from me come to me on my hill. I still have the *bundukis*, and as you all know, my sons are excellent shots!' And I drove straight into them and made them jump out of the way. They saw you there at the holiday, so I let them think we were all there.

"Well, you see, he was so brave when he was talking in front of everybody, but he is quite a cowardly bully. They did come to the hill, but weren't brave enough to come in person, even at night. Instead, they put the grass on fire. And you know, in December there has been no rain for weeks, it is very dry. After two nights of putting out the fires, Paga, Mum and the boys, ... I mean ...and, Pascal's speech about brick houses with *manzanza* roofs didn't change our grass camp to something less flammable ...

"Well, we thought that discretion is the better part of valour. It was better to take Paga and Ona across the river, for safety. *Je? Ai?* Hm?

"I had put some of our own men to open a road to the Lamia, through our own place, and to prepare a ford across the river, as a back door for us, just in case. So at night, we drove out, with whatever we could put into Polonia. We wanted to leave Paga and Mum and John and Richard, who had to go to school soon, on the other side and come back, Bill and me, before morning, to go on as usual. But Polonia stuck. The stones just turned under the wheels. It took all night to get

337

across with the tractors pulling and the *watu* pushing. When we got back, in the morning, they had destroyed everything that we hadn't taken with us.

"Well, you see, at that point, we didn't really have much hope of being able to do anything on Kagando. And the fires were destroying the coffee. So now we are sitting on the Uganda side, just trying to get out as much of the equipment as we can. Perhaps we can salvage a few things. What we will do with it, I don't know, but if we take it, we have it. If we leave it, we don't have it anymore."

He carried on, a bit, about the Stanleyville people who had taken over much of Kivu province and about how Pascal had obviously been influenced by them. Pascal didn't have the brain to figure out the logic behind his claim to our property.

Three and a half decades after the events took place, Mum wrote me these notes. They cover much of what she would have told me as we drove.

"Barry Clegg visited us on New Year's Eve, to see if we were all right. We toasted the New Year with something or other, and Jacobo got drunk on John's potato wine, which hadn't finished fermenting.

"A few days before New Year - the end of Dec - two young men from Fort Portal, junior Govt. officials, sent by the P.C. [Provincial Commissioner, square brackets like these are my comments] appeared from over the river, to tell us that if we had to leave, the P.C. would send *askaris* [constables] up to the Lamya. They could not come into the Congo, but it was felt that their presence on the Uganda side of the river would discourage the *Force Publique* from following us into Toro country.

"They left in the afternoon. Dad & the boys took them down to the ford in the pick-up. While they were gone, (inexplicably?) the *matete* began to burn everywhere around the house. Paga, [our] Pascal & I were helpless - every black person had miraculously disappeared, although the place had been swarming with Watalinga just half an hour before. We watched the fire coming at us - and worried what had happened or could happen to Dad & the boys; the road was just a narrow track. The wind changed, however, and the flames went away from the house - Pascal, standing beside me on the hilltop looking down on the flames said 'Now I know what Hell

338

looks like.' It looked black, after the fire burned out, but the pickup crew came back safe. They had driven into the coffee nursery, which was fairly open and also wet, being surrounded by marshy ground, till the fire was over."

She continued, in a later session.

"New Year Barry Clegg came to check on us.

"The next thing we heard was that every *Mzungu* had to hand in all firearms* - this would have left us defenseless, & we didn't do it. We buried them in the veg. garden behind the huts, at night. Happy Congolese boasted: "Yes, the *Wazungu* are now helpless, they (you) can't shoot us when we come to take over whatever we want" - etc. On Jan. 3rd our Tanganyika Africans came an & said they had heard the *Force Publique* were down with [Chef] Pascal Saa Mbili, and were about to deal with all the Europeans in the district - now that the guns were gone. I knew that if any soldier had laid hands on me, Paga would go for him & probably get beaten to death - I knew I could take risks for myself, but not for my old father, two young boys & Bill, just 20. I said - It's time to go.

"Reluctantly & with bad conscience - because after all, not every Congolese was against us, we loaded what we could onto Polonia & went across the river - not without drama, but safely & without any *askaris*, as it happened. Paga didn't want to go, absolutely not! But he couldn't stay by himself. James didn't want to go, obviously, to abandon just about everything we owned. It was really my decision. But even with the guns (which we had dug up again!) we couldn't take it up with soldiers armed with machine guns, or whatever - not even with the help of Banandi armed with spears & bows & arrows who had been promising to defend us for days!

"Some time before all this happened, John took the silver & Grossmama's gold tea set across the river and left it with Joashi. Mrs. J. put it under her bed & didn't tell anybody it was there. She didn't go away from her house for days - but sat at the door & said she didn't feel too well when the other women asked why she wasn't coming to the market. We got it all intact, once we were in Uganda.

"Around then, Bill went to Fort Portal on the motor bike,

---

* In the margin, Mum inserted the note: "Pauline said this had happened earlier on." It had. This was a repeat of the order.

to tell the PC we would probably be needing his *askaris*. He was so tired that he fell asleep while waiting for the PC to be ready to see him - probably the first & only time anyone ever did so!

"Just before that, de Jaeger was invaded by soldiers, who looted his *duka*, & sat in his house drinking his beer. He sent a message to Bill asking him to come, as he had something to say - I think he wanted him to bury or un-bury the money from the *duka*. The whole countryside was un-easy, *matete* burning, drums beating, etc. & the buffaloes were uneasy too. Bill sat down on the road to think what to do next & (it was full moon) felt something looking at the back of his neck & a buff. snorted just behind him. He also saw a fairly thick stick lying on the road & thought that it would be better than no weapon at all - so he leant over to pick it up - it wriggled & shot off into the *matete* - Bill said he didn't even stand up before he began to run; Congo vipers are very poisonous. It was the morning after this adventure that he went to Fort Portal & fell asleep in the Boma - I think so! Strange how much I've forgotten or mixed up the dates. Anyway, we left on Jan. 4th - Steph's birthday [eight years later]."

And Bill wrote these comments after seeing a draft of this story, also thirty-five years after the events happened:

"... the sequence of events is much as I recall - I do have vague memories, though, of us - you, me and perhaps John and Rich, going together to take you back to de Poerck's after Christmas 1960 in Dad's caravan - on the way back to our place I had a prang - not far from Talya and came back to you. When we eventually got back to Watalinga (John, Rich & I) we found roadblocks, etc., etc., - which was the start of the local chiefs' trying to take over the expat shambas. I may be wrong, but I do think it was all one trip."

One more year later, Bill and I were talking, late into a night, when I asked him if he had any more comments on the way I had recorded the events. His remarks are in Appendix III.

CHAPTER TWENTY-FOUR

While Mum and Dad began to tell me their story, we got into the camper. Dad thought it would be a good idea for us all to go back together to the place near Bundibugyo where Bill was keeping an eye on the things that had been salvaged. He suggested that I could help get some more things out and we could talk about the future.

I said something like: "Can I get back to Mutwanga by Monday morning? Now I know you're all right, I should get back there."

Mum didn't wait to hear what Dad might say. "Don't go back! If you go, I'll never be able to sleep a wink."

We talked about it a bit. It didn't take long for me to agree that I should not go back, at least not immediately.

We stopped briefly at the Cleggs and brought them up to date.

We drove down the escarpment to Bundibugyo and on to the Uganda side of our Lamia. There was Bill, looking as though he had had all of two hours of sleep in the last week. He was encamped in a mud and wattle house, the home of Joashi, a Ugandan and a Protestant schoolteacher. Joashi had offered it and put it at our family's disposal for as long as we needed it. He and his family had moved out to make room.

The first night, I sat in the VW pickup with a rifle across my lap, trying to stay awake. For good measure, I had Sims' old Browning automatic in my pocket. In over ten years of trying, nobody had ever been able to free up its action. It behaved like a solid piece of metal. Maybe, as I sat on sentry duty, I could work on it to free it up. It might come in handy as something other than a paperweight. I had ammunition for it, which, though it was twenty years old, had been kept dry. Bill joined me. He wasn't sleeping comfortably on Joashi's bed. We would both watch for a spell, then one of us would go and sleep.

At dawn there was a tap on the pick up's window: "Bill! Is this Bill? Or is it Carl?"

It was an American voice. Bill and I woke up to find a couple of white men standing there.

"Your father said that we could use this way out if the situation got bad. We found the way, but we can't get the cars across the river. Can you help?"

Bill and I tried to straighten out our cramped limbs as we asked them a couple of questions about their vehicles and then drove one of de Jaeger's tractors to the river. De Jaeger had put all his rolling stock there, to be out of harm's way during this little flare up.

The American missionaries had been coming, in convoy, from the other side of Butembo. I think they had been on the road for two nights. They wanted only to get the women and children across the border into Uganda, and the men were planning to head back. When they had got as far as Beni, they had taken a small detour to Ouisha, which was a part of the mission network. There they had heard about the problems getting out the normal way over the Kasindi border. Dad had stopped at Ouisha, recently, and had told Dr. Becker and the missionaries there about a back way out through his place, that could be used in an emergency. They felt this was an emergency, and here they were. People had tried to stop them. Trees had been cut down across the road. There were armed Congolese following them on foot. They were tired. They were worried. They were so near to safety, and yet so far.

Things looked very bad.

There was a line of over a dozen cars, most of them big American sedans, one or two pickups. The first one was in the river, unable to get across. The round stones just rolled under the car wheels, as they had under Polonia's and every other vehicle's, except the tractors'. As the wheels rolled, they dug a small hole and the car just rested on the stones. Pushing didn't help.

We hitched the car to the tractor using a long rope that one of the missionaries must have produced, we didn't have one, and pulled the car across in about one minute.

Things looked much better. It was fully daylight, too, which always makes situations look less bleak.

We let the second car get stuck, hitched it up and pulled it across. We got smart and hitched the rest of them before they got into the cold water. This went on for a few more cars. Bill was doing the work, so I went down the line of cars, to see how many more were there.

The last car belonged to Dr. and Mrs. Becker. Dr. Becker

and I were standing beside his car, talking, when Chef Pascal appeared, at the head of a long column of his tribesmen. They all carried spears, bows and arrows and *machetes*. If I was reading the signs right, they did not look friendly.

Maybe things were not that much better! Daylight doesn't help when it shows you things like that!

I thought about the pistol in my pocket, still useless. I wished I hadn't fallen asleep before I had fixed it. Then I was glad it wasn't working. It couldn't have done anything against a few hundred men. So I wished, even more fervently, that it were not in my pocket, bulging a little too prominently, looking very pistol-like. I didn't mind not looking helpless in this situation, but I also did not want to look threatening. I remembered my little act of bravado after midnight mass at Christmas. I thought I'd better turn and leave, one rash or misinterpreted move by me could turn a bunch of people into pin cushions.

Before I turned away, Chef Pascal greeted me, not with a snarl, but with a hurt look and almost a whining tone: "Bwana Kallo! What's up, then? What are you doing? Why are you helping these people to run away from here? What are you doing to me? Doctor Becker? What are we going to do if you leave? Who will give medicine to our sick?"

This didn't sound very dangerous, but it was not yet really safe. There were still hundreds of spears, arrows and machetes that might be looking for blood. You can, sometimes, predict the actions of rational men. In their present state of mind, Pascal and his crowd, between them, were several measures short of a full ration.

Dr. Becker said: "You should have thought of that earlier. Anyway, you have cut down trees across the road so no one can pass. We cannot go back, even if we want to."

Chef Pascal answered: "We will take the trees away at once." He continued to talk to Dr. Becker, for a while, and then walked along the shrinking line of cars, clucking.

In a few minutes, all the cars had been pulled through, but one. We made ready to pull Dr. Becker's car, and we asked him to move it forwards to where the rope could reach it.

He said: "We're going back. We only came to show the way and to see the convoy safely this far. Our work is in Ouisha. We can't leave it."

Mrs. Becker agreed.

They wished their companions good luck and God speed, and they got in the car, turned and drove back. The crowd of Watalinga, who were still milling about with their weapons, parted to let them through and closed again behind them.

I am quite certain that Dr. Becker's mind was not changed by anything Pascal said. He had never intended to leave.

I couldn't see the Watalingas offering any signs of welcome, nor could I discern any signs that they deserved Dr. Becker's life. But he could. That's what made him what he was. Fifteen years later (December 29, 1975), Time Magazine did a cover article on the saints of the modern era. Among people like Mother (perhaps still Sister) Teresa, was a surgeon, Dr. Carl Becker, aged 81, still accompanied by his wife, Marie, running a mission hospital in a remote place in the Ituri forest, in a country called Zaïre.

With the cars gone, Chef Pascal left. His men followed him, a bit reluctantly. It was going to be much less fun removing the roadblocks than it was putting them there.

We went on with our day.

Our day consisted of going back on to our land to try to salvage some more of the equipment. The stuff that had taken Paga and Dad decades to collect and all of us seven months to refurbish, we picked over in a few hours. I didn't even go up onto the hill. Bill had told me what I'd see there. I didn't need to. Indeed I didn't want to see it for myself. I wanted to get out.

We were not exactly in an expansive and friendly mood when we got back to Joashi's house. Shortly after we got there, Mpendawatu came sauntering along, jauntily, to see what he could see. It was the first time I had seen him since the little incident with the coffee shillings. I got up and went towards him. I must have been looking less than friendly, because after he greeted me from about twenty paces, he stopped, hesitated, then turned around and ran as fast as his new shoes would let his duck feet carry him. He knew I knew about the money. I ran a few paces after him for effect, the big rifle somehow in my hands. I stopped. What was I trying to do? What was the point? I wouldn't have wanted to catch up with him.

When we had gathered everything that we could reasonably save on the Uganda side, there remained a small hurdle. There was one smaller river between the place we had it all piled and the beginning of the road. The real road ended effectively at a rickety bridge. This structure, made from blue gum trees cut down and laid side by side, tied together with string and covered with smaller branches and earth, posed no problem to pedestrians, nor any difficulty to motorcycles. It posed only a small problem to the camper and the pickup, but a major one to Polonia. I'd already seen what Polonia's load did to weak structures, and I didn't want to see it again. If this bridge failed, Polonia would topple ten feet onto a stony river bed. We spent a good part of a day cutting trees to put alongside the existing ones and to brace the span. After we stood back and looked at it the third time and were about to tell each other that we thought two or three or more tree trunks would do it, Bill and I saw Marcel start Polonia towards it.

"*Sogeeni!* Move out of the way! I'll go 'top speedi' and before her weight hits the bridge, Polonia will be across. Watch!"

We jumped out of the way and watched, expecting another disaster on top of all the other ones. 'The devil looks after his own', according to Sims, and he must have been watching. Or else Marcellian physics still had some merit. The bridge sagged. It creaked and cracked, it threatened to - no, it promised to break. But it held. Marcel smirked.

We pulled our things away from the border, further into Uganda. Some clothing shoved into every bit of free space in the caravan, a few things in the pickup, a small load in Polonia and two beaten up tractors were all we had to show for nearly a century and a half of man-years of work in Africa. The farm in Rongai was gone, Dad's money in France was gone. Our work on Kagando would be visible from the air for a number of years, as a scar on the brow of the hill, and on the plain because we had disturbed the vegetation in the *kipaniyés*. And there was a minor graveyard of incongruous equipment as evidence that some outsiders had been there. All of it would be of no possible use to anybody.

Only the freshness of the *matete* for the next couple of seasons would be of use to the buffaloes whom we had temporarily displaced less than thirty months earlier. It was just waiting for the rain to come before springing up with increased vigour where we had cultivated. The *matete* and the *mbogo,* the buffaloes could have the last laugh, together.

Bad as it was, it would still get worse. Weeks later, Dad would park the camper outside the Queens Hotel in Nairobi, while he and Mum visited Astrid von Kalckstein there. The camper would be broken into and every last stitch of clothing and some other possessions would be stolen out of it. This would happen not half a mile from the church in which Mum and Dad began their married life together, almost exactly twenty-four years earlier.

We left the Bundibugyo area via Kilembe. The Cleggs told us that a day or two after I hadn't shown up at Talya, Manoélé had turned up in Kilembe looking for me. They had told him Mum and Dad's story and that I had gone with them to help them, but that they didn't know my plans beyond that. He didn't know the way, so he had waited around for a day or so and had gone back.

I wanted to make a final decision about my return, but only knew what I'd seen at the Lamia river, and, of course what Mum and Dad thought about it.

We stopped in Katwe. We could get late news from the Greek owner of a shop there. He was an outpost of the Greek trading community that ran the Congo commerce. For the few people still going back and forth to the Congo through Katwe, his shop was a stopping point, so he heard everything. He told us that things were deteriorating fairly fast in Kivu Province since its takeover by the Orientale people. He gave some details and repeated some stories that he had heard.

That was enough for me to make my decision. I left the Talya keys with him. I asked him to have them sent through to Mr. Milingos, a half Congolese, half Greek trader, a friend of the de Poercks, who, he said, was committed to staying. Milingos would see Jacques on his visits to town, if the latter ever came back from his last exit.

I regretted that I was just going to disappear from the people of Talya, without taking proper, face to face leave of them. I felt I was acting no better than the scores of *colons* whose behaviour I had mocked with them.

That was only one of many regrets, and I couldn't dwell on all, or even any of them.

I wrote a letter to Mr. de Poerck.

CHAPTER TWENTY-FIVE

Pauline was already in Nairobi and had a job in a bank. The isolation and the ever-present frustrations of Kagando had brought her to a wise decision to try to start a career for herself in a better place. Maybe she just saw the inevitable several weeks sooner than we did. She was living at the YWCA, had been for a few months.[43]

John and Richard headed back to Saint's, for the last time by train from Kasese. They completed their schooling there.

Bill stayed around in the Bundibugyo and Fort Portal area with Dad for a few weeks to organize the things, to sell Polonia and the tractors and otherwise mop up. He later went on to Nairobi and got a job in a bank with which he stayed for his entire working-for-pay life.

Everybody was kind enough to suggest that I, having turned twenty-one, was under the biggest pressure to start to find a career. When Paga was taken to Njoro, I was dropped with the Williamsons in Nairobi. Jack Williamson had been missionary, teacher, linguist, insurance agent, and farmer, and now he had turned into an Anglican priest. He was an associate rector at the Nairobi Cathedral. There I started a process, with Jack's help, in which I narrowly avoided signing up with the RAF (I took and passed their qualifying exams, and was about to go for my second interview) and through some other twists and turns I landed up a full scholarship student in the United States.

I think Mum and Paga stayed with the von Kalcksteins in Njoro for a while. Paga survived a prostate operation to live a very active life with the family, for about six more years. He suffered a stroke in his ninety-first year, while replanting his roses in the garden he shared with Mum in Nairobi, and died in about an hour. I am happy that by then Valerie and I were

---

[43] There she had as a roommate, a cheerful, amusing, pretty, blonde girl named Gillian Bowers. That accident of fate may explain why Jill was unable to avoid Bill's attentions. She got even with him by marrying him and turning him into a sedate, well behaved, mature banker.

"back" from America, so he got to know her over a period of eighteen months.

When we were all in Nairobi for a short while, immediately after leaving Kagando, Dad tried to get some attention focused on the situation in the Congo. Not the fact that there were European refugees streaming out of there through East Africa by the train full, that was already in the news every day. He wanted to bring it to the attention of the world that the legitimate, constitutionally elected government of Kivu Province had been taken over by the cancerous Province Orientale, home of Lumumba, under the leadership of Gizenga, Lumumba's protégé. He wanted to point out that the future of the Congo would be very shaky if the tribal problems that were showing up were allowed to grow. He made some calls. He was quite excited to tell us that he had arranged an interview with a reporter. Maybe they'd want some photos for human interest, we should come along. What the world would do with that bit of news, I don't think he knew, but it was his duty to pass it on.

The world, through its information gatekeeper, The Daily Nation, yawned. A picture of five freshly bathed, neatly combed and newly clothed young people appeared in the Nation with a caption saying they had recently left the Congo. Ho, hum! Dad's interview was never published.

All of Dad's hopes for his own and his family's future had gone up in smoke, in fires set by African hands. His forty-year-old dream of growing coffee in Africa never came true. He grew coffee for other people, he grew some coffee plants, but he never harvested his own crop. (Ironically, for fun, Valerie bought a coffee plant in a pot, sold in America as a novelty. Thirty-five years after our effort in the Congo came to an end, there are twelve coffee cherries reddening on this plant. It's her little joke; Val is more successful than any of us ever were at growing coffee).

However, Dad held no grudge. He felt that the trouble was due to ignorant people being misled more than by evil people doing intentional harm. His reaction was true to form. Most of the rest of his later efforts to earn a living in Africa, and even after his forced retirement to Germany, all of his time and energy, were directed towards projects that would enhance the economic future of the independent countries or minimize the threat of inter-tribal fighting. He believed that the already evident tribal conflicts would inevitably grow to something much bigger with the departure of the colonial governments. Sad to say, he was not far off the mark. Within a month of independence in Zanzibar, the streets literally ran with Arab blood. While the Tutsi-Hutu massacres in Rwanda and Burundi have been widely reported, the massacres in the Congo jungles have not. Even Kenya, relatively stable compared to its African neighbours, has seen its share of tribal pogroms.

When Dad had done whatever he could about Kagando, he looked for something to do and became a paid employee for the first time in his life, managing a farm near Thompson's Falls. He soon found paid employment an unnatural state to be in and took a much more entrepreneurial path in the growing tourism industry, which he saw as the foundation of the future of the newly independent states' economies. To make the roof over the family's head pay for itself, he started a boarding house and took up a job for which he had to be on the road almost all of the time. He left Mum running a house with seven or eight paying guests whom she had to feed two hot meals a day, while he went off to try to build his future and that of the new Kenya, concurrently.

Over and above the PGs, Mum had her own family of Paga, Bill, who lived at home, on and off, and John and Richard, who had become day students while they finished up at Saint's. And she had a zoo's worth of birds, a jackals and dogs that Pauline found for her to keep. Pauline had married. She and her husband, Frank were living a somewhat nomadic life, being posted from place to place by the Civil Aviation Authority of the East African High Command and couldn't easily keep the animals themselves. Dagobert, Jakopo, the ducks and the chickens had remained on Kagando, of course, but they had been replaced. Mum no longer had her *Neu Affenheim*, she now had a *Neu Tiergarten*, which is close, after all, even if it doesn't have the same ring.

At about the time I returned from America after four years, with a bride, Dad was in the middle of a project. He had found a broken down, rattly, trailer caravan, and was going to fix it, so he had it in pieces on the front verandah. To get into the house, you had to step through the door-hole in the side frame of the caravan, which was leaning against the house, and that was before you even got to the bird cages.

It is to this menagerie that I brought Valerie, who had been raised in real civilization, with indoor plumbing, real toilet paper, electricity and all those niceties, to introduce her to my family. For all the change in four years, nothing had changed. I'm glad she was ten thousand miles from home and couldn't easily run home to her mother. I'm glad Dagobert decided to stay on Kagando, I might not have got her past that sentinel. I'm glad I wasn't bringing her to Kagando to introduce her.

But I'm really glad that I needn't have worried, she is resilient and has a sense of humour. In this family, as in Africa, as in life, resilience and a sense of humour are essential equipment.

By the way, I also took Val to Bagamoyo. You recall that, two decades earlier, Dad had fulfilled at least one of his goals by taking his family there. Does this make a tradition? It is about as long as the famous tradition of naming every miserable child Maria. It is probably healthier, too. I broke the latter tradition, so my children need feel no obligation to go to Bagamoyo.

We were able to keep track of only a few of the rest our cast of characters after we left Bundibugyo.

Pascali, our cook, and the other Warundi stayed behind, their three-week trips that had become three years long now indefinitely prolonged. If they ever got back to Urundi, they only traded the then present frying pan for a coming fire.

Marcel absconded with all the tools and went back to his woman under Kagando Hill. The other Wachagga, including Meku, stayed with him, for a while. Six years later, in a lightening visit to the Ngare Nairobi area with Valerie, that we made just before we left East Africa again, I asked a farmhand if he knew who was now living in our old house. He said that it was a man named Marcel. That would be quite like him. We drove past the Portals, which were still standing. The road was overgrown, obviously no longer in use, and though I could have found the way around, I couldn't bring myself to drive up the hill.

Mum heard that Père Jean was sent to a mission at Marakujipu, in the hills near Butembo, when it got to be too dangerous near the Uganda border. He died quite soon

350

afterwards, some said it broke his heart leaving the mission that he had founded. We never heard what happened to Père Rombaud. He may have retired to Belgium or to some other mission.

Van der Zichelen and Paepe disappeared from our knowledge.

Roger de Poerck came to Nairobi a few times in his FAO work, and visited Mum and Dad. He came once when I was back in Nairobi, and we had a friendly cup of tea or a Tusker Lager together at the New Stanley Hotel. He had never been back to Talya, though he had chartered a small plane in Uganda and had flown over it once. He bore me no apparent grudge for having abandoned Talya.

He told me that the Talya neighbour, the one who had been the garage operator in Belgium, had toughed it out and stayed on with his whole family. For this effrontery, he had been beaten and left for dead, and, for what was left of him, he might have preferred to have been dead.

Raphael de Jaeger also visited the family in Nairobi, from time to time. On one such visit, I got to see him. He had stayed in the Congo. He had bought himself a small plane. He asked the salesman where the ignition key went, what the various dials, levers and pedals were for, paid in cash and flew off with it. Heck, he could drive a *camionette*, a *tracteur*, or anything else with a *moteur*, why should a plane faze him? He was flying around the Congo, navigating by following the roads which were few and therefore not easy to confuse. He would make a point of appearing in a town that was just about to fall to an attacking force, be it rebels, the Force Publique or the UN. In each place, he would be sure to find some deal to be transacted at a very attractive price. He had done that for four or five years, making himself a good living, perhaps a small fortune. He told us it wasn't as dangerous as it sounded, because the Force Publique usually advanced with their vehicles in reverse, to be better prepared to retreat, and he had learned to avoid the only really dangerous people, the mercenaries.

There is a very sad footnote to his story.

De Jaeger couldn't learn to swim as fast as he learned to fly. Perhaps water is less forgiving than air. He was on holiday in Goma, on the northern tip of Lake Kivu, with a colleague. His friend was swimming in the cold lake, got a cramp and shouted out for help. De Jaeger, who couldn't swim a stroke, not even the doggie paddle, jumped in to save him and drowned.

I have two pictures in my mind's eye. One is Raphael de Jaeger drowning. The second is of the tenth generation of descendants of the buffaloes we displaced, dodging the same Watalinga traps, in the same *matete,* unaware of the irony of my interpretation of their ancestors' "blessing" of our home, in fact, unaware that we were ever there. Buffaloes are less talkative than ducks (I know from direct observation), so the stories about our short visit were likely not to have been passed down from generation to generation in *kimbogo.*

Sometimes, I see another version of the image of the buffaloes. In it they are very aware of our having been there. They are telling each other the same funny story, embellishing it, having the last buffalo laugh. (I don't always interpret well what I observe, even directly). Their ancestors had greeted us with a copious, welcoming, house-warming blessing. We had responded with very anti-social behaviour, going as far as to shoot dead some members of the welcoming committee. We paid the price for our behaviour, and the buffaloes relished the irony of it.

These images suggest some lessons that might find a place next to Dad's and Jock's lessons:

First: "If you can't swim, stay out of the water."
Second: "Read the buffalo droppings right."
Third: "Don't shoot the Oracle."

Poor, heroic, stupid Raphael. You jumped into the water, impulsively, for the best of reasons. You never went into a town in the wild upheaval that was post-independence Congo without knowing who was where, whom you were facing and how to get out. When you jumped into Lake Kivu, you forgot all your rules that had helped you survive very dangerous situations for over five years. You had no idea how you were going to do what you set out to do in there, you had no idea how to get out. But, for all of that, I know you couldn't just stand there.

We jumped into the apparently calm waters of the Congo, deliberately, though we could do no more than a poor doggie paddle. To do what we wanted to do, we needed to be able to swim. We needed to know how far we had to go, which stroke was best suited, how to pace ourselves. We needed to know how far our doggie paddling would take us and we needed an idea of what we would do when we learned a stronger stroke.

We needed a plan to get revenue immediately, and we needed to stick to the plan, hang the coffee, hang the tests, hang the roof, the bricks and the foundations for the house, hang even the Mulching System. All of those other things were academic if we didn't get in new revenues before the cash ran out.

Those things were also academic for another reason, the subject of the next lesson.

When you are in a situation in which buffaloes can leave their droppings in your living room, you can be excused for thinking that the future is probably not going to be easy. You probably would have to work at it to arrive at the conclusion that it is going to be rosy. We were shown other, less symbolic, less subtle signs that things would be difficult, even that they might be impossible. But even during the night that Dad moved the family over the Lamia, he was convinced, and so were we all, that we would outlast the troubles. Now, with more than three decades of hindsight, we know that that was improbable. Being "fair" and "decent" to "our" people, even being liked and respected by them, or even just tolerated by them, would not save us or our enterprise from the revolutionary forces that would be unleashed with the end of colonialism. We felt we were innocent. Of what we were innocent I don't know, but it doesn't matter. In revolutions innocent bystanders get hurt. We probably were in a state of mind that wouldn't let us read the signs realistically, or honestly. *We* could handle difficult. *We* didn't quit. *We* weren't like the Belgians, who ran at the first 'BOO!' *We* could tough it out.

We could delude ourselves!

Of course, most of the clearer signals came when we were committed to the point that there was no going back, and when we didn't have any place to run to. In those circumstances, you do what you have to do. That's what pioneers did in America. It's what pioneers have done, everywhere. It is also what de Jaeger thought he was doing when he tried to save his friend.

We didn't "read the buffaloes' droppings right" in a most fundamental way, long before we built the camp, long before we ever moved to the Congo. We convinced ourselves that the water we were jumping into was calm. We saw the surface, and

353

it appeared calm. We didn't ask ourselves more than superficially if it really was so, or if would remain so. We went to the Congo, not to avoid independence in East Africa, because we didn't think we had anything to fear from the latter, but for the better opportunity that the land there and the abundant water offered us. And we convinced ourselves that it was not risky to do so, for there would be stability in that country because independence would not, indeed could not, be granted by Belgium, *because the Congo was not ready*. That is probably the weakest reason for independence not to be granted, and possibly the strongest reason to expect revolution rather than evolution as the medium for the inevitable change.

This brings me back to the doggie paddling, again. Our finding ourselves doggie paddling in the troubled waters of the Congo was a result of many factors, some of our own doing, some purely circumstance. We survived it, figuratively, with nothing more than our tattered swimming trunks left to show for our effort. While we were rather ill-equipped and unprepared for our swim, and while we may have been foolhardy to undertake it, or even if we had no attractive alternative but to undertake it, we were fortunate, somehow, to have been washed ashore by a current we hadn't even seen. Then we were even more fortunate to be able to try something else, somewhere else. We survived the crisis, and we still had opportunity.

To be honest, I think when we found ourselves *ngambo*, looking over at the smoldering remains of our work on Kagando, I think that I was at least partly relieved that we were freed from what seemed to be an impossible situation and an unattractive future. No money left, no sizable crops in sight for about another year, just a lot more of the same hard work. Hard work and watching and hearing the effects of the worries on Dad's health and demeanour. Partly reilieved? Why don't I just say it? I was glad!

The poor people of the Congo have essentially been doggie paddling since they were shoved into the water over three decades ago. True, they demanded to be allowed into the water, that is, their self-appointed leaders demanded that they be allowed in. The Congolese were woefully ill-equipped and even worse prepared for their venture than were we, and their stakes were higher. There is no shore close to them nor are any currents likely to wash them onto one, if it were there. They have perished by the hundreds of thousands. Some say by the millions.

They couldn't walk away from their future.

Zaïre's waters have not calmed yet. Nor have their leaders shown any signs of caring more for their drowning people than for their personal numbered bank accounts overseas. The people will have to doggie paddle for a long time to come, and many more of them will not make it.

Yet, for all of their miseries, the Congolese may be better off now than they ever were under Leopold. That is a damning statement about the white legacy in that country. We Europeans came back to the place where our common ancestors took some of the first steps towards civilization by inventing barbed hunting tools, as long as five or ten thousand generations before the earliest known similar development in Europe, and, at the end of our visit, in the aftermath of our interference, we left the other descendants of the same people, to continue my metaphor, all but drowning. In that context, I think my little discussion with the PDP official in Mutwanga was a little ironic.

I think back on the people that we had around us, back then. I recognize some of them in the people I have around me now, and I remember some lessons I learned from them. I'd like to think that, despite my youth and inexperience, I also taught them something, anything, in return.

Marcel, for all his faults, taught me about machines and gave me confidence to approach them as their master rather than as their victim. He was an intelligent man. Had he had a different education, he could have done very different things with his life. Ironically, he had the same dream, much earlier than I did, to go to America. He wanted to train at International Harvester's factory, to become the best Farmall mechanic in East Africa. He never got that opportunity. He might already have been the best one, and he never could have found out.

Basikania was a diplomat and a gentleman. He knew his place as a chief, as a father to his people, and yet didn't put himself before them. He could control his anger and disappointment in public and keep his dignity. He was a man of honour, even if the Belgians treated him like a clown.

Pascali, our cook, was an optimist. He could face every day of his life with a big smile and a big heart. He could get away with murder on the strength of his personality.

Pascal Saa Mbili, the chief of the Watalinga, was a clown and had a personality that was murder. He acted like the bullies I had known in school, as long as he thought he had control. The moment he was uncertain of where he stood, he deflated like a punctured balloon. And he was walking proof that you can't make a silk purse out of a sow's ear.

Augustin was an opportunist, in some ways. He made himself available and was willing to do anything, thereby making himself indispensable to us.

Manoélé, in Mutwanga, was a bit like Augustin, but more approachable. He was much more spontaneous, while Augustin was guarded.

Michel demonstrated that mission boys are not saints. And that a smile can be skin deep.

In a different time and place, in a different context, I could see having a beer with some of these guys after work, and being able to talk about work, the football scores, or something. But that wouldn't have happened then. It couldn't have happened then.

I'd like to think that, once the heat of that January moment cooled, a few of our companions, retainers and neighbours were as sorry to see us gone as we were, after our own emotions cooled, to have lost them. I'd like to think that our brief presence among them was benign, even a bit beneficial to at least a few of them. I'd like to think that we were more to them than a source of wages, iodine, aspirins and amusement. I'd like to think that along the way we saw signs of genuine warmth towards us or concern for us from some people. I think we saw it in Melile. I think Mum saw it in Pascali, who stayed on the burning hill with her and Paga. And she saw it in the Wanandi who offered to defend them against the other tribes and the armed soldiers. I like to think that perhaps Manoélé's trip to look for me in Kilembe was motivated as much by a concern for me as for himself.

But it is for them, not for me, to judge and to confirm that. I'm told I often misread signs.

I'd like to think, also, that the sign on the road in the Ituri Forest, "Elephants Have Right of Way," is being honoured. I fear it is not. As long as there is value to some eople in elephant body parts, they are doomed to extinction.

APPENDIX I

NOTES ON SWAHILI PRONUNCIATION

Vowels:
"a" as in f**a**ther example, w**a**tu.
"e" as in t**a**ke t**e**mbo.
"i" as in f**ee**t K**i**l**i**manjaro.
"o" as in **o**b**o**e M**o**shi.
"u" as in m**oo**n Ar**u**sha.
Doubling a vowel only lengthens it, there is no change in the nature of the sound.
"aa" as in b**aa**, as in black sheep, or as in "Ah!".
"ee" as in double t**a**ke NOT as in f**ee**t.
"oo" as in a long b**o**w NOT as in f**oo**t.
A doubled vowel syllable usually has the emphasis in a word.
jog**oo** would rhyme with **o-BOE.**
When two vowels come together, each keeps its own sound.
f**ai**da, profit, is said: f**a-i**da, with "a" as in father and "i" as in feet, NOT as in faith.
Maas**ai**, the final syllable almost rhymes with "die".

Consonants
"f" as in **f**at, never as in o**f**
"g" as in **g**ot, never as in **g**in
"s" as in **s**in, never as in vi**s**it

Don't insert anything that isn't written between "m", "n" and "w" and any consonant they come up against.
"m" before a consonant at the beginning of a word is said as a syllable, and in two syllable words, it is stressed: **m**tu, man, is said: **mm'**-tu. In longer words, as in Mpendawatu, it is pronounced, but not stressed. If you call yourself a Mutalinga, you could be excused for saying Mupendawatu. That's the kind of thing that the thousand mile trip from the coast has done to Swahili to make it into Kinguana.
Mtu, man, is sometimes said mutu, by settlers. It is never said umtu. **Mbwa,** dog, is sometimes said *umbwa,* never

mubwa, never *mbuwa*, never, ever *umbuwa*. Even if it sounds acceptable, and if you hear otherwise perfectly decent seeming people say it, you don't really want to sound like a *mutu-umbwa* person, if you can help it. These **m** and **w** sounds really separate the pongos from the people who know. If you can say *bwana*, you can say *mwana*, child. Slip a "b" in there, drop the "-na" and remember to stress the "m" and you have an almost perfect *mbwa*. I know someone who thinks there is no such thing as a perfect *mbwa*, at least not alive today, but we'll let him argue that point somewhere else. Don't feel terrible if you can't get it, there are otherwise educated sounding people who have problems with certain simple English sounds (viz nucular and realitor), and they are allowed to live.

"nd"at the beginning of a word or syllable sounds like "nd" in fund, with no preceding vowel sound, i.e. not "und" or "ind" and it is never "nid".

"ng"as in finger , or as in singer.

APPENDIX II

Mum (Fiona) wrote these notes about her family, her childhood, and the first few months at Rongai. These are her own words. Where I add my comments, I use square brackets [like these]. I transcribe them here without using them to go back and edit my own recollections of that history. The inconsistencies in details of our stories are entirely due to my incomplete or faulty memory. I do not think that they detract in any way from either story.

<u>Grandparents</u>
When we were small Jock & I liked nothing better than to hear about our parents' life in Scotland. Maybe it was because it was so different from our own life in Tanganyika - anyway, in the evenings we would sit round the table with the lamp & sometimes play dominoes, or cribbage & sometimes listen to tales of Stonehouse & my grandparents' farm. My grandfather John Davidson & his wife Helen (Helen Vessie Wilson) had nine children, three daughters & six sons. The farm was mainly fruit, apples & strawberries, but also a dairy which supplied the hospital in Hamilton with milk and butter. After my grandfather's death, the farm was sold & an extension of the hospital was built on it. My grandparents died before I was born - & anyway in those days Africa and Scotland were very far apart - but we had a photo of them. Grandfather sitting in a chair, & grandmother standing beside him. He was blond & blue-eyed & had a beard. My mother said he was the kindest, gentlest man she ever knew - her uncle John. Grandmother was dark haired and brown-eyed (so was my father & he resembled her) & a matter of fact, busy person - with nine children & a farm & dairy to look after. The first farm was on a ninety-nine years lease, which came to an end when the children were still young. They moved to the Tofts, nearer to town, and it was there that my grandmother saw a ghost. She had set aside a small room at the top of the stairs to be her private place. In it she had a round table, with a grape vine in a pot (!) of which she was very proud because she had grown it from a grape pip. History related that her three younger sons once wired a bunch of white currants to it, hoping she would

359

think it had produced grapes. Needless to say, she was not taken in. Anyway, one evening she remembered that she wanted to water her vine and hurried up the stairs to do so while it was still light. She opened the door & to her astonishment there was no table, no vine, but an armchair with "lugs" [colloquial Scots for "ears", I guess it was a wing chair] & an old lady in a cap sitting in it. The old lady looked round the side of her chair & said "Are you biding here noo?" Grandmother was so taken aback that she ran down the stairs & when she plucked up her courage to go back, there was no old lady & no chair, but just the vine on its table. Being a practical person, I'm sure she watered it, but she was sorry she had run away instead of finding out who the old dear was - she never saw her again.

My grandfather did not approve of some sermons preached by the minister in the village church, so the family had to walk quite a distance to the next village on Sundays. The horses had to have their day of rest - & driving [in a buggy] on a Sunday was unthinkable anyway, so everyone rose early & set off to be in time for the morning service - where they could rest & hopefully not sleep, till it was over & they walked home again. One old uncle had a better idea, he invented his own religion which he called "The Enlightened Lights". He remained the only member & it died with him, nobody seemed to know any details of what he believed, he can have had no missionary ambitions.

My other grandfather, Walter MacIntyre, ran away from home when he was about sixteen. His mother died when he was quite young, & his sister Elizabeth cared for him and his two brothers & his father. There was some upset & Walter fell out with his father & ran away to Glasgow, where he thought he could find work. It seems he was earning a few pennies by holding the horses for people who were shopping, & one pair of horses belonged to a well-to-do lady who took a fancy to him & asked him about himself - in the end she took him home with her to look after the horses & generally help & eventually almost adopted him. When she died, she left him her business - providing everything people needed for horses and carriages etc. There he met & married my grandmother Jane Gentles. We were told he was a fine tall man, very good looking & he had red hair. Jock was said to resemble him (-at least his hair

360

was red!) whereas I was blonde & blue-eyed like my grandfather Davidson.

My grandmother only met her father-in-law after her husband died - she wrote to him & he came to Glasgow for the funeral. He never spoke, and only later she found out that he spoke no English, only Gaelic, so she never knew what he might have said. The doctors said my grandfather died of "inflammation of the bowels", but it must have been appendicitis & it was before operations for appendicitis became quite ordinary; one just had to take one's chances & maybe recover. My mother often spoke of her mother, but I never had a clear picture of her. She was not very tall, had brown hair & was particular about her appearance! She died when my mother was twenty, of cancer of the liver. They had been to the doctor together & when she came out of the consulting room & mother asked "What did he say?" she answered (putting on her gloves) "He says I'll be all right in about six months," but in less than that time she was dead, and her daughters decided to go to Africa.

Mother had brown, curly hair that never grew very long, but during her mother's illness it began to go white - so that we always knew her with grey-white hair, wavy and pretty but no longer curly. She had hazel eyes, we used to say they were heather mixture, like sock wool, because they had brown flecks in them. She wasn't very tall, & plump rather than slim, & she was the most courageous woman I ever knew. She would try anything, no matter how impossible it seemed & every blow of fortune only made her look around for a way out of the difficulty - and she usually found one. She must have despaired sometimes in secret, but she never let us know it, difficulties were there to be faced & mastered & we rather despised people who sat down & wept or gave up in the face of adversity.

[Africa]

My father and mother went out to Africa in 1902 and 1910 respectively. They had known each other all their lives, for their mothers were half-sisters, and my mother spent a good deal of her childhood on the farm in Stonehouse, where her aunt Helen Davidson lived. My grandmother MacIntyre felt that her small, delicate looking daughter needed country air, fresh eggs and milk, and the company of her nine cousins would be good for her, although all except Walter, the youngest, were older than Nan. At home in Glasgow there was only her sister Margaret (Peg), who was fourteen years older, for my grandmother's other five children had died in infancy, leaving just the first child and the last. My father, William, was the middle cousin, and was eight years older than his cousin Elizabeth Agnes [Nan] and it was with Tom and Walter that she played. My grandfather Walter MacIntyre died when my mother was two, so she did not really remember him, though she could recall him standing before the fire, and it was his long legs she remembered best. Peg, who was clever with her hands, had a passion for trimming hats, and became a milliner. The huge hats with feathers and flowers, veils and ribbons that were worn at the time gave her plenty of scope and her 'creations' were much admired. She did not marry, and when my grandmother Jane MacIntyre died and my mother felt she could no longer stay in the house, the two decided to sell everything and emigrate to South Africa. Their cousin Bill had been home on a visit in 1907, and had told them what a lovely country it was, and they felt certain that Mother, a trained teacher, would easily find work, while Peg would be able to make beautiful hats for the fashionable ladies of Pretoria or Johannesburg. So they sold their possessions and sailed for Durban. The ship took six weeks to make the trip down the West coast of Africa and round the Cape of Good Hope, and I expect Mother was sea-sick most of the time. Still, they arrived in Durban and took the train to Pretoria, where cousin Bill had found rooms for them, and where they found work, just as they had expected. About a year later my parents were married, and the three moved into a house together. Peg lived with them until her death in 1921.

My father was considered by his mother to be the delicate one of her family and she felt that a farmer's life would be too strenuous for him. She hoped for a while that he would become a schoolmaster, or a Minister, but when it became clear that he had no inclination for study, she apprenticed him to a draper in Hamilton. He had to rise at four in the morning to catch the early train to work and came home on the last train in the evening, not a very easy life for a fourteen year old boy. However, he finished his apprenticeship, and worked for a while in Hamilton. When he was twenty-five, he and a friend decided to try their luck in South Africa. For a while he worked in Bloemfontein, and later with Becketts in Pretoria. In 1907 he went back to Scotland for the first and only time, and it was during this holiday that he had praised South Africa to his two cousins, and he must have really meant it, for he was not given to meaningless enthusiasm.

After they married, my parents bought a plot of land in Pretoria West and built the house 456 Frederick Street, more poetically named Tulloch-Morvern by my father, for Davidson and MacIntyre country. Here their three children were born, Margaret Jean who only lived a few hours, a year later, in February 1917 Fiona Elizabeth, and in November 1920 my brother John Campbell. I remember Dr. Sanders coming into the dining room where I was eating my porridge to say: "Well, Fiona, you've got a baby brother." I was disappointed, I wanted a sister, but the doctor said: "He's got red hair. I turned over the whole basket, and he was the only one with red hair."

It must have been shortly before Jock was born that my Aunty Peg went to Scotland and, when she came back, she brought Aunt Maggie with her. She was my grandmother MacIntyre's younger sister, and. of course, half sister of my grandmother Davidson, and was the only one of that generation we ever saw, all my grandparents were dead before I was born. She planned to make her home with us, for my mother was her favourite niece. When Jock was about six months old Aunty Peg died. she came home from work one evening, and went onto the garden, just as usual, but when she didn't come to supper and Mother went out to call her she found her lying in the garden, unable to move or to speak. The doctors said that a clot of blood had gone into her brain. She was ill for some days, and though she seemed to know the people around her, she was not able to speak, and was quite helpless. One morning my father said that the angels had come for Aunty Peg in the night, and that he was taking me to Mrs. McLennan for the day. I liked Mrs. McLennan well enough, but I was sad that I hadn't seen the angels, and I wasn't used to being away from home, so was not very co-operative, and fed my lunch to the cat. He was quite pleased, but both Mrs. Mc and I were relieved when Father came to take me home. Soon after this, Aunt Maggie decided to go back to Scotland to live. She hated the thunderstorms we had in Pretoria in the summer, they really frightened her, and she felt she would be happier back in the old country. The storms were really impressive, sometimes there was hail as well, so bad that it broke tiled roofs and killed chickens that were too small or too silly to take cover. Every year lightening killed people who were caught in the open, so one could understand Aunt Maggie, in a way. But on the whole the climate was good. In winter we had frost, and icicles hung from the roof, and from the garden tap, but it never snowed, and when the sun came out the ice melted. The frosty air in winter gave my mother asthma and hay-fever, and arthritis made her hands painful, so she and a neighbour, Jean Aitken decided to rent a house in Warner's Beach near Durban together, and to take P.G.s [paying guests] to help pay the rent. They planned to spend the winter months there and to go back to Pretoria in the summer, but in the end my mother stayed on with Jock and me. She shared the house with Sister Loxton, who had been her nurse when I was born. My Dad was by now manager of Beckett's Cash Sales, but he planned to get a job in Durban so that we would be living in a warmer climate, but before he found anything suitable something else happened.

I had worn glasses since I was five, and it was time for them to be checked. My mother took me to an optician in Durban, a Mr. Reynolds - I think she found his name in a newspaper. I didn't mind going to have my eyes tested because if I behaved well we always went to a book shop afterwards, and I could choose any book I wanted as a reward. Probably my mind was on books, for I do not remember Mr. Reynolds and my mother having said much of interest, but they seem to have had an important conversation in which Mr. Reynolds told her that he had a number of farms in Tanganyika, formerly German East Africa. He was looking for a few people who wished to invest a little capital, the farms were on the foothills of Kilimanjaro in coffee-growing country and were sure to make fortunes for their owners in a very short time. He assured my mother that the climate was excellent, no Malaria, the water was very good - "straight from the snows of Kilimanjaro", in fact it seemed like an answer to the problem of where to live. Mr. R. was willing to sell us three hundred acres of the best coffee land, as he said, part of one of the farms. He was so sure my parents would be satisfied that he promised to exchange the land for three hundred acres of the farm that he was keeping for

364

himself if they did not like it. My mother wrote all this to my father in Pretoria, and he came to Warner's Beach, and to Durban to meet Mr. Reynolds. Soon everything was settled, the house n Pretoria was sold and we left for Tanganyika. We sailed from Durban, in the Guildford Castle, the trip should have taken ten days, but we were delayed in Beira, where there was a strike and it was fourteen days before we landed in Tanga.

We had to wait a day or two for the next train to Moshi, there were only two a week at that time, November 1924. It was very hot, and Jock and I were not used to having to wear hats, or rather topees [pith helmets] whenever we left the house. we were glad when we could take the train at last for it would be cooler when we left the coast. Our compartment was like a small room, with a washroom next door, there was no corridor. The Collie, Mac, was not allowed to travel with us, he had to be put in a sort of box under the guard's van, normally used for transporting goats. The train left in the evening, and just before dark, while the engine was taking on water at a station there was a great shouting and scurrying on the platform, and we saw Mac running along the train. Mother opened the door and whistled, and he leaped in, very relieved to have found us. After that the Guard let him stay with us. The locomotives burned wood in those days, in the daytime they produced lots of smoke, at night streams of sparks could be seen, they must have started many a bush fire. Early in the morning we saw Kilimanjaro for the first time, Kibo pearly pink in the dawn, and Mawenzi grey and rocky beside him, higher than anything I had ever seen. Soon we were in Moshi, which would be our nearest town from now on. Besides the railway station, there was a Post Office, a small hospital, one European shop, a straggling collection of "dukas" run by Indians, catering for the Africans. Then, of course, there was the Boma, where the Government offices were, and the Standard Bank. The only hotel was run by a Greek, whose African name was Bwana Tumbo [Mr. Belly]. Here we took the only available room and started looking for transport to take us to Ngare Nairobi. We had hoped to leave at once for our farm, but firstly the only two trucks in town were busy carting the coffee harvest down from the mountain, and secondly our packing cases had been left behind in Korogwe, halfway from Tanga. My father quite rightly felt we must stay in Moshi until they were sent after us, there would be no hope of communicating with the railway, we would be rather cut off from everything. It took ten days for the cases to catch up with us, and during this time I had my first attack of malaria, my mother bought two kittens from a passing toto [Swahili for child] and collected advice from the few white women in town as to what supplies to take with us, how to make potato yeast and banana vinegar, and doubtless more valuable hints about life at the Back of Beyond. At last the two trucks were free, and we loaded our possessions. We set off, Dad and Jock with Mac on one truck, Mother and I and the kittens, by now named Kibo and Mawenzi, on the other. In theory the trip should only have taken a few hours, but one of the trucks was in rather bad condition, and kept boiling and spouting steam from its radiator, so we constantly had to stop and wait for it to cool down before water could be filled in and we could go on again. Whenever we passed a river, we stopped to fill the water cans; so that progress was slow. At first the road was good and the bridges over the first rivers had been built by the Engineering Corps in the War, but after the third river there were only fords, the road became less and less recognizable as a road until finally there was just a track through the bush. We saw no animals, and no sign of people till we reached the Sanya river. The banks were very steep, and our faulty truck would never have climbed the far bank if about twenty Wachagga had not miraculously appeared and pushed it through the water and up the other side. Soon after this we emerged from the bush into the plains, a completely different country. Kilimanjaro soared into the sky on our right, to our left was beautiful Meru, and far away before us we could see Longido blue in the evening light, for by now the day was almost over. There had been a grass fire some time before, and the plains were covered with short green grass, clumps of pink and white flowers, and the scattered bones of countless cattle. The driver told us they had died of Rinderpest, and that the Masai had moved away with the remainder of their herds, he seemed to be relieved that they were gone. Away on the grassy slope below the forest on Shira [the western part of the Kilimanjaro massif] we saw a roof shining in the last rays of the sun. Mother said "I hope that is not where we are going, it looks so lonely" but we were going further on across the plain, and at last lights appeared, then a house, dogs barked and people came out of the house as the drivers stopped, relieved to have reached somewhere at last. It was the home of a South African family, who had settled there some years before, old Mr. Visser, his sons and a married daughter with her husband and children. They took us in to supper, and would have kept us over night, but our drivers were anxious to off-load us and our boxes and get back to Moshi. They said the truck would do better at night when it would not be so hot, but they were afraid to stay all night in such wild country where there might be leopards behind every bush. Our new friends gave them instructions how to find the Weber farm where we were going, and where there was a house we could use until we had built our own. It was not very far away, and the Africans made haste to unload everything, they even carried most things inside before they drove off, leaving us behind in the darkness which our hurricane lamp did very little to disperse.

The house was solidly built of stone & still had a corrugated iron roof, but all the doors & windows had been removed & the cement floors were covered a foot deep in dry leaves & grass, so the first thing we unpacked was a broom. Jock and I sat on a packing case & held each other up - we were so tired & everything was so strange. Soon bedclothes were unpacked & we were asleep on a makeshift bed on packing cases, the doors blocked by the biggest cases for my mother had the uneasy feeling that the Africans might have been right in expecting leopards at every turn. Luckily there was a strange room in the middle of the house with no windows & that was our bedroom for the first night! Mac shared our room - leopards like dog-meat better than anything. The kittens slept in their basket, tummies full of milk that Mrs. Joubert had given us.

Morning brought its own problems, for although we had the raw materials for breakfast & even a few pots and pans available, we had no stove & no water. My father set off to find the river, which must be quite close by & fairly soon came back with a bucket of water. This I examined closely because Mr. Reynolds had told us it came "straight from the snows of Kilimanjaro" which had appealed to my imagination. It was good clear water & we soon had tea & something to eat. There were three stones & charred bits of stick in one corner, so we cooked on three stones & life was one long picnic. Dad contrived shutters and doors so that we felt safe at night.

A day or so later Mr. Joubert went with Dad to see where our three hundred acres were. He and his brothers-in-law felt sure from the plan that Reynolds had given us that he had sold us a large hill, known as Leuw Kop (Lion Hill) and it turned out they were right. It was hopeless to think of farming there, there was no water anywhere near & the slopes were far too steep to be planted. I think my father must have been daunted, but my mother said all we had to do was to write to Mr. R. & remind him of his promise to exchange the land, & in the meanwhile we should find his other farm & see which part of it would suit us, & with this in mind, we set off one morning to visit our three neighbours, Mr. Fabic, "Old Renton" & the Arnesens. Mr. Fabic was a bachelor, from Czechoslovakia. He invited us into his house and gave us tea. His English was not too fluent, but it seemed he had a coffee nursery planted near the river, about 20 oxen & a wagon, & a small window with glass in it of which he was very proud - & rightly, it was the only glass window for miles around. we left him & walked further on dusty paths, downhill to Renton's farm. The grass was tall & yellow like wheat, here & there were thorn trees & bush. We saw a herd of giraffe on the side of a hill. It was sunny and warm, the mountains looked blue & far away. We came to a cattle kraal of thorns, a few huts and a wagon. Out of one hut came Mr. Renton. Everyone called him "Old Renton" & he had a grey beard, grey hair & blue eyes in a sunburned face. I knew him for twenty years & he never looked any older. He offered us more tea, but Jock & I preferred playing with the baby goats that jumped around everywhere. Mr. Renton's next trip to Moshi was almost due & he promised to post the letter to Reynolds. He said if we didn't want to wait for him, we could send a runner [the forty miles] to Moshi - but we had no-one to send, so the letter was left & we crossed the river to look for the Arnesens. They lived in a mud & wattle house, very cool under its thatched roof. Arnesen was Norwegian & he said he had picked his farm from the top of Longido, during the War (1914-18!). His wife was a South African of English descent & they had two children, the boy Jock's age & the little girl 2 years younger. They gave us lunch, & the cook later produced cakes for tea, baked in oval herring-tins in an oven cut into an ant hill. Arnie knew where Kuhn's farm was and promised to go there with my Dad, to see what the land was like. They would have to walk. nobody had a car - no roads - nor horses, because of the Tsetse fly belt & only Old Renton had an obstreperous donkey called Neddy. Donkeys were said to be immune to fly, but each trip to Moshi cost Old Renton an ox or two even though he tried to get through the fly belt at night, when the Tsetse were asleep & didn't bite. Taking their guns, the two walked over to Kuhn's farm. High up a little river towards the forest was the house - the lonely roof my mother had seen on the trip out from Moshi. As they came up to it a large leopard leaped out of a window & disappeared before they realized what it was. A little further on they stumbled over a skeleton in the grass in front of the door. But they didn't spend very long at the house, because the land they thought most promising was lower down the river. In the evening Dad came back quite worn out, but satisfied they had found what we wanted. I think it took quite a few letters before Reynolds was finally convinced that he must exchange the land, but at last we began building a mud & wattle house on our farm, Rongai. By this time we had a houseboy called Asmani & a factotum named Kafue. Kafue and my Dad walked to Kibongoto, which was the nearest source of labourers - in fact, I think Kafue went ahead & arranged for two "fundis" to meet them somewhere. Kibongoto was not a town or a village, but a whole district & it would have been like looking for a needle in a haystack if the way had not been prepared. Kafue had been instructed by my mother, who was becoming quite good at Swahili & the two fundis were engaged to build our house & to bring enough workers with them. Their first task was to build huts for themselves & the labour force because walking the five miles from Weber's to Kuhn's was inconvenient and time consuming. One morning, on their way to work they came upon a large lion who was eating a kongoni - he seemed to be alone & everybody yelled and banged on everything they were carrying. The lion reluctantly withdrew & the boys fell upon the kongoni & cut it up. One of them came back to us with meat in a basin. Everybody was happy to have so much meat. Dad always remembered the lion lifting his head out of the kongoni's belly & the blood dripping off his whiskers.

We had come to Ngare Nairobi in Nov. 1924 - by April '25 we moved to Rongai. Fabic hired us his ox wagon & drivers to move our possessions & we set out quite early one morning. Jock & I were quite happy at first to ride on the wagon. We could not follow the track over the hills, which would have been shorter, but had to go down to the "road" on the plains as being easier on the oxen. it soon became clear that the team was not equal to pulling the load. The oxen were young & the drivers inexperienced. After a while my mother set off with the kittens in their basket & an African carrying provisions & milk - she said she would have a meal ready when we came. My father, never very good at waiting for anything had long since walked ahead with Mac. Jock & I stayed on for a while, then he said he wanted to go to his Mummy (he was only 4) so finally an old man named Tugi went with us & we set off on foot. It took us some time to walk across country, but we were at the new house long before the wagon arrived after dark. The new house was built of "wattle & Daub" & had three rooms, plus a kitchen and storeroom. It was near the end of the slope, about 3 miles from the Kilimanjaro forest, on the little Rongai river. When we went there, there was water in the river - no one warned us that as the dry season went on the water retreated further & further up the river till at last it was only to be found quite near the forest boundary.

There was a lot of game in those days, kongoni, Thompson & Grant's gazelle, zebras, wildebeest and 20 oryx who used to walk down to drink in the evening silhouetted against the sunset. A lion family lived in the korongo [a dry gully or valley] - a big black maned lion and his wives & several half-grown cubs. We used to hear them hunting at night; the lion would come roaring down the valley & drive the game down to the lionesses who lay in wait to kill some unfortunate beast as the herds ran down to the plains.

It was a good life for children, we felt as if the world belonged to us & we were wonderfully free. Nothing would hurt us, if we kept our eyes open & there were endless things to be discovered. Everything was new and interesting. It must have been difficult for my parents, in a new land far away from doctors, schools, shops, post office - almost everything familiar. Both Dad & I had bad attacks of malaria, Jock too, Mum seemed to have escaped infection in Beira on the trip up the coast. Apart from this we were healthy & busy. Dad bought a Fordson tractor & a plough & harrow. He ploughed 20 acres in front of the house & planted maize - we had a very good first crop & everyone felt optimistic. Coffee plants were bought to save time & a coffee nursery was started near the river, which still had water in it, though rather less than when we arrived. We measured land for the coffee plantation, putting in pegs where the holes for the little trees were to be dug. When it rained they were planted. Nobody realized that it was far too low & too dry to plant Arabica coffee, our ignorance of the land & the climate was only equaled by our enthusiasm & optimism. Anyway, the rains were not good in the next years & we had to dig a water furrow with its intake a good way up the river in order to have water at the house. Later this proved to not to be far enough up the river, though we had plenty of water when it rained enough to bring the river down.

Jock & I did lessons every morning - I had to learn arithmetic & grammar. I had been reading everything I could lay my hands on for years & read history & geography as happily as anything else. Robinson Crusoe suited our life-style very well, so did the Swiss Family Robinson. Lorna Doone, Rob Roy McGregor & Quentin Durward were my companions for years. My uncle Robert Davidson sent us books from his school in Drummore & he sent me the Children's Newspaper too.

At first we had no near neighbours, but fairly soon the two next door farms were sold - Gararagua to Col. Stevens & the rest of Rongai to Mrs. Gayer. Both farms had managers & both managers had motor cars so that we were no longer so isolated.

APPENDIX III

On a rare meeting, Bill and I were talking late into the night. We got on to the events leading up to our departure from the Congo. After agreeing that we could never, ever, have guessed that sometime in the future we would be sitting together in Florida, where he would have come to escape the English winter, I tried to check my memory against his.

"Actually, Carl, I have to say that I haven't read very much more of your stuff. Some of that was too painful."

"What bothers you about it still?"

"Oh! A bunch of things. It was not a very good time. Who do you think had to make the decision to leave? What was I? Nineteen? Dad must have been paralyzed, or just not thinking. I had to ask things like: 'How much money is there? How much income is there? How long will it last before there is absolutely nothing? A month? What can we do when we are forced to leave with not a single franc?'"

A bit later, "You remember that old Chagga 'expert', or robber, - "

"Meku?"

" - who spent two years getting water down from the Lamia, using dozens of men? He didn't bring the water on to the hill. Said it wouldn't go! I took the old theodolite out, improvised a measuring pole and in three days I had water just below the house. De Jaeger looked at the water and asked how I did it. I told him I could do something like it for him. He said: 'Do it,' and I did. With the theodolite, I brought him water where he could use it, and I didn't have to go to the top of the Lamia to do it."

This suggested a relationship with de J that I wasn't aware of.

"You know that, earlier, the old man and I had had a major falling out and I had quit?"

"No! If I ever heard it, I've forgotten"

"Just after you went to de Poerck's, and I think Pauline had already gone to stay with Rene and Joe Cassel, we were dealing with that big block we had opened up just under the little river by Paepe and van der Zichelen. What was it called, the Litikira? We had planted some mangy tobacco plants in it. I had said we shouldn't waste the effort and the money, but Dad went ahead,

372

anyway. We planted the field and waited for it to grow, which it did only reluctantly. It never looked good. Eventually, it sort of looked ripe, getting some yellow blotches, but it was too weak and thin and small. We held off harvesting, waiting for it to get some weight on the leaves, which wasn't happening and didn't look like it would ever happen.

"You know how you can tell when it should be picked? If it has gone yellow and you bend the leaf in your fingers, and if it is stiff enough to snap, it is ready? Well, I tested it and decided that we were only risking it getting worse before it got better, so I began harvesting with all the men.

"In the middle of the day, after the picked leaves had been lying in the sun ..."

"Wilted," I said.

"... totally limp, by this time, along came Dad, from somewhere, and he tested the picked leaves, which, of course, didn't snap. He was furious. He exploded. He yelled at me about it, in front of everybody, telling me I'd ruined it, and us, and so on.

"I just had had it. I told him he had better do it himself. I got on Pauline's little old BSA bike and rode off. I don't know where I was going, but I had to cool off.

"I bumped into de Jaeger, who took one look at me and said: 'Guillaume, you've just had a fight with *le patron*, haven't you?' I admitted it. He had been after me for weeks to come work with him, and he didn't miss a beat. He said 'Come on over right now and start with me.' I went.

"I spent the rest of the day in his fields with him. He said: 'This is how you prune coffee,' and we pruned coffee for a few hours. Then he showed me some other things. At the end of the day, he said: 'Now you know how to prune and to whatever else, start doing it tomorrow. I'll pay you seven thousand francs a month. I'm off for a week.' And he left. Then I went home for the night. When I got there, Dad said 'Well, son! We are very busy. There is a lot to be done.' I said 'Yeah! You've got a lot to do. So have I! Good luck.' And I told him about my new job."

"Did you stay at home, or did you move over to de J's?"

"I moved. I lived at de J's for several months."

"Did you ever see any of your pay?"

"Yes, I got paid," Bill said, "but it went into the general kitty, mostly.

"You remember that I had a deal with Dad? He had promised me that if I got a good School Cert. I could go on to Egerton College [the agricultural college in Njoro]. On Flakey's recommendation I went back to Prince o' for one term, to see what my School Cert. results were. 'You've totally wasted your time here, and I can't let you waste another space here. But you are intelligent and we can't throw you out without another chance, if you need it, to get a decent School Certificate, without which you won't stand much of a chance in life. And so on and so forth ... ' Well, when he read out the results, he said: 'What's this? Isenburg? a Division A? This is not what we expected!' I told him it was exactly what I expected and planned. It was going to get me what I wanted.

"What I wanted was to go to Egerton, and I should have done it. But, when it came down to it, I listened to all the talk, and it seemed that the Congo might have promise, so I went along, giving up on Egerton.

"Then, when we saw we weren't going to make it there, and we'd wasted all that time and effort ... I guess I resented it all, a bit.

"De Jaeger told me that he had financed van der Zichelen's whole plantation. Now, since v d Z had abandoned it, the plantation was his, de J's. He had a mortgage on it. If, along with whatever else he had me do on his other places, I worked that plantation long enough to pay off his debt and interest, getting a salary while doing so, I could have it for myself! That was a real plantation, already producing papaine, and the coffee wasn't far from maturing.

"If we had hung on for a while, I would have been set up nicely! But that's rather academic, isn't it? We couldn't have held out there any longer."

We agreed on that. And that at 2:00 a.m., not being as young as we were thirty-six years ago, we couldn't have held out talking any longer. As youths, we craved to lengthen our sleep at the end of the night. Now, our age demands we get it at the beginning. And, in the morning, Bill was to have his turn as the professor. In his single, long career in banking he had, somehow, picked up the game, or curse, of golf, which, in my various careers, by a different somehow, I had escaped. He was going to get even with me by introducing me to it.

374

Made in the USA
Middletown, DE
07 January 2023

21476895R00215